JOHN MORLEY
Liberal Intellectual in Politics

John Morley, *c.* 1883

JOHN MORLEY

Liberal Intellectual in Politics

D.A.HAMER

Formerly Professor of History, Victoria University of Wellington, New Zealand

EER
Edward Everett Root, Publishers, Brighton, 2019.

EER
Edward Everett Root, Publishers, Co. Ltd.,
30 New Road, Brighton, Sussex, BN1 1BN, England.

edwardeverettroot@yahoo.co.uk

JOHN MORLEY
Liberal Intellectual in Politics

D.A.HAMER

Classics in social and economic history series, no. 9.

© the estate of the late David Hamer, 1968, 2019.

This work first published in 1968.
This edition © Edward Everett Root Publishers 2019.

ISBN: 978-1-911204-69-5 Paperback.
ISBN: 978-1-911204-67-1 Hardback.

The rights of the author and of the author's estate have been asserted under the Copyright, Designs and Patents Act 1998 as the owner of this work.

All rights reserved. No part of this publication may be reproduced, stored in a retrieval system or transmitted, in any form or by any means, electronic, mechanical, photocopying, recording or otherwise, without the prior permission of the copyright owner.

Cover design by Pageset Limited, High Wycombe, Buckinghamshire.

PREFACE

THE main theme of this study is the interplay between the political ideas and principles of John Morley and the various situations and problems in which he was involved as a practical politician. Approximately the first quarter of the book is devoted to a survey of the development of his thought, his 'frame of mind', in the intellectual context of the 1860s and 1870s and in relation to his own personal situation. From this basis I move on to examine certain aspects and themes of his journalistic and political careers, selected for emphasis mainly because of their relevance to this thought-practice motif.

Morley was so substantially involved in both the intellectual and the political life of the period 1867 to 1914 and wrote or said so much about the implications of this dual career that we can investigate in him with very considerable thoroughness the relationship of thought and practice in late-Victorian Liberalism. This I have concentrated on doing. Although the work is, for the most part, developed chronologically, detailed biographical narrative is kept subordinated to the main thematic and episodic treatments. Aspects of Morley's personality, and general biographical material, are brought in from time to time, but are not examined continuously or principally.

In so far as Morley is remembered today, it is probably mainly as the author of the *Life of Gladstone*. Neither his literary nor his political achievement was of a very durable kind, and it is doubtful if his books are read very much now or the record of his political career remembered by many in any detail.

In the mid—and late—Victorian literary world Morley attained a solid second-rank status. His principal achievements were in the realm of biography—monumental studies of two Liberal politicians, Cobden and Gladstone; three shorter historical biographies —of Cromwell, Burke, and Walpole; and a series on leading French thinkers, writers, and political figures of the eighteenth and early nineteenth centuries, ranging from short essays on such men as Turgot, Robespierre, and de Maistre, to full-scale lives of Voltaire, Rousseau, and Diderot. In addition he wrote numerous reviews and essays, mainly on literary and historical topics. One of his most influential works was *On Compromise*, a series of essays on the principles and conditions governing political conduct, that was published in 1874 and became a source of inspiration for young Liberals over the next few decades. I do not make any detailed critical assessment of Morley's literary work. For the purposes of this study its main interest has been as providing evidence of the development of Morley's ideas. In particular, I point to a close connection between the biographical nature of so much of his literary composition and the individualism that was so strong a feature of his political creed.

A great part of Morley's literary output was published between 1867 and 1882 in the *Fortnightly Review*, of which he was then editor. There can be no doubt that Morley was among the leading editors of reviews in the late nineteenth century. The *Fortnightly*, which was founded in 1865 (and was, in fact, during Morley's editorship a monthly publication), became in his hands one of the most successful and influential Victorian journals of opinion. In the early part of this book I investigate what Morley hoped to achieve through his editorship of the *Fortnightly* and how far his hopes were realized.

As for intellectual history, it is possible to discern in Morley quite a few of the features of the 'Victorian frame of mind' as described by W. E. Houghton in his book on that subject. I place particular emphasis on Morley's being an intellectual preoccupied with the consequences of loss of religious faith. In Morley we see also the coming together, though scarcely the integration, of numerous different strains of thought and great intellectual influences of the previous century and of the Victorian age. The ideas of John Stuart Mill, of Auguste Comte and the positivists, of Carlyle, of Edmund Burke, of the eighteenth-century French *philosophes*, of Cobden and the Manchester School, all have a prominent place in his intellectual development.

But Morley was also an 'intellectual in politics', and it is from this angle that I try to study him in this book. The balance in his career between intellectual interests and practical political activity was remarkably even, and there was constant interaction, very often tension, between the claims and attractions of the two 'worlds' in which he existed. He himself was very conscious of being an intellectual—or, as he would put it, a 'doctrinaire' or a 'theorist'—in politics, and he thought and wrote a great deal about the peculiar characteristics and difficulties of this role. His career therefore provides excellent material for reflection on the motives which cause intellectuals to become politicians and on the nature of their conduct thereafter. Morley displays, for instance, many of the classic symptoms of indecision, shrinking from commitment, and paralysis in the face of demands for action, that are often regarded as stemming from an intellectual's awareness of the existence of many aspects to a situation. Throughout his career he was obsessed with problems of 'expediency' and 'compromise', with defining how a man with principles and beliefs should accommodate these to the conditions of practical politics, when he should speak out and when keep silent, and so forth. I draw attention also to his growing dislike, amounting almost to fear, of a purely introspective, intellectual existence. I relate this to his awareness of a connection between mental instability and the absence of clear guiding principles and 'systematic' ideas, and I trace how he sought relief through involvement in the world of action, first in complementary relationships with men of great practical ability, such as Joseph Chamberlain, and then later in becoming a practical politician himself. The nature of Morley's interest in practical politics is in this way related in part to the mid-Victorian intellectual predicament. This is done in another way through the theme of Morley's tendency to concentrate on 'one question at a time'. This tendency emerges during the early chapters as a product of his loss of religious belief and failure to discover any intellectual 'system' of thought to be a substitute and is then traced through the various phases of his political activity.

The book is concerned also with the history of the Liberal party in the late nineteenth and early twentieth centuries. Morley was a

Liberal M.P. for twenty-five years, from 1883 to 1908, and was a member of Liberal cabinets over altogether about thirteen years (1886, 1892–5, 1905–14), as well as being a prominent member of the party's leadership in periods of opposition, notably between 1886 and 1892. Through a study of Morley's career as a liberal intellectual in Liberal politics it is possible to appreciate more fully the confusion with regard to ideas and policies which underlay so many of the difficulties of Liberal political practice in this period.

I pay particular attention to Morley's relations with various political leaders, such as Chamberlain, Gladstone, and Harcourt, because these seem to me very relevant to the major themes. Two examples of this relevance are: the theme of the 'complementary' nature of these relationships, of the man of ideas attaching himself to men of great practical talents; and the crisis over the succession to Gladstone as Liberal leader in 1894, when Morley's behaviour was, in my view, considerably affected by basic ideas and principles that I examine earlier in the book.

The policy issues that appear prominently in this account are surprisingly few in relation to the length of Morley's career in politics. This is partly to be explained by Morley's habit of concentrating on single questions and subordinating all else to them. I begin with Morley's involvement in the 1870s in the agitations of the Nonconformist pressure groups, the National Education League and the Liberation Society; but very soon Ireland and imperialism take over and occupy much of the rest of his career in constant alternation. What has particularly interested me about this has been the relationship between his preoccupation with these two issues and his attitude to the general condition of Liberal politics. My interpretation of this relationship has bearings that go beyond the career of Morley alone, and I hope to be able to examine these more fully in another work.

Morley was Irish Secretary in 1886 and again from 1892 to 1895, and thus principally responsible, with Gladstone, for the preparation of the first and second Home Rule Bills. In addition, he played a major role between 1886 and 1892 as exponent of the home-rule policy to which the Liberal party had become so suddenly committed. To this period I devote considerable but not, I think, dis-

PREFACE ix

proportionate attention. After 1895 a ten-year period which was dominated by his opposition to imperialism ended rather bizarrely in his acceptance of the office of Secretary of State for India, which he was to hold until 1910. My treatment of his work as Indian Secretary is brief, even though this was his longest period in office and greatest opportunity for substantial achievement. The reason for this brevity is that there has now been published an exhaustive account of this aspect of Morley's career in Professor S. A. Wolpert's *Morley and India 1906-1910*. To have gone over the same ground in detail when the work had already been so well done would indeed have been a superfluous labour, and so I concentrate instead on surveying fully Morley's earlier career.

Manuscript collections which contain large numbers of letters written by and to Morley have been opened up recently in numerous places. I refer in particular to the Asquith and Bryce papers at the Bodleian, the papers of Joseph Chamberlain at the Birmingham University Library, the papers of Frederic Harrison at the L.S.E., the papers of Lord Rosebery and Lord Haldane at the National Library of Scotland, and the papers of Lord Spencer and Sir William Harcourt which remain in private possession. The Gladstone papers in the British Museum, long accessible, also contain a great deal of material relevant to Morley; there are letters in many other collections referred to in the bibliography; and in addition the Bodleian Library at my suggestion purchased from the Library of Congress in Washington microfilms of over four hundred letters from Morley to Andrew Carnegie which are now available in the Bodleian and are of great interest to students of Morley and as a commentary on public events from 1892 to 1918.

This book could not therefore have been written without full and generous assistance from the staffs of the various libraries in which I worked, and I am most grateful for having received this in all cases. In addition to the libraries referred to above, I would like to mention the Foreign Office and India Office Libraries and the Library of Imperial College in London, the Central Library in Newcastle, and the National Library of Ireland in Dublin.

PREFACE

I wish to make a special reference to the Morley Library at the Ashburne Hall, Fallowfield, Manchester. Morley's very large library now belongs to the University of Manchester and is housed at the Ashburne Hall. It contains very little material of primary relevance to Morley's career, but I did find in it two items of considerable interest. The collection of books written by Morley himself includes a proof copy of the book which he wrote but did not publish (see below, page 320): 'Ten Years of Ireland' or 'A Chapter in the History of Ten Years', a largely factual and narrative survey of the Irish question in the 1880s. There is also a commonplace book containing numerous entries in Morley's own hand. A few extracts from this are quoted in an appendix. I am most grateful to the Librarian at the Ashburne Hall for showing the collection to me and letting me consult the books in it.

I wish also to express my appreciation of the kindness of Lord Harcourt in allowing me access to the papers of Sir William Harcourt at Stanton Harcourt, and of Lord Spencer in granting me permission to consult the Spencer papers at Althorp.

I wish to acknowledge with thanks the permission of the following to quote from works published by them: Ernest Benn Limited (Askwith, *Lord James of Hereford*; Hamer, *Papers of Lord Rendel*; Harris, *Auberon Herbert*; T. P. O'Connor's *Memoirs*); Jonathan Cape Ltd. (Massingham, *H.W.M.*); Cassell and Company Ltd. (Sir A. Chamberlain, *Down the Years* and *Politics from Inside*); Constable and Company Ltd. (Mills, *Sir Edward Cook*); William Heinemann Ltd. (A. Harrison, *Frederic Harrison*); Hodder and Stoughton Ltd. (Lord Haldane's *Autobiography*); Hutchinson and Company Ltd. (Sir A. Fitzroy's *Memoirs*; Mallet, *Herbert Gladstone*; Spender and Asquith's *Life of Asquith*); Longmans, Green and Co. Limited (Trevelyan, *Grey of Fallodon*); Macmillan & Co. Ltd. (Garvin, *Life of Chamberlain*; Viscount Gladstone, *After Thirty Years*; Gooch, *Life of Lord Courtney*; Hardy, *Early Life of Thomas Hardy*; Hirst, *Early Life and Letters of John Morley*; Lady Minto, *India, Minto and Morley*); Methuen and Company Ltd. (Lucas, *The Colvins and their Friends*; Scott, *Life and Death of a Newspaper*); John Murray Ltd. (Hutchinson, *Diaries of Sir Algernon West*; Morgan, *John, Viscount Morley*).

PREFACE

I am also grateful to Mr. Robert Rhodes James for having given me permission to quote from his two books, *Lord Randolph Churchill* and *Rosebery*, and for letting me see copies of letters from Morley to Rosebery at a time when the Rosebery papers were not accessible.

I wish to express my gratitude to Mrs. A. E. Croft for her very efficient and helpful work in connection with the typing of the manuscript of this book.

This book is based on an Oxford doctoral thesis which I submitted in 1964. I count myself fortunate to have had my work at Oxford supervised by Mr. R. B. McCallum, at that time Master of Pembroke College. His constant kindness and interest eased my path considerably.

D. A. HAMER
University of Lancaster

July 1968

CONTENTS

John Morley, c. 1883 — *Frontispiece*
(Photograph by the Radio Times Hulton Picture Library)

	Abbreviations	xv
1	The Early Years: Personal and Intellectual Crisis	1
2	A New Faith: Positivism or Millism?	16
3	The Emergence of an Individualistic Social Theory	33
4	An Intellectual in Politics	53
5	The Quest for New Principles	64
6	The Single Great Question: A Substitute for System	81
7	Morley and the Politics of Nonconformity	96
8	Morley and Chamberlain, 1873–1883	112
9	Ireland and Imperialism, 1879–1885	129
10	Chamberlain's Radical Campaign, 1885	147
11	The Rift with Chamberlain, 1885–1886	162
12	The Home-Rule Issue	183
13	The Liberal Party and the Home-Rule Preoccupation	195
14	Morley and the Maintenance of the Great Irish Policy	210
15	Coercion	228
16	The Search for New Liberal Policy, 1886–1890	240
17	Two Crises: The Eight-Hour Day and the Parnell Divorce	255
18	The Collapse of the Great Irish Policy, 1891–1894	271
19	The Change of Liberal Leadership, 1894	285

CONTENTS

20 Problems of Liberal Policy, 1894–1898 — 296
21 Imperialism and Liberalism, 1896–1902 — 311
22 Surviving in a New World — 329
23 The Liberals in Office, 1905–1914 — 343
24 Morley and the First World War: The Last Years — 360
Conclusion — 377
Appendix — 386
Bibliography — 390
Index — 403

ABBREVIATIONS

Works by Morley are referred to, without repetition of the author's name, by the following abbreviations. [Rest of full title is enclosed in square brackets.] For editions used, see bibliography.

Burke
[*The Life of Richard*] *Cobden*
Critical Miscellanies
[*Oliver*] *Cromwell*
Diderot [*and the Encyclopaedists*]
Edmund Burke [: *a Historical Study*]
[*The Life of William Ewart*] *Gladstone*
Indian Speeches [*1907–1909*]
Memorandum on Resignation [*August 1914*]
Miscellanies Fourth Series
Modern Characteristics [*A Series of Short Essays from the Saturday Review*]
[*The Struggle For*] *National Education*
On Compromise
Politics & History
Recollections
Rousseau
Studies in Literature
Voltaire
Walpole

Other abbreviations:
B.M.	The British Museum
F.R.	*The Fortnightly Review*
Handbook of Home Rule	J. Morley, 'Some Arguments Considered', in J. Bryce (ed.), *Handbook of Home Rule* . . ., London, 1887
Hansard	*Hansard's Parliamentary Debates*

ABBREVIATIONS

I.O.L.   India Office Library
N.D.C.   *Newcastle Daily Chronicle*
P.M.G.   *Pall Mall Gazette*

N.B. Letters to and from Morley are located, unless an indication to the contrary is given, in the collection of papers of his correspondent. Fuller information on these collections is to be found in the bibliography. Where a letter is referred to simply as 'To Harrison', 'To Harcourt', etc., the writer of the letter is Morley.

The three figures given in references to *Hansard*, e.g. 3, 250, 1168, relate to the series, the volume, and the column or columns where the speech is to be found.

The following abbreviations are used for works by other people. [Part omitted in square brackets]

[F.W.] Hirst, *Early Life & Letters* [*of John Morley*], 2 vols., London, 1927.

[J.S.] Mill, *Utilitarianism,* [*Liberty, and Representative Government*], Everyman edition, 1910.

I

THE EARLY YEARS: PERSONAL AND INTELLECTUAL CRISIS

JOHN MORLEY was born in Blackburn in 1838. His father, an Anglican surgeon, intended that he should enter holy orders; and the conflict that developed between them when Morley, at Oxford, in the late 1850s, began to find the foundations of his Christian faith being eroded, formed one of the principal influences over his intellectual development. On finding that Morley no longer wished to take up a clerical vocation, his father wrathfully cut off his allowance and obliged him to leave Oxford in haste with a pass degree only.[1] Morley then had to spend several penurious years in London seeking to establish himself in a professional career, either in law or in journalism, and subsisting as best he could on the proceeds of 'penny-a-lining'. It is essential to explore the impact on him of this personal crisis if we are to understand the development of his thought in the following ten or so years.

There can be no doubt of the profound emotional shock which the rift with his father caused him or of his preoccupation thereafter with finding some way of relieving the pain and grief and of remedying the psychological disturbance. In his biographical writings we can detect again and again echoes of his personal predicament in his examination of similar crises in the lives of other men who, in spite of these early setbacks, went on to become famous and achieve great things. Thus Diderot's father withdrew all financial support from the future editor of the *Encyclopaedia* when he refused to follow either of the occupations which the father had intended for him, and so the young Diderot was obliged to live on his wits in Paris, as was the young Morley in London. When Voltaire's father attempted to bind him to a legal career, they

[1] *Recollections*, I, pp. 5–7, 17, 31. Hirst, *Early Life & Letters*, I, pp. 7, 16–17.

quarrelled. When the young Edmund Burke decided that he preferred a literary career, his father, 'who had set his heart on having a son in the rank of a barrister', finally 'withdrew his son's allowance, or else reduced it so low that the recipient could not possibly live upon it'. Burke then turned to literary work for a livelihood, 'like so many hundreds of smaller men before and since'.[1] One may perhaps see in this an attempt to mitigate the individual, personal pain involved in the crisis in his own career by generalizing it into something of common occurrence in the early lives of men of talent. In his writings we are sometimes aware of a sense of guilt about his own share in the family rift. In *On Compromise*, which he published in 1874, he discusses the question of when it is seasonable and prudent to make known one's opinions, especially on matters of religion, and declares, with obvious reference to his own experience: 'When we come to declaring opinions that are [, however foolishly and unreasonably,][2] associated with pain and even a kind of turpitude in the minds of those who strongly object to them, then some of our most powerful sympathies are naturally engaged. We wonder whether duty to truth can possibly require us to inflict keen distress on those to whom we are bound by the tenderest and most consecrated ties.' The problem was how 'to reconcile unflinching honesty with a just and becoming regard for the feelings of those who have claims upon our forbearance.'[3] And his answer to those perplexed by this problem again shows his desire to generalize the solitary, personal pain out of the experience. The fact is, he writes, that because 'our own is characteristically and cardinally an epoch of transition in the very foundations of belief and conduct', it is inevitable that intellectual development should be 'a tale not of concord, but of households divided against themselves', of 'the son against the father'.[4]

Morley's willingness to generalize thus on the basis of his personal experience obviously stemmed in part from a consciousness that it was an experience undergone by others in his own day;

[1] *Diderot*, I, p. 15. *Voltaire*, pp. 46, 48. *Burke*, p. 13.
[2] This is omitted in the version published in *F.R.*, July 1874, p. 104.
[3] *On Compromise*, pp. 148–9. *F.R.*, July 1874, p. 104.
[4] *F.R.*, Apr. 1874, p. 437; July 1874, p. 106.

and some of the influence of *On Compromise* over the young liberal intellectuals of the late nineteenth century is clearly attributable to its relevance to this aspect of their predicament.[1] One of them was later to say of *On Compromise* that 'in his youth it was a great release from difficulties which had pressed hideously'.[2] W. E. Houghton has described the feelings of loneliness, alienation, and disintegration experienced by Victorian intellectuals as a result of estrangement from family and friends over a change of belief. 'When doubts issued in conversions to another Church or to outright agnosticism, Victorian families were torn asunder.' He quotes Bagehot's description in 1855 of the age as one when 'intellectual change has set father and son at variance'.[3] Two of Morley's closest friends had strikingly similar experiences. In 1854, not long before Morley himself went to Oxford, Leslie Stephen had entered holy orders, in part because he was tempted by the prospect of a tutorship and life at Cambridge, and in part because he did not wish to offend his father, who wanted his son to have a career in the Church. Even at that stage, however, his Christian faith was very superficial, and soon he found it slipping away altogether. Before he could bring himself to reveal his true position and give up his fellowship at Cambridge, he suffered severe mental anguish through fearing 'what grief his determination would cause to some of his family who were nearest and dearest to him'. Like Morley, having taken the plunge, he moved to London, where he was 'driven to the occupation of penny-a-lining'. It was while working on the *Saturday Review* that he made Morley's acquaintance, and the fact that by 1873 Morley had become one of the only two friends with whom he professed to feel fairly confident of establishing thorough sympathy in conversation was surely not as 'odd' as Stephen thought it was.[4]

[1] For this influence, see below, p. 246.
[2] Augustine Birrell as quoted by H. Laski in a letter to Holmes, 12 Feb. 1924, M. D. Howe (ed.), *Holmes-Laski Letters. The Correspondence of Mr. Justice Holmes and Harold J. Laski 1916–1935*, I, 1953, p. 593.
[3] W. E. Houghton, *The Victorian Frame of Mind 1830–1870*, New Haven, 1957, pp. 81, 83.
[4] F. W. Maitland, *The Life and Letters of Leslie Stephen*, 1906, pp. 131–4, 146–7, 158, 163, 173, 235. Morley, *Recollections*, I, pp. 116–17.

Then there was Frederic Harrison, who, after a strongly religious upbringing, decided not to enter the Church when he lost his faith at Oxford in the early 1850s. He tells in his memoirs of how the intensity of the language with which he denounced the Church of England in justifying this decision caused his mother great pain. He describes a letter which he wrote to her defending himself against her imputations of 'unchristian presumption' and 'irreligion' as 'an example of the cruel domestic sufferings of affectionate men who found their genuine convictions met by the sorrow and remonstrance of those dear to them', and as 'a specimen of the pressure put by the elders on the thought of the rising generation'. In 1863 he wrote in his diary about an article which he wrote critical of the Church: 'The shock that it caused my mother will remain the dark cloud in which the matter is covered round in my memory. The blow must have come to her some time. All that I had done for years to prepare for it was of no avail. This is but one case of the dreadful anarchy in which we live'.[1] Shortly afterwards Harrison and Morley became close friends, and their thinking began to move in a direction the significance of which we can understand in terms of the desire to overcome this 'anarchy' and personal unsettlement.

In *On Compromise* Morley declares that there is becoming apparent a tendency in thought which can bridge this gap between the generations and prevent the profession of dissent from Christianity from causing such sharp disruption of personal relationships. The modern dissenter, although not accepting Christianity, nevertheless 'explains it by referring its growth to the better, and not to the worse part of human nature, to men's cravings for a higher morality'; and, as a result of this understanding, the 'tendency of modern free thought' is more and more towards the preservation of continuity with 'the old faith' by 'the extraction of the first and more permanent elements' of it 'to make the purified material' of a new faith. This will be a new synthesis which is certain to 'stand as closely related to Christianity as Christianity stood closely related to the old Judaic dispensation'. Those who build this 'new creed by which men can live' will look

[1] F. Harrison, *Autobiographic Memoirs*, I, 1911, pp. 39–40, 97, 142–7, 208.

for material to 'the purified and sublimated ideas, of which the confessions and rites of the Christian churches have been the grosser expression'. 'Just as what was once the new dispensation was preached *a Judaeis ad Judaeos apud Judaeos*, so must the new, that is to be, find a Christian teacher and Christian hearers. It can hardly be other than an expansion, a development, a readaptation, of all the moral and spiritual truth that lay hidden under the worn-out forms.' And it is this which, according to Morley, will make the sharpness of personal conflict such as he had experienced less and less necessary. '[There is] some cause for thinking that dissent from the current beliefs is less and less likely to inflict upon those who retain them any very intolerable kind or degree of mental pain. . . . If a believer finds that his son, for instance, has ceased to believe, he no longer has this disbelief thrust upon him in gross and irreverent forms. Nor does he any longer suppose that the unbelieving son must necessarily be a profligate.'[1] In this we can see Morley striving to come to terms with the crisis in his life in two ways. First, he generalizes the conflict with his father into something for which he could feel little personal responsibility because its development was an inevitable consequence of his having been born into an age of transition in thought and belief. But, secondly, he is able to re-establish a sense of continuity in his life by stressing that the true nature of this transition as one to a new faith developing out of and closely related to the old is now becoming apparent.

On Compromise was written in the early 1870s, in other words about ten years after the rift with his father. What had happened in the interim was that Morley had been searching for the new faith or system of belief which was to be a replacement for the old of the kind described above. It was a quest that could only have been encouraged by its close relationship to one of the major intellectual preoccupations of the day. The assumption that the age was one of transition from one system or faith to another was widely held by Morley's contemporaries in the intellectual world. The question usually asked was not whether a new creed would emerge but what the new creed which must inevitably emerge

[1] *On Compromise*, pp. 151-5, 163-4. F.R., July 1874, pp. 104-9.

would be.¹ And it is obvious that the reason why so many intellectuals, like Morley, thought in terms of system and synthesis was that they, too, wanted a substitute for the Christian religion, faith in which they had themselves lost or were losing, and which could no longer claim to be a comprehensive creed in the sense of providing the organizing principles of belief for most educated people. A new faith was needed, wrote John Stuart Mill, because 'the philosophic minds of the world can no longer believe its religion, or can only believe it with modifications amounting to an essential change of its character'.² Mill described the 'utility' principle as having been, 'in one among the best senses of the word, a religion' for him;³ and his essays on religion, published posthumously, show how he had come to incline towards religion as a major element in the renovation of thought. In fact, the writings of Mill and the controversy over positivism⁴—two of the main influences over Morley's intellectual development—show that the period of this development, between 1860 and 1875, was one of intellectual crisis in which the spread of religious uncertainty and doubt produced a strong craving for order in thought and belief.

To many of the intellectuals of the day anarchy seemed to prevail in the realms of thought and belief. This is clear enough from the articles in the review which Morley edited after 1867. In 1868 Walter Bagehot wrote in the *Fortnightly*: 'An instinct of revision is felt to be abroad in human opinion, of which thinking men want to know the direction, and wish, if they could, to see the end.' A year later Frederic Harrison declared: 'There is abroad a strange consciousness of doubt, instability, and incoherence.'⁵ Morley's own writings reflect an awareness of living in an age of transition and confusion. In *On Compromise* he writes of changes taking place in the realm of thought that are creating a condition of constant fear and misgiving. People had the 'hurried uneasy mien' of those

---

¹ Houghton, pp. 1–14, 77–83.
² Mill, *Autobiography*, 6th edition, 1879, p. 239.
³ Ibid., p. 67.
⁴ See below, chapter 2.
⁵ *F.R.*, June 1868, p. 645; Nov. 1869, p. 471.

PERSONAL AND INTELLECTUAL CRISIS 7

who live 'amid earthquakes', and seemed to be numbly waiting for they knew not what: 'all is doubt, hesitation, and shivering expectancy.'[1]

As to the remedy for this situation there was a large measure of agreement among the intellectuals. Mill summed up their attitude when he argued that the prevailing confusion in matters spiritual and intellectual could be ended only by 'the evolution of some faith, whether religious or merely human', in which men could really believe.[2] There was widespread concern for the discovery of some system or some great comprehensive unifying principle that would replace anarchy by order. Harrison suggested that the age was characterized by a craving for organic, systematic belief. 'At bottom', he wrote, 'mankind really longs for something like a rule of life, something that shall embody all the phases of our multiform knowledge, and yet slake our thirst for organic order.'[3] Matthew Arnold believed that the individual needed to have 'an Idea of the world in order not to be prevailed over by the world's multitudinousness'. Order in thought was essential also, he wrote, for the harmonizing of 'all the multitudinous, turbulent, and blind impulses of our ordinary selves'.[4] In *Liberty, Equality, Fraternity*, James Fitzjames Stephen pointed to the great desirability of working towards a situation in which 'we were all of one mind' about 'the nature of men and their relation to the world or worlds in which they live', and in which 'the divided forces of mankind' could be united 'upon one foundation of moral and spiritual truth, and directed towards a set of ends forming one harmonious whole'.[5] A. J. Balfour noted how prevalent was the demand for a scheme of knowledge which 'shall give rational unity to an adequate creed' and for an all-reconciling theory 'by which each inevitable claim of our complex nature may be harmonised' and belief unified 'into an ordered whole compacted into one coherent

---

[1] pp. 36–7. *F.R.*, Apr. 1874, p. 437.
[2] Mill, *Autobiography*, p. 239.
[3] *F.R.*, Nov. 1869, pp. 471–2.
[4] L. Trilling, *Matthew Arnold*, 1939, pp. 32–3. Arnold, *Culture and Anarchy: An Essay in Political and Social Criticism*, 1869, p. 225.
[5] 1873, pp. 63–8.

structure'.[1] To T. H. Huxley even free thought was a phenomenon of transition. He hoped that one day it would 'organize itself into a coherent system, embracing human life and the world as one harmonious whole'.[2]

Morley's own personal need for belief must have been strongly reinforced by the prevalence of these attitudes among the writers and thinkers with whom he was most closely associated. The nature and purpose of his intellectual activity were clearly laid out for him. Mill's influence on him was profound, and Mill said of this 'transitional period', and of its being able to end only when some new faith had been evolved, that, 'when things are in this state, all thinking or writing which does not tend to promote such a renovation, is of very little value beyond the moment'.[3] The positivists would have restricted intellectual activity to whatever was deemed to facilitate the transition to the 'positive' era.

The problem, as it appears in Morley's writings, is in particular one of the effect which lack of order in thought and belief can have on personal conduct and character. Like many other Victorian thinkers, he was worried about the absence of agreed standards of right and wrong and definitions of moral obligation and duty. Henry Sidgwick wrote in 1878 that many of his contemporaries felt 'no general doubt' as to the existence of an ideal of Duty, but did not know how it could be 'concretely realised here and now—there are so many competing methods and so much to be said on both sides of so many questions'.[4] Worried about the absence of 'clear-shining moral illumination' and of some means of ascertaining what duty might be in given circumstances, Morley eventually tried to provide such a means through the principle of 'compromise' as defined and explained in his book on that theme. He stated his aim as to relate rules concerning 'the expediency of compromise and conformity' to 'actual conditions' so as to 'transform them into practical guides and real interpreters

---

[1] Quoted in K. Young, *Arthur James Balfour. The Happy Life of the Politician Prime Minister Statesman and Philosopher 1848–1930*, 1963, pp. 152–7.
[2] Quoted in L. Huxley, *Life and Letters of Thomas Henry Huxley*, 2nd edition, 1903, p. 111.
[3] *Autobiography*, p. 239.
[4] A. S. and E. M. S., *Henry Sidgwick. A Memoir*, 1906, p. 337.

of what is right and best in thought and conduct, in a special and definite kind of emergency'.[1] Morley saw an intimate connection between acceptance of a synthesis or religion and certainty about rightness in conduct. A synthesis is an interpretation of the whole of existence, an explanation of every part in terms of the whole and of the whole through every part. This, Morley believed, provides the basis for a 'natural' morality, according to which that is right or good which conforms to the ordering of the totality and is thus 'organic' or natural, while that is wrong which defies the natural order of things. In 1868 Morley wrote that the definition of 'wrong' which he favoured was 'non-conformity to the requirements of the surrounding conditions'. The 'high moral type' was 'that which best meets the requirements of the situation'. Morality was rooted in a 'vision of what social circumstances demand', and behaviour in response to such a vision was what Morley termed 'expediency'.[2] He was later to refer approvingly to Holbach's principle that 'we must seek a base for morality in the necessity of things';[3] and we shall see how his approach to politics was shaped by his belief in the existence of a natural order which it was man's duty to discover and to which he should make his actions conform. He once wrote that a government 'which keeps most close to morality in its political dealings' is also keeping 'close to the nature of things' and will enjoy 'that success which rewards conformity to the nature of things.'[4]

What created additional difficulties in Morley's day for those who sought guides for conduct in the reality of 'nature' was that it now appeared that, if there was any order in 'nature', it came only through the fortuitous selection of species, through the inter-

[1] F.R., Apr. 1874, p. 426. On Compromise, p. 3. Cf. also F.R., July 1870, p. 8, and Critical Miscellanies, I, p. 153.
[2] F.R., Mar. 1868, p. 337. 'Expediency' and 'morality' seem to have been interchangeable words for Morley; thus in his article, 'Edmund Burke', in F.R., Feb. 1867, pp. 136–7, he refers to politics as having 'expediency for its standard' and being concerned 'with a shifting expediency', but when it was republished as a book these phrases became 'morality for its standard' and 'with practical morality'. Edmund Burke, pp. 20, 23.
[3] F.R., Aug. 1877, p. 282.
[4] F.R., May 1881, p. 645.

actions of chance and force. Morley described 'the Darwinian hypothesis and the mass of evidence for it' as having 'startled men into a sense of the precariousness of the official foundations of virtue and duty'. 'How were right and wrong to hold their own' against this new 'conception of the Universe'?[1] Morley always, however, strongly resisted the application of Darwinian principles to morals and politics. If this, then, was not the true 'nature of things', what was? Perhaps there was no order and meaning in nature, after all. But Morley refused to accept this. For, so long as there was no generally accepted synthesis which explained the parts and fragments of life by their relationship to the whole scheme of things, so long could there be no agreement on 'right' and 'wrong', no common understanding of what was 'natural' and therefore 'moral'; and so the anarchy of the age would intensify. Therefore, there must be found a system representing a vision of the organic relationships of all things one to another.

Morley believed that firmness, order, assurance of thought are among the most fundamental of all human needs. Most people, he once wrote, are content to 'accept the traditional system of their time' without scrutinizing 'its internal coherence' too closely or paying too much heed to 'its logical weight and consistency', because they 'want a religion to live by, or perhaps to die by'. He acknowledged that there are 'those who think almost any fabric of common and ordered belief better for men, than the seeming chaos of intricate and multitudinous growths which now overspread the field of European opinion'. The need for a 'firm ordering of our knowledge' is a 'prime demand of human nature'.[2] A 'craving for mental peace may become much stronger' than 'passion for demonstrated truth' and lead people into accepting systems.[3] Thus the desire for order in thought and belief can be rooted in fear of mental disorder and disintegration.

In Morley's writings there is a very strong emphasis on the connection between order in thought and order in mind and character. He admitted that a 'too common drawback to great

[1] *F.R.*, Aug. 1877, p. 271.　[2] *F.R.*, Jan. 1867, p. 10. *Voltaire*, p. 39.
[3] *Rousseau*, II, p. 255.

openness of mind' was that it produced loose beliefs, vacillating opinions, and feeble convictions, 'appearing, shifting, vanishing, in the quicksands of an unstable mind'.[1] Opinions were a very important part of character, and 'a commanding grasp of principles, whether they are public or not, is at the very root of coherency of character'. Personality becomes 'broken, incoherent, and fragmentary' if a man's opinions are not 'reasoned and consistent'. Morley praised Rousseau for having 'cared extremely that the opinions which he did hold should be a solid and undisturbed part of himself: not an element of fever, agitation, aggression, but the integral substance and all-pervading essence of a collected character and an even life'. Order in belief, he wrote, 'emancipates us from the paralysing dubieties of distraught souls', and a sense of the realtionship of things is 'the master-key and prime law of sanity'. What was so wrong about the disjointed, dispersive nature of his contemporaries' beliefs was that it 'fritters character away, breaks it up into discordant parts, and dissolves into mercurial fluidity that leavening sincerity and free and cheerful boldness, which comes of harmonious principles of faith and action'.[2]

The connection between consciousness of intellectual 'anarchy' and fear of mental instability in the careers of many Victorian writers and thinkers has been copiously documented by W. E. Houghton in his *Victorian Frame of Mind*. The positivists, the system-makers with whom, as we shall see, Morley was most closely associated, constructed their system partly in order to confer freedom from the paralysing and disintegrating effects of mental confusion. J. H. Bridges, a positivist, attributed mental and physical illness directly to absence of ordered belief; while Frederic Harrison urged Morley to commit himself to positivism in order to enjoy 'peace & security of mind' and 'feel the infinite peace & rest & strength of a cohesive intellectual, social, & practical system all developed together'.[3]

The relevance of this to Morley's own situation is obvious when

[1] F.R., Jan. 1874, p. 2. *Critical Miscellanies*, III, p. 55.
[2] *On Compromise*, pp. 120–3, 135. F.R., May 1872, p. 499. *Critical Miscellanies*, I, p. 180. *Rousseau*, I, p. 12.
[3] F.R., Aug. 1869, pp. 140 ff. Harrison to Morley, 10 Feb. (1874).

we consider his proneness to moods of melancholy and depression, his great fear of the purely intellectual, introspective life, and the strain under which he was often put by extreme nervousness and sensitivity. In early manhood his awareness of relationship and meaning in life had received a severe double blow—in his religious beliefs, which were disintegrated and not replaced by any single new set of beliefs; and in his personal circumstances, the rift with his father, who died in 1862 and was scarcely ever referred to thereafter by Morley, being accompanied by several years of what appear to have been considerable hardship and loneliness in London. The struggle to re-establish a sense of relationship and meaning in his life seems to have been a difficult one.

Erich Fromm has described three stages in the mental disintegration which sets in once a man has lost a sense of meaning and connection in life: doubt, or paralysis of the mind; paralysis of the ability to act; and finally melancholy and depression verging on the suicidal.[1] All three stages are clearly present in Morley's situation. Frequently he seems afflicted by the paralysis of doubt, and his spirit is oppressed by the 'paralysing' impression that at the bottom of all things human 'lies emptiness and nothingness' and 'all the works that are done under the sun are vanity and vexation of spirit'. In the early 1860s he wrote of 'the paralysing doctrine' of the meaninglessness of life, in 1870 of 'the paralysing dubieties of distraught souls', in 1878 of the paralysing effect of a 'sceptical and centrifugal state of mind'.[2] In *On Compromise* there is frequent reference to doubt, inconclusiveness, and incoherence as characteristics of the modern intellect. There is 'a deadly weakening of intellectual conclusiveness', a general 'reluctance to commit one's self', and thought is 'distracted, wavering, confused'.[3]

We shall see later how indecisiveness and inability to fix on and follow through a course of action characterized Morley throughout his life.[4] As for Fromm's third stage, Morley's temperament was subject to recurring melancholy, which would tend to plunge him

[1] E. Fromm, *The Fear of Freedom*, 1942, p. 15.
[2] *Modern Characteristics*, pp. 231–5, 258–63. *Critical Miscellanies*, I, p. 180. *Studies in Literature*, p. 303.
[3] pp. 17–18, 21, 28, 37, 127–8, 133–5.
[4] See below, p. 64.

into moods of depression and extreme pessimism. In an essay of 1865 entitled 'Nineteenth-century Sadness', he refers to 'minds who love to reflect habitually on the confusions and miseries in which man is bound'.[1] This is a very accurate description of the kind of 'nineteenth-century' mind which his *Recollections* in particular reveal Morley himself as having had. The *Recollections* contain a strikingly large number of meditations and disquisitions from throughout his career on themes of mortality and of the meaninglessness and mystery of human existence.[2] The scene of autumn and fading light and human loneliness which he conjures up with such beauty at the end of the book is a perfect representation of the imaginative world in which he spent his life. He seemed haunted by the vision of life as but 'a gruesome mask of shadows' played out in the 'gray ghostly light' that was all that ever-present intimations of mortality would allow.[3] 'You talk of death and life', he once wrote to Rosebery. ' 'Tis a strange dance of shadows.'[4] There is evident a strong connection between his melancholy and his loss of religious belief. When in his biographical studies he dwells on the severe mental struggles which his subjects have undergone in regard to religion, his generalizations give his descriptions an unmistakable personal application. For example, in *Cromwell* he refers to 'those painful struggles with religious gloom that at one time or another confront nearly every type of mind endowed with spiritual faculty'.[5] In his early essays written for the *Saturday Review* and published in book form in 1865 as *Modern Characteristics*, we can see something of the effect on him of his recent loss of faith. He writes of a 'feeling of the worthlessness of all our aims and objects of endeavour' as 'one of the very few convictions which, in some form and at one time or another, come home to all the world'. No man is 'entirely unsusceptible' of such a 'chilling persuasion', and to some it is 'a source of real torment'.[6] In *Voltaire* he writes that, as a man grows older, aware-

[1] *Modern Characteristics*, p. 231.
[2] e.g. I, pp. 275–6, 284, 381–2; II, pp. 75, 113–30, 361–7.
[3] *Voltaire*, pp. 44–5. To Chamberlain, 26 Mar. 1877.
[4] 25 Aug. 1892, quoted in R. R. James, *Rosebery* . . . , 1963, p. 269.
[5] 2nd edition, 1904, p. 14.
[6] *Modern Characteristics*, pp. 231–5, 258–63.

ness of 'the vast space' of the 'eternal sea' and of the narrowness of the confined space of human life 'oppresses the soul with a burden that sorely tries its strength'.[1]

Morley's life seems to have involved a constant struggle to preserve an evenness and balance of mind and temper. An emotional instability would be revealed in sudden, violent changes in mood; and at times it seemed that beneath his customary graciousness and urbanity there were serious, almost volcanic, stresses at work. When reference was made to Morley's 'philosophic calm', Sir Henry Campbell-Bannerman is said to have retorted: 'Ah! wait till you know Morley better; there is no one who can boil up heat so unexpectedly.'[2] From his own experience he knew how over some quite trivial matter Morley could produce an 'unseemly display of temper'.[3] Lord Esher found Morley 'quick tempered'; T. P. O'Connor refers to his 'violent outbursts of rage'; Lord Rosebery said that he could be 'extraordinarily irritable'.[4] Morley himself was aware of an 'old Adam of impatience' in him that could lead to a vehemence in discussion which he would later regret.[5]

The fact is that Morley often lived in what he called 'a state of super-excitation'.[6] When writing *Rousseau*, for example, he confessed to a friend that the work 'is straining me—and I am in danger of exaltation . . . I am hopelessly without a sedative, moral or physical'.[7] His proneness to emotional unbalance, and his fear of what this might lead to, were clearly the main causes of his determination throughout his literary and political careers to prevent the predominance of emotional influences. He described himself as a man who had not been 'an emotionalist'.[8] He strove to keep

[1] pp. 44–5.
[2] Quoted in Sir Almeric Fitzroy, *Memoirs*, II, 3rd edition, n.d., p. 472.
[3] See F. E. Hamer (ed.), *The Personal Papers of Lord Rendel*, 1931, p. 165.
[4] M. V. Brett (ed.), *Journals and Letters of Reginald Viscount Esher*, I, 1934, p. 181. T. P. O'Connor, *Memoirs of an Old Parliamentarian*, I, 1929, p. 296. J. W. Robertson Scott, *The Life and Death of a Newspaper* . . . , 1952, p. 42.
[5] Cf. to Congreve, 13 May 1874, B.M. Add. MSS. 45241, f. 65. For an example of such vehemence and Morley's regret for it, see *Gladstone*, III, pp. 460, 479.
[6] To Harrison, 14 Jan. 1875.   [7] To Harrison, 5 Jan. 1873.
[8] Quoted in A. Harrison, *Frederic Harrison. Thoughts and Memories*, 1926, p. 177.

himself free of that 'unrestrained passion' which he considered one of Burke's main failings. Burke's language, he once wrote, 'burns with too consuming a blaze for the whole to diffuse that clear, undisturbed light which we are accustomed to find in men who have trained themselves to balance ideas, to weigh mutually opposed speculations, in short, to argue and to reason . . . '.[1] The sovereignty of reason and the control of emotion became his guiding principles; and his career involved a constant effort to shield the 'clear, undisturbed light' of reason from the forces that menaced it with extinction.

'Peace of mind' depended, then, on order in thought. We shall now trace the successive stages through which Morley's intellectual development passed as he searched for some principle or system that would confer that order on his thinking.

[1] *F.R.*, Feb. 1867, pp. 137–8. *Edmund Burke*, pp. 25–6.

2

A NEW FAITH: POSITIVISM OR MILLISM?

FOR a time it seemed that Morley might be finding the new system of belief in the positivist philosophy of Auguste Comte. The ideas of Comte, a pioneer French sociologist, had strongly interested and influenced John Stuart Mill in the 1830s. Morley was probably introduced to them by James Cotter Morison, one of his tutors at Oxford, and then in London he entered the circle of the positivists through his literary association and personal friendship with George Eliot and G. H. Lewes, his predecessor as editor of the *Fortnightly Review*. The system and the friendship of some of its adherents, notably Frederic Harrison, 'laid strong hold' upon him, and he drew close to formal acceptance of the positivist creed.[1] In his difficult, lonely early years in London the appeal of this small, self-confident group of intellectuals must have been very strong.

Morley often later acknowledged the importance of Comte's writings as an early intellectual influence. In this confused, 'transitional' phase the ideas and emphases of positivism shaped his thinking and provided organizing principles for his literary work. Thus, he acquired the positivists' enthusiasm for French culture and thought, and most of his early literary exercises were studies in this field. In these the ideas of Comte very often provide the basic assumptions for his structure of comment and interpretation. He later said that it was the French Comtist, Pierre Laffitte, who 'in the many conversations we had together' did 'more than anybody else to furnish the key and the direction to my French studies'.[2] In 1868 he gave as one reason for writing on Joseph de Maistre the influence of this early nineteenth-century conservative thinker on Comte, for, 'accepted or detested, Positivism is

---
[1] *Recollections*, I, pp. 68–70.
[2] Ibid., I, 69, 81.

being every day more and more clearly perceived to be the great battle-field of modern philosophic and social controversy'.[1]

After the crisis of his loss of Christian faith Morley was searching for some new means of re-establishing a sense of meaning and purpose in human existence, of relating the individual to society and to the movements of history. Postitivism, with its stress on individual achievement within a process defined by sociological laws, enabled him in his literary works to depict individuals operating in a meaningful social and historical context. Its stages and laws and explanations of the processes of change and of the improvement inherent in them made history seem ordered and charged with purpose. As a result Morley could write of Comte in 1871: 'That my whole idea of history is his, is certain'.[2] In the *Recollections* he describes how the Comtists showed him history as 'an ordered course'.[3] In an essay of 1870 he claimed that, by revealing 'the succession of social states', 'the great fact of social evolution' leads one to find 'a natural and observable order' in human development. By studying human societies in the different states through which they have passed, one can develop a sense of order in history and thus be able also to predict the future.[4] It is scarcely surprising to find him even writing of 'the religion of history', with the study of history becoming 'an instrument of moral training'.[5]

Comte's thesis that European civilization was now passing through the anarchic transitional period preceding the 'positive' era, which would be founded on scientific thought, provided both an explanation of the Victorian religious and intellectual predicament and the assurance that a new ordering of ideas was shortly to emerge. To Morley the mid-nineteenth century was like the age before the introduction of Christianity.[6] His view of history, derived from his study of Comte, was that since the sixteenth century, when the disintegration of the old synthesis, Christianity,

[1] *F.R.*, May 1868, p. 483.
[2] To Harrison, 9. Dec. 1871.
[3] I, pp. 69–70.
[4] *F.R.*, Feb. 1870, pp. 133, 138–9.
[5] *F.R.*, Jan. 1867, p. 17. Cf. *F.R.*, Aug. 1867, pp. 226 ff.
[6] *Recollections*, I, p. 19.

had begun, a new synthesis, connected with the development of science and sociology, had been forming. Since human beings could not bear mere negation and craved the 'mental peace' that only order in thought and belief could afford, Christianity had survived even the destructive efforts of the *philosophes* of the eighteenth century. It would, in fact, finally disappear only as the result of 'the slow steadfast growth of some replacing faith'. Morley believed that the great remedy for the anarchy of modern thought was 'possession of a new doctrine', the establishment of a religion that would be, as Christianity had been, the 'supreme, penetrating, controlling, decisive part of a man's life'; and it was to the Comtist 'religion of humanity' that he seemed for a while to be looking for the 'indispensable synthesis'.[1]

Positivism, he wrote, shows 'the direction which is almost necessarily taken by all who attempt, in however informal a manner, to construct for themselves some working system of faith, in place of the faith which science and criticism have sapped'.[2] And he himself was one of those engaged in this effort. His early writings show confidence that positivism can provide the desired new religion-synthesis. In *Rousseau* he asserted that, possessed by the new religion of progress and humanity, 'we shall move with an assurance that no scepticism and no advance of science can ever shake'. Then 'each fresh acquisition in knowledge', each new 'widening of experience', instead of disintegrating thought and belief as was the case in the nineteenth century, would 'only kindle new fervour' and make even 'wider and firmer' the 'positive base' of the new faith.[3] In another essay he described how the new 'system of life' and 'social faith', based on science and history, conferred a sense of 'a self-sustaining order and a self-sufficing harmony' in all the 'faculties and parts and energies of universal life'. His description stresses the benefit which he sought above all else, release from doubt and paralysis of will. 'The active energies are not', he claimed, 'paralysed by the possi-

---

[1] Ibid. *Diderot*, I, pp. 4–5. *Rousseau*, II, pp. 255–6. *Voltaire*, p. 293. *On Compromise*, pp. 36, 42. F.R., Feb. 1875, p. 153; Apr. 1874, pp. 437, 440.
[2] *On Compromise*, p. 152. F.R., July 1874, p. 105.
[3] II, pp. 277–81.

bilities of enfeebling doubt, nor the reason drawn down and stultified by apprehension lest its methods should discredit a document, or its inferences clash with a dogma, or its light flash unseasonably on a mystery.' Unlike the old synthesis, this 'scientific and rounded interpretation of the facts of life' has 'a harmony' so developed that 'freshly found truths' made belief all the more 'ample and elaborate'. The positivist synthesis and the worship of humanity can provide a cure for religious gloom as well:

> The last appalling stroke of annihilation itself is measured with purest fortitude by one, whose religious contemplation dwells most habitually upon the sovereignty of obdurate laws in the vast revolving circle of physical forces, on the one hand, and, on the other, upon that moral order which the vision and pity of good men for their fellows, guiding the spontaneous energy of all men in strife with circumstance, have raised into a structure sublimer and more amazing than all the majesty of outer nature.[1]

Progress, ordered movement, inevitable improvement—these are the themes of the system in which Morley wanted to believe. The system would re-establish a sense of continuity and order in human affairs, as in Morley's own life. It would give meaning to the change and flux and movement that were felt as the predominant characteristics of the modern world by showing them to be the conditions of inevitable evolution into a better order. Like any system of thought, positivism professed to reveal the future course of human development. From it Morley derived confidence in the certainty of progress. The record of human experience may seem to be one of anarchy and discord, and this impression may paralyse; but, Morley wrote, fortified by the insight which such a system affords, the interest of historic study lies in 'tracing, amid the immense turmoil of events and through the confusion of voices, the devious course of the sacred torch' of social progress. History does have a 'real subject', and that is 'the improvement of social arrangements'. When men are overwhelmed by an impression of multitudinousness and disorder, they should appreciate that what they are seeing and feeling most immediately is not the whole of

---

[1] *Critical Miscellanies*, I, pp. 220, 236–9. F.R., Dec. 1870, pp. 657, 666–7.

reality but only interruptions in a general process. History is 'a record of social growth and its conditions', but within that there is also a record of 'interruption and misadventure and perturbation'. To convey this idea Morley used the metaphor of the railway, machinery functioning in accordance with ascertainable mechanical laws, which was to Victorians the great symbol of material progress and was often employed by them to express the 'idea of history'.[1] History was, he wrote, like a locomotive on a line. Although there could be and were frequent delays and disasters, owing to the carelessness of men at the controls or to obstructions on the line, the fact remained that it was 'the "law" of a locomotive engine to run on the rails', and those rails led to one terminus and no other. To most people history is no more than a confusion of 'broken machinery' and 'fragments', the products of these delays and mishaps. But it is not so. A few minds, whose faith confers social vision, can discern the 'great lines of the future' stretching onward all the time. History is not merely fragments and turmoil, but has meaning, the meaning of progress and improvement, understood only by these few minds.[2]

Nevertheless, by the early 1870s it was growing obvious that Morley was finding this new synthesis as little acceptable as he had found the old. This development can in part be traced to the growth of a new and opposed intellectual influence over him, the influence of John Stuart Mill. One major difference between Morley and leading English positivists was that he was introduced to the system slightly later than they were. Frederic Harrison, E. S. Beesly, and J. H. Bridges were all at Wadham College, Oxford, in the early 1850s, and there a dominant intellectual influence was that of Richard Congreve. Congreve, in fact, resigned his Wadham fellowship in 1855 upon deciding to dedicate himself to positivism, and he was later to become its 'high priest' in England. Morley, on the other hand, was not at Oxford until the end of the decade, when, as he testifies, Mill's *On Liberty*

[1] Cf. H. House in N. Annan and others, *Ideas and Beliefs of the Victorians*, 1949, p. 71.
[2] *F.R.*, Jan. 1867, p. 16; Aug. 1876, pp. 168–9; Apr. 1874, p. 453. *Critical Miscellanies*, I, pp. 4–5. *On Compromise*, pp. 81–2.

POSITIVISM OR MILLISM?

appeared and made a great impression on young intellectuals.[1] In 1864 Mill published his *Auguste Comte and Positivism*, explaining why, having once been strongly attracted to and influenced by Comte's thought, he had finally rejected it as a system. A year later Morley began what soon developed into a very close friendship with Mill. According to Morley, his own inherited nonconformist outlook and disposition to oppose authoritarianism in the realm of thought and belief were now 'confirmed by the influence of Mill' and of men to whom Mill introduced him, such as Spencer, Tyndall, and T. H. Huxley. It was Huxley, for instance, Morley recalled, who 'bitterly condemned official Positivism as Catholicism minus Christianity'.[2]

In order to understand why Mill's influence replaced that of positivism it is necessary to consider why it made such an impact on Morley. The relationship between them was established because Mill was impressed by an article entitled 'New Ideas' published by Morley, anonymously, in the *Saturday Review* in October 1865. Mill wrote to Morley asking to make his acquaintance and saying of the essay—which was indeed, as Morley later acknowledged, 'the pure milk of the Millite word'—that 'it shows an unusual amount of qualities which go towards making the most valuable kind of writer for the general public'.[3] It is obvious that Mill saw in Morley a writer who could do much to disseminate his own ideas. By 1867 he was commending Morley as 'one of our best and most rising periodical writers on serious subjects—moral, social, and philosophical, still more than political'.[4] Morley would send him articles, and Mill would offer his comments.[5] The development of the Millite side of Morley's thinking proceeded also through his admission to that select circle of Mill's friends who dined with him on Sunday evenings.[6] Morley became a regular

---

[1] *Recollections*, I, p. 60.
[2] Ibid., I, p. 69.
[3] Ibid., I, p. 52. Hirst, *Early Life & Letters* I, p. 52; *In the Golden Days*, 1947, pp. 165–6.
[4] H. S. R. Elliot (ed.), *The Letters of John Stuart Mill*, II, 1910, p. 95.
[5] See, e.g., ibid., II, pp. 64–5, and Morley to Mill, 2 Mar. 1873, Mill-Taylor MSS., vol. II, letter 241, ff. 562–3.
[6] *Recollections*, I, p. 52. Hirst, *In the Golden Days*, p. 166.

visitor at Blackheath, and Mill's interest in his career extended even to offering to relieve him temporarily of his editorial burdens when Morley was in poor health.[1] Mill's principle of 'Liberty' now became for Morley 'the true doctrine'.[2] And carefully Mill would try to reduce the positivist aspect of Morley's thought. We find him on one occasion correcting a tendency in Morley to employ meaningless abstractions when writing about practical politics.[3]

But all this would not have been enough without the very considerable impact on Morley of Mill's personality, for we must bear in mind that it was the need to resolve an urgent personal crisis which had impelled Morley in the direction of a new faith such as positivism. To counter the positivist influence Mill needed to provide an equivalent answer to personal problems—and he did. F. W. Hirst noted that one of Morley's 'favourite topics' of conversation was 'his friendship with John Stuart Mill'.[4] 'The most virtuous and truth-loving man that I at least have ever known', was Morley's description of Mill.[5] As we have seen, Morley worried about the possibility of disintegration of character by confusion in thought. But Mill seemed to him to have preserved to the end a unity and a 'completeness' of character, and in this lay 'one of the secrets of Mr. Mill's peculiar attraction for young men'.[6] Mill fascinated Morley because he seemed to have achieved that unifying of 'single elements' which Morley was so anxious to secure in his own thought.

Mill had entered Morley's life at a particularly critical time. In 1865 Morley was still struggling to make a living at anonymous 'penny-a-line' journalism, forced to suppress or distort his own views to suit those of his employer.[7] No doubt he was still afflicted by the pain of his quarrel with his now deceased father,

---

[1] Elliot, II, pp. 278–9, 284–5, 292–3.
[2] *On Compromise*, p. 239. Morley to Helen Taylor, 16 Oct. 1873, Mill-Taylor MSS., V, letter 235, f. 198.
[3] Morley to Mill, 2 Mar. 1873, Mill-Taylor MSS., II, letter 241, f. 562.
[4] Hirst, *In the Golden Days*, p. 165.
[5] Morley to Carnegie, 6 Feb. 1905.
[6] *F.R.*, June 1873, p. 671. *Critical Miscellanies*, III, p. 41.
[7] Cf. *Recollections*, I, p. 117.

and still thinking of the career in the Church that might have been his had he chosen to keep silent about his loss of religious convictions. His essays indicate that this was a period of intellectual confusion and anxiety for him. And now the greatest English philosopher and political thinker of the day had gone to the trouble of seeking him out and welcoming him into his select circle, and was encouraging and advising him.

In Mill's teaching, now reinforced by constant contact with Mill himself, Morley was able to find reason for believing that he had acted rightly in his rift with his father. In Mill's exaltation of nonconformity, of the refusal to conform for the sake of a comfortable life, Morley saw revealed a higher duty even than that to one's own father—a duty to speak the truth as one saw it and express one's individuality. Mill enabled him to find release from the guilt and remorse which he had felt since that crisis at Oxford. In this way Mill's influence became a substitute for that of positivism which as a new 'religion' had been seen as healing over the great break in Morley's life. In his essay on Turgot in 1870 we can see him beginning to express his discovery of the new liberating principle. It was Mill himself who urged Morley to write this essay, Mill being a great admirer of the 'god-like Turgot'. In the character of the great eighteenth-century French statesman Morley professed to find a 'model, and abiding influence' that provided a chart and compass 'in respect of civil conscience for the day'.[1] But the real influence would seem to have been that of Mill, who probably directed Morley to Turgot to find the qualities that he himself most admired. That Morley is writing about his own early life in the light of Mill's teaching emerges quite clearly. What he meant by a guide 'in respect of civil conscience' can be seen from a passage describing Turgot's decision to 'abandon all idea of an ecclesiastical career'—for which his father had intended him—'and the advancement which it offered him'.[2] Turgot, wrote Morley, being a man of high morality and intelligence, felt an honourable repugnance from entering into an engagement 'which would irrevocably bind him for the rest of his life either always to hold

[1] Ibid., I, pp. 57, 81–4.
[2] In Turgot's case, however, the father accepted the son's decision.

exactly the same opinions, or else to continue to preach them publicly after he had ceased to hold them privately'. The prospect of worldly comfort and benefit was outweighed for him by the thought of the 'horror and disgrace' of a situation where he would have to stifle his intelligence and outrage his conscience. Morley's conclusion that, had there been on either side in France before the revolution 'a hundred righteous men like Turgot, 'the end might have been other than it was', is unmistakably linked to Mill's insistence on the vital necessity for social progress of there being a few men who stand out and refuse to conform.[1]

Thus Morley moved towards justifying his own conduct in the terms of Mill's philosophy. The culmination of this tendency is in *On Compromise*, 1874, where he discusses at length Mill's ideas on intellectual nonconformity and the practice of Millite 'liberty'. The aim of the work itself he defined as being to 'seek some of the most general principles which ought to regulate the practice of compliance', and to decide under what circumstances the right to think and speak and act freely becomes 'a positive duty in practice'.[2] A passage with obvious personal relevance is that in which he discusses what he calls the 'coarsest and most revolting shape which the doctrine of conformity can assume, and its [degrading] consequences to the character of the conformer'. This is the entering into holy orders of a man who has little or no sincere religious faith, but desires money and social rank. After denouncing the 'moral improbity' of dissimulation and hypocrisy of this kind, he remarks also on 'the intellectual improbity which it brings in its train, the infidelity to truth, the disloyalty to one's own intelligence'. He imagines what it would be like to be such an impostor—that is, what his own life would have been like had he obeyed his father. Life would go on, and the impostor would grow ever more remorseful about the waste of his intellectual powers. The intellect would be corrupted 'in an atmosphere of mean purpose and low conception of the sacredness of fact and reality'. After this there is a long section full of vivid detail concerning the horrors of the life of such a dissembling clergyman. Finally he generalizes by reminding us that the depravation that

[1] F.R., Aug. 1870, pp. 171–2.   [2] F.R., Apr. 1874, pp. 425–6.

follows 'the trucking for money of intellectual freedom and self-respect' 'attends in its degree each other departure from disinterested following of truth, and each other substitution of convenience, whether public or private, in its place'.[1]

Other sections of *On Compromise*, already referred to, deal directly with conflict over religion between parent and son, and discuss in detail what claims parents have on children in regard to forbearance in expression of opinion.[2] Within the framework provided by Millite principles Morley is able to generalize personal situations and liberate himself from the particular, isolated feelings hitherto associated with them. He is even able to look at his father's conduct in a new and detached way. Wishing to illustrate the lightness and lack of real conviction with which religious faith is now held, he writes: 'Are we to suppose that it is firm persuasion of the greater scripturalness of episcopacy, that turns the second generation of dissenting manufacturers in our busy Lancashire into churchmen? Certainly such conversions do no violence to the conscience of the proselyte. He is intellectually indifferent, a spiritual neuter.' In fact, Morley's father had been a religious dissenter until he settled in the Lancashire town of Blackburn, whereupon he had turned to the Church of England, even although, as Morley observed, his outlook remained fundamentally nonconformist. Morley could scarcely have written the passage just quoted without being aware of its relevance to the conduct of his father. He went on to describe this type of 'conversion' as the 'unspeakably ignoble' 'social consequence' of the revolution taking place in 'the whole spiritual basis of thought'.[3] Thus he could feel that his father's reaction to his own change in religious professions was unjustified. His father and he had both been subjected to the same temptations; both were victims of the consequences of living in 'an epoch of transition in the very foundations of belief and conduct'.

By 1874 Morley could afford to feel that he had been right in admitting his loss of religious faith, even though he had thereby

---

[1] *On Compromise*, pp. 87–94. F.R., June 1874, pp. 721–3.
[2] *On Compromise*, pp. 148–69.
[3] F.R., Apr. 1874, p. 437.

sacrificed his chances of a good degree and preferment in the Church. He was now a success. His father had been wrong, whereas it seemed to Morley that the course of his life offered proof abundant of the rightness and virtue of Mill's principles. The connection between Mill's influence and the personal passages in *On Compromise* emerges clearly from Morley's essay on the death of Mill, in which he writes: 'That guilty and grievously common pusillanimity which leads men to make or act hypocritical professions, always moved his deepest abhorrence.'[1] Yet Morley's father, far from praising his son's refusal to be such a hypocrite, had practically disowned him on learning of it. Not surprisingly, therefore, it would seem that, just as Mill's teachings on 'liberty' and nonconformity entered the gap left by the religious faith which Morley had lost, so Mill himself came to fill the place of the father who had tried to force hypocritical conformity and the continued and false profession of that religion on to his son. Morley in his later life seldom referred to his father, yet he mourned the death of Mill as a son mourns the death of a father. He wrote that Mill had the 'gift of intellectual fatherhood' and that his friends 'must always bear to his memory the affectionate veneration of sons'.[2] Writing to Helen Taylor after Mill's death, he called him 'the best and wisest man that I can ever know' and 'one whose memory will always be as precious to me as to a son'.[3]

We can now understand why it was that Mill's influence so powerfully checked and replaced that of the positivists. Its effect was soon obvious to Harrison and others of his positivist friends, and in the early 1870s one can discern a struggle between them and Mill's influence for control over Morley's intellectual development. Harrison pressed him to commit himself to some system of thought and attacked his insistence on preserving an open mind and using the *Fortnightly Review* as a forum for 'the unbiassed expression of many and various minds'.[4] To Harrison this attitude

[1] F.R., June 1873, p. 672. *Critical Miscellanies*, III, p. 43.
[2] F.R., June 1873, p. 669. *Critical Miscellanies*, III, pp. 37–8.
[3] 10 May 1873, Mill-Taylor MSS., V, letter 233, ff. 193–4.
[4] Morley in F.R., July 1870, pp. 118–19.

exemplified the worst features of the Millite philosophy. 'I dare say you are right on Mill's principles', he wrote to Morley in 1874; and went on, 'Mill as I always tell you is the origin of evil. I am a Comtist not a Millite, & specially repudiate the doctrine of liberty of speech. The truth is when you & I quarrel that is only because we do not politically recognise from what utterly different systems of thought we set out. Congreve is consistent in regarding Mill as one of the poles & antidotes to Positivism.'[1]

After 1870 Morley seemed to be growing increasingly anxious to rid himself of the label of 'positivist', to diminish the appearance of connection with positivism, to atone for praise bestowed on Comte and admissions of indebtedness to his ideas by emphatic statements of dissociation. In this he was like other writers of the day who, anxious to influence the English public, felt their efforts to be hindered by any strong appearance of association with positivism—an appearance which the positivists, for their part, were determined to fasten on to as many leading intellectual figures as possible. Their attempts to do this were a major cause of the attacks made on positivism by John Stuart Mill and others of his circle, such as Herbert Spencer and T. H. Huxley.[2] The foreignness of Comte's thinking aroused uneasiness about being identified with it in English eyes. Mill argued that it contained many of the bad features of French thinking;[3] and Morley began

[1] 10 June [1874].
[2] Cf. H. Spencer, 'Reasons for Dissenting from the Philosophy of M. Comte', appendix to *The Classification of the Sciences*, 2nd edition, 1869; *An Autobiography*, II, 1904, p. 487. J. S. Mill, *Auguste Comte and Positivism*, 4th edition, 1891, pp. 2–3. T. H. Huxley, 'On the Physical Basis of Life', *F.R.*, Feb. 1869, p. 141; 'The Scientific Aspects of Positivism', *F.R.*, June 1869. Cf. Morley to Huxley, 13 Jan. 1869: 'I fully understand the vexation with wh. you have undergone the popular or archiepiscopal confusion about every scientifically minded person being a Comtist; and I hope your protest will do something to clear people's heads.' Huxley MSS., General Corr., vol. 23, f. 12.
[3] According to Mill, Comte's passion for 'unity' reflected' an original mental twist very common in French thinkers', and his positivist religion showed that 'mania' for regulation by which Frenchmen are distinguished among Europeans'. Harriet Taylor helped to turn Mill decisively against Comtism by pointing out to him how 'Comte is essentially *French*, in the sense in which we think [the] French mind less admirable than [the] English'. *Auguste Comte and Positivism*, pp. 70, 140, 153. F. A. Hayek, *John Stuart Mill and Harriet Taylor. Their Correspondence and Subsequent Marriage*, 1951, p. 118.

to condemn what he considered the excessive Frenchness of positivist attitudes. He rebuked Congreve for an alleged disposition to denigrate England and see France as equivalent to the Western world, and deplored Comte's failure to understand such phenomena of English development as the colonies, the parliamentary system, and Protestantism.[1] Also held against Comte was the striking resemblance of his 'religion' to Roman Catholicism. Morley attacked what he saw as Comte's depreciatory treatment of Protestantism and its associated merits—the critical spirit, free inquiry, the use of reason, liberty of conscience.[2] He felt the positivist support for France in the Franco-Prussian war to be much too extreme, and found their endorsement of the activities of the Communards embarrassing and wrong. He himself was developing a considerable admiration for Prussia. Soon he and Harrison were quarrelling bitterly over Bismarck's policies towards the Roman Catholic Church, which he applauded, but Harrison condemned, thus seeming to prove his pro-Catholic bias. In 1874 he summed up the development of his thinking thus in a letter to Richard Congreve:

The discussion on the war of 1870 revealed to me how much further off either my training or my temperament or both had left me from you, than I had thought. I was amazed and even struck with consternation. So I am now when Harrison talks of Bismarck's anti-papal policy. When I saw your application of Comte's principles in 1870, and when I see your application of them now . . . , I feel that I don't understand those principles. So I fall back on the critical, individualist, scheme of things, wh. my protestant upbringing and the influence of Mill have made congenial to me.[3]

The growing divergence between Morley and the positivists, the struggle by the latter to counter Mill's influence, and Morley's changing attitude towards systems of thought, can all be studied in his correspondence with Frederic Harrison. Early in 1871 he was accusing the positivists of having become 'worshippers of

[1] Morley to Harrison, 3 Jan. 1873. *F.R.*, Apr. 1882, p. 514.
[2] *Voltaire*, pp. 177-8. *F.R.*, Jan. 1867, pp. 7-12; May 1868, p, 481. Morley to Harrison, 26 Oct. 1872.
[3] 8 Jan. 1874, B.M. Add. MSS. 45241, ff. 61-2.

abstractions' and followers of 'an absolute method'. They were now 'penetrated with the vices of French political thinking', and had turned into a 'sect' that tended merely 'to iterate the formulas of the master, instead of constantly applying, translating, and vivifying them'. Harrison now called him 'the Positivist heresiarch', and told him that the other positivists 'all see you are not *Comtist*'.[1] Morley's study of Voltaire, which appeared at the end of 1871, gave even more conclusive proof of his rejection of the positivist system. Comte was no admirer of Voltaire; nor was Harrison, who welcomed the news that Morley was to write on him, as he expected that Morley would treat Voltaire very severely. He even pleaded with Morley not to be too harsh![2] But the work proved to be far more unfavourable to Comte than to Voltaire. Morley rebuked Comte for underestimating Voltaire, and explained the cause of Comte's attitude as being that 'everyone who has a system to defend' was the enemy of Voltaire, who 'destroyed the reigning system of his day, with engines that seem to point with uncomfortable directness against all other systems'. Morley now took the opportunity, while acknowledging numerous obligations to Comte, of expressing 'final inability to follow him in his ideas of social reconstruction'. Mill had triumphed. Morley compared Comtist and Millite remedies for the anarchic condition of modern thought, and concluded that 'far wiser and safer' than desperately grasping for any kind of firm order was a patient working forward towards social reconstruction by the cultivation of the individual intelligence and the open-minded investigation of all that it might discover.[3]

These declarations shocked the positivists. 'The brethren', Harrison informed him, 'are not satisfied with your attitude towards them; & I must admit that your book distinctly severs you from Comte morally & intellectually'. The book 'does show', wrote Harrison, ' & the others feel it with as much regret as I do, that you are very sensibly outside of the Positivist body'.[4] Morley

[1] Morley to Harrison, 25 Apr., 7 May 1871. Harrison to Morley, 9 June [1871].
[2] 'Damn him gently, & give the poor devil a drop of water between the turns of the torment you conscientiously administer'. 21 June [1871].
[3] *Voltaire*, pp. 36–7, 177–80. F.R., Oct. 1871, pp. 459–60.
[4] 20, 23 Dec. [1871].

now cultivated the kind of open-mindedness which he had commended in *Voltaire:* 'My mind is not made up. I don't know Comtism . . . well enough . . . I want three or four more years of reading of him, & of social observation. I believe I shall become more and more Millite, less and less Comtist. But I must wait.'¹

After Mill's death in 1873 Harrison seems to have determined to make a last effort to restore positivist influence over Morley. In order to break the hold of Mill's principles he sought to emphasize the importance of the positivist element in Morley's intellectual development and to undermine his confidence in Mill. On one occasion he told Morley that 'Millism' was a 'thin, poor & arid system', a 'barren world' of 'liberties, & rights, & arguments', and suggested that Mill—and hence anyone who followed him—might be found 'on the reactionary side of human progress in the long run'.² On another he wrote:

> You & your utterances are saturated with Comte, as Mill was, to a degree you may not suspect. Your Voltaire, your Rousseau is full of Comte. . . . that system is your whole intellectual substratum, & all that is living in your action & thought comes from principles of which that system is the incarnation. . . . To my mind Mill in all that he is great is an English version of Comte . . . Mill went so far with Comte & belonged to the same current of philosophy so far (apart from any question of originality) that I think he ought to have [acknowledged] the intellectual parentage more truly. . . . I wonder at the jejunity of the mind [Mill's] which has stirred so much transient enthusiasm.³

Harrison tried to foster in Morley a consciousness of intellectual confusion and of the advantages of a system in this regard:

> Purge your intellectual mind & live cleanly. I really am low & sick at heart when I think of the muddle you are getting into. Make a tabula rasa of your opinions, & rebuild the edifice anew on true Positive lines. All that is great & new & strong in you is in the Positive strain. . . . Into the inter-stices of that great & coherent conception, you have let wild shoots & roots of Millite individualism & Rights thrust up & shake the fit of the blocks. . . . Purge clear out these Atheisms, & Sectarianisms, & limitless Rights of men & women to live their own

¹ 9 Dec. 1871. ² 7 Jan. [1874]. ³ 11 Jan. [1874].

lives on individualist principles. Have a rest & go in for 12 months for the quiet all round consideration of Comte . . . to feel the infinite peace & rest & strength of a cohesive intellectual, social, & practical system all developed together.[1]

The 'grand question' to which every man must direct his thoughts was, 'Shall there, can there be a religion?' 'By *religion*', Harrison explained, 'I mean a systematic order of life, organised & formulated.' 'Now you have hardly settled that question yourself,' he reminded Morley.[2] He tried to convince Morley that this should be the aim of his intellectual activity: 'Do you reject this systematisation [positivism]. Do you accept it. Do you modify it. Whichever of these you do, your business is only this. If you have another religion—Millism—or be it Morleyism—to supersede it teach us this.'[3]

But, so far as particular 'systematisations' were concerned, there could be no doubt that Harrison had failed to reverse Morley's movement away from positivism. 'That you have a coherent doctrine is to me not quite demonstrable, far otherwise,' he had told Harrison in 1873; 'it won't come in our time.'[4] In 1876 he thus described the effect on him of reassessing Comte for an article in the *Encyclopaedia Britannica:* 'Comte provokes me more than ever. I have read and read and meditated and re-meditated— and at the end of it my whole soul revolts—and how *you* [Harrison] of all men on this bright planet have gone over to such an idol doth perplex me by day and by night.'[5] In the article he wrote that the basic feature of Comte's system, 'the abstract idea of Humanity, conceived as a kind of Personality', could not produce any 'effective unity' of thought by enabling men to agree on 'the right and wrong' of given courses. The 'erection of Humanity into a Being' was just 'utilitarianism crowned by a fantastic decoration', and the Comtists were 'no better off than other utilitarians in judging policy, events, conduct'.[6] Positivism was not adequate as a system, 'not competent to control and to direct', he wrote in 1882.[7] Towards the end of his life he remarked

[1] 10 Feb. [1874].   [2] 10 Oct. [1875].   [3] 1 June [1874].   [4] 13 Feb. 1873.
[5] To Harrison, 15 Sept. 1876.   [6] *Critical Miscellanies*, III, pp. 378–80.
[7] F.R., Apr. 1882, pp. 503–4.

'how foolish he himself had been in getting excited about Comte'.[1]

But he found equally unacceptable Harrison's insistence on the urgent necessity of adhering to a system. In rejecting Comtism he had developed and employed arguments which did seem to 'point with uncomfortable directness against all other systems'. We must now consider further his intellectual situation after the ebbing of his faith in positivism.

[1] M. D. Howe (ed.), *Holmes-Laski Letters*, I, 1953, p. 438.

3

THE EMERGENCE OF AN INDIVIDUALISTIC SOCIAL THEORY

MORLEY developed a distinction between 'protestant' and 'catholic' attitudes to systems of thought. The majority of people took a 'catholic' attitude in the sense that they were content to 'accept the the traditional system of their time' without worrying very much about its 'internal coherence' or 'logical weight and consistency'. This was because they wanted 'a religion to live by, or perhaps to die by', 'not one that may be pulled to pieces and then put together again without injury'. On the other hand, 'there are a few minds who detest a logical weakness, and refuse to obey the precepts of the system in which it exists'. In his own day there had emerged, he argued, a growing divergence between those who, afraid of whither the investigation of logical weaknesses might lead, 'fall back into systems in which logic has no place', and those who 'courageously grasp the sound principle at the bottom of Protestantism', receptiveness to the findings of an open, critical mind, 'and carry it out at all hazard'.[1]

Morley himself moved more and more towards the 'protestant' attitude, and his search for system in thought and belief was as a consequence increasingly controlled by what might be called the claims of objectivity, which disabled him from accepting simply for subjective reasons any system of thought which offered itself. Although he believed that the 'master-key and prime law of sanity' was a sense of order and relationship, the exact words which he used to define this were, a 'sense of the *actual* relations of things to one another in the *objective* world'.[2] That is, the only kind of system which he could believe in and which could therefore give him peace of mind was one reflecting an order known

[1] *F.R.*, Jan. 1867, pp. 10–11.
[2] *Rousseau*, I, p. 12. My emphasis.

and proved to exist in 'things'. In his essay on Byron he defined as characteristic of the modern intellectual condition this inability to accept a system of thought independently of the question of whether or not it reflects a really existing order:

> One living as Byron emphatically did in the truly modern atmosphere, was bound by all the conditions of the atmosphere to have mastered what we may style the natural history of his own ideas and convictions; to know something of their position towards fact and outer circumstance and possibility; above all to have some trusty standard for testing their value and assuring himself that they do really cover the field which he takes them to cover. People with a faith and people living in frenzy are equally under this law; but they take the completeness and coherency of their doctrine for granted.[1]

This Morley could never do. To him, as to Condorcet, 'distinct grounds for the faith that was in him' were as essential as 'the faith itself'.[2]

Morley came to believe that form must be organic, must draw out and express an order inherent in 'the actual relations of things'. It must not be artificial or imposed. If no order or meaning is discernible, then freedom must continue until further knowledge does yield a sense of order. Only through free inquiry can truth, and hence organic form, emerge. The objection to systems was that in a situation of constant augmentation of knowledge such as existed in the nineteenth century any system purporting to be all-embracing would have to ignore incompleteness and inadequacy or tentativeness of information and would not therefore be organic. Comte had, after all, constructed his system after deciding to read no more books, and in the controversies with Huxley and others his followers tended to dismiss criticisms of the incompleteness of the knowledge on which his grand hypotheses were founded. Morley believed that truth was gradually emerging and that form would therefore also be slowly revealing itself as long as men were patient, careful, and alert, and did not succumb to that impatience which he considered had characterized most

---

[1] *F.R.*, Dec. 1870, p. 665.
[2] *F.R.*, Feb. 1870, p. 131.

French philosophers, from Descartes to Comte. These thinkers, declining to 'rest on an uncompleted interpretation of existence', had insisted on a 'hasty supplement of unconcluded analysis by what is virtually an à priori synthesis'. Voltaire was the exception. He trusted to the individual to build 'by the motion of his own faculties' a new order in 'action and belief', and was 'perhaps the one great Frenchman who has known how to abide in patient contentment with an all but purely critical reserve, leaving reconstruction, its form, its modes, its epoch, for the fulness of time and maturity of effort to disclose'.[1] But Diderot also received praise for being content to observe all the complex and multitudinous elements of life 'playing freely around him' without feeling any 'haste to compress his experience into maxims and system'.[2] In the interpretation of these elements, Morley believed, there should ideally be 'a free stream of ideas spontaneously obeying a sense of order, harmony, and form'.[3]

He felt strongly averse from interfering with natural, organic growth and imposing any artificial order. *Rousseau* was a study in the evils that seemed to him to result from the imposition of systems. Rousseau, ignoring 'the complex tangle of the history of social growths' and the organic quality of manners, customs, and opinions with their intricate involvement in the constitution of human nature, tried to construct a system 'which might be imposed upon all societies indifferently by a legislator' determined 'to wipe out existing uses, laws, and institutions, and make afresh a clear and undisturbed beginning of national life'. But, Morley declared, such an attempt to 'impose a system from without' can never succeed; social change has to be 'slowly wrought out by many minds, with popular assent and co-operation, at the suggestion of changing social circumstances and need'.[4]

The same objection applied to the argument that artificially created systems of thought were justifiable because through developing mental stability they created order in personality.

[1] *Voltaire*, p. 38.
[2] *Diderot*, I, p. 22. F.R., Feb. 1875, p. 162.
[3] *Diderot*, I, p. 42. F.R., Apr. 1875, p. 488.
[4] *Rousseau*, II, pp. 125–30.

'Human nature' was too complex and organic a phenomenon to be safely treated in this way. Morley criticized Comte for having 'thought to impose a system of culture without taking sufficient account of human nature'.[1] By contrast, Rousseau was, in this respect at least, worthy of praise, because, since he 'cared extremely that the opinions which he did hold should be a solid and undisturbed part of himself', he had 'sought unity of character in the development of the spontaneous qualities of human nature' and had rejected Christianity for having 'imposed a system from without'.[2] In *On Compromise* Morley condemned those who would tolerate erroneous, ungrounded beliefs for the sake of 'the maintenance of that coherency, interdependence, systematisation of opinions and motives, which is said to make character organic, and is therefore so highly prized by some schools of thought'. In his view, so long as error is an element in belief, there can be 'no value in coherency and harmonious consistency as such', for error itself vitiates character. The 'advantages that we desire to preserve' in character cannot come from the creation of system on a basis of error; their only proper source is 'some true opinion or just motive or high or honest sentiment' 'springing from man's spontaneous and unformulated recognition of the real relations of things'. It would be both wrong and unnecessary to yield to impatience in one's longing for firmness of belief. A sense of order in 'the real relations of things', the objective world, may be 'very faint in the beginnings of society', but it 'grows clearer and firmer with each step forward, until in a tolerably civilised age it has become a force on which you can fairly both count and lean with a considerable degree of assurance'.[3]

What Morley feared above all was loss of contact with reality. An artificially developed system might confer boldness and decisiveness on a man's conduct, but, because of its inadequate relationship to reality, it always ultimately proved an untrustworthy guide. At first the man with an artificial system is at an advantage, because he is free from 'qualifying propositions and

[1] A. Harrison, *Frederic Harrison. Thoughts and Memories*, 1926, p. 177.
[2] *F.R.*, May 1872, p. 499.
[3] *F.R.*, Apr. 1874, pp. 450–1.

AN INDIVIDUALISTIC SOCIAL THEORY 37

multitudinous limitations'. 'A man who handles sets of complex facts is necessarily slow-footed, but one who has only words to deal with, may advance with a speed, a precision, a consistency, a conclusiveness, that has a magical potency over men who insist on having politics and theology drawn out in exact theorems like those of geometry.' Rousseau, for example, by not caring whether his words bore any relationship to 'complex facts', was able to 'assume an air of certitude and precision' which captivated his disciples and gave them, too, 'a supreme and undoubting confidence'.[1] One such disciple was Robespierre; but, although he gained at first through this confidence, he soon found himself 'amid the perplexities of practice' 'paralysed and bewildered by his own principles'. The reason for this was the failure of his system to reflect 'the actual relations of things'. 'The teaching of Rousseau was ever pouring like thin smoke among his ideas, and clouding his view of actual conditions.'[2] The very attempt to think systematically could produce confusion and incoherence even worse than before. By contrast, the ideal which Morley set before himself was that of Burke, who, after 'examining the relations among political ideas in the light of political practice', 'constructed from them a complete and coherent system of his own'.[3]

Morley therefore rejected the temptation to commit himself to positivism or any other system before he was convinced that it represented a natural, organic order. Long, patient waiting was the alternative; in the meantime, the mind must be content with incomplete knowledge, with fragments, areas of light, hints of the truth. What effect did the acceptance of this situation have on Morley's intellectual activity?

As he found the prospect of arriving at a satisfactory synthesis of all aspects of human experience becoming ever more remote, Morley's view of the world grew increasingly limited until man seemed to him to be confined in a small circle or a corner within

---

[1] *Rousseau*, II, pp. 134–8.
[2] *Critical Miscellanies*, I, pp. 55–6. *F.R.*, Aug. 1876, p. 195.
[3] *Edmund Burke*, p. 20.

a vast, mysterious darkness; and it was from and in this circle that he began to feel that he had to work in order to discover pattern and meaning in life. He thus described his feelings about man's place in the universe: 'Nobody who has asked himself fruitless questions—why the race of man inhabits the earth, or, what is the final upshot of the endless series of successive transfusions among forms of life and growth—is likely to deny that outside the ever-widening circle within which reason reigns and works there lies the sombre and sterile land of mystery eternally unfathomable.'[1] For many centuries Christian belief had illuminated and made intelligible the whole of life: 'truth had been conceived as of the nature of a Real Universal, of which men had full possession by the revelation of a supreme divinity. All truth was organically one; and the relations of men to something supernatural, their relations to one another, the relations of outward matter, were all comprehended in a single synthesis, within which, and subject to which, all intellectual movement proceeded.' But the 'advancing spirit of inquiry' had undermined that synthesis;[2] and now all that was left was a 'sense of the puniness of man in the centre of a cruel and frowning universe', man confined to 'the narrow land of rational certainty, relative, conditional, experimental, from which we view the vast realm that stretches out unknown before us, and perhaps for ever unknowable', and 'the great gulf which is fixed round our faculty and existence on every side'.[3] Frequently there appear in his writings images that suggest a feeling of being hemmed in and restricted by a menacing environment. In *On Compromise* those whose beliefs are firm are depicted as living in a tower while all about the air is 'full of missiles' and the ground

[1] *F.R.*, June 1868, p. 505.
[2] *Voltaire*, p. 35.
[3] *F.R.*, July 1870, pp. 11-15. For the occurrence of similar images describing man's place in the scheme of things in the writings of contemporaries, see J. H. Bridges (a positivist), *The Unity of Comte's Life and Doctrine* . . ., new edition, 1910, p. 49; G. W. E. Russell (ed.), *Letters of Matthew Arnold 1848-1888*, I, 1901, p. 289; M. Arnold, *Culture and Anarchy: An Essay in Political and Social Criticism*, 1869—the frequent imagery of 'light' struggling against darkness, as also in Arnold's poetry, e.g. 'Dover Beach' ('the darkling plain'); T. Carlyle, *Sartor Resartus*. . ., 1897, pp. 4, 78, 132, 144. Morley's appreciation of Carlyle's use of this imagery is seen in his essay on Carlyle, *F.R.*, July 1870.

is shaking.[1] In *Voltaire*, written when he was in his early thirties, he thus described how the world appears to a man who has reached that stage of life: 'The narrowness of the cribbed deck that we are doomed to tread, amid the vast space of an eternal sea with fair shores dimly seen and never neared, oppresses the soul with a burden that sorely tries its strength, when the fixed limits first define themselves before it. Those are the strongest who do not tremble beneath this grey ghostly light . . . '[2]

It is Morley's literary work that shows most clearly his effort within a consciousness of this situation to explore particular areas of experience and seek in them intimations of the universal and principles for systematic understanding. The literary form that he chose was the biographical study, and this predominates in his literary output. Morley wished to work from the concrete and particular experiences towards the achievement of a more general understanding. The only full-scale discussion of principles which he wrote was *On Compromise*. He was never at ease with the abstract and theoretical, and, although he joined the Metaphysical Society, he read only one paper to it.[3] His major literary effort was a series of studies of French thinkers and writers of the eighteenth century—Voltaire, Rousseau, Diderot, Vauvenargues, Holbach, Turgot, Condorcet. These were written between 1870 and 1878 and varied in length from short essays to full-scale biographies. It appears that the series was systematically planned under the general theme of a 'survey of the intellectual preparation of the French Revolution' and that he hoped to follow it with a study of the revolution itself. Of this only 'Robespierre' appeared, in 1876. In it is plainly evident an intention to study how the French proceeded to 'translate the word' of the *philosophes* into 'social action'.[4] Thus we see how he worked to the general from personal, particular situations.

The study of these individual circles of human experience was

---

[1] pp. 36–7. F.R., Apr. 1874, p. 437.   [2] pp. 44–5.
[3] This was paper 72, dated 11 Dec. 1877, and entitled 'Various Definitions of Materialism'. See A. W. Brown, *The Metaphysical Society: Victorian Minds in Crisis, 1869–1880*, New York, 1947, p. 135.
[4] F.R., Aug. 1877, p. 259. His letters to Chamberlain, 29 Apr., 10 Oct., and 24 Oct. 1877, and 3 Jan. 1878, show him 'working away at my Fr. Rev^n'.

Morley's 'favourite form of composition'.[1] In a letter to Harrison in 1876 he made a characteristic juxtaposition of attitudes when, after referring to the Metaphysical Society and his lack of interest in 'these abstract things', he described how he had just met Gladstone and felt very much attracted to his personality.[2] Even in the writing of history he found it hard to comprehend and describe general movements and forces. Everything was translated into terms of 'great men'. He wrote history as biography. At the beginning of *Gladstone*, indeed, he complains of the 'difficulty of fixing the precise scale between history and biography'.[3]

Morley's principle was to take the lives of individuals for his starting-point, especially great men who could be considered to have contributed in some way or other to human progress, and to try to develop through contemplation of them an understanding of the conditions and forces governing and promoting such progress. He once defined progress as, 'first, the multiplication and elevation of types of virtuous character; and next, the practical acceptance of these types by the general sentiment'.[4] For the guiding of 'social action' there were needed 'theories of human nature' and of 'the character of man'.[5] In force of character, Morley believed, could be found the secret of a strength that would enable man to understand and to master the complex conditions of his existence. Of Burke, for instance, he wrote: 'The fiery glow of his nature fused all his ideas into a tenacious and homogeneous mass ... wrought by an inborn ardour of character.'[6] Strength of character seemed to him to have been the secret of Mill's success in continually absorbing new ideas and facts without 'disturbing the organic structure of the whole' of his thought.[7] The spectacle of character fascinated him, especially the 'complex interplay' of innate conditions of temperament and fixed limitations of opportunity with 'that character, which is first their

---

[1] Hirst, *Early Life & Letters*, I, p. xiv.
[2] 16 Feb. 1876.
[3] I, p. 2.
[4] F.R., Mar. 1868, p. 332.
[5] F.R., Apr. 1882, p. 503.
[6] F.R., Mar. 1867, p. 303. *Edmund Burke*, pp. 46–7.
[7] F.R., Jan. 1874, pp. 1–6. *Critical Miscellanies*, III, pp. 55–64.

creature and then their master'. Here was man, within the circle of his own individuality, reaching out towards the materials of his environment and conquering them by the force of his character.[1] To Morley the central point in the study of human affairs, in the absence of systematic principles for understanding the whole, had to be character. Character alone is 'real'.[2] Morley praised Rousseau for having shifted the 'point of view' of social criticism away from 'knowledge' and 'the acquisition of truth' to character, so that one could study the 'whole range' of 'external circumstances and relations' by seeing their effect on character.[3] In the hope of arriving at general conclusions from his contemplation of character Morley deliberately cultivated a systematic broad-mindedness and many-sidedness in relation to it. He was most anxious to exclude moral judgement or anything else that could give a distorted, artificially inspired view of human character. Since a character is 'much else besides being virtuous or vicious', why, he asked, 'rush to praise or blame, to eulogy or reprobation, when we should do better simply to explore and enjoy?' Character, not dogma, should be the central consideration, and we should develop 'wide sympathy and many-coloured appreciativeness'.[4] From this could come that comprehensiveness which could form the basis of a systematic understanding of human existence. It is impossible, he wrote, 'for us to know too much of plans of life which rest on principles opposed to our own'. The writings of our antagonists should be studied 'to pick up the fragments of truth and positive contribution, that so nothing be lost'. It is essential to appreciate 'the infinite diversity of effort that goes to the advancement of mankind'. If we do, we can rise to 'a point of view so lofty and so peculiar that from it we are able to discern in men and women something more than, and apart from, creed and profession and formulated principle'—'their character or humanity'.[5] Of Burke, Morley wrote that his appreciation of 'the

[1] *Voltaire*, p. 98.
[2] *Critical Miscellanies*, III, pp. 166–7.
[3] *F.R.*, May 1872, pp. 499–500.
[4] *Critical Miscellanies*, I, pp. 182–6.
[5] *Modern Characteristics*, p. 208. *F.R.*, May 1868, p. 482. *Critical Miscellanies*, II, pp. 258–9; I, p. 185.

many conditions, possibilities, and "varieties of untried being" in human character and situation' gave 'an incomparable flexibility to his methods of political approach'.[1] He himself tried to acquire the same flexibility in his literary methods. One of his first studies was of the arch-conservative writer, Joseph de Maistre; and he later tried very hard to overcome his dislike of Rousseau in order to explore the numerous unconventional aspects of that philosopher's character.

Since Morley justified the study of character as a means of arriving at principles of conduct, it is scarcely surprising that he tended to try some generalizing and to begin the elevation of 'virtuous types' by the idealizing of the characters of those whom he especially admired. Here was an example of his attempt to reach out from particular areas of experience to relate them to the ordering of the totality. This was, in any event, an age when much importance was attached to idealized biography. In *Physics and Politics*, which appeared in the *Fortnightly Review* soon after Morley became editor, Walter Bagehot claimed that in every nation there was a struggle between types of character. The type which would prevail would be the one made to appear most attractive.[2] Arnold in *Culture and Anarchy* complained that no ideal of the 'best self' was being presented to Englishmen.[3] Even Mill seemed in *On Liberty* to be asking that 'the intelligent part of the public' be made to appreciate the value of that ideal of the nonconforming individualist which Morley tried to define more precisely in *On Compromise*.[4] Each of these men was suggesting in his own way that what he believed to be good character should be illustrated and made attractive in order that dangerous social trends—respectively, the triumph of a bad type of character in the Darwinian struggle for existence, 'anarchy', and conformism—might be averted. Morley, as we have seen, wrote of social progress as coming through the elevation and acceptance of types of virtuous character.

---

[1] *Burke*, p. 308.
[2] Bagehot, *Physics and Politics*, 1906, p. 43.
[3] p. 118.
[4] Cf. Mill, *Utilitarianism*, . . . , 1910, p. 131.

AN INDIVIDUALISTIC SOCIAL THEORY

There was another important influence which probably encouraged Morley to idealize his characters. F. W. Hirst, who had known Morley personally for many years, wrote that Morley believed that biography should be 'a means of edification' and that the biographer had a 'high function' to 'immortalise in sublime prose' the characters of great men.[1] This notion of the biographer as a kind of high priest performing a religious function has an obvious resemblance to the positivists' cult of great men or secular saints. Like Morley, the positivists believed that the movements and forces of human progress could best be understood through the study of the lives of great individuals; and Morley was certainly influenced by them. In 1867 he wrote that, through the Comtist encouragement of gratitude to great men for their benefactions to mankind, history 'becomes an instrument of moral training, and acquires an aspect of practical moral significance'.[2] Noel Annan has suggested that in Victorian times agnostics found in biography the means of illumining a morality divorced from Christianity.[3] Morley was undoubtedly trying to create out of the biographical subject something like the positivist 'saint'. In *Voltaire* he laid down a 'rule to keep ourselves as much as we can in contact with what is great', because 'it is little edifying to the character to rake among the private obscurities of even first-rate men'.[4] On reading Froude's *Erasmus* he found objectionable what he termed its 'cynical taste' and 'cheap satirical realism', which he considered 'falser than even over-idealism'. 'I don't see how these lectures can do young men any good', he wrote.[5] When a friend once drew his attention to certain foibles of Mill and Gladstone, Morley was 'mightily offended' at such lack of 'reverence' and declared that he himself would not 'lay hands' on such great and virtuous men.[6]

It is true that Morley himself explicitly rejected any idea of

[1] Hirst, *Early Life & Letters*, I, p. xv.
[2] *F.R.*, Jan. 1867, p. 17.
[3] N. G. Annan, *Leslie Stephen. His Thought and Character in Relation to his Time*, 1951, p. 222.
[4] p. 101.
[5] *Recollections*, I, p. 280.
[6] Morley to Carnegie, 6 Feb. 1905.

writing hagiography. It is not, he wrote in *Voltaire*, 'the office of history to purvey heroes'; history should not be 'distorted into a new hagiographa'. He argued that veneration of great men, 'if it is to be an intelligent mood, implies insight into the inmost privacy of aim and motive, and this insight, in the case of those whom circumstance raises on a towering pedestal, we can hardly ever count with assurance on finding faithful and authentic'.[1] Here again we can see in him the conflict between his anxiety to retain contact with firm reality, and his craving for order and system. Because of this craving he did constantly tend to introduce system and meaning into the fragmentary and incomplete knowledge which he admitted was all that he possessed. Harold Laski once distinguished Morley from Boswell as biographers by Boswell's 'infinite genius for little things'.[2] Morley did not like little things. He wanted order and unity and tidiness among the multitudinous elements of life, and longed to snip off what he would call the 'ragged edges'. The frame of mind in which he wrote about people is evident from his preparations for writing. According to Hirst, his table 'was always clear and free from papers, which he kept in drawers', and he liked to sit down to write 'in clean linen'. Morley once wrote to a friend: 'I wonder whether you agree with me in the garb proper for writing. Like Buffon, I insist upon shaving and clean linen before sitting down to composition.'[3] This composition itself often took the form of the obscuring or omitting of detail and the tidying up of other people's characters. Just as he disliked a desk littered with papers, so he disliked a history littered with 'insignificant facts, sterile knowledge, and frivolous antiquarianiam'.[4] This urge to introduce order and tidiness can be seen in his description of the quarrel between Frederick the Great and Voltaire. After observing how distressing this episode is to those who 'crave dignity and admission of the serious in the relations of men with one another', he proceeds to rearrange the fragments into a fitter pattern: 'One

[1] p. 185. *F.R.*, Oct. 1871, p. 463.
[2] M. D. Howe (ed.), *Holmes-Laski Letters*, I, 1953, p. 39.
[3] J. W. Robertson Scott, *The Life and Death of a Newspaper*, 1952, p. 24. E. A. Helps (ed.), *Correspondence of Sir Arthur Helps, K.C.B., D.C.L.*, 1917, p. 294.
[4] *Diderot*, II, p. 212.

would rather that even in their estrangement there had been some grace and firmness and self-control, and that at least the long-cherished illusion had faded away worthily . . . It jars on us . . .'[1] *Gladstone* shows much evidence of a similar idealizing tendency. In it he deliberately gave little space to 'domesticities', because he was working to a 'theory of the right plan and scale', which was 'to impress the world with his [Gladstone's] greatness'. For this reason Morley considered that 'every super-addition of detail of ordinary kind would be dubious in art & in effect'.[2] Morley once commented on Burke's admiration of the country gentleman that Burke 'clothed his favourite with ideal qualities which ought, even if they did not, to have belonged to that position'.[3] The same may well be said of Morley's depiction of Gladstone. Very often in reading the work one feels that Morley's Gladstone is not so much the real historical figure—it was, after all, very early for any attempt to get him in perspective—as Morley's ideal individual, a titanic figure subduing the tumultuous elements of life by force of character.

The idealization can be seen, in fact, as deriving in part from Morley's desire to bring order into his own life, for this led him to create the kind of character which he himself would have liked to have. When related to his own life, his biographies appear as extremely personal works, used by him to explore his own situations and resolve dilemmas. He liked to create characters which seemed to have the power to understand and to master multitudinous circumstance.

The idealization, the generalization imposed on the characters of individuals, proved, however, to be premature. Morley had failed to discover either within or connecting his biographical subjects any generalizing principle or any substantial clue to the meaning and conditions of human progress. His diverse characters continued to be simply diverse, unrepresentative, 'isolated and incoherent', as Morley said that Carlyle's 'heroes' were. Nothing

[1] *Voltaire*, p. 207. *F.R.*, Oct. 1871, p. 474.
[2] Morley to Mrs. Drew, 21 Sept. 1903, Mary Gladstone MSS., B.M. Add. MSS. 46240, ff. 93-4. Compare Laski's complaint that Morley presented Gladstone in 'continuous evening dress'. Howe, *Holmes-Laski Letters*, I, p. 39.
[3] *Burke*, p. 162.

linked them. Nor within them did he succeed in uncovering the secret of 'force of character'.

He remained unable to discover and define a comprehensive context within which the conduct of individual men could be connected and be given meaning. He felt that there was something wrong and deficient in interpreting history simply through a Carlylean emphasis on 'heroes'. He condemned 'Hero-Worship' on the ground that it laid the foundation of a 'barbaric and cynical' ideology which would make 'greatness identical with violence, force, and mere iron will'. The great man must not be viewed in isolation, for he is greatly influenced—and limited—by the context of his activity. 'Hero-Worship' was no more than a 'vagabond polytheism', and at its shrine 'each altar is individual and apart'. No 'effective unity' or world-view emerges from it, for the heroes are isolated figures unrelated to one another.[1] The context is simply omitted, unexplained, and uncomprehended; and yet, Morley wrote in *Cromwell*, 'in spite of the fine things that have been said of heroes, and the might of their will, a statesman in such a case as Cromwell's soon finds how little he can do to create marked situations'. He has gradually to learn how to control 'circumstances for which he is not any more responsible than he is for his own existence, and yet which are his masters, and of which he can only make the best or the worst'.[2] But how are these circumstances to be understood? Morley appeared haunted by a continuing sense of mystery about the context of individual effort. In *Voltaire* he claimed as a 'great historical principle' 'that besides the prominent men of a generation there is a something at work underneath, a moving current on whose flood they are borne'. But to define this 'something' was a work beyond him. The statesman, and any man without a systematic understanding, can have no 'deep and far-reaching sight of consequences', but must grope step by step.[3]

Central to Morley's difficulties was the idea of progress itself. Looking back over the nineteenth century in his *Recollections*, he

---

[1] *Studies in Literature*, pp. 179–80. *Critical Miscellanies*, I, pp. 170, 190–1.
[2] *Cromwell*, pp. 236–7.
[3] *Voltaire*, pp. 307–8, 184. *F.R.*, Oct. 1871, pp. 462–3.

AN INDIVIDUALISTIC SOCIAL THEORY 47

saw as its most remarkable feature the way in which belief in progress had become 'the basis of social thought' and had even 'taken the place of a religion'.[1] He himself at first seemed very confident about the practicability of the concept as a means of providing historical explanations and connecting the actions of individuals. In 1867 he argued that in studying a great man the chief object should be to estimate his contribution to 'the cause of the collective progress of mankind'. History has to do with individuals only as 'the originals, the furtherers, the opponents, or the representatives of one of those thousand diverse forces which, uniting in one vast sweep, bear along the successive generations of men as upon the broad backs of sea-winds to new and more fertile shores'.[2] Later he wrote of 'their relations to the great forward movements of the world' as the criteria for judging great men.[3] But, just as in 1877 he reached the conclusion that 'there is no guidance in the conception' of 'Humanity', so in 1878 he admitted that 'the general device of Progress' provided no unifying principle.[4]

The belief in progress did fulfil the same purpose as a religious belief. Morley could not bring himself to think of man in complete isolation. He was anxious to believe that there was some beneficent force in the universe, some general force, independent of man, that was producing improvement. He later wrote that 'faith in Progress' as 'a certainty of social destiny, as the benignant outcome of some eternal cosmic law', was in the nineteenth century 'the mainspring of Liberalism in all its schools and branches'.[5] Liberalism laid stress on the individual; and, if there were no such law of progress, the individual might well be discouraged from exerting himself, might be paralysed, by the feeling that life was ultimately meaningless and without inherent order.[6] But was belief in such a law itself compatible with an individualist ethic? Morley went on to point out that 'faith in Progress' has also been 'a superstition' and 'a kind of fatalism', and as such had

[1] I, p. 27.
[2] F.R., Mar. 1867, pp. 306, 309. *Edmund Burke*, pp. 55, 63.
[3] *Diderot*, I, pp. 7, 9.
[4] *Studies in Literature*, p. 305. *Critical Miscellanies*, III, pp. 378–80.
[5] *Miscellanies Fourth Series*, p. 293.
[6] Cf. *Modern Characteristics*, p. 235.

been fraught with peril, 'first to the effective sense of individual responsibility', and then to the 'successful working of principles and institutions of which that responsibility is the vital sap'.[1] For, if progress was inevitable, then what need was there of human effort? It was obviously with the object of resolving this dilemma, so that the individual could be at the same time inspired by the conviction that he was working in harmony with inevitable laws of progress and yet discouraged from leaving all to these forces, that Morley began to identify progress with individual effort and to say less and less about inevitability. Thus a systematic concept began to disintegrate. 'Progress', he would insist, 'is very far from being of the nature of an automaton. It wants human agents to keep it at work.' He still believed in progress, 'but only on condition of enlightened and strenuous effort on the part of persons of superior character and opportunity'. He deplored the way in which an uncritical belief in 'evolution' was tending to 'place individual robustness and initiative in the light of superfluities' and to furnish 'in some minds a plea for a kind of philosophic indifference towards any policy of Thorough, as well as an excuse for systematic abstention from vigorous and downright courses of action'.[2]

But Morley needed 'ground for the faith that was in him'; and he had to recognize that his understanding of the context within which individual effort occurs remained insubstantial. All that he was left with was the individual himself, isolated, unconnected within any general system to other individuals. In 1882 he wrote of how fortunate the Benthamites had been to be guided by 'carefully formed theories of human nature', of 'the character of man, his proper education, his potential capacities'.[3] No such theories had formed themselves out of his own biographical studies. The nature of these studies changed. The old enthusiasm for exploring the multitudinous variety of human character disappeared, and

---

[1] *Miscellanies Fourth Series*, p. 293.
[2] *Modern Characteristics*, p. 143. F.R., Mar. 1870, p. 373; Apr. 1874, p. 435; Aug. 1874, pp. 228–33. *On Compromise*, pp. 31–2, 206, 209–20.
[3] *Studies in Literature*, p. 346.

his biographies became less personal and more narrowly political.

His thought failed to develop, as he had hoped it would, beyond the individual towards a more general social understanding, and the one certain thing that he could always say about himself was: 'I am, and always have been, a pretty strong individualist.'[1] If the surrounding world was dark and unexplained, within the circle of the individual there could at least be order and light. At the end of the *Recollections* he wrote of the world-view of the agnostic. From within his own being he 'watches the recurrent motions of the universe, not sure whether it is all entanglement, confusion, dispersion; or is it unity, order, providence? Is it a well-arranged cosmos, or chaos?' In such perplexity the only sound rule is: 'If all is random, be not random thou.'[2]

The individual remained the starting-point and basis for Morley's social and political thinking. He insisted that there was the greatest chance of social progress if the freedom and self-respect of each individual were strengthened and he were left alone as much as possible. After Mill's death Morley vigorously defended against James Fitzjames Stephen's attack the doctrine that 'mankind obtain a greater sum of happiness when each pursues his own, under the rules and conditions required by the rest, than when each makes the good of the rest his only object'.[3] He maintained that social improvement was effected, not by outcry against society's 'collective characteristics', but by 'the inculcation of broader views, higher motives, and sounder habits of judgment, in such a form as touches each man and woman individually'. Because society is 'only a name for other people', the individual should be encouraged to develop 'a sense of responsibility for his own character' and not 'lay the blame on Society'.[4] Institutions, which in their form and influence may represent the 'collective characteristics' of a society and which develop laws and properties of their own, were to him little more than 'other people'. Laski, in fact, noted how Morley had been

[1] *Hansard* (Lords), 4, c. 1144.
[2] II, pp. 363-4.
[3] *F.R.*, Aug. 1873, p. 253. *On Compromise*, p. 278.
[4] *Diderot*, II, p. 12.

unable in his thinking to 'make the transition from character to institutions'.¹ Morley confessed to finding speculation about 'political institutions, government, and the like' 'curiously barren'.² His social theory remained no more than a belief that social good would come out of the diverse and free actions of individuals.

But the individuals to whom he looked in particular were those 'of superior character and opportunity'. Morley's individualism was strongly élitist. He believed, as we have seen, in tracing social development and studying historical tendencies through the lives of 'great men'. In *On Compromise* he argued that what is important in a nation's life is 'the mind and attitude, not of the ordinary man, but of those who should be extraordinary'. Social discussion should centre on the 'best men in the country'—and on them alone.³ He was unable to develop a belief about all men or about society as a whole. Inspired by the positivists' 'religion of humanity', he had written in *Rousseau* that 'instincts of holiness' would now be attached to 'the long brotherhood of humanity seen and unseen' and to 'the great unseen host of our fellows who have gone before us and who are to come after'. Such a faith was, he insisted, 'no rag of metaphysic floating in the sunshine of sentimentalism'.⁴ Nevertheless, as he lost his enthusiasm for Comte's 'religion', his devotion to the 'unseen host' also melted away to be replaced by an élitist individualism. There were markedly élitist features to positivism in any case and these not surprisingly were what remained with him.

Élitism became a dominant feature of Morley's political thinking. The only book which he wrote on political principles, *On Compromise*, is fundamentally élitist. In it he writes of rule by an élite as a necessity because of 'the indigenous intellectual haziness of the majority of men'. He assumes a clear division between those 'who are possessed by the special progressive idea' and those who are not, and writes about what should be the conduct of 'the

---

¹ Howe, *Holmes-Laski Letters*, I, 344.
² To Gladstone, 3 May 1896, B.M. Add. MSS. 44257, ff. 207-8.
³ *On Compromise*, p. 9.
⁴ *Rousseau*, II, pp. 277, 279.

instructed or intellectually privileged class'. The book can indeed be read as a kind of manual on conduct for the élite or those who ought to be the élite of mid-Victorian England. It is such a work as great ages of élitist individualism tend to produce, a *Prince* or *Courtier* of Victorian liberalism. Morley addresses his readers in terms such as these: 'The fact that others do not yet share our opinions is the very reason for our action.' In one section he discusses how an élite character is formed.[1] We shall see later how *On Compromise* did become a major influence on a group which saw itself and was seen by Morley as a developing élite—the young liberal intellectuals of the late nineteenth century.

The inspiration for *On compromise* can be found in Mill's *On Liberty* and *Representative Government*, which discuss and seek to define the intellectual climate and the political institutions respectively within which the 'best men' can most freely and fruitfully work. To Mill a small minority were 'the salt of the earth', the source of all social progress; and he and Morley were most concerned that this élite should be conscious of its role and alert to pressures that might impede its operation. *On Compromise* is essentially an expansion of a passage in *Representative Government* in which Mill condemns the able man who compromises with his own opinions. Like Morley after him, Mill calls such behaviour 'treason against his especial office; abdication of the peculiar duties of mental superiority, of which it is one of the most sacred not to desert the cause which has the clamour against it, nor to deprive of his services those of his opinions which need them the most'.[2] 'New Ideas', the essay by Morley which first brought him to the attention of Mill, discusses the responsibility of such men for propagating the ideas on which social progress depends.[3] *On Compromise* develops this theme and deals in particular with the practical details connected with its application.

On Compromise was written partly as a defence of Mill's ideas against the attacks on them by James Fitzjames Stephen in *Liberty, Equality, Fraternity;* and Morley's refutation of Stephen's charge

[1] *On Compromise*, pp. 9, 32, 120–5, 212, 225.
[2] Mill, *Utilitarianism*, . . . , 1910, pp. 122, 322.
[3] *Modern Characteristics*, p. 136.

that Mill had helped to foster 'anarchic democracy' shows his keen awareness of the élitist aspects of Mill's philosophy. He pointed out that *On Liberty* was 'one of the most aristocratic books ever written', and quoted various 'aristocratic' statements from it:

> that miscellaneous collection of a few wise and many foolish individuals, called the public. . . . No government by a democracy or a numerous aristocracy ever did or could rise above mediocrity, except in so far as the sovereign Many have let themselves be guided by the counsel and influence of a more highly gifted and instructed One or Few. The initiation of all wise or noble things comes and must come from individuals; generally at first from some one individual. . . . On any matter not self-evident, there are ninety-nine persons totally incapable of judging of it, for one who is capable.[1]

His own writings show the strong influence of such attitudes. He referred to a ceaseless struggle 'between the obstructive indolence and inertia of the many and the generous mental activity of the few'. Only a few possessed 'the special progressive idea': over against them was 'that immense mass of disinterested stupidity which exists in all countries', consisting of people who cannot be penetrated by argument, who cannot or will not reason and think, and who 'simply follow blind, inveterate prejudice, because change, or the thought of change, disturbs their mental ease'.[2]

Thus Morley came to place the role of the individual at the centre of his understanding of the conditions of social development. His élitism was a substitute for the general social theory which continued to evade him.

---

[1] *F.R.*, Aug. 1873, p. 246.
[2] *Rousseau*, II, p. 235. *On Compromise*, p. 212. *F.R.*, July 1868, p. 107.

4
AN INTELLECTUAL IN POLITICS

IF one attaches such great importance to individualism and to strength and force of character, one is bound to exalt those characteristics which give individual character the greatest force and firmness and distinctiveness. This is all the more likely when the individualism is as markedly élitist as was the case with Morley's. Furthermore, Morley had deliberately examined the phenomenon of force of character in order to discover the general principles and conditions that governed human progress, and he had failed. All that remained was strong character as a phenomenon in and by itself. Now, one of the most remarkable features of Morley's writing is the frequency with which he uses images and expressions suggesting energy and power. He habitually presented his characters in terms of a constant outpouring of energy, and the reader can hardly avoid concluding that Morley looked on the exercise of power as in itself an admirable quality no matter what might be the end to which the power was being applied.[1]

Morley once wrote: 'For the unreflecting portion of mankind the spectacle of energy on a large scale has always irresistible attractions; vigour becomes an end in itself and an object of admiration for its own sake.'[2] Thus, as with Carlylean 'hero-worship', he knew that there was something wrong with such feelings; and yet there is an unmistakable presence of the same attitude in his own work. Something of his confusion appears in a passage on Rousseau in which, after complaining of the difficulty

---

[1] For examples, see *Gladstone*, I, pp. 186–9, 218, 231, 279, 463, 550; II, pp. 42, 203–4, 284; III, pp. 88, 537–8. *Cromwell*, pp. 14, 347, 407. *Critical Miscellanies*, I, p. 55. *Burke*, p. 78. *F.R.*, Feb. 1867, p. 133. F. W. Hirst, *In the Golden Days*, 1947, p. 179.

[2] *Cobden*, II, p. 64.

of discussing Rousseau's character 'without putting on the mask of the prig', he goes on as if excusing not only the rest of mankind but also himself for not putting it on: 'Those whom the moralist justly condemns are constantly reprieved by a world which willingly forgets the multiplicity of circumstances surrounding conduct and character, and fixes with perfect admiration upon the extraordinary display of any one singular human quality—energy, tenacity, fortitude, devotion.'[1]

He was, in fact, caught between two conflicting tendencies in contemporary thought and also between, on the one hand, inclinations arising out of his personal position and, on the other, the promptings of reflections on the moral implications. He was well aware of the importance of considering the effect of any exertion of energy. For example, the 'unreflecting portion of mankind' had admired the vigour of Palmerstonian foreign policy, but what should have been noted—and condemned—was the way in which that policy had 'involved waste of our resources' and had 'diverted attention from the long list of improvements that were so sorely needed within our own gates'. Now the idea that energy was a good in itself was reappearing in dangerous new ideologies of *realpolitik*, 'Might is Right', and what Morley called 'neo-Palmerstonianism'. In his 1897 Romanes Lecture on Machiavelli, which he intended as an attack on 'the Bismarckian gospel of Force and Fraud, which now masters Europe, and has some foothold in England', he argued that, 'after all has been said, energy as an abstract theory is no better than a bubble'.[2] In a lecture in 1912 he described the doctrine that the characteristics most to be admired in a statesman are 'strength of will, courage, massive ambition, passionate joy in the result', as encouraging 'the sinister school of political historians, who insist that the event is its own justification, that Force and Right are one'.[3]

But, on the other hand, there were numerous mid-Victorian political philosophers whose thought did exhibit a marked

---

[1] *F.R.*, May 1872, p. 495.
[2] *Cobden*, II, p. 64. Morley to Gladstone, 28 Dec. 1896, Gladstone MSS, B.M. Add. MSS. 44257, f. 228. *Miscellanies Fourth Series*, p. 53.
[3] *Politics and History*, p. 33.

tendency towards what Arnold condemned as Hebraism or the worship of fire, strength, and energy.[1] Goldwin Smith, who was Regius Professor of Modern History at Oxford when Morley was an undergraduate there,[2] asserted in his lectures of 1861 on the 'Study of History' that 'effort is the law, if law is it to be called, of History'. The 'end and key of history' is 'the formation of character by effort'.[3] The belief that energy can be a good in itself can also be found in the writings of Mill. According to Mill, effort is the great bulwark against the relapse of humanity into barbarism. He extols the active type of character, therefore, as the great source of human progress. Even 'misdirection of energy' is better than absence of it, and the chief value of human striving does not consist in 'the amount of actual improvement' that results.[4] In Morley's early writings a similar attitude appears. Effort and energy are presented as the source of all improvement.[5] The abundant outpouring of energy is a great feature of the new religion described by him in *Rousseau*.[6] There is apparent the same tendency as in Mill to concentrate on the intrinsic importance of the exertion of any kind of energy. He expresses admiration for the man who, having realized how little one individual's effort can achieve, 'yet finds in effort his purest pleasure and his most constant duty'.[7]

With one side of his nature Morley deeply admired the strong men of this world, its Cromwells and Straffords, its Bismarcks and Fredericks, even if with another side he detested them because of what they stood for or had done. Haldane noted that it was 'the man of affairs, the soldier, the diplomatist, or the ruler, who moved Morley most' and that he 'admired men of action'.[8] J. H. Morgan considered that men of iron exercised an almost hypnotic

---

[1] For Arnold, cf. *Culture and Anarchy: An Essay in Political and Social Criticism*, 1869, p. 173.
[2] Cf. *Recollections*, I, p. 8.
[3] G. Smith, *The Study of History. Two Lectures*, 1861, pp. 40–1, 49, 55–6.
[4] *Utilitarianism*, . . . , 1910, pp. 118–19, 211–14.
[5] *Rousseau*, II, p. 184. *Critical Miscellanies*, II, p. 258. *On Compromise*, pp. 209–20.
[6] *Rousseau*, II, pp. 235, 278–80.
[7] Ibid., I, p. 151. *Critical Miscellanies*, II, p. 77.
[8] [Lord Haldane], *Richard Burton Haldane. An Autobiography*, 1929, pp. 97–9.

attraction over Morley's imagination.¹ He seemed to approve of the leadership of such men for at least the early stages of political evolution—a Peter the Great for calling a nation from stagnation in barbarism or a Frederick for imposing social renovation and administrative reform.² In his own career as Secretary of State for India he was to dream of playing such a role himself and recall often how the 'men of iron' in history had acted in similar circumstances. 'I have often thought', he once confessed, 'that Strafford was an ideal type, both for governor of Ireland in the 17th century, and governor of India in the 20th century.' On one occasion, steeling himself to order the deportation of Europeans who had committed serious offences, he recalled that 'Strafford would have done it in Ireland, and I don't suppose old Oliver would have thought twice about doing it either in Ireland or anywhere else'.³ But at other times his attitude appeared rather one of revulsion. Thus he commented once on the 'hopeless mess' into which Bismarck had come as a result of his church laws: 'I'm all against your "autoritaire". I don't believe in it, and I never did. Your Cromwells and Fredericks don't do their work half as well as slow sober free American citizens.'⁴

Several other reasons can be suggested for his fascination with 'men of iron'. One is that in them he could contemplate that achievement of a mastery over circumstances which he himself was unable to find. His writings abound in awe-struck descriptions of great statesmen wrestling with circumstances and conquering them by sheer strength of will and character.⁵ Sometimes, when beset by obstructions and oppressed by the disorderliness of the conditions within which he had to work, he would long for power such as theirs to sweep it all away. He once wrote from the India Office: 'I am the least in the world of a Cromwell, but I am

[1] J. H. Morgan, *John Viscount Morley An Appreciation and Some Reminiscences*, 1924, p. 30.
[2] *Voltaire*, pp. 186–92, 307.
[3] To Lord Minto, 19 Sept. 1907, 3 Jan. 1908, I.O.L. MSS. Eur.D. 573/2, f. 238; /3, f. 7.
[4] To Chamberlain, 17 June 1883.
[5] See *Cromwell*, p. 236; *Voltaire*, p. 284. Footnote 1, p. 53 above contains other examples.

beginning to understand in a way I never understood before, how impatience at the delays and cavillings and mistaking of very small points for very big ones, at last drove him to send his counsellors packing.'[1] Here lay the attraction for him of a man such as Parnell, 'a man of temperament, of will, of authority, of power; not of ideas or ideals, or knowledge, or political maxims'[2]; that is, an uncomplicated man able to ride boldly over difficulties unhampered by the doubts about principles and ideals and facts that usually paralysed Morley.

Morgan wrote of Morley's being attracted to his opposite,[3] and Morley's admiration for men of action and power, and his emphasis on energy, may not be unrelated to the marked femininity of his character to which many of those who knew him have testified. Thus, to Lord Rosebery he appeared a 'petulant spinster' and 'such a perfect lady'. Sir Henry Campbell-Bannerman described him as 'that old-maidish Priscilla', and T. M. Healy mocked him as the 'Grand Old Maid'. Lord Rendel wrote that he was 'femininely sensitive in personal matters'; J. A. Spender referred to his 'shrinking, almost feminine sensibility', and Sir Algernon West to his 'sensitive and almost feminine character'. Asquith 'regretted John Morley's feminine susceptibilities'. Harold Laski thought that he had 'basically a feminine mind with the difficult vanity of a brilliant woman'.[4]

But, thirdly, and most important from the point of view of our study of an intellectual in politics, Morley, although he was both talented and successful as a writer, was constantly beset throughout his career by a craving for a life of action. He once remarked that the 'bane' of his life had been a continual conflict between the

[1] To Lord Minto, 20 Aug. 1909, I.O.L. MSS. Eur.D. 573/4, f. 178.
[2] *Gladstone*, III, p. 304.
[3] Op. cit., p. 30.
[4] F. E. Hamer (ed.), *The Personal Papers of Lord Rendel*, 1931, p. 164. J. W. Robertson Scott, *The Life and Death of a Newspaper*, 1952, p. 42. Sir S. Lee, *King Edward VII. A Biography*, II, 1927, p. 443. T. M. Healy, *Letters and Leaders of My Day*, I [1928], p. 255. H. G. Hutchinson (ed.), *Private Diaries of the Rt. Hon. Sir Algernon West, G.C.B.*, 1922, pp. 205, 212. J. A. Spender, *Life, Journalism and Politics*, I, 1927, p. 70. J. A. Spender and C. Asquith, *Life of Herbert Henry Asquith*, I, 1932, p. 71. M. D. Howe (ed.), *Holmes-Laski Letters*, I, 1953, pp. 126, 340.

claims of literature and of politics.¹ His entry into Parliament in 1883 he described as the consequence of a 'wish to be somebody else';² and many of his contemporaries expressed surprise to see the anxious striving of this man of letters to appear a man of affairs. After visiting the House of Commons in 1886, Thomas Hardy wrote: 'Morley kept trying to look used to it all, and not as if he were a consummate man of letters there by mistake.' A year later Hardy observed him again at a Royal Academy dinner: 'Morley tried to look a regular dining-out-man-of-the-world, but really looked what he is by nature, the student.'³ Haldane considered that Morley should have remained a writer, as he was 'not by nature a man of affairs'.⁴ After he had lost his seat in 1895 Gladstone himself tried to persuade him 'not to return to political life, for which he was not naturally fitted'.⁵

Morley seemed at times oppressed by a sense of the futility of trying to be 'somebody else' and by a longing to 'be himself' again. On the eve of being elected to Parliament, for instance, he wrote to a friend: 'You are right about the mire of politics; but I have floundered into the mess somehow, and I don't see my way out of it just yet. I used to think that I could perhaps improve politics; so far it looks as if politics had rather *dis*-improved me.'⁶ In 1887 he declared himself to be prepared 'cheerfully and without hesitation' to exchange politics for the editorship of a daily newspaper: 'It would cost me no pang to throw parliament and platform into the second place. Writing comes much more easily to me.'⁷ But eight more years of vigorous political activity were to elapse before in 1895 this mood swept over him again. 'I want to *write*, which I can & not to speak, which I cannot', he once said.⁸ He seemed to be constantly contradicting himself. Thus, in 1905, only two months after telling a friend that 'I have another

¹ *Recollections*, I, p. 228.
² Ibid., I, p. 188.
³ F. E. Hardy, *The Early Life of Thomas Hardy 1840-1891*, 1928, pp. 234, 261.
⁴ Haldane, pp. 95-7.
⁵ Hutchinson, *Diaries of West*, p. 334.
⁶ To T. H. Huxley, 22 Jan. 1883, Huxley MSS., General Corr., vol. 23, f. 77.
⁷ To Gladstone, 10 Apr. 1887, B. M. Add. MSS. 44255, f. 191.
⁸ To Campbell-Bannerman, 3 June 1903, B. M. Add. MSS. 41223, f. 122. To Spencer, 31 May 1901.

calling that I do better and like better' than politics,¹ he accepted the exceptionally strenuous new work of Secretary of State for India. It is easy to understand what T. P. O'Connor meant when he wrote that the 'inner conflict between the man of letters and the man of politics in Morley pursued and paralysed him all through his life'.² When Morley looked back over his life as it neared its end he appeared very conscious that it had not been a unity, that it had been disorganized by this continual oscillation between interests. He feared that the *Recollections* would 'be found rather fugitive and fragmentary', as 'its pages are constantly straying from letters to politics, and from politics to letters'.³ Having 'had two trades—letters and politics', and wishing also to say something about his views on religion, he now found it very difficult to 'manage three steeds of this sort'.⁴

Again and again he felt himself impelled back to the work which came most naturally to him—that of a man of letters. And yet one finds in his comments on this kind of career a curious inclination to disparage it and also what can only be described as a fear of becoming completely immersed in it. He had the strange habit of going out of his way to belittle the man of letters and to humble himself before men of affairs. On one occasion, when Sir Algernon West said that he felt humbled by 'deep' discourse on history between Morley and Gladstone, Morley replied that such an attitude was 'wrong; that the world was governed by men of action, not by men of books, and that [West's] life was far more important towards the government of the world than his life of literature'.⁵ Why should he have wanted to make this point when he felt himself being admired for his achievement as a 'man of books'? In *Voltaire* he wrote thus of 'the position of the mere literary life in the scale of things': 'To have really contributed in the humblest degree, for instance, to a peace between Prussia and her enemies in 1759, would have been an immeasurably greater

[1] To Spencer, 11 Oct. 1905.
[2] T. P. O'Connor, *Memoirs of an Old Parliamentarian*, I, 1929, pp. 293-4.
[3] To Mrs. Carnegie, 10 Aug. 1917.
[4] To Bryce, 19 Aug. 1917. A particular passage in the *Recollections* to which this obviously applies is I, pp. 186-9.
[5] Hutchinson, *Diaries of West*, p. 30.

performance for mankind than any given book which Voltaire could have written.'[1] The same 'scale of things' was implied in a comparison which he made between Macaulay, 'a historian criticising or describing great events at second hand', and Burke, 'a statesman taking active part in great events'.[2] He claimed that the work of an administrator such as Turgot was emphatically 'worthier and more justly satisfactory' than the writing of 'nearly all literature'.[3] When Lord Ripon wrote to him in 1903 about the *Life of Gladstone*, he made this reply: 'I always feel how flimsy a thing mere literary narrative must seem to the actor in great events.'[4] He seemed to envy anyone who had been a success in the practical sphere. In the papers of John Burns there is a memorandum by Burns on this theme: 'Often Morley has said to me, how I envy you, Burns. I *think* whilst *you act*, I write while *you do*. I have no trains over the bridges, no Parks to walk in which I have secured, no steamboats on the Thames as result of my work like you . . . .'[5]

Why was it that Morley developed so strong a dislike for the 'mere literary life'? The answer is to be found in his fear of the effects of the self-consciousness and introspection which characterize the life of the man of letters. We have seen how concerned he was that order in thought and belief should be discovered because of his fear of the mental instability which could be the consequence of continuing disorder or disintegration. The failure of his search for systematic belief reawakened in him this fear and developed in him a 'longing for active political life in preference to mere study'.[6] He shrank from a life which would involve absorption of the self in the broodings of a solitary, confused mind. In *Voltaire* he wrote of 'the inhuman egotism', 'so nearly inevitable and in any wise so revolting, of men of letters and men of science'.[7] In *Rousseau* the 'egoistic character that loves to brood and hates to act' is described

---

[1] *Voltaire*, p. 17.
[2] *Critical Miscellanies*, I, p. 285. F.R., Apr. 1876, p. 510.
[3] *Critical Miscellanies*, II, p. 148.
[4] To Ripon, 16 Feb. 1903, B.M. Add. MSS. 43541, f. 104.
[5] Memo dated 10 Jan. 1925, B.M. Add. MSS. 46283, ff. 119–20.
[6] F.R., Jan. 1870, p. 32.
[7] *Voltaire*, p. 200.

as 'big with catastrophe'. 'In many this brooding egoism produces a silent and melancholy insanity.'[1]

The alternative to this kind of existence, the remedy for melancholy and depression, is a life of action. 'Excessive personality', that is, the extreme sensibility and self-consciousness of the literary man, can be dangerous and unhealthy when left alone; but 'when militant is often wholesome'.[2] In *Voltaire* he maintained that 'the only sure safeguard' against the 'inhuman egotism' of men of letters was 'active interest in public affairs'.[3] And it was in such a life of action that he himself was to seek relief from the confusion and doubt that beset his intellectual position. He once referred to 'the urgent necessity which every one of us has felt, at some season and under some influence, of filling up spiritual vacuity by energetic material activity'.[4] He described the 'active life' and the 'necessity for active industry' as antidotes for 'morbid broodings'.[5] In *Voltaire* he wrote of 'industry' as that which can free a man from religious melancholy, just as he was later to see the 'instinct of action' as having enabled Cromwell to emerge from his 'painful struggles with religious gloom'.[6]

The inclination to turn away from confusion in thought and belief towards absorption in 'work' and 'industry' seems to have been a marked characteristic of mid-Victorian intellectuals. The exceptions included those such as the positivists who believed that they had found a new religion and were not conscious of disarray in their own ideas. Morley and Frederic Harrison, for instance, found themselves diverging sharply in their attitudes to the life of 'action'. It seems that Morley's growing involvement in practical politics perplexed Harrison, who found his life's justification in positivism and had no great practical ambitions. According to Harrison's son, Morley once told him: 'We parted company on that issue. I can do more good—in life; your father can do more good—through books. I try to lead them, your father wishes to

[1] *Rousseau*, I, p. 277.
[2] Ibid., II, p. 234.
[3] *Voltaire*, p. 200.
[4] *F.R.*, Dec. 1870, p. 663. *Critical Miscellanies*, I, p. 230.
[5] *Rousseau*, I, pp. 71, 255.
[6] *Voltaire*, pp. 44–5. *Cromwell*, p. 14.

reform them.'¹ Morley frequently condemned any attitude or philosophy of 'quietism'. He admired Holbach's *System of Nature* in so far as it was 'a protest against ascetic and quietist ideals', and quoted Holbach: '*Action . . . is the true element of the human mind*; no sooner does man cease to act, than he falls into pain and weariness of spirit.' A man who adhered to the 'ideal of quietism' of Rousseau's Emile 'should perish, lest his example should infect others with the same base contagion'. He disliked socialism because he considered that it was infected in this way, as it was associated with 'pity instead of effort, meditation instead of struggle', 'self-sacrifice instead of energetic pushing'.²

He himself appears to have been influenced by two thinkers in particular, by 'Mill's exaltation of the active type of character', and by 'Carlyle's praise of work' and prescription of it as the remedy for confusion in thought.³ He came to believe that 'the only safeguard for the minds who love to reflect habitually on the confusions and miseries in which man is bound is Mr. Carlyle's "Gospel of Labour"'. 'Carlylism' supplied 'the only deliverance possible' from this 'morbid brooding'.⁴

What this involved, of course, was that movement of interest from religion to politics which was to become so marked a phenomenon in late Victorian England. Morley's career is a good example of what Beatrice Webb meant when she noted in 1884 that 'that part of the Englishman's nature which has found gratification in religion is now drifting into political life'.⁵ As we have seen, he became aware of how 'belief in Progress' had taken 'the place of a religion as the inspiring, guiding, and testing power over social action'.⁶ When he wrote of Turgot as 'one of the men to whom good government is a religion', he made this comment: 'The decay of a theology that places our deepest solicitudes in a sphere beyond this, is naturally accompanied by a

---

¹ A. Harrison, *Frederic Harrison. Thoughts and Memories*, 1926, p. 177. Cf. Morley's letter to Frederic Harrison of 7 May 1871.

² *Diderot*, II, pp. 192–3. *Rousseau*, II, pp. 233–4. *Recollections*, I, p. 289.

³ *Recollections*, I, p. 281.

⁴ *Modern Characteristics*, pp. 231–2. F.R., July 1870, pp. 11–15.

⁵ B. Webb, *My Apprenticeship*, 1929, p. 163.

⁶ *Recollections*, I, p. 27.

transfer of these high solicitudes to a nearer scene.'[1] Of a statesman of his own time whom he greatly admired he wrote that his 'whole mind was possessed by the high needs and great opportunities of society, as the minds of some other men have been possessed by the aspirations of religion'.[2]

In part this explains why Morley became an 'intellectual in politics'. It is possible to interpret his embarking upon a political career through reference to certain tendencies in his thought and to a desire to satisfy certain personal needs. For various reasons he did not find satisfaction and peace of mind in the purely intellectual life, and he turned to the world of action to supply the deficiencies. He was an intellectual in politics, not so much because he wished to study the practical application of certain ideas as because he feared the consequences of excessive intellectualism.

[1] *F.R.*, May 1877, p. 725.
[2] *Cobden*, I, p. 120.

5
THE QUEST FOR NEW PRINCIPLES

ALTHOUGH Morley transferred his interest increasingly to the realm of political action, he did not escape from the problem of lack of system, order, and coherence in thought. For he realized that political conduct, too, needed to rest on a firm basis of systematic principles. He became very concerned about the chaotic condition of modern politics, and would deplore the absence of 'the cohesion of a political creed'. It was unfortunate, he believed, that there was no 'body of systematic political thought at work in our own day', no 'system of political or social principles, connected with one another, bearing with united pressure in a common direction, and shedding light now on one, now on another, of the problems which circumstances bring up in turn for practical solution'.[1] The consequence of such a situation was that the politician acted in an incoherent and unguided way or found himself increasingly paralysed by doubt. One of Morley's own principal weaknesses as a practical politician was indecisiveness, the result of such doubt and uncertainty. He was constantly tormented by the agony of having to decide on a course of action. F. W. Hirst observed of him: 'His difficulty or weakness is in taking action.' T. P. O'Connor recalled that, 'when he was talking about his work as Secretary for India, he mentioned among its many hardships that of always having to take decisions. He was not a man who wanted to take decisions. . . .'[2] And yet he was determined to develop a career in the world of action. The key to the overcoming of his indecisiveness seemed to be the acquisition of a system.

[1] *F.R.*, Apr. 1878, pp. 602–4; Apr. 1882, p. 503; Oct. 1882, pp. 520–1. *Studies in Literature*, pp. 302–5, 346–7. *Politics and History*, p. 4.

[2] Hirst, *In the Golden Days*, 1947, p. 188. T. P. O'Connor, *Memoirs of an old Parliamentarian*, I, 1929, p. 295.

THE QUEST FOR NEW PRINCIPLES 65

Morley was very impressed by Burke's famous definition of the value of prejudice: 'Prejudice is of ready application in the emergency; it previously engages the mind in a steady course of wisdom and virtue, and does not leave the man hesitating in the moment of decision, sceptical, puzzled, and unresolved. Prejudice renders a man's virtue his habit, and not a series of unconnected acts. Through just prejudice, his duty becomes a part of his nature.'[1] He would observe with some envy how persons with 'anything in the shape of a vigorously compact system' 'always come to the front for a season in times of distraction'. Such persons, always 'ready with a deduction and a phrase for each case as it arose', tended to stand out 'like a needle of sharp rock, amid the flitting shadows of uncertain purpose and the vapoury drift of wandering aims'. He often studied examples of intellectuals who tried to become men of action. For instance, he attributed Byron's weakness in this attempt to the fact that he was 'without a faith', 'had no firm basis for his conceptions', and 'was aware that he had none'. Morley's conclusion is of great significance with regard to his own career: 'Only the man arrives at practical strength who is convinced, whether rightly or wrongly, that he knows all about his own ideas that needs to be known. . . . The strong man is not conscious of gaps and cataclysms in the structure of his belief, or else he would in so far instantly cease to be strong.'[2]

But the words, 'whether rightly or wrongly', remind us of the difficulties which Morley found to be in the way of his accepting systems of thought. He had to have a faith that was related to reality, was grounded in 'the actual relations of things', reflected an already existing and inherent order. We have already seen how his objection to artificially created and imposed systems extended to politics, in the case of Rousseau, for example. He was strongly opposed to the importation into politics of abstractions and absolute concepts. Burke's maxim that 'nothing universal can be rationally affirmed on any moral or any political subject' became

[1] Quoted in *Edmund Burke*, pp. 280–1. *Burke*, p. 252. F.R., Apr. 1870, p. 420.
[2] *Rousseau*, II, p. 135. *Critical Miscellanies*, I, p. 26. F.R., Aug. 1876, p. 180; Dec. 1870, p. 665.

a basic feature of his thought.[1] Mentioning Burke as an influence, he would condemn the 'abstract, absolute' thinking of the French revolutionaries and assert that 'political truths are always relative, and never absolute'.[2] The positivists offended, in his opinion, by being 'worshippers of abstractions' and followers of 'an absolute method'.[3] We can frequently find him applying criticism of this kind to other people's interpretations of particular political situations. Thus he once rebuked Harrison for discussing the problems of Ireland on 'the assumption of rigid & absolute principles—without the measure of the truly special circ[um-stanc]es of Ireland—wh[ich] needs quite peculiar ways of dealing with it'.[4] When Harrison wrote an article on the German Church laws in 1874, Morley went to the lengths of appending an editorial note in the *Fortnightly Review*, alleging that 'it is merely doctrinaire to criticize a specific piece of legislation from the point of view of abstract principle without reference to foregoing circumstances. Such criticism has its interest, but it is not politics . . . the matter cannot be decided by any one cut-and-dried principle.'[5] Many years later he was thus to reject interpretations of the great parliamentary crisis of 1909–11 as a clash between the hereditary and democratic principles: 'I am a theorist, but I detest the introduction of abstract principles into the great practical difficulties of this nation.'[6]

He always opposed the use of abstract phrases. His objection to them was twofold. First, they distort and obscure one's view of reality. He saw as an example of 'the widespread mischief that may be inflicted by the predominance of an unsound metaphysical abstraction' the attempt by the British Government to enforce a pedantic 'right' on the American colonies. 'The actual bearings of circumstances, so visible to anybody who, like Burke, looked

---

[1] *Edmund Burke*, p. 20. F.R., Feb. 1867, p. 136. *Burke*, p. 244. P.M.G., 7 Mar. 1881.
[2] *Studies in Literature*, pp. 176–7.
[3] To Harrison, 25 Apr. 1871.
[4] To Harrison, 21 May 1872.
[5] F.R., Feb. 1874, pp. 293–4.
[6] *Hansard*, Lords, 6, cc. 990–1.

upon them from the point of practical sense, were hidden from the sight of men who surrounded themselves with a hazy medium of abstract and universally applicable ideas.'[1] In his own commentaries on political issues he would try to banish 'the slippery illusions of phrases and abstract principles'. Thus he wrote about attempts to justify British imperialism in southern Africa: 'The disguise of great abstract words hides from us what our alleged civilizing influence in South Africa really comes to.'[2] Secondly, slogans and phrases 'make fanatics';[3] that is, they cause feeling to predominate over reason and produce a loss of self-control resulting in excesses such as the connivance of Robespierre in the most horrible crimes or the behaviour of the Communards whom Morley called 'phrase-mongering curs'.[4]

He insisted that feeling in politics must be kept under strict control, yet another point on which he parted company with the positivists. Harrison told him that Mill 'reasons, argues, & syllogises about Politics. And all his followers & believers do the same. . . . Now you ought not to reason about politics. The part of the intelligence is very small. It is only to enable you to express articulately your passions. Politics is a matter of feeling. . . . Mill teaches you all to chop logic in politics—very good logic, no doubt, but you ought to feel with a mysterious force of nature.' To this Morley replied that he must insist on the application of reason to politics. Harrison's contention that 'the master-science of society goes by "force of nature"' was equivalent to wishing to subject everything to the rule of 'hysterics'. 'As you say', Morley wrote, 'it makes political action so simple.'[5] Emotionalism breaks down the individual's defences against both external and internal disorder—external as when Dickensian sentimental benevolence is helpless amid 'the surging uncontrollable tides of industrial and economic forces';[6] internal as when the 'cruelty

---

[1] *F.R.*, July 1867, pp. 53–7. *Edmund Burke*, pp. 143–51.
[2] *F.R.*, May 1879, p. 658; Apr. 1879, p. 561.
[3] *Rousseau*, II, p. 146.
[4] *Critical Miscellanies*, I, pp. 57–8. *F.R.*, Aug. 1876, p. 196. To Harrison, 20 Mar. 1871.
[5] Harrison to Morley, 20 Feb. [1871]. Morley to Harrison, 22 Feb. 1871.
[6] *Cobden*, I, p. 99.

inherent in sentimentalism' appears after the latter has been allowed full sway over men's actions. It was men carried away by Rousseau's 'sophistry of the emotions' who perpetrated the excesses of the French revolution.[1] The 'true motive and deepest passion' of the statesman should be, not 'emotional sympathy', but 'positive and scientific feeling for good order and right government.'[2] Morley once condemned Carlyle for subordinating reason and a balancing judgement to the 'dictates of a kind heart' and 'swift and peremptory resolution'.[3] 'I have no frenzy,' he said to Austin Harrison in 1909; 'and my social enthusiasm has little of the splendid vision of your father [Frederic Harrison] who is an emotionalist.'[4]

But, nevertheless, Morley saw in the possession of ordered and systematic principles the only way in which a man involved in political action could find guidance and the assurance of continuity and coherence. Where, then, could he find such principles without encountering these various dangers?

Morley did accept, with Burke, that politics is 'an empirical art with expediency for its standard'.[5] But might it not be possible to make the very application of this standard and of the principle of 'utility' to politics into something systematic? There was, after all, the attitude of the Benthamites to serve as an example here. To Morley Benthamism was the most recent 'school' of systematic politics. While acknowledging that in many respects its ideas were now outmoded, he also often referred to the precedent when lamenting the lack of any such school in his own day. In his writings there appears a strong element of what could be termed nostalgia for the Benthamite situation. Again and again he refers to and praises the systematic nature of their political attitudes.[6]

---

[1] *Critical Miscellanies*, I, p. 147.
[2] *Cobden*, I, p. 99.
[3] *Critical Miscellanies*, I, pp. 147-8. F.R., July 1870, p. 6.
[4] A. Harrison, *Frederic Harrison. Thoughts and Memories*, 1926, p. 177.
[5] F.R., Feb. 1867, pp. 136-7.
[6] *Studies in Literature*, pp. 303-4, 346. F.R., Apr. 1882, pp. 503-4. For the survival of this 'nostalgia' in English political thinking, cf. J. Plamenatz, *Mill's Utilitarianism Reprinted with a Study of the English Utilitarians*, 1949, p. 145.

It would seem that in his own search for principles that were firm and systematic and yet could also be applied easily and consistently to emergencies as they arose, 'utility' and 'expediency' presented themselves as the best available. At times he seems even to want to find in utilitarianism a comprehensive creed or 'religion'. In 1869 he wrote of it as 'practically the dominant creed of the time', a creed which 'fits in more naturally and closely with ruling tendencies of other kinds, than any other substitute that offers for the creeds that are failing'.[1] As for politics, it might be possible to have a philosophy of government based on 'the conception of expediency and convenience'; for was not the whole nation now bound together politically by a general agreement on the principle of 'the greatest happiness of the greatest number' and on the desirability of measuring every proposal with regard to the standard of 'the highest public expediency'? Even the Tories had developed the habit of claiming that, for example, low taxation or a state church would bring benefit to the whole community.[2]

We have already seen how Morley associated 'expediency' with a natural morality, defining it as the achievement of conformity with the order inherent in 'nature'. 'Expediency' therefore usually involved arriving at arrangements such as would allow that order to manifest itself. Morley's deepest hope was that through the free play of forces natural order would emerge. The action of a politician would be ordered and consistent if only he allowed himself to work in harmony with natural forces. He should rely on natural, organic processes, in which, Morley believed, was inherent a tendency of progress. The man who tried to force what Morley called *political* change',[3] without possessing those systematic principles that developed from an understanding of natural order, was bound to suffer frustration and incoherence. There was 'no short cut in life', he argued. 'It was useless to attempt "sudden reformation" or "reformatory rebellion". There was no such thing as progress "by force, or book, or candle". Only "stages" mattered and it was idle to be in advance of one's

[1] *F.R.*, May 1869, p. 538.
[2] *Rousseau*, II, p. 183. *F.R.*, Dec. 1868, pp. 684–6.
[3] To Lord Minto, 26 Mar. 1908, I.O.L. MSS.Eur.D. 573/3, ff. 83–4.

time.'¹ The great task must be to discover what these 'stages' were, what was the natural order inherent in the scheme of things.

'My mind is not made up', Morley finally informed Harrison; and he cultivated an open-mindedness that might best reveal to him the order in the free play of natural forces. This was the way to arrive at a sense of system such as could guide through the perils and emergencies of political action. In his attempt to work towards this lies much of the significance of Morley's editorship of the *Fortnightly Review*, the episode which first brought him into a position of prominence in the country's intellectual life.

Morley became editor of the *Fortnightly* in 1867 on the retirement from that position of G. H. Lewes only two years after the founding of the review. One important question yet to be decided was what relationship his work here was to have to his desire for achievement in the sphere of practical politics. In 1865 he had written an essay debating 'the respective rewards of literary or speculative and political pursuits' and concluding that a clear choice between them was possible only for the few men who were obviously fitted to be outstanding in one of them, such as Mill or Gladstone. For most men the choice lay between secondary positions in either, and at this point Morley preferred literature, as he considered that a second-rank writer could achieve more than a second-rank politician. The writing of history or criticism, in any event, seemed to him an excellent preparation for a political career.

. . . a man may form sound political judgments notwithstanding the more serious attention which he pays to non-political ideas and subjects. In fact it is sufficiently notorious that some of the most sagacious statesmen have been also profound abstract thinkers and inquirers in other departments. The two characters, in their fullest measure, are not frequently combined. Still, it is clear that intenser interest in abstract subjects does not of necessity extinguish all practical interests.²

However, the friendship of Mill, which began later that year, and Mill's own entry into Parliament caused Morley to make a much

---

¹ Harrison, *Frederic Harrison*, p. 177.
² *Modern Characteristics*, pp. 197–205.

more optimistic estimation of the possible impact on practical politics of thinkers and writers. In 1867 he wrote about the association of Mill with John Bright:

> For the future, whoever attempts to estimate the direction and momentum of social tendencies in this country must count upon a close and ever-increasing sympathy between culture and democratic opinions, or he will omit what is probably the most important of all elements in the conformation of our political and social future. The extreme advanced party is likely for the future to have on its side a great portion of the most highly cultivated intellect in the nation, and the contest will lie between brains and numbers on the one side, and wealth, rank, vested interest, possession in short, on the other.[1]

But disillusionment soon followed with Mill's defeat at Westminster in 1868, Morley's inability to obtain the candidatures which he sought at Preston and in his home town of Blackburn in the same year, and his defeat, at the bottom of the poll, when he had succeeded in gaining a Liberal candidature at the Blackburn by-election in 1869. The alliance of 'brains and numbers' remained a dream 'for the future'. Politics were not yet ready for him. Morley consoled himself by reflecting that the able man could serve his country and propagate his ideas just as well outside as inside the Commons. The 'disappointment of a highly honourable ambition' could be easily repaired, because a man of capacity and self-respect is always able to find 'other and hardly less effective ways of making a mark on the opinion and policy of his time'. Nevertheless, the electors should not pass such men over, and the fact that they were doing so indicated that representative democracy was not yet working as it ought.[2]

He now seemed to feel that he could best make an impact on practical politics by seeking detachment for a while and, through his literary work, attempting to master by some comprehensive understanding the confusions and difficulties of the day. In 1873 he wrote of an 'effort after detachment' from the 'noisy and multitudinous' 'speculative distractions of the epoch'. This effort

---

[1] F.R., Apr. 1867, pp. 491–2.
[2] F.R., Sept. 1868, p. 330.

would take the form of 'criticism of the past, the only way in which a man can take part in the discussion and propagation of ideas, while yet standing in some sort aloof from the agitation of the present'.[1] A strong influence on Morley at this stage was clearly that of Matthew Arnold. In *Culture and Anarchy* Arnold had advised young intellectuals after the 1867 Reform Act to stand back from ordinary political activity, from 'the rougher and coarser movements going on round us', and to seek a superior, comprehensive appreciation that would prevent action from being 'random and ill-regulated'. Because present 'disorders and perplexities' were in large part attributable to confusion and weakness in thought, it was more important to search for 'a firmer and sounder basis for future practice' than to engage in the work of 'bustling politicians'.[2] It was Arnold who advised Morley to take the editorship of the *Pall Mall Gazette* in 1880 with the argument that there he would be 'more useful, happier, more yourself, than in Parliament'.[3]

Morley very quickly turned the *Fortnightly* into one of the leading literary and political reviews of the day. The secret of his success lay in the way in which he as editor responded to, and developed the *Fortnightly* to express, the most vital characteristics of an age of great intellectual growth and fluidity. The model which he had in mind was the Encyclopaedia of the French *philosophes* of the eighteenth century, in other words, 'a centre, to which active-minded men of all kinds might bring the fruits of their thought and observation'.[4] Indeed, in the *Recollections*[5] he explicitly compares the *Fortnightly* and the Encyclopaedia as centres in their ages 'for the best observation of fresh flowing currents of thought, interest, and debate'. A unity, it was hoped, would emerge from the comprehensiveness of such an enterprise. Morley once described the Encyclopaedia as 'a sort of substitute for a philosophic synthesis', providing 'a provisional rallying-

[1] *F.R.*, Apr. 1873, p. 470.
[2] Arnold, *Culture and Anarchy*, 1869, pp. 53–4, 250–7.
[3] *Recollections*, I, p. 187. G. W. E. Russell (ed.), *Letters of Matthew Arnold 1848–1888*, II, 1901, p. 195. Arnold to Bryce, 6 Apr. 1880, Bryce MSS.
[4] *Diderot*, I, p. 190. *F.R.*, Sept. 1875, p. 389.
[5] I, pp. 85–6.

point for efforts the most divergent', a focus of unity which yet did not require anyone to sacrifice 'points of essential independence'. In this way 'a body of incoherent speculation' could be given at least 'an external look of system'; and so the progressives of that day were able to confront the conservatives, that is, the Church, with 'a similar semblance of organic unity and completeness'.[1] According to Morley, he derived this analysis of the significance of the Encyclopaedia from Comte. It is therefore obviously rooted in Comte's assumption that such an enterprise was a phenomenon of transition to a permanent systematization of opinion.[2] It is quite evident that Morley saw the *Fortnightly* in a similar light. In it, too, as in the Encyclopaedia according to his description, a 'band of writers, organized by a harassed man of letters', and comprising most of the great names in the literature of the day,[3] dealt with the most varied topics. It, too, was not 'a single body with a common doctrine and a common aim'. But could it, like the Encyclopaedia, appear to be such a body and generate out of itself the 'spirit of system'?[4]

As he insisted in his correspondence with Harrison, Morley was determined to maintain the *Fortnightly* as 'an organ for the unbiassed expression of many and various minds,' and he refused steadfastly to commit it to the consistent advocacy of a particular sect or system.[5] He used his editorial control, not to shape all contributions into conformity with an editorial bias, but to preserve a balance and to encourage the natural emergence of truth by the free expression and interplay of as many points of view as

[1] *Voltaire*, p. 355.
[2] Cf. Hariet Martineau's edition of *The Positive Philosophy of Auguste Comte*, II, 1875, p. 297.
[3] To mention only some of those who wrote for the *Fortnightly* during Morley's editorship: Mill, Bagehot, Matthew Arnold, A. C. Swinburne, W. T. Thornton, J. E. Cairnes, A. V. Dicey, T. H. Huxley, Herbert Spencer, Robert Lowe, Sir Henry Maine, George Meredith, A. J. Balfour, Octavia Hill, H. M. Hyndman, Henry Sidgwick, W. S. Blunt, J. A. Froude, Henry Fawcett, Viscount Amberley, James Bryce, Joseph Chamberlain, F. W. Newman, E. A. Freeman, the Earl of Carnarvon, Leslie Stephen, Auberon Herbert, Mark Pattison, Henry George.
[4] *F.R.*, Feb. 1875, p. 155; Sept. 1875, pp. 360–1, 387 ff.
[5] Cf. Morley's note on '*The Fortnightly Review* and Positivism' in *F.R.*, July 1870, pp. 118–19.

possible. This creative flexibility did much to make the *Fortnightly* great, in that it enabled it to convey and embody the full spirit of movement forward and experimentation that marked an age of challenge to orthodoxy and constant discovery in science. No contributor to the *Fortnightly* was allowed to dominate it. Morley himself was sparing in his own contributions. He usually insisted that all who wrote for it should sign their articles in order that there should not appear to be any '*auto-Fortnightly*' or 'universal essence and absolute *idea* of *Fortnightly*'.[1] It became famous rather for the variety of its contributors and of the opinions which they expressed and for the frequency with which 'new ideas' were brought forward in it.

What was the significance of Morley's work on the *Fortnightly Review* from the point of view of practical politics? To appreciate this, we must bear in mind that his editorship began in the year of the passing of the second Reform Bill. The widening of the franchise to include many working men creates the context within which Morley saw his work as having great practical importance. The task which he believed himself to be engaged in was the development of ideas and principles that would guide practical politicians in these new and potentially dangerous circumstances. What he was most concerned to help the politician with were the emergencies which could be expected to arise with much greater frequency and unpredictableness in the strange situation of the extended franchise. The need was for principles firm and comprehensive enough to enable the politician to keep his footing amidst the constant surge of 'emergencies'. In 1882 he wrote that, although there was a great number of perplexing and dangerous questions 'with which time and circumstance are rapidly bringing us face to face', it remained true that the 'practical statesman must deal with emergencies under all these heads as they arise' without the guidance of systematic principles.[2] That Morley himself was concerned to help remedy this deficiency can be seen from *On Compromise*, where he defined his task as to find 'a guide for

---

[1] Ibid.
[2] *F.R.*, Apr. 1882, pp. 503–4.

practice' by the transforming of vague rules about the expediency of compromise and conformity into 'practical guides and real interpreters of what is right and best in thought and conduct, in a special and definite kind of emergency'.[1]

In Morley's writings after the extension of the franchise there appears a consciousness of impending 'emergency' associated with fear of what destruction the sleeping giant of the working-class electorate might wreak when it awoke to the potential of its new strength. In an article of September 1867 he warned of 'precipitate, irregular, and undurable changes' if Europe were engulfed in another revolutionary flood and the English people were thereby stirred to appreciate the uses of their new power. Change might then come 'with a rush, carrying us we know not whither', and provoking 'the hateful calamities of reaction'.[2] From this time on he was haunted by the thought that changes were one day going to be made 'with hurry, heat, and violence'. Since political action was now seen as 'one of the most direct and powerful means of shaping social circumstance', men's thoughts would certainly turn 'with vehemence into political channels' as the need for social change pressed more heavily on their minds. There was danger of a sudden passionate outbreak by 'those classes, whose only tradition is a tradition of squalor and despair'. Such an outbreak would interrupt the gradual processes of 'natural' social improvement and drive 'the possessors of superior material power back into obstructive trepidation'. That the common people were 'the depositories of power' would be apparent 'whenever they choose to unite in the use of it', although so far 'the old social organization' was serving to 'neutralise the new distribution of power'. 'Household suffrage as yet is only a thing on paper. We have still to feel its reality. The new possessors of power are still hardly aware that it is theirs.' But one day they would awake or be awoken, and then, Morley warned his readers, 'they will make terribly short work with a good deal that you hold precious now'. The middle classes must see that a gulf was 'ready to open at the feet of them and the institutions' to which they were attached. For the unskilled

[1] *On Compromise*, pp. 3, 226.
[2] F.R., Sept. 1867, pp. 359–66.

working men were 'one day very likely to invent cries of their own, that will bring destruction' and 'will trample, efface, obliterate'.[1]

It was therefore of vital importance that change be prepared for, and the work of doing this seemed to Morley to be the particular province of himself and his associates. He once defined their task as 'the modification and instruction of the current feelings and judgments of our countrymen' so as to 'ripen them for change'.[2] In this, as in so much else, he was following along lines laid out for men such as himself by John Stuart Mill. Mill had written that the people were 'very far from being in a fit state of preparation' for the great issues being brought to the forefront by 'the progress of democracy and the spread of Socialist opinions'. The responsibility for ensuring that the entry into 'a better order of things' was peaceful and not accompanied, as had been the Reformation, by a century of violence lay with 'the moral and intellectual movement of the next ten or twenty years'; consequently, there would be 'abundance of occupation for moral and political teachers'.[3] Such a 'teacher' was Morley, and here was his occupation. Morley's own detailed studies of the intellectual condition of France before the revolution led him to find the dangers of unprepared change exemplified in the history of that era. To him the 'want of preparation in the public mind for every great change as it came' was one of the most striking circumstances of the Revolution' and explained 'the violent, confused, and inadequate manner in which nearly every one of these changes was made'.[4] His great argument was the need to forestall the cycle of revolution and reaction by being ready for change. In *Cobden*[5] he referred to the Anti-Corn Law League as an example of the effectiveness of such preparation. The League's 'energetic propagandism' made people believe 'in a general way' that free trade was good, and then when a crisis arose, requiring prompt decision, they knew at once what the right solution was. Men such as himself, he would say, discussed

[1] *F.R.*, Dec. 1868, pp. 681–2, 693; Oct. 1871, p. 466; Sept. 1873, p. 320; Oct. 1873, pp. 420–2. *Voltaire*, pp. 191–2. *National Education*, pp. 86, 107–11.
[2] To Harrison, 25 Apr. 1871.
[3] H. S. R. Elliot (ed.), *The Letters of John Stuart Mill*, I, 1910, p. 170.
[4] *Critical Miscellanies*, II, p. 197. *F.R.*, Jan. 1870, p. 34.
[5] I, p. 406.

reforms because they wished 'to anticipate the time when the need of such alterations shall have become peremptory and irresistible'.[1] He argued for the importance of preparing opinion by constant discussion of 'unfamiliar but weighty and promising suggestions' in case an issue should be forced on unexpectedly soon.[2]

Morley set a very high estimation on the responsibility and function of those, like himself, who formed opinion in such a situation. He had written of how in eighteenth-century France men of letters had replaced priests as 'the teachers, the guides, and the directors of society' and had assumed 'spiritual power'; and in his own relations with the practical politicians, Chamberlain and Dilke, he would refer to himself in contrast with them as 'the spiritual Power'.[3] This notion of the preparing of opinion as a priest-like function is reflected also in his summons to 'instructed men' to embark on 'missionary effort' and his description of the man with a new idea as 'the holder of a trust'.[4] The idea that writers and journalists and formers of opinion were the real power in the land was widely held at the time, not least by the intellectuals themselves, and one can see how the belief was a factor in creating Morley's own position. Thus Goldwin Smith, expressing pleasure at Morley's defeat at Westminster in the general election of 1880, claimed that Morley would have 'ten times more influence' as an editor, because 'power is quitting Parliament and passing to the leaders of opinion'.[5] Matthew Arnold declared that, as the 'centre of movement' was now 'in the fermenting mind of the nation', 'his is for the next twenty years the real influence who can address himself to this'. He is probably, Arnold wrote, 'more in concert with the vital working of men's minds, and more effectually significant, than any House of Commons' orator, or practical operator in politics'.[6] Morley agreed that the power of

[1] *F.R.*, Dec. 1868, pp. 684, 693.
[2] *On Compromise*, pp. 98–9. *F.R.*, June 1874, p. 725.
[3] *Diderot*, I, p. 16. *F.R.*, Feb. 1875, p. 160. To Chamberlain, 21 Oct. 1881. To Dilke, 13 June 1882, B.M. Add. MSS. 43895, f. 156.
[4] *F.R.*, July 1868, pp. 113–14; Aug. 1874, pp. 230–2. *On Compromise*, pp. 213–18.
[5] A. Haultain (ed.), *A Selection from Goldwin Smith's Correspondence*, n.d., p. 91.
[6] *Culture and Anarchy*, pp. 270–1.

opinion, and therefore of those who formed it, was greater than that of Government or Parliament. The man who concentrated 'the currents of common sentiment or opinion' was the real shaper of policy. The 'official chiefs' could do no more than accept it from his hands. Those who thought deeply on political and social questions and propagated their ideas were the real leaders, 'not the men who come in at the eleventh hour and merely frame the bills for Parliament'.[1]

The élitism of Morley's attitude is very apparent. His response to the new political situation which he saw created by the second Reform Act was to stress the importance of establishing the ascendancy of a progressive and 'instructed' élite. Indeed, he defined as one of the major issues in the development of 'modern democracy' 'how the rule of numbers is to be reconciled with the rule of sage judgment'.[2] In 1868 he deplored in particular the voters' failure 'to recognize the necessity of giving supreme political power to supreme political intelligence'.[3] There would, after all, be numerous questions which 'the ignorance of the constituencies makes them incompetent to judge'. The leadership of men with 'instructed' minds was essential for dealing with these. Morley insisted that there would have to be an élite whose minds were 'trained'—'either by systematic and directed thought, or—like patricians—by the habits and tradition of public affairs and great duties'.[4]

What is especially impressive is his confidence in the ability of such an élite to assume control. An obvious influence here was Comte's thesis, endorsed and developed by Mill, that 'the moral and intellectual ascendancy, once exercised by priests, must in time pass into the hands of philosophers, and will naturally do so when they become sufficiently unanimous, and in other respects worthy to possess it'. Mill had long argued that the multitude needed to have an authority in questions of political philosophy

[1] *Cobden*, I, p. 153. *F.R.*, Feb. 1875, p. 299.
[2] *Studies in Literature*, p. 54.
[3] *F.R.*, Sept. 1868, p. 330.
[4] To Chamberlain, 28 Jan. 1876. To Lord Minto, 24 Jan. 1908, I.O.L. MSS. Eur.D. 573/3, f. 26.

and that they would be prepared to repose 'unlimited confidence' in this authority so long as 'the instructed classes' were in 'something like a general agreement in their opinions on the leading points of moral and political doctrine'. What was most important —and here we can see the significance of a forum for debate among intellectuals such as the *Fortnightly* provided—was that 'the instructed' be persuaded 'to recognise one social arrangement, or political or other institution, as good, and another as bad, one as desirable, another as condemnable'.[1] Morley believed that in 'times of distraction', of 'uncertain purposes' and 'wandering aims', power goes to those men who know their own minds best, and have the clearest, firmest, most systematic principles to guide them. The period after 1867, with the revolutionary potentialities of the masses still held in check by their inertia and ignorance, was just such a time. All depended on the existence of 'united authority' among 'the instructed'.

Morley was confident that, so long as 'the instructed' knew their own minds, they could have a strong influence over the new voters. In 1877 he told a group of miners that there ought to be as much contact as possible between working men and 'careful and disinterested watchers of events' such as himself, for in nine cases out of ten where a great body of people had 'gone wrong', the cause had been a failure or lack of leadership on the part of 'those who know better', but had refused 'to go down into the crowd, and honestly and courageously to tell them their minds'.[2] He was always confident that 'dangerous quackeries and fooleries' in the minds of working men would pass away provided that what he called 'the "directing classes" keep their heads, and are not afraid . . . of speaking the truth'.[3] Thus he believed that the more turbulent and violent features of trade unionism had been eliminated as a consequence of 'active fraternization . . . with the leaders of the workmen by members of the middle class, who represented the best moral and social elements in the public opinion of

---

[1] Mill, *Autobiography*, 6th edition, 1879, p. 212; *Dissertations and Discussions*, I, 1859, p. 474; *Utilitarianism*, . . . , p. 184.
[2] *F.R.*, Mar. 1877, pp. 392-3.
[3] To Lord Minto, 24 Jan. 1908, I.O.L. MSS. Eur.D. 573/3, ff. 26-7.

their time'.[1] 'You may depend upon it', he once wrote, 'that if they are decently and considerately handled, the British demos are all right.'[2]

It might have been argued that there was a danger in the proposed activities of this élite of the 'instructed' in that the criticisms and the new ideas put about by their predecessors, the eighteenth-century *philosophes*, had been followed by the disintegration of the social fabric, the collapse of the political institutions, and the violent excesses of the revolution. But Morley was confident that no such consequences could come from the propagation of new ideas and social criticisms in England. No matter how ardently new ideas were preached, society would not dissolve unless 'already in a condition of profound disorganization'. There was no instance in history of 'mere opinion making a breach in the essential constitution of a community, so long as the political conditions were stable and the economic or nutritive conditions sound'. And England was such a community. 'We look about us in vain for any of the essential conditions of a violent overthrow of the social fabric.' Because England was not suffering from 'intolerable material evils', as France had been in the eighteenth century, Englishmen could absorb safely far more stimulus and exhortation to change than the French had then been able to. Discussion in the *Fortnightly* of possible future dangers was therefore to be seen solely as 'a warning to those above, and not an invitation or an incitement to those below'.[3]

The people were waiting to be led. What mattered were the type of leadership and the wisdom of the ideas they were offered.

[1] *Cobden*, I, p. 299.
[2] To Lord Minto, 24 July 1908, I.O.L. MSS. Eur.D. 573/3, f. 223.
[3] *On Compromise*, pp. 254–64. F.R., Dec. 1868, pp. 684, 689–90; Nov. 1870, p. 588.

6

THE SINGLE GREAT QUESTION: A SUBSTITUTE FOR SYSTEM

So long as the new voters did not appreciate the full scope of their power but were content to act in accordance with the initiative of others, the question of what kind of issue was to be put before them was of vital importance. To what ends were they to be encouraged to use their power? What were they to be told that politics were about? In his preface to the 1872 edition of *The English Constitution* Walter Bagehot, one of the principal writers on politics for the *Fortnightly Review*, urged politicians not to 'raise questions which will excite the lower orders of mankind' or which referred only to their special interests. There was a danger of upsetting the 'delicate experiment' of democracy. These 'ignorant men, new to politics, should have good issues, and only good issues, put before them'. Bad issues were such as would bind the 'lower orders' together as a class, or excite them against the upper classes, or make them believe that all their wants could be met by legislation and a bottomless Government purse.[1] Morley himself was most anxious that issues should not be raised that would make the working class a factor by itself in politics. 'I don't recognise the workman as such, except in economic controversy', he once remarked. 'Do let us try to give a *national*, not a class tone to English politics.'[2]

Here, then, was the principle that should direct the 'missionary effort' of the 'instructed' élite. Their task was to lead the people away from ideas of using their power for class ends and to instil in them instead ideas of national purpose. In this way the dangers that Morley predicted for the time when the people awoke to an awareness of their power could be averted. By developing political

---
[1] Bagehot, *The English Constitution*, 2nd edition, n.d. [Nelson], pp. 18–23.
[2] A letter of May 1874 quoted in Hirst, *Early Life & Letters*, I, p. 300.

principles and strategies along these lines the 'instructed' would be performing a service for practical politicians of greatest importance. They would guide the newly enfranchised in such a way as to turn them from thoughts of class to thoughts of nation. In the year of the Reform Act Morley wrote of the urgent need for 'a vivid *national* impulse', some cause that 'would knit all classes of us together into a single nation' and cover over the 'many subordinate diversities of temper, and aim, and moral complexion'. The basic condition for strength and stability of government in a democracy was the derivation of 'its life and motive power directly from the collective impulses of a whole people'. In order that the 'whole nation' might soon be 'concentrating all its energies, organizing all its practical resources, under the direction of a strong executive, for national objects', it was necessary to find policies that would 'generate a collective national impulse' and allow for the effecting of 'the National Will'.[1]

Curiously enough, in view of his later career as a strong anti-imperialist, he seemed at this stage to favour an active foreign and imperial policy as a means of uniting the nation by concentrating its attention on what was going on outside of itself. Thus he argued that 'the keen and excited movement at present taking place in the order of our political ideas' ought to be completed and 'the forces to which it is due' given further expression by being carried 'beyond the questions of parliamentary and administrative reform at home, up to the not less momentous questions connected with the national colonies and dependencies'. A negative foreign policy was 'fraught with danger to our internal safety and health', for, while intervention in Europe to keep the peace would express 'the just social impulses natural to [the] history and position' of England, the 'bulwark of liberty', England was 'sure to find, sooner or later', if these impulses were discouraged, 'that the forces which she has thus kept back from their regular modes of expansion have found outlets and channels within her own borders less regular, and therefore more perilous and uncertain'. The development of a 'virtuous imperial opinion', a new national 'morality' involving 'beneficent rule' and 'the diffusion of good

[1] *F.R.*, May 1867, p. 628; Sept. 1867, pp. 363-4.

government' over the world, was more likely than issues of internal reform to 'generate a collective national impulse'.[1]

But, whatever was the form to be taken by the 'national impulse', there could be no doubt that the creation of it was the especial work of the 'instructed classes'. Morley would refer to the younger progressive thinkers of the day in such terms as 'the National party' and 'the party of active humanity' and 'political initiative'. The reason for this was that they aimed to bring about the 'growth of a greatly enlarged conception of national life and activity'. Whether or not the new electors will choose 'to follow the most able and disinterested leaders they can find, in a policy which shall restore the national energy and power by renovating the national morality and social virtue', would depend on 'the number of men who can be found with will and faculty to help, in the press and on the platform, in the creation of this virtuous imperial opinion'. But he was confident that as soon as 'any struggle or crisis or moment of urgent need' arose the importance would be appreciated of the guidance of those 'who have the highest conception of a national life, the most elevated vision into what is desirable and what is possible, the least care for themselves and the most care for the multitude of the people'. The radicals who wrote in the *Fortnightly* would 'stir national opinion' and 'enlarge and emancipate the national life', and so eventually the era of 'balanced parties and weak governments' would end.[2]

Morley several times referred to himself as addressing and appealing to 'the influential class'.[3] It seems that he regarded this as a combination of the enlightened, progressive element in the middle class and the working-class leadership of the day. On the one hand, he told Chamberlain that he could not 'reach the respectable middle class safely by any other way' than by writing for the *Fortnightly*.[4] On the other hand, he wrote of the working

[1] F.R., Sept. 1866, p. 257; May 1867, pp. 621–8; Sept. 1867, pp. 364, 368; July 1868, pp. 109–10, 114.

[2] F.R., Sept. 1867, pp. 362–3; July 1868, pp. 113–14; Dec. 1868, p. 694; Oct. 1870, p. 480. To Chamberlain, 17 Aug. 1873, 18 Jan. 1875. To Richard Congreve, 4 Feb. 1874, B.M. Add. MSS. 45241, f. 63.

[3] To Harrison, 9 Sept. 1873. To Chamberlain, 11 Sept. 1873.

[4] To Chamberlain, 11 Aug. 1873.

men as 'needing instruction' by the press and being likely to accept it 'more readily and zealously' than the middle class because they were 'less hindered than other classes by fixed ideas'.[1] Morley considered that the *Fortnightly* had 'about 30,000 readers in the most influential classes'.[2] Thus it certainly did not reach the mass either of middle-class people or of working men directly. What he seems to have seen it doing was reaching the opinion-leaders in these classes, who in their turn would disseminate the ideas and help to create a 'national opinion'.

One group with whom he believed it especially important to establish close contact was the practical politicians. They needed the help of men such as himself. Their immersion in the constant flood of immediate tasks made it necessary that others should be looking ahead, developing a wider view, and preparing opinion. The 'keenest and busiest politician' often had 'less of a true general impression than one to whom politics are only a secondary interest because he has other things to attend to'. The man 'outside the bustle of party politics' could 'watch the movement of forces' and develop a presentiment of 'the difficulties and interests that will engage and distract mankind on the morrow'.[3] Morley argued that there should be some link between political responsibility or 'respect for what is instantly practicable' and intellectual responsibility or the 'search after what is only important in thought', for otherwise the practical politician might lose sight of larger questions beyond those which bear directly on 'the material and structural welfare of the community'. He ought to be reminded that these larger questions exist and that it is important to try to find answers for them.[4] On the other hand, only through contact with practical men could the philosopher hope to make his ideas a force in practical affairs. He could not do it on his own. Indeed, Morley professed inability to find any 'satisfactory example of great political advantages being secured by the direct contact of minds, long habituated to abstract ways of surveying things, with

[1] To Harrison, 25 Apr. 1871. *F.R.*, July 1868, pp. 113–14.
[2] To Chamberlain, 11 Sept. 1873.
[3] *On Compromise*, p. 98. *P.M.G.*, 14 Aug., 26 Dec. 1882. *F.R.*, June 1874, pp. 724–5; Apr. 1876, p. 513. *Critical Miscellanies*, I, p. 291.
[4] *On Compromise*, pp. 109–10. *F.R.*, June 1874, p. 729.

the things themselves, which are mainly known to them through this diffracting medium'.[1] Morley's evaluation of his own position was clearly involved in this; and that others felt about him in a similar way is indicated by Beatrice Webb's observation on him: 'surely not a man of statesmanlike grasp or of practical sagacity? An "intellectual", delighting in "the order of thought", not in "the order of things".'[2] For Morley 'the type of the relations proper for the philosopher in regard to political action' was the relationship of Adam Smith, who developed his opinions 'undisturbed by the harassing necessity of modifying them so as to meet particular practical exigencies', and the younger Pitt, who assimilated these opinions and 'proceeded to apply them in practical and modified forms to the solution of actual problems'.[3] There was also the relationship of Rockingham and Burke, combining 'the clever and indefatigable party-manager, with the reflective and philosophic habits of the speculative publicist'.[4] Would it be possible for Morley to find somebody able and willing to play Rockingham to his Burke, Pitt to his Smith?

We have now to see how Morley fared in his work of discovering principles that could guide through the complexities of political practice. The basic issue was whether debate among the leading 'progressive' and 'instructed' thinkers of the day, presided over and organized by Morley as editor of the *Fortnightly Review*, would lead to the emergence of 'natural' agreement on principles. Morley possessed the classic liberal belief that natural order can and does evolve out of the free play of forces, whether in the intellectual, the economic, the social, or the political sphere. But at this time this fundamental assumption was itself coming under mounting attack from many thinkers who were maintaining that 'liberty' produced 'anarchy', not order, and that the régime of 'liberty' was bringing about a great crisis in which principles of authority were urgently needed. The problems which confronted Morley in connection with the contemporary intellectual

---

[1] *Edmund Burke*, pp. 282–5. *Macmillan's Magazine*, June 1883, p. 125.
[2] B. Webb, *My Apprenticeship*, 1929, p. 305.
[3] *Edmund Burke*, p. 284.
[4] *Burke*, pp. 92–3.

condition were, then, that these thinkers neither believed that there was a natural order waiting to be revealed nor were prepared to wait for the slow evolution of system and order through the 'natural' processes of open-minded investigation and free debate and discussion. Thus Matthew Arnold wrote urgently about the anarchy he believed to be inherent in intellectual and political freedom and called for principles of authority to counteract it and to make 'the frame of society in which we live, solid and seaworthy'.[1] Writing a year later Morley showed himself aware of such attitudes. In his essay on Carlyle he referred to 'the profoundly important crisis in the midst of which we are living' and to 'the moral and social dissolution in progress about us'; and, giving examples of types of relationship—social, industrial, political, intellectual, 'spiritual'—he praised Carlyle for having drawn attention to 'the anarchy that prevails in all these, and the extreme danger of it'. There could be no doubt of 'the urgency of the problem': society must have an 'organizing policy'.[2] Then in 1873 James Fitzjames Stephen produced in his *Liberty, Equality, Fraternity* a powerful assault on Mill's 'Liberty' principle; and Morley, preparing a reply after Mill's death, wrote: 'In truth the stream is setting rather strongly the other way just now—which is all the better reason why one should maintain the true doctrine.'[3]

Morley's reaction to these criticisms gradually manifested itself during the period from 1870 to 1874. Increasingly he appeared interested in the possibility of establishing some temporary substitute for 'system', some provisional arrangement that would bring with it all the advantages of a system of thought while not itself being a hardened system. From now on, underlying the development of Morley's thinking, and shaping its course, was a concern for finding some principle of reconciliation between analysis and synthesis, freedom and order, criticism and construction, some means of easing the predicament of 'a generation distracted between the intense need of believing and the diffi-

[1] F. Neiman (ed.), *Essays, Letters, and Reviews by Matthew Arnold*, Cambridge, Mass., 1960, pp. 5–6. Arnold, *Culture and Anarchy*, 1869, pp. 53, 64–8, 87–91, 166, 253–7, and *passim*.
[2] *F.R.*, July 1870, pp. 8, 22. *Critical Miscellanies*, I, pp. 137–8, 153.
[3] To Helen Taylor, 16 Oct. 1873, Mill-Taylor MSS., vol. 5, f. 198.

culty of beliefs'.[1] In 1874 he wrote that 'the co-ordination of Criticism and Belief, of Liberty and Duty', ought to be 'one of the prime objects' of 'mental discipline' in view of 'the circumstance of our being in the very depths of a period of transition from one spiritual basis of thought to another'. The essential purpose of this reconciliation was to cause men 'to have the spirit of system, yet never to construct a system', and so to achieve 'a union of the advantages of an organic synthesis, with the advantages of an open mind and unfettered inquiry'. The result would be to combine 'organic with critical quality, the strength of an ordered set of convictions, with that pliability and that receptiveness in face of new truth, which are indispensable to these very convictions being held intelligently and in their best attainable form'.[2] Acknowledging that 'men can never live by analysis alone', Morley suggested that it might be possible to have a kind of system flexible enough to allow modification in response to increases in knowledge and 'unforeseen changes in the current of human affairs'[3]—those 'emergencies' for guidance in which he believed rigid, artificial systems to be especially unsuitable.

We have seen how, with Morley's realization of his inability to accept the positivist system, his view of the world appeared to shrink until he saw man as confined in a small circle or corner, and how through his biographies he endeavoured unavailingly to discover a sense of order connecting the individual areas of life and experience. But now the possibility developed of finding the firm base of provisional order in the context of particular, fragmentary experience. Noel Annan has written of the position of the Victorian rationalist and agnostic who, unable to arrive at any understanding of the general 'scheme of things', nevertheless 'labours on, now in this vineyard and in that, striving to bring order into one small corner of the chaos which surrounds him and to which he inescapably belongs'.[4] T. H. Huxley, for example, saw man's position in this way: 'Why trouble ourselves about

[1] Lord Acton, quoted in *Recollections*, I, p. 16.
[2] *Diderot*, I, p. 205. F.R., Sept. 1875, p. 397; Jan. 1874, pp. 1–6. *Critical Miscellanies*, III, pp. 55–64.
[3] *Voltaire*, p. 293.
[4] N. G. Annan, *Leslie Stephen*, 1951, p. 284.

matters about which, however important they may be, we know nothing and can know nothing? We live in a world which is full of misery and ignorance, and the plain duty of all of us is to make the little corner he can influence somewhat less miserable and ignorant than it was before he entered it.'[1]

When in *Voltaire*[2] Morley wrote that 'the indispensable synthesis' cannot 'soon again be one and single for our civilisation' and that allowance must therefore be made for the possession by other people of systems just as capable as one's own of guiding and inspiring conduct, he was referring to a situation in which, in the absence of a common frame of reference, thinkers were each trying to make their own corner of the world, their own fragmentary experience, into a microcosm of order and a substitute for system. Morley himself explained how it was possible to achieve a sense of fixedness and stability by turning in on the personal, particular corner of experience: 'Our globe is whirling through space like a speck of dust borne on a mighty wind, yet to us it is solid and fixed. And so with our lives and all that compasses them. Seen in reference to the long aeons, they are as sparks that glow for an indivisible moment of time, and then sink into darkness, but for ourselves the months are threads which we may work into a stout and durable web.'[3]

It was in Carlyle's 'Gospel of Labour' that Morley found, not only relief from intellectual confusion and 'religious gloom', but also a means of reconciling the claims of freedom and order. Writing of the modern intellectual's condition of perpetual, paralysing doubt and lack of faith, he declared that 'there is in Carlylism a deliverance from it all; indeed, the only deliverance possible'. This was Carlyle's advice to 'leave the region of things unknowable, and hold fast to the duty that lies nearest'. Writing in 1870, Morley suggested that, after the 'indefinite aspiration' of youth, 'larger fulness of years and wider experience of life' make men increasingly disposed 'to apply actively and contentedly to the duty that lies nearest, and to the securing of "that infinitesimallest

---

[1] Quoted in N. Annan and others, *Ideas and Beliefs of the Victorians*, 1949, p. 221.
[2] p. 293.
[3] *F.R.*, Apr. 1873, pp. 470–1, 477.

product" on which the teacher [Carlyle] is ever insisting'.[1] Morley's own political career followed exactly this pattern. Near its end he wrote of 'having been accustomed for most of my life to concentrate upon one subject at a time'.[2] He had taken up a series of single great subjects or Carlylean 'duties', each one totally replacing the one before it and being concentrated on temporarily in isolation. Each represented a withdrawal into a particular corner of experience and an attempt to find in that corner a base and a microcosm of order.

The single great question was the temporary substitute for a system of thought. The characteristics which in his preoccupation with it each assumed were exactly those of the organic yet 'open' and 'pliable' ordering. One can see this by considering the paradox that Morley's own tendency to concentrate on special issues in politics was associated with a frequently stated hostility to the narrow outlook of the specialist. 'Human things have many sides and many aspects,' he would insist. It was wrong, therefore, for a man to 'confine himself to one way of looking' at them. He admired Mill because Mill was 'not a specialist—a man with one or two ideas, or one or two subjects, or some solitary interest', but tried to master 'the largest conceptions which belong to the greatest number of subjects'. He seemed to see much disadvantage and inadequacy in concentrating on a single subject at a time. Sense of proportion may be destroyed by the way in which a special interest 'effaces other questions'. While too wide a view may paralyse one 'for the purposes of action', there was 'no more fatal error in human affairs than to mistake a fraction of a case for the whole' and 'no more fatal error in politics than only to be able to see one thing at once'. The 'scientific specialist', for example, because of 'the narrowness or minuteness of the specialist's conception of Truth', was the most likely of all men to lose 'the social and humane point of view' and to forget 'care for Freedom and Humanity'.[3] The explanation for this apparent conflict between his

[1] *F.R.*, July 1870, pp. 11–15. Cf. Carlyle, *Sartor Resartus*, 1897 edition, p. 156.
[2] To Lord Minto, 14 Feb. 1908, I.O.L. MSS. Eur.D. 573/3, f. 40.
[3] *Miscellanies Fourth Series*, p. 17. *F.R.*, July 1867, p. 123. *P.M.G.*, 2 Aug. 1880. *The Times*, 16 Sept. 1899, p. 8, c. 2. To Gladstone, 7 Apr. 1880, B.M. Add. MSS. 44255, ff. 13–14.

theory and his practice lies in the way in which he always tried to make his specialisms as comprehensive as possible. He once praised Carlyle's thought for being comprehensive, 'ever in the tiniest part showing us the stupendous and overwhelming whole'.[1] It was in 'the tiniest part' that he himself found the point of effective compromise between the requirements of wholeness and of order. Through failure to find a system of thought, he was obliged to be a specialist, but he endeavoured to develop as much as possible of a 'spirit of system' within his specialism. It is, in fact, impossible to understand his political career without taking into account the effect of his detestation of the narrowness of the specialist's point of view.

Morley did not want to ignore all other questions. Rather did he hope that his single great subject could cover them all over like an umbrella. Its function was to enclose and bring into a temporary ordering in relationship to itself all the complexities of the general situation and thus create within its own area a 'spirit of system.' We may call this function 'focalising', a word used by Morley to describe a new style of writing which he believed to be rendered necessary by the increasing complexity of thought. In this style 'the rays of many sidelights', qualifications, and difficulties 'are concentrated in some single phrase'; and 'focalizing words and turns of composition' produce out of complex ideas an 'intensely elaborated kind of simplicity'.[2] In the same way Morley's great political questions focused upon themselves all the diversity and complexity of politics; and their chief characteristic was exactly such an intensely elaborated simplicity, the product of the effort to compress within the bounds of one issue many devious and unconnected aspects of thought and practice. For example, he once referred to the Irish question as 'a microcosm', 'wrapped up' in which were 'nearly all the controversies of principle which will agitate the political atmosphere for our time': 'The functions of the State, the duties of property, the rights of labour, the question whether the many are born for the few, the question of a centralised imperial power, the question of the

---

[1] *F.R.*, July 1870, p. 12.
[2] *Voltaire*, pp. 122–3.

pre-eminence of morals in politics—all these things lie in Irish affairs.'[1]

The single great questions were not systems, as they represented only fragments of an entire situation; but by developing in them the 'focalizing' function Morley was able to realize his ideal of acquiring the 'spirit of system' without having constructed a system. They were a means of temporarily resolving the dilemma that the only alternative to an artificially and prematurely created synthesis appeared to be to have no order whatever in one's thinking and no guidance for one's conduct. By fixing his attention on a single question and relating all else to it, Morley acquired a provisional sense of order in his thought and practice. The single great question became a microcosm of order, appeasing the craving for system and harmony while allowing to continue a probing into the darkness for wider conceptions of truth and order.

In the single great questions it seemed possible also to find an 'organizing policy' that would not violate the sacred principles of freedom nor check the free play of forces on which the ultimate evolution of natural order still depended. These, in particular, were to be the features of each 'organizing policy':

(i) Each question embodied the principle of freedom and represented within itself the free play of forces. Thus disestablishment, for which, according to Morley, he 'who is most in earnest for the free play of social forces, is bound before all other men to press', was founded on opposition to 'the interference of the State' —'with the religious concerns of the people'.[2] In his land policy he opposed artificial restrictions. He opposed coercing the Irish and advocated leaving them alone to manage their own affairs in their own way. He condemned imperialism as interference in the natural development of other peoples.

(ii) As each question was not a system but only part of a situation, it also gave scope for the continuing free play of forces and evolution of order outside of itself.

(iii) Each question was presented by Morley as a 'national' issue; that is, it was alleged to raise an issue within which the

[1] *F.R.*, Sept. 1868, p. 327.
[2] *F.R.*, Feb. 1875, pp. 298–9. Cf. to Chamberlain, 17 June 1883.

interests of the whole nation were concentrated and on which the attention of the whole nation should be focused. It was seen as checking the tendency towards politics based on class division.

The single great question was intended by a man whose deepest faith was in 'liberty' and the 'free play of forces', but who was conscious of the prevalence of 'anarchy' and of a longing for 'authority', to provide a provisional principle of ordering that would preserve the integrity of his faith and allow 'freedom' to continue to operate.

The relevance of all this to the condition of nineteenth-century liberalism is obvious. In liberalism there were appearing the general characteristics of intellectual life at this time—shapelessness, disunity, 'anarchy'. Morley deplored what he saw as 'the flaccid and aimless state of Liberalism', and blamed the modern 'sceptical and centrifugal state of mind' for tending to 'nullify organized liberalism and paralyse the spirit of improvement'.[1] Liberal politics were coming to be the politics of fragments, of diverse sectional demands for reform. In 1873 Chamberlain wrote to Morley complaining that 'At present there are only individual Radicals, each specially interested in some part of the whole. . . . There are Leagues and Associations and Unions but no party. . . .'[2] In 1874 Chamberlain remarked on 'the prominence of special questions' in the election campaign: 'The organizations of the Alliance, the Liberation Society, the National Education League, the Anti-Contagious Diseases Acts Association, the Home Rulers, the Women's Suffrage Association, and others—all consisting mainly of Liberals—were everywhere pressing their claims and striving to make their concession the crucial test.'[3] Gladstone, too, was at this time deploring the existence of so many reform questions, 'each with a group of adherents to a special view, but incapable of being pursued by common and united action'. He listed nine of these, on none of which did he know to exist 'a plan desired by the entire party, or by any clear and decisive majority of it'.[4]

[1] To Helen Taylor, 24 Feb. 1877, Mill-Taylor MSS., vol. 5, f. 234. *Studies in Literature*, p. 303.
[2] 19 Aug. 1873.
[3] *F.R.*, Oct. 1874, p. 413.
[4] *Gladstone*, II, pp. 502-3.

The basic problem was that it was extremely difficult for what was supposed to be the party of change to evolve concepts of order out of the flux and movement in which it had its being. Morley himself had not been able to find a principle of change that would give 'effective unity'. For example, when in *Rousseau* he used the expression, 'the Revolution', to sum up the changes that had occurred in the Western world in the last hundred years, he had to admit that those who had participated in this movement were not agreed on any 'given set of practical maxims', and then he had to accept Mill's protest that, 'in dealing with practical politics, the expression is either meaningless or dangerous'.[1] In 1878 he wrote that the only motto which liberals could find to adopt was 'the general device of Progress', each 'interpreting it in his own sense, and within such limits as he may set for himself'.[2]

He soon came to find in the single great question the only satisfactory means of cohering reform politics in the absence of systematic principles. He believed that a party which devotes itself to more than one reform question at a time is doomed to disunity and confusion if there is no underlying principle strong enough to bind the questions together. He saw groups of supporters of diverse reform policies, not as simply adding to a sum total of strength for liberalism, but as tending to its disintegration by the way in which they competed with one another. Each issue in a programme was just one more element of friction if no comprehensive principle existed to give it an organic connection with each other issue. It is, he wrote in *Cobden*,[3] 'the besetting weakness of reformers and dissidents of all kinds' to press forward their own special questions and thus increase 'the elements of friction' in reform politics. The 'antagonism generated' by each question is only 'made worse by the antagonism belonging to every other', and there is thus 'called up a whole host of enemies together'. Cobden, by contrast, was a reformer who achieved notable success because he preferred to 'deal with one [subject] at a time'.

[1] *Rousseau*, I, pp. 1–5. Morley to Mill, 2 Mar. 1873, Mill-Taylor MSS., vol. 2, f. 562.
[2] *Studies in Literature*, p. 305. *F.R.*, Apr. 1878, p. 604.
[3] I, pp. 203–4.

This was the mode of action which Morley sought to encourage in the reform politics of his own day. When in 1873 Chamberlain drew up for the radicals a programme of four 'planks', Morley urged him to omit three of them. 'Shall we not fight with most effect', he asked, 'by stirring the Nonconformists & leaving other people alone?' For Chamberlain's programme would 'run the risk of alienating those who dislike one article from supporting the other three'.[1] In other words, there was no ideological connection strong enough to make supporters of, say, 'Free Land' necessarily and logically also supporters of 'Free Church' or 'Free Schools'. Indeed, Morley expressed grave doubts whether the Nonconformists, whose policy 'Free Church' was, would follow on to 'the touchy ground of free land and free labour'.[2] The answer was to find a single issue on which radicals and liberals could concentrate.

Morley believed, moreover, that taking one step at a time was the best way of achieving reform in England because it came out of a great historical tradition and because it represented most naturally the particular political genius of the English people. He argued that 'it is a characteristic of the English mind' that 'we hardly know how to reconcile ourselves to accept more than one general principle at a time, and then it must be exhibited in its practical application to a special case then and there before us'. A quality 'often noticed in the people of this country' was that of 'not being able to be passionately in earnest about more than one thing at once'.[3] In opposing Chamberlain's idea of a wide programme, Morley remarked: 'Englishmen are not touched by big programmes. They distrust *generalia*. They like to go step by step.'[4] The successes of the great agitations for the abolition of the slave trade, Catholic emancipation, parliamentary reform, and free trade made concentration on a single issue now seem the most effective way whereby a reformer could secure the attention of the English public. Historical precedent was obviously a major in-

[1] To Chamberlain, 18 Aug. 1873.
[2] To Harrison, 6 Sept. 1873.
[3] *F.R.*, Feb. 1867, p. 139. *Macmillan's Magazine*, Oct. 1884, pp. 468–9.
[4] To Harrison, 20 Aug. 1873.

fluence on Morley's own political practice. Thus he suggested to Chamberlain that he reshape his programme into the '*thorough* and *broad* treatment of one great issue—just as Bright & Cobden won a hearing for their other opinions by sticking for some years to Free Trade'.[1] In the 1880s his own practice as advocate of the home-rule policy was clearly not unrelated to what he had learned from his examination in the *Life of Cobden* of the politics of a man who always acted according to the 'maxim that he could only do one thing at a time' and had used a single great issue as a means of concentrating the energies of radicals.[2]

These, then, were the ideas which were to shape Morley's approach to the issues of practical politics with which he came into increasing contact from 1870 on. We turn now to follow a more strictly chronological account of his career as an 'intellectual in politics'.

[1] To Chamberlain, 18 Aug. 1873.
[2] Cf. *Cobden*, I, pp. 203–4; II, pp. 36–41, 112, 121.

7
MORLEY AND THE POLITICS OF NONCONFORMITY

As Carlyle had recommended, it was to 'the duty that lies nearest' that Morley first turned his attention—to the question of the grievances of English Nonconformity, 'nearest' to him in terms of personal experience and upbringing. A Wesleyan mother, a church-going father of Wesleyan origin and continuing strong Nonconformist frame of mind, attendance at a school which 'abounded in the unadulterated milk of the Independent word, and perhaps accounted for nonconformist affinities in some of the politics of days to come'[1]—the reasons for Morley's interest in the revolt of the Nonconformist churches against the 1870 Education Act are not difficult to discover. One might say that he was as much a Nonconformist minus Christianity as the positivists, Comte or Congreve, were Roman Catholics minus Christianity. The uncertainty of his position, related perhaps to his basic desire to preserve continuity in his life, is reflected in his telling an audience of Nonconformists on one occasion that 'he was not a Nonconformist—or rather he was a Nonconformist and something more'.[2] His writings contained numerous laudatory references to Nonconformism and Protestantism.[3] He made determined efforts to associate his own position with that of the Nonconformists. 'We', too, are 'Dissenters', he claimed.[4]

Morley's antagonism to the Established Church can be seen to have involved a considerable amount of feeling derived from personal experience. In his attacks on the Anglican clergy he would frequently deplore the way in which 'in a time of active scientific

[1] *Recollections*, I, pp. 5–6.
[2] *The Liberator*, 16 May 1874, p. 88.
[3] Cf. *On Compromise*, pp. 41–2, 113. *National Education*, pp. 3, 7.
[4] To Harrison, 22 Aug. 1873. Cf. *P.M.G.*, 18 Aug. 1882.

inquiry' men who comprised an important section of the 'intelligent and instructed classes' bound themselves at about the age of 23 'never again to use their minds freely so long as they live' and had from then on to 'move through the world of light and knowledge, of discovery and criticism and new truth, with bandaged eyes and muffled ears'. There can be no doubt that he had in mind how close he himself had come to this at the age of 23. One can appreciate the feeling behind his depiction of the privileges of the Church as temptations to able young men to induce them to enter a career of intellectual hypocrisy.[1]

There was a marked anti-clerical tone in much of his early political writing. The expressions which he used in reference to the Church of England—'champion of retrogression and obstruction', 'ally of tyranny', 'organ of social oppression', 'champion of intellectual bondage', encourager of 'coarse, ferocious, intolerant, and obstructive political impulses in the nation', 'resolute' enemy of 'justice, enlightenment, and freedom'[2]—are very reminiscent of criticisms of the Roman Catholic Church made by the *philosophes* in the eighteenth century, and indeed Morley seems to have imagined that the great cause of the radicalism of his own day might be to fight the same battle over again.[3] Already, before 1870, he was calling 'Ultramontanism' 'one of our own deepest difficulties' because of the Irish problem.[4] The controversy over the 1870 Education Act found him in a very anti-clerical mood. He declared, for instance, about the Paris Commune that 'I shall not flinch if they decapitate or flagellate all the bishops and curés in Paris'.[5] He saw the criticisms of the Anglican clergy within a European context. 'While the statesmen of every other country in Europe, from Austria downwards, were fully aware that the priests had too much power, it was left', he wrote, 'for liberal leaders in England to find out that priests had too little power, and straightway to hasten to make it greater.'[6]

[1] *National Education*, p. 60. F.R., Oct. 1874, p. 504.
[2] *National Education*, pp. 3–7.
[3] *Critical Miscellanies*, I, p. 152. F.R., July 1870, p. 7. *Diderot*, I, p. 9.
[4] F.R., May 1868, p. 482.
[5] To Harrison, 14 Apr. 1871.
[6] F.R., Sept. 1873, p. 310.

At this time Morley was showing himself increasingly anxious to organize his journalistic work around some definite theme. He began referring to an intention of starting 'an energetic political crusade' or a 'new social movement' in the *Fortnightly*.[1] He first suggested as the theme an attack on 'Privilege'. Was not this, after all, the great principle that underlay all reform movements over the previous hundred years?[2] In 1868 he claimed that the disestablishment in Ireland 'means the death-blow to all Privilege which cannot show some cause beyond prescription why it should be spared'.[3] The attack on 'Privilege' might well be a cause that would attract the new voters. There was, he alleged, an 'underlying connection' between 'a vigorous industrial movement and the impulse towards the abolition of privilege'. It was well known that 'the artisans are, as a class, the resolute enemies of Privilege', and one could therefore expect to see the organization of trade unions and the overthrow of privilege 'perfected at the same time, because most of the conditions that lie about the root of the one are also at the foundation of the other'.[4]

But it will be remembered that he also believed Englishmen to be unable to 'accept more than one general principle at a time, and then it must be exhibited in its practical application to a special case then and there before us'. In the early 1870s, as his hopes of finding a satisfactory general system receded, such began to be more and more the characteristic of his own thinking, and, late in 1872, he started to concentrate his attention on one 'special case' of privilege—the strengthening by the 1870 Act of the privileges of the Church of England in the sphere of education.

Morley argued that no State or parish money should be given to denominational schools. The Act had virtually handed over elementary education to the Church. The Liberals, committed in 1868 to resist denominational ascendancy, had in 1870 given to Church of England schools nearly three-quarters of all money provided by the State for primary instruction. He claimed that

[1] To Harrison, 11 Oct., 1 Dec. 1871.
[2] *F.R.*, Feb. 1867, pp. 134–5. *Edmund Burke*, p. 17.
[3] *F.R.*, July 1868, p. 108.
[4] *F.R.*, Mar. 1867, p. 312. *Edmund Burke*, pp. 68–9.

teaching in Church schools was of a low quality because these schools existed, not to provide improved education for the working classes, but to maintain the 'dogmas and shibboleths' of religion. The administration of educational funds in rural areas remained in the hands of the clergy, and thus a great chance had been lost of 'enlisting the interests of laymen in the greatest of national objects' and strengthening habits of local self-government.[1]

He now became involved in the work of the National Education League, a Nonconformist organization formed to fight the 1870 Education Act; and it was when attending a conference of the League in July 1873 that he made the acquaintance of Joseph Chamberlain.[2] He at once sensed Chamberlain's great potential as a radical leader and wrote enthusiastically about him as 'decidedly a leader for an *English* progressive party'.[3] Chamberlain, for his part, was impressed by Morley and asked him if he would help in the work of 'advertising & advocating the "New Political Movement" ', which, he said, was in urgent need of 'intelligent defence and explanation' because of the misrepresentations of it in the press.[4] Morley grasped the opportunity eagerly. Inviting Chamberlain to launch the new movement with a manifesto in the *Fortnightly,* he suggested that Chamberlain might 'take the Fortnightly for your platform, just as Ld. Salisbury takes the Quarterly for his'.[5] To Harrison Morley wrote excitedly[6] that 'now is the opportunity for opening our campaign, of wh. we spoke together last year'.

What was this 'new political movement' that Morley wished to help develop? It was not seen by him as merely another political party. Morley distrusted party organization as introducing an artificial and unnatural element into political life. Organization

[1] To Harrison, 17 Dec. 1872. *National Education, passim.*
[2] *Recollections,* I, p. 148. J. L. Garvin, *The Life of Joseph Chamberlain,* I, 1932, pp. 156-7.
[3] To Harrison, 17 July 1873.—i.e. a party not tainted by association with French thought and revolutionary violence, as were the positivists.
[4] Chamberlain to Morley, 19 July 1873.
[5] To Chamberlain, 11 Aug. 1873.
[6] 17 Aug. 1873.

can bury 'the vital part of a movement under a dreary and depressing fussiness', 'choking the most earnest spirits with dusty catch-words'. The abandonment in a month of the traditions of centuries or the principles of a lifetime—those organic growths which alone give a party or system inner vitality and coherence—can readily be accepted as advantageous for 'the rapid and easy working of the machine'.[1] He found party politics 'hollow and essentially insincere', and complained of 'the hollowness and the hypocrisy characteristic of so much of the mere party debating of the House' of Commons.[2] He once wrote that there was 'something revolting to the intellectual integrity and self-respect of the individual' in the surrender to party of 'personal action, interest', and freedom of judgment, and he even admitted to Chamberlain that he was not altogether without sympathy for opponents of the 'caucus', as 'I'm a bit of an individualist myself.'[3] The 'party man' was obliged to approach political problems 'with something of a sinister interest in solving them in one way rather than another' and did not dare 'to press a principle against the beck of a whip or a wire-puller'.[4]

Morley believed, however, that party division was something artificial that would prove to be neither an essential nor an enduring element in the British political system. He described 'party government' as 'a comparatively novel excrescence in our system, and . . . no vital element in it'. It was an historical 'accident', not a necessary component of parliamentary politics. It was when the party system was in abeyance, with parties coming together to agree on national solutions to problems, that substantial accomplishments were made in British politics. Party division made government 'impossible and absurd by telling off one half of your ablest men to construct the edifice, and the other half to pour shot and shell into them while they are engaged in the work'. He was confident that the party system would soon collapse through the brittleness of its own artificiality; and he wrote of 'spent forces',

[1] *Cobden*, I, p. 205. *On Compromise*, pp. 97–8. *F.R.*, June 1874, p. 724.
[2] *F.R.*, Oct. 1870, p. 480. T. P. O'Connor, *Memoirs of an Old Parliamentarian*, I, 1929, pp. 293–4.
[3] *Burke*, pp. 75–6. To Chamberlain, 20 Oct. 1878.
[4] *F.R.*, Feb. 1867, p. 138. *On Compromise*, pp. 118, 127.

'the final years of party', and 'that possible fusion among leading men, for which the destruction of the old parties, already morally consummated, is preparing the way'.[1]

In his desire to see the existing party conflict replaced by his 'new political movement' Morley was in part reacting to his own experience with party politics. After his failure in 1868 to secure Liberal candidatures at either Preston or Blackburn he wrote articles attacking the system which he believed to be frustrating men like himself. He complained that the new Parliament would not represent the new electorate because, although the voters could 'decide whether the Liberal nominee or the Tory nominee shall go to Parliament', they had 'no power whatever in settling that the nominee on either side should be the best and fittest man who can be induced to offer himself.' The 'local juntos', being 'naturally timorous of new ways', gave no chance to the 'new man' who 'stands only on his merits', Instead they brought forward candidates of a 'respectable and stereotyped conventionality', Party 'sits with deadly weight upon us'. The House of Commons would be full of 'golden mediocrities from Lombard Street and the Exchanges all over England'.[2]

Repeatedly he now expressed his contempt for the existing parties whose 'playing at two violently opposite sides' seemed to him a sham. Politics had become an 'ignoble field of small and base personalities' about whose conflict was 'an air of infinite meanness'. Liberalism had become a matter of 'mere entrances and exits on the theatre of office', and Conservatism, which could be based on principles, was being debased by 'aristocratic adventurers and plutocratic parasites' into 'some miserable process of "dishing Whigs" '.[3] But he was not objecting only to the type of party division which then operated. Party division itself, as something sectional and disruptive, seemed to him a thoroughly undesirable feature of the political scene. For, if artificiality were replaced by naturalness, but division remained, might this not

---

[1] *F.R.*, Sept. 1868, pp. 325–36.
[2] *F.R.*, July 1868, p. 112; Sept. 1868, pp. 326–31; Dec. 1868, p. 693.
[3] *F.R.*, Sept. 1868, pp. 322–4; Oct. 1870, p. 480. To Harrison, 17 Dec. 1872. *On Compromise*, pp. 124, 126.

mean the introduction of class divisions into politics? Articles written in the *Fortnightly* at this time by E. S. Beesly, the positivist and champion of trade unionism, show that this prospect was apparent to people in Morley's circle. Beesly agreed that the old party divisions would soon disappear because of their artificiality and irrelevance in the new electoral conditions. But he went on to claim that the boundary between parties would now conform to the 'natural and eternal' division between working men and non-working men. Once the distracting influence of aristocratic privilege had been removed, politics would be related to the separation between employers and employed, 'a natural and fundamental condition of society'.[1] Morley, on the other hand, maintained that the only 'true and substantial division' now was that 'between the Obstructionist party and the National party, between the party of Privilege and the party of the Nation'. And that was a division that must soon disappear.[2] We have seen how Morley stressed the importance of developing 'national' politics and spoke of his own work in this connection. The 'new political movement' was to be a broad, national, non-sectional movement completely opposed in form and spirit to the traditional political party which 'deadens and disperses the political energies, the patriotic sympathies, the civil impulses, of the nation at large'.[3] Through such a movement would come the end of that political confusion which Morley clearly saw as associated both with the artificiality of existing parties and with the development of class tension. Then 'all this talk about classes shall be at an end' and 'every citizen shall be able to rise to the conception of a national life, and every politician to follow and grasp the idea of united and national action'. England had 'need to pray for, and to effect, national unity' in face of 'organic questions'. The old parties could not cope with these; but there would develop a third 'party', a 'party' of a different kind, 'the party of active humanity' and 'of the republic in its true sense'.[4] In a letter to Harrison in 1872 he

[1] *F.R.*, July 1867, pp. 17–18; Mar. 1869, p. 352.
[2] *F.R.*, Sept. 1867, pp. 362–4.
[3] *F.R.*, Sept. 1868, p. 325.
[4] *F.R.*, Oct. 1870, pp. 480, 487–8; Nov. 1870, p. 591.

referred to 'our tiny flock' as 'the only true version of an Opposition', because it stood out against the system whereby two parties played at being opposed to each other, but were really a 'family party' together.¹ After the general election of 1874 he wrote to Richard Congreve: 'We must now, I suppose, prepare for a long period of balanced parties and weak governments—until your questions and mine have had time to ripen in men's minds.'² The implication was that once these questions had ripened the perpetual division and oscillation between two artificial parties would be ended and politics would become firm and stable because based on a mature, unified national opinion.

The new 'party' was to be different in that it would be extra-parliamentary, in direct contact with public opinion instead of confined within the artificiality of parliamentary life. In 1875 Morley told Chamberlain that 'it is clear that for all the things that you and I hope to see done, we shall have to work out of doors'.³ In this way, he hoped, the new radicals would be able to seize the initiative from the Liberal party which at present posed as the 'party of progress'. 'The moment is the most favourable possible', he told Chamberlain in August 1873. The Whigs were being 'thrust out of the running', and, he insisted, 'it is not they, but we, who shall reap the benefit of the reaction wh[ich] will certainly set in before the Tories have been three years in office'.⁴ Were a radical campaign to be opened now, in five years' time, when the Tories were 'played out', people would turn to 'the Radicals who know what it is they want, and are not afraid of saying so', not to the Whigs who would have become 'permanently fossilized'.⁵

The new political movement had scarcely been inaugurated when the crucial question arose of the form which its agitation should take. Chamberlain's manifesto, which appeared in the *Fortnightly*

[1] 17 Dec. 1872.
[2] 4 Feb. 1874, B.M. Add. MSS. 45254, f. 63.
[3] 17 Jan. 1875.
[4] 11 Aug. 1873.
[5] To Harrison, 17 Aug. 1873.

of September 1873, advocated a programme of 'Free Church, Free Land, Free Schools, and Free Labour'; but Morley, as we have already seen, urged concentration on the single issue of 'national education'. Chamberlain considered this issue to be too narrow and lacking in force.[1] But Morley showed his idea of how the new radicalism should develop by offering to be 'the mere penman of the Education cause' and then writing a series of articles on 'The Struggle for National Education'.[2] At this stage, however, the conflict was not serious, for Chamberlain himself soon appeared willing to accept the mode of agitation preferred by Morley. The chaotic multitude of 'special questions', which he saw as characterizing Liberal activity in the 1874 elections, led him to compare those elections with the elections of 1868 and conclude that the voices of the special interests were silent only when there was a 'larger issue' felt to be of sufficient magnitude to justify the postponement of all minor subjects'. By late 1874 he had decided that it was necessary to consider 'which of the many practical applications of Liberal principles has the first claim to be selected as the next rallying cry of the Liberal party'.[3]

What Morley wanted was a *proper definiteness* in the programme of the new movement. This is how he described the strategy which he wished to see followed:

What seems to me desirable is that the world shd. know that there is a group—a very small one—of men with a good many years of work before them who mean to press certain principles on the constituencies irrespective of the old and worn-out party grooves; men who know what they want, who believe they can in time bring the people over to them, and who intend intrepidly to go to work without more loss of time. . . .

What has to be done is to convince the public that there is a set of men—of whom you [Chamberlain] are the most prominent—who mean to press forward with a programme. Now is this not done by *thorough* and *broad* treatment of one great issue. . . .[4]

And this one great issue was to be 'national education'.

[1] To Morley, 19, 23 Aug. 1873. Cf. Morley to Chamberlain, 18, 22 Aug. 1873.
[2] To Chamberlain, 4 July, 6 Aug. 1873.
[3] *F.R.*, Oct. 1874, pp. 413, 418.
[4] To Harrison, 22 Aug. 1873. To Chamberlain, 11, 18 Aug. 1873.

Morley became temporarily absorbed in the question, and saw it as absorbing within itself other important issues—the development of national life, the extension of local self-government, the attack on privilege, the education of the working classes. His aim was to present it in 'its true importance as the most serious of national concerns'.[1] He opposed any form of presentation that would be sectional or suggest that the issue was just part of a greater whole. Thus he insisted that it should not be viewed 'as a part of the old wrangle between church and chapel'. There must be no 'restriction of criticism to the 25th clause &c.' The argument should be presented '*as a whole*' and public opinion educated on 'the *whole question* of sectarian as against national teaching'.[2] He argued that it was a particularly appropriate issue to occupy the attention of the new electorate. 'The assumption by the nation of duties which had hitherto been left to the clergy, came foremost', he claimed, 'among the hopes of those who had been most ardent in the cause of parliamentary reform.' Here, indeed, was a means of enforcing precedence on the many reform interests demanding attention after the Reform Act. 'It was the first article in that programme of improvement and a higher national life, for which, and for which only, parliamentary reform had ever been sought by sensible men.' In 1867 he had written of the need for 'a collective national impulse' that would unify the new democracy. Now he described 'distrust of clerical influence' as 'one of the soundest and shrewdest of all our national impulses'.[3] He also claimed that the issue was the best embodiment of true liberal principles. 'Liberalism in 1868', he wrote, 'meant this hostility' to denominationalism 'more than any one other thing'. 'This was the centre of the party creed', 'the first article', 'foremost among the hopes of reformers'. 'If liberalism means anything at all beyond a budget of sounding phrases', then it must mean opposition to priestly control over education.[4] Thus this one issue could be used to provide definition and order in a very confused situation.

[1] To Chamberlain, 4 July 1873.
[2] To Chamberlain, 4, 23 July 1873.
[3] *National Education*, pp. 16, 60. F.R., Aug. 1873, p. 149; Sept. 1873, p. 308.
[4] *National Education*, pp. 16, 71. F.R., Aug. 1873, p. 149; Sept. 1873, p. 314.

Nevertheless, he himself soon began to think that this issue must be viewed within a wider context. One might have expected that, if he did come around to this way of thinking, the larger issue within which he placed 'national education' would be that of educational reform in general. But it was not so. The reason is that he had a rather limited attitude towards education. His inability to develop education as a 'great issue' can be appreciated in the light of his insistence that universal education was not a panacea for social ills. Education should develop in working men self-reliance and self-respect, but should not be depicted as able to provide the answer to the problems of society.[1] His élitism was also a limiting influence. He refused to support any move towards a general system of free secondary education, and was concerned mainly that some better education be devised for the middle classes, so that, among other consequences, the quality of political leadership would be improved.[2]

The greater issue which he came to see as incorporating that of 'national education' was disestablishment. As early as 1872 he was beginning to believe that 'you can only thoroughly consider the Educat[io]n policy in connection with disestablishm[en]t' and that, viewed in this way, what Forster's Act had done was to give the parson a great opportunity to use his control over education 'to create in the villages a strong pro-church feeling, when the battle [over the establishment] comes'.[3] The Act had created for the Church 'a new platform, a new instrument, a new organ of power —paid for by public money'.[4] Gradually 'national education' became superseded by, and absorbed into, the larger question. In itself it had become confused and complicated, unable to provide the firm rallying-point that radicals needed. By 1876 Morley was advising Chamberlain to make 'an emphatic statement that the Educat[io]n Q[uestio]n is over for some years, and that when it reappears it can only be to withdraw every sou from the voluntary schools'. 'The Radicals', he said, 'wd. be grateful for a clear note

---

[1] *National Education*, pp. 95–6, 113, 118, 120.
[2] Ibid., pp. 116, 148. To Chamberlain, 3 Nov. 1878.
[3] To Harrison, 17 Dec. 1872.
[4] *National Education*, p. 59. F.R., Sept. 1873, p. 308.

of this kind.'¹ The question had to be dropped completely, not to reappear unless in a definite, uncompromising form. Nobody must be in any doubt that it was no longer the great issue, and it must not be allowed to confuse the situation for whatever was. 'I shall not come to the [Education] League Meeting', Morley declared in January 1875. 'The Education Question is now a subordinate branch of the Disestablishment Question. My voice would be for cutting a loss, and letting the League quietly slip into the background, for a time at any rate'.² In later years he admitted that the issue had not, in fact, aroused great enthusiasm in the nation.³ After 1885 he was anxious that the Liberals should not try to make much of the issue lest they should give offence to their Irish Roman Catholic allies.⁴ Thus it was sacrificed to the primacy of what happened to be the great question of the time.

We can see Morley trying to perform the work of discerning 'the great lines of the future' in an observation which he made in 1872 that a settlement of the education issue in the way that he himself favoured would be 'worthy of a statesman preparing the future on the extending lines of the present', lines which represented 'dominant tendencies towards disestablishm[en]t, secularism, &c.' Disestablishment 'is one day inevitable, isn't it?' he remarked.⁵ In the latter part of 1873 he was thinking of the prospect if Goldwin Smith should return from Canada to England, for Smith seemed 'the natural leader of a disestablishment movement'; and he urged Chamberlain to work with himself in preparing a practical scheme of disendowment.⁶ 'There seems every reason to think', he wrote in May 1874, 'that the disestablishment and disendowment of the Church is likely to be the next foremost great question in England.' That month he attended and addressed a conference of the Liberation Society, the Nonconformist pressure group working for this reform. The Liberationists were

[1] To Chamberlain, 28 July 1876. Cf. to Harrison, 28 July 1876.
[2] To Chamberlain, 18 Jan. 1875.
[3] *Hansard*, 4, 46, 228 [Feb. 1897].
[4] Cf. to Gladstone, 2 June 1891, B.M. Add. MSS. 44256, ff. 147-8.
[5] To Harrison, 17 Dec. 1872.
[6] To Harrison, 26 Sept. 1873. To Chamberlain, 11 Sept. 1873.

'trying', he said, 'to widen their base, so as to include even such non-sectarian persons as myself.' After the conference he wrote that he intended during the next year 'to state the case in a broad and national shape' and 'to frame some rational scheme of disendowment'. He did, in fact, assist the Liberation Society to prepare such a scheme.[1]

When in October 1874 Chamberlain, apparently converted to the strategy of concentration on one issue at a time, came out in the *Fortnightly* in favour of disestablishment as 'the next rallying cry of the Liberal party' and the 'only one great question of immediate interest of Radical politicians on which the party may be summoned to unite or to re-form',[2] Morley was delighted. Here was a 'responsible spokesman' taking up disestablishment from 'the party point of view'. 'I am cordially with you', he wrote, 'about the importance of making Disestablishment and Disendowment the next move. The Establishment is really the key to the whole obstructive position.' And he discussed with Chamberlain plans 'to launch Disestablishment as a party and political movement'.[3] By February 1875 he felt confident enough to say that it was 'now clear on all sides that the Church question is . . . the next page of the Liberal Programme'.[4] During the next two years he was to work hard to promote the question in the *Fortnightly*.

Disestablishment appealed as a great question because of 'the simplicity of the main issue': 'the relations of Church and State are capable of being submitted in a single question, "Shall the Church be disestablished and disendowed?" In answering this no elector will be confused by the intricacies of the problem. . . .' By contrast, an alternative issue, the reform of land tenure, was full of 'numerous and complex' difficulties and 'innumerable details'. Disestablishment must be promoted on its own.[5] Like 'national education', this great question appealed as a possible

[1] To Helen Taylor, 7 May 1874, Mill-Taylor MSS., vol. 5, f. 205. *The Liberator*, 16 May 1874, p. 88. Hirst, *Early Life & Letters*, II, pp. 1-10.
[2] *F.R.*, Oct. 1874, pp. 413, 418, 420.
[3] To Chamberlain, 13, 19 Sept., 16 Nov. 1874.
[4] *F.R.*, Feb. 1875, p. 303.
[5] *F.R.*, Feb. 1876, pp. 304-5.

defining and ordering factor in reform politics. Early in 1875 Morley complained that it was 'impossible to devise even a plain working definition of a Liberal' or 'to name a single object which it is the special and express note of a Liberal to desire'.[1] A year later, however, he was referring to disestablishment as 'the one bond of union between the most important groups of liberals' and 'a cause to which a greater number of liberals of all kinds may be expected to rally than to any other cause whatsoever'.[2] He saw it also as an issue that could provide national unity. He hoped that out of it might come a 'great combination of Dissenters with workmen' based on the principle that 'no class . . . can now lead, it must be *men*—from whatever class'.[3] When at the Liberation Society's conference in May 1874 R. W. Dale spoke of 'the influence which they might exert upon the working men', Morley warned of the need for care lest agitation of such a kind might produce 'a division of the nation into classes'. He urged the Liberationists to 'make this movement a political and national one', and he tried to show them how they could present the disendowment issue 'in its civic and national aspect' with the Church of England appearing as 'the nation in one of its aspects'.[4] In November 1874 he told delegates to a conference in Manchester that 'the advocates of disestablishment should increasingly aim at producing a general conviction that the interference of the State with the religious concerns of the people is productive of great political and social as well as religious evils; that the question is, therefore, one of national and not of merely sectarian interest; and that on its settlement will largely depend the future prosperity and peace of the country'.[5]

But a persistent theme throughout Morley's connection with the Liberation Society was the difficulty of reconciling the nature of the Society as a vehicle for expressing the grievances of a particular section with the idea of turning the disestablishment movement into a broad, national, supra-sectional campaign. The

[1] F.R., Feb. 1875, p. 296.
[2] F.R., Jan. 1876, p. 151.
[3] To Harrison, 3 Oct. 1873.
[4] *The Liberator*, 16 May 1874, p. 88.
[5] *The Liberator*, 9 Nov. 1874, p. 190.

sectionalism of the movement continued to shape its development. After the conference in November 1874 Morley told Chamberlain that, while 'our Dissenters have the root of the matter in them' and their enthusiasm remained an essential asset, the movement ought to be broadened politically, especially 'in the direction of the artisans'. 'The Liberation Society is even now not national—not political enough.' He proposed that a lay or 'non-dissenting' meeting be held in Birmingham with only one clergyman (R. W. Dale) on the platform 'and not a word to be said about the "freedom wh. is in Christ Jesus" '.[1] By July 1875 he was worried that the advocates of disestablishment remained 'very unpopular & rather weak and *mal vus*' and that the question was not being sufficiently 'discussed and stirred'.[2] In November he urged Chamberlain to 'touch the general public' in a speech and to 'remember that you are talking, (if well reported) not only to Dissenters, but to political England'; and a month later he begged him to call a meeting in Birmingham to pronounce disestablishment 'a political, and no longer a nonconformist, quest[io]n'.[3] But Morley himself found difficulty in having the question presented in this way in the *Fortnightly*. He arranged for an article by Dale on disestablishment to be published in the issue of March 1876, but was disappointed with it, finding it 'merely nonconformist', 'still distinctly Nonconformist in tone', and lacking in appeal for 'the secular liberal'. He decided that he himself would have to 'sit down and write a couple of papers on disestablishment, purely political and social'.[4]

But these papers were never written. Disappointed at its failure to become a great, national issue, he lost his enthusiasm for disestablishment, too. Writing in May 1876 he admitted that there were three serious problems about it. First, as work on a practical scheme of disendowment proceeded, a host of difficulties and complexities of detail arose to disintegrate what had once appealed as a simple, clear-cut issue. Secondly, he had begun to doubt whether

---

[1] To Chamberlain, 16 Nov. 1874.
[2] To Chamberlain, 14 July 1875.
[3] To Chamberlain, 12 Nov., 20 Dec. 1875.
[4] To Harrison, 22 Mar. 1876. To Chamberlain, 25 Feb. 1876.

it was, after all, a safe question for agitation in the new political situation. Disendowment would involve interference with property on a large scale; and there was a danger that the issue might 'bring the nation to the edge of a civil war'—in other words, wreck on the shoals of sectionalism that very unity within the nation which he had been looking to such a movement to foster. Indeed, six months earlier Morley agreed that W. E. Forster had 'a point to be met' when Forster said to him: 'You are going to plunge the country into a conflict almost like a civil war, for the sake of a change wh. *may* profit your sacerdotal foes.' Now Morley was wondering whether the issue was worth such a risk. Thirdly, there was the fact that it was fundamentally and unalterably a sectional issue. The only real enthusiasts for it were people 'who live in exclusively dissenting circles, or have no opportunities for surveying our society widely in its varied strata'.[1] Chamberlain, for his part, became disenchanted with the idea of concentration on a single great issue as a means of unifying reform politics, and turned in 1877 towards party organization instead as an 'umbrella' over a programme of reforms.

One lesson that clearly emerged from this failure to find in disestablishment a great, unifying, national cause was the difficulty involved in trying to develop such a cause out of what was entirely an internal issue, that is, one of the many sectional interests that were already within and disintegrating reform politics. We shall see how later great questions taken up by Morley were of a different kind.

[1] To Harrison, 8 May 1876. To Chamberlain, 12 Nov. 1875.

8

MORLEY AND CHAMBERLAIN, 1873–1883

IN Morley's opinion the success of the new political movement would depend not only on the kind of issues which it worked to promote but also on the kind of leadership which controlled it. He now saw the chance to evolve the leadership of a progressive élite which he had become convinced was essential in the new political circumstances. He wanted the world to see that 'there is a group—a very small one—of men' who 'know what they want' and 'intend intrepidly to go to work' to bring the people over to the principles in which they believe.[1] The kind of group which most interested him is seen first in the Radical Club, founded in 1870. This club was intended to combine political thinkers and writers with practical politicians. Half its members were to be M.P.s. Morley himself became a member, and so did many of the leading contributors to the *Fortnightly Review*.[2] Indeed, Morley seems to have tried to effect a similar combination in the pages of the *Fortnightly*, and the idea was carried on in his efforts to evolve the new radical 'party'. Commenting on the distinction between those interested in politics from an academic standpoint and those practically involved, he wrote: 'The possible strength of the PARTY lies in the combination within its ranks (!) of the two types.'[3]

But his ideas on the form of leadership, like those on the form of agitation, developed in the direction of favouring greater concentration. The importance of a single individual of great practical ability who could lead the radicals became increasingly apparent to him. Mill's views on the reasons for the ineffectiveness of the

---

[1] To Chamberlain, 11 Aug. 1873.
[2] S. Gwynn and G. M. Tuckwell, *The Life of the Rt. Hon. Sir Charles W. Dilke, Bart., M.P.*, I, 1917, p. 100.
[3] To Chamberlain, 31 Jan. 1876.

Philosophic Radicals of the 1830s may well have influenced his thinking on this. Mill attributed the failure of this other group of radicals which had formed just after a Reform Act to their lack of a leader who would 'either have forced the Whigs to receive their measures from him, or have taken the lead of the Reform party out of their hands'. Mill himself had tried to guide and inspire the radicals through his writing; but he had come to appreciate that what was needed was 'one who, being himself in Parliament, could have mixed with the Radical members in daily consultation, could himself have taken the initiative, and instead of urging others to lead, could have summoned them to follow'.[1] Morley was soon looking for a possible candidate for such a role. In 1871 he wrote to Frederic Harrison: 'I shd. like to see you in power: in a Cabinet, one day.'[2] But Harrison had no such practical ambitions, and Morley's meeting with Joseph Chamberlain in 1873 revealed to him a much more impressive potential radical leader.

Chamberlain did not entirely conform with the ideal of political leadership held by either Morley or Mill. Mill had defined as the type of leader needed by the Philosophic Radicals 'some man of philosophic attainments and popular talents'.[3] Morley's ideal may be seen in his description of John Pym's 'double gift' of being at once practical, a 'master of tactics and organizing arts', and also 'elevated', 'the inspirer of solid and lofty principles'.[4] But Morley's account of Chamberlain stresses that he did not possess such a 'double gift'. 'In general ideas' Chamberlain's equipment did not seem to Morley to be 'particularly wide'. He was content simply to meet 'events and forces as they arose'—those 'emergencies' for guidance in which Morley thought systematic principles so necessary for the practical politician. But at least Chamberlain 'knew enough to be sharply interested in any general ideas that were from time to time presented to him'. 'His mind was open to ideas.'[5] On the other hand, Morley fully appreciated Chamberlain's fine practical talents. What is especially significant is that in

---

[1] Mill, *Autobiography*, 6th edition, 1879, pp. 196–7.
[2] 25 Apr. 1871.
[3] Mill, *Autobiography*, p. 196.
[4] *Cromwell*, p. 43.
[5] *Recollections*, I, pp. 155–6.

this appreciation he often showed an acute awareness of his own lack of such talents. 'That is going to be your line—the man of office, power, function, great affairs', he once told Chamberlain, adding: 'Only don't look down, by and bye, on the poor devils of prophets in the wilderness. . . .'[1] When Chamberlain rebuked him on one occasion for advancing 'Utopian' arguments, he accepted the description, even although, he added, it was made by 'a member of the Cabinet whose success as practical and non-Utopian statesman is so dazzling'.[2]

It is clear that he saw his relationship with Chamberlain as complementary, with each man compensating for what the other lacked. In this way was realized the 'double gift' which was his ideal of leadership. As a result, furthermore. Morley could satisfy his own longing for an active political career by the closeness of his identification with the progress of a man who really was fitted to be a success in such a career. Austen Chamberlain has described his impression of the complementary nature of the relationship. Each man 'opened a new world to the other'. Morley, 'the university man, the disciple of Mill', author and political thinker, 'was a stimulating companion to a man who had left school at sixteen and, though he had afterwards read widely for himself, had no pretensions to be a scholar'. Chamberlain found that Morley 'opened many windows through which till then he had had no chance of looking'. He was deeply impressed by Morley's knowledge and learning. He once remarked that 'one evening with John Morley would do more for his son than many days' teaching at Rugby'. And Morley found his own characteristics complemented by Chamberlain. To him, 'the scholar and philosopher and publicist, the intensely practical life which [Chamberlain] led, immersed in the work of administration whether of city or country, was something equally new'. Morley, comments Austen Chamberlain, 'had what almost amounted to a craving for public life . . . he longed for the limelight and the perils and the triumphs of the platform'.[3] For a time the friendship

---

[1] To Chamberlain, 23 Dec. 1876.
[2] To Chamberlain, 14 Feb. 1885.
[3] A. Chamberlain, *Down the Years*, 1935, pp. 197–8.

of Chamberlain provided a vicarious satisfaction of this craving.

Descriptions of complementary relationships of a very similar kind occur frequently in Morley's writings. For example, this is his comment on the differences between Turgot and Condorcet: 'They belonged to quite distinct types of character, but this may be a condition of the most perfect forms of sympathy. Each gives support where the other is most conscious of needing it.'[1] Burke and Dr. Johnson seemed to him 'the two complements of a single noble and solid type'.[2] Cobden and Bright were 'the complements of one another; . . . their gifts differed, so that one exactly covered the ground which the other was predisposed to leave comparatively untouched'.[3] We have seen how he even developed what might be called a theory of complementariness in regard to relations between intellectuals and practical politicians. Morley saw himself as 'the Spiritual Power' supplying ideas to a man who, if without many of his own, 'liked and valued any contribution from my own modest stock of that commodity'.[4] And Chamberlain acknowledged that the preparation and propagation of ideas were Morley's 'special province'.[5] Morley was Adam Smith to Chamberlain's Pitt, Burke to Chamberlain's Rockingham. Chamberlain was 'the clever and indefatigable party-manager', he the 'speculative publicist'. Morley made this distinction quite plain. For example, informing Chamberlain of a plan to write commentaries on current events for the *Fortnightly,* he warned: 'don't be surprised if the thing comes out rather more literary, general, semi-meditative, critico-philosophical, than you have bn. expecting.'[6] Advising Chamberlain to defer a certain action for a few weeks, he explained that in this question of timing was involved one of those subtle distinctions on which turn the most crucial points of practice, but which are not appreciated in the 'rough brawling of politics'.[7] When Chamberlain criticized him for not being prac-

[1] *F.R.,* Jan. 1870, p. 22.
[2] *Burke,* p. 156.
[3] *Cobden,* I, p. 193.
[4] *Recollections,* I, p. 155.
[5] Chamberlain to Morley, 13 Mar. 1874.
[6] To Chamberlain, 9 Dec. 1875.
[7] To Chamberlain, 14 Nov. 1880.

tical enough, he was quite prepared to admit to the weakness and rely on their association to remedy it: 'I always told you, I am an academic politician at bottom. Luckily I know the weaknesses incident to the character; and am only too glad to have them set right by a good friend of another type.'[1]

Chamberlain made Morley feel satisfied with his literary work by showing a practical outlet and purpose for it. When he assigned to Morley the work of propagating radical ideas, he told him that 'whenever the present prosperous state of trade gives way to commercial distress the seed you have sown will spring up'.[2] Morley's craving for an active political career abated temporarily. He turned down a suggestion in 1873 that he should stand for Parliament: 'I will be as useful to the cause with pen as with tongue or vote. . . . I shall be happiest of all to remain the mere penman of the Education cause.'[3] His feeling of completion and satisfaction through this association can be seen in a letter mentioning how Chamberlain was inspiring his writing: 'You put me on the scent, and if I have done any good to your cause, that's only a fair return.'[4] He frequently invited Chamberlain's comments and criticisms on what he had written as if anxious to make it express the unity of their relationship. Of one article, which he significantly wished to appear unsigned, he said: 'I would write it; you would see it; and we would thus do it together, as it were.' 'I regard it as indispensable', he went on, 'that I shd. talk to you before writing. A mere literary shot will do no good—unless it represents more than the words of an isolated writer.'[5] When he commenced his monthly commentaries he sought to make them reflect the complementary nature of their relationship by asking for Chamberlain's assistance: 'I count upon that, and without it, should not enter upon the affair . . . two heads are better than one, and previous discussion with you will always make my own ideas clearer. . . .'[6]

[1] To Chamberlain, 31 Jan. 1876.
[2] Chamberlain to Morley, 13 Mar. 1874.
[3] To Chamberlain, 6 Aug. 1873.
[4] To Chamberlain, 29 Sept. 1873.
[5] To Chamberlain, 18 Jan. 1875.
[6] To Chamberlain, 9 Dec. 1875.

For as long as they were allies in this way the two men were extremely close friends. 'We were like brothers until '86', Morley later told F. W. Hirst; and when this was reported to Chamberlain, his eyes filled with tears.[1] 'The interest of co-operation in public work is enhanced a thousandfold by private and personal attachment', Morley once wrote;[2] and he certainly did seem to live through Chamberlain's own experiences. 'I really fear London *at first for* you', he wrote when Chamberlain became an M.P. 'It will seem so cold and *unhomeish*.' After Chamberlain's first speech in the Commons, Morley was 'in high spirits', writing of how Chamberlain's success was also his friends' 'in a very important sense'.[3] It is not surprising that he hoped that they would always 'stick together' because 'it makes an immense difference—to me at any rate'.[4] The way in which Morley lived through Chamberlain can be seen in the letters which he sent to Chamberlain, worrying about and for him, advising and guiding him, and showing a great longing for him to succeed as a practical politician. In Chamberlain Morley saw the means of vicariously fulfilling his own wish to succeed as a man of action, and into his letters he poured the doubts and feelings that would have been perfectly appropriate had it been his own career that was the object of them. Every success or set-back in Chamberlain's career was as if it had happened to himself. In fact, it was happening to that other self, the man of action that he always wished to be. To him Chamberlain was strong, active, unselfconscious, extroverted.[5]

He gave Chamberlain copious advice on tactics, trying to bring out for the benefit of the practical politician the wider considerations affecting them such as an outside observer could best appreciate. For example, in 1875 he urged Chamberlain to enter the Commons as soon as possible: 'It would give you a better chance of making your individuality tell than when the party gets back into power again, and the party chiefs will have prestige

[1] Hirst, *In the Golden Days*, 1947, p. 169.
[2] To Chamberlain, 19 Dec. 1884.
[3] To Chamberlain, 10 July, 5 Aug. 1876.
[4] To Chamberlain, 29 Apr. 1877.
[5] Cf. to Chamberlain, 10 July 1876, 29 Apr. 1880.

at their backs against independent men.'[1] From 1873 on he kept up constant pressure on Chamberlain to seize his chances for getting into Parliament.[2] As soon as Chamberlain was elected in 1876, Morley asked to have a full day's discussion with him: 'There is a good deal to be said between us.'[3] He now gave Chamberlain very detailed advice on how to conduct himself in Parliament. He suggested a proper time for taking his seat, gave him some hints on his first speech, and advised him to stand 'well out of the ruck', take 'an austere, cool, firm, semi-isolated line', and let a party form gradually around him.[4] Morley's practical ambitions, expressed in his attitude to Chamberlain, soared ever higher, and he kept continually before his friend the greater goals to be aimed for.[5] He identified Chamberlain with the great men of power whom he admired so much. Thus he wrote when Chamberlain was afflicted with gout: 'Old Chatham's gout and the craziness that went with it, cost us the American colonies. And your gout may be as expensive some day.'[6] A royal commissionership was hailed by Morley as a first step on the road to 'office, power, function, great affairs'.[7] After the Liberal victory in 1880 he was most insistent on Chamberlain's trying to secure a '*serious* and decent post', and fought his reluctance to take office.[8] When Chamberlain was appointed to the Cabinet, Morley was most anxious to maintain their alliance. 'Ten minutes with you three times a week', he wrote, 'would be of great value to me and perhaps to the rest of the world. I see plenty of other important people, but you would be worth the whole lot and pack of them, because we understand one another, and have the same objects.'[9] Austen Chamberlain could recall the dinners at his father's London house at least once a week during this period when

[1] To Chamberlain, 28 May 1875.
[2] To Chamberlain, 22 Nov. 1873, 6 Feb. 1874, 28 May, 3 June, 12, 28 Nov. 1875, 14 Jan. 1876.
[3] To Chamberlain, 29 June 1876.
[4] To Chamberlain, 5 July 1876.
[5] Cf. to Chamberlain, 7 Jan. 1876.
[6] To Chamberlain, 7 July 1876.
[7] To Chamberlain, 23 Dec. 1876.
[8] To Chamberlain, 12, 19 Apr. 1880.
[9] To Chamberlain, 6 June 1880.

the two men would discuss the political questions of the day.[1]

Nevertheless, there were present in their relationship tendencies which threatened to disturb its complementary harmony; and one of the most important of these was Morley's growing dissatisfaction with his own side of the association, stemming from continuing failure to discover systematic principles. For, if the ideas of the 'spiritual adviser' were themselves incoherent and unorganized, then the value of his advice to the practical politician was greatly diminished. Anxiety about the unsystematic nature of his work is evident as early as 1875, when in *Diderot* he discussed Comte's description of the weakness of a man of letters, an editor such as Diderot, in an age of transition. A man engaged in an enterprise such as the Encyclopaedia—or the *Fortnightly Review*—lacks an organic doctrine, an effective discipline, a definite, comprehensive aim. His activity is characterized by 'dispersiveness'. He popularizes 'detached ideas' by dressing them up 'in varied forms of the literary act', and guides men 'by judging, empirically and unconnectedly, each case of conduct, of policy, or of new opinion as it arises'.[2] In other words, the work of an editor involved many of the problems of intellectual activity regarded as most serious by Morley and other contemporaries—the lack of connection or system among ideas, for example, and the absence of guidance for particular 'cases' 'as they arise'. When Morley embarked on his commentaries on current events, he wrote of the problem of combining such work with the preaching of 'a regular set of principles'.[3]

From 1873 on Morley made numerous attempts, while carefully preserving the position of the *Fortnightly* as a forum for free and general discussion, to develop its attachment to some cause or principle. First came Chamberlain's manifesto, the invitation to him to make the *Fortnightly* his 'platform', and Morley's own work, published in the *Fortnightly*, as 'penman of the Education cause'. Then there was the campaign for disestablishment. When Chamberlain wrote in the *Fortnightly* announcing that this was

[1] Chamberlain, *Down the Years*, p. 197.
[2] *Diderot*, I, p. 18. *F.R.*, Feb. 1875, pp. 160–1.
[3] To Chamberlain, 9 Dec. 1875.

the 'next page of the liberal programme', Morley was very pleased that the *Fortnightly* was giving 'the *mot d'ordre* to the radical press'; in other words, supplying radicals with a sense of direction and purpose.[1] But these great questions disappointed, and the search for a commitment remained unfulfilled. In 1877 Morley proposed a new weekly review, to be 'staunchly the organ' of the radical 'party'. He would be the editor, but would be associated with Chamberlain and Dilke on a board which would meet each week to 'discuss the line to be taken' on subjects suggested by himself.[2] But nothing came of this project, and by the end of the year he was looking to another possible focus for his journalism. Inviting Gladstone to contribute an article on the Eastern question, he pointed out how 'staunch' the *Fortnightly* had been 'in its editorial portion' to what Gladstone had 'persuaded the best part of England to regard as the true cause'. He does indeed seem to have been anxious at this time to find something to be 'staunch' to. The qualification, 'in its editorial portion', is significant as separating Morley from his contributors on whom he had been unwilling to impose any commitment and who, in keeping with the idea of the *Fortnightly* as an open forum, had been enabled by him to advance a remarkable variety of opinions on the Eastern question.[3] He kept pressing Gladstone for an article as an encouragement, 'not to myself only, who need none,—but to waverers and doubting friends'.[4]

A further confession of the failure of his policy of free and open discussion to produce firmness of attitudes appeared in a review of the correspondence of a former editor of the *Edinburgh Review*, published in 1878. Again taking an opportunity to discuss the problems of an editor, he showed that he was worried that, although eleven years had elapsed since he had become editor of the *Fortnightly*, there was still no sign of agreement among its contributors. He felt that the authority of 'an organ intended to lead public opinion towards certain changes, or to hold it steadfast

[1] To Chamberlain, 19 Sept. 1874.
[2] To Chamberlain, 19 Apr. 1877.
[3] Cf. R. T. Shannon, *Gladstone and the Bulgarian Agitation 1876*, 1963, p. 217.
[4] To Gladstone, 27 Nov. 1877, 30 Sept. 1878, B.M. Add. MSS. 44255, ff. 2–3, 6–7.

against wayward gusts of passion'[1] would be a hundred times greater 'if all the writers in it were inspired' by a 'thorough unity of conviction'. He hoped that such a group might yet emerge, but was not sure what would inspire it. Perhaps the success of the French Republic, or the example of the United States, or even 'some trouble within our own borders', would 'lead men with open minds'—still his faith was in openmindedness—to a great principle that would unite them 'in a common project for pressing with systematic iteration for a complete set of organic changes'. But until such time 'the only motto that can be inscribed on the flag of a liberal Review is the general device of Progress, each writer interpreting it in his own sense, and within such limits as he may set for himself'.[2] When, four years later, Morley gave up the editorship of the *Fortnightly*, he devoted a valedictory article largely to deploring the absence of system in political thinking, and pointed out that the 'original scheme of the Review, even if there had been no other obstacle, prevented it from being the organ of a systematic and constructive policy'. Nevertheless, he claimed, although it had been open to 'opinions from many sides', there had been a certain 'common drift' or 'undefinable concurrence among writers coming from different schools and handling very different subjects'—perhaps owing to 'the fact that a certain dissent from received theologies' was 'found in company with new ideas of social and political reform'.[3] There had been at least a 'spirit of system'.

Between 1877 and 1881 Morley made a detailed study of one school of political thought which, he admitted, had attached its views on 'special political questions' to 'a general and presiding conception'.[4] In Cobdenism he found a set of principles adhered to with 'strength and fervour' by 'a political school'. Cobden, 'fully possessed by the philosophic gift of feeling about society as a whole, and thinking about the problems of society in an ordered connexion with one another', had 'definite and systematic ideas of

---

[1] This must refer to recent changes of public feeling on the Eastern question.
[2] *Studies in Literature*, pp. 304–5. F.R., Apr. 1878, pp. 603–4.
[3] F.R., Oct. 1882, pp. 518–20.
[4] F.R., Apr. 1878, pp. 602–3.

the way in which men ought now to travel in search of improvement' and 'attached new meaning and more comprehensive purpose to national life'.[1] However, Morley did not emerge from his study of Cobden's ideas convinced that these could provide a system of thought for his own day. In 1882 he wrote:

> it is not so many years ago since it seemed to some as if the Manchester School had found a key that would unlock all the secrets of a wise policy. It is only simpletons who disparage the real utility of the Manchester principles . . . but it is not well to claim for them a higher place than belongs to a number of empirical maxims, subject to the limitations common to all such maxims. There are whole departments of social institutions . . . about which the Manchester School, quite naturally and rightly, never professed to have anything to say.[2]

It would appear that, in spite of Chamberlain's increasing success in the practical sphere, Morley grew less and less content with his own 'speculative' or 'critico-philosophical' sphere and began to think about beginning an active political career on his own account. In 1877 he was faced with the necessity of making a crucial decision about his career. Chamberlain and other radicals had been talking for some years of wanting to see him in Parliament. Chamberlain wrote to him in 1873 that 'I should think it a very great gain to our cause if you could find a seat, and . . . I shall do my best to secure this result'.[3] Jesse Collings argued in 1876 that the 'next thing to do' after the election of Chamberlain himself was 'to get Morley into Parliament'.[4] In 1877 Chamberlain mentioned Morley several times to Joseph Cowen as a possible candidate for Newcastle.[5] But then Morley suffered a severe illness, and this persuaded him to accept Chamberlain's advice and offer of financial assistance to write his history of the French revolution; in other words, as Morley put it, to 'cut off all parliamentary aspirations and stick to my lawful and natural

---

[1] *Cobden*, I, p. 89. *F.R.*, May 1881, p. 634.
[2] *F.R.*, Apr. 1882, p. 504.
[3] Undated, but placed in sequence in the Chamberlain Papers for early Aug. 1873. It has an obvious connection with Morley to Chamberlain, 6 Aug. 1873.
[4] Collings to Chamberlain, 22 June 1876, Chamberlain MSS., J.C.5/16/8.
[5] P. Corder, *The Life of Robert Spence Watson*, 1914, p. 222.

trade'. 'Now I know where I am—without dispersion', he wrote. Chamberlain had rebuked him for his 'ingenious turn for swinging to and fro' on this matter, but Morley assured him that he did not for a second doubt the wisdom of his decision or think of it 'otherwise than with contentment and comfort'. And yet, within two months, as his health began to improve, the 'swinging to and fro' recommenced. When Cowen pressed him about a Newcastle candidature, he complained of being unable to say 'a plain and final No' because 'saying No to him means my final departure from politics—and it takes my breath away to think of the icy plunge'. After a few days of 'wrestling with the Lord', he decided that 'finally to shut the door against the only *real* chance I have ever had, or probably ever shall have of the H. of C., is more than I can do in my reviving health'.[1] This was the turning-point.

There were two major difficulties in the way of his embarking on a political career. The first was his financial position. The set-backs which he encountered at Preston and Blackburn in 1868 and 1869 led to his writing some bitter articles in the *Fortnightly* complaining about the expensiveness of electioneering and the consequent near-monopoly of successful candidatures by rich men. 'Nobody', he wrote, 'understands and respects the power that wealth gives a man more clearly than I.' At that stage he called himself 'a poor man who lives up to his income'.[2] When Chamberlain urged him to stand for Parliament in 1873, he pleaded inadequacy of financial resources as a reason for not doing so.[3] During the decade he struggled to build a sound financial basis, but, apart from gradually increasing insurances, he was able to save almost nothing.[4] Chamberlain seems to have helped him, however, and in the early 1880s the *Life of Cobden,* his editorship of the *Pall Mall Gazette,* and his work as a reader for Macmillan and Co., must have improved his position considerably. In 1883 he was reported

[1] To Chamberlain, 10, 24 Oct., 27 Dec. 1877, 3 Jan. 1878.
[2] To Harrison, 25 Aug. 1873.
[3] To Harrison, 17 July 1873. To Chamberlain, 6 Aug. 1873 (in this he offers to pay £750 towards the expenses of a candidature at Hastings if Chamberlain's election fund provides the rest).
[4] To Harrison, 25 Aug. 1873, 14 Jan. 1875. To Chamberlain, 12 Dec. 1876.

to be assuming the editorship of *Macmillan's Magazine* 'so as to secure a modest income and adequate leisure for his political life'.[1]

Secondly, his views on religion proved a disadvantage at a time when radicalism was so closely linked with the Nonconformist churches. In 1873 he was reluctant to stand for Parliament because he thought that his 'notorious heterodoxy' would make him 'unwelcome to the dissenters'.[2] Chamberlain was very concerned about this handicap. Certain articles in the *Fortnightly* in 1875, when the radical campaign was developing, caused Chamberlain to warn him of 'the great inexpediency of mixing up our religious or non-religious beliefs, with our politics'. Morley replied that he agreed, but could not 'honourably desert or ignore' those freethinkers who looked to the *Fortnightly* for 'arguments and counsel'.[3] Morley did try to make himself more acceptable to the Nonconformists. An address to a conference in 1876 'allowed the Dissenters', according to Morley, 'one more chance of seeing and hearing a Freethinker without shying', and he tried to show them that they 'need not fear infidel ravings'.[4] But not long after Chamberlain was telling Jesse Collings[5] that Morley was 'a splendid fellow and I wish he were in Parliament but his expressed views on religious subjects are awfully against him. I suggested his name to Sheffield but they said it would not [do] and I fear there are very few constituencies which would overlook *printed* nonbelief.' When in 1880 the Nottingham Liberals refused him their nomination, he was told that 'the theology did it'. He declared himself now 'thoroughly savage at the pious Non-Cons'; 'the theologians were too strong for me. They could not stand my heresy and offered a resolute opposition from first to last.' He wrote to Chamberlain in despair: 'if Nott[ingha]m cannot get over my heterodoxy, I don't believe any other place will.'[6]

But he may have become accustomed by this stage to look to

---

[1] F. E. Hamer (ed.), *The Personal Papers of Lord Rendel*, 1931, p. 222.
[2] To Chamberlain, 15 July 1873.
[3] To Chamberlain, 27 Dec. 1875.
[4] To Chamberlain, 16 Feb. 1876.
[5] 30 June 1876, Chamberlain MSS., 5/16/54.
[6] To Chamberlain, 21, 24 Apr. 1880. S. H. Harris, *Auberon Herbert: Crusader for Liberty*, 1943, p. 223.

this factor to explain any such set-back and therefore have failed to take account of another handicap under which he laboured—his lack of roots in any particular community and its politics. Thus an important factor at Nottingham in 1880 seems to have been that his successful rival, Arnold Morley, was a well-known local man and son of the Nottingham industrialist and philanthropist, Samuel Morley, whereas he was regarded as a ' "carpet-bagger", sent at a moment's notice from the alien Caucus Central Office'.[1] Yet it was only a nation-wide influence such as Chamberlain's, transcending local interests, which was really going to secure Morley his opportunity. Indeed, Chamberlain pointed out that it was 'only large Radical boroughs like Nottingham that would be able to return' him.[2] In 1880 Morley did finally stand, without success, for Westminster, about the nearest approach to a community of his own that he now had.

Some years earlier Morley had professed a contempt for Parliament and had seen the new radicalism mainly as acting on public opinion 'out of doors'. But Chamberlain had always been concerned for the development of a radical party within Parliament itself, and Morley's attitude came more and more to correspond with his. His concern to reconcile the free play of forces with the possession of a 'spirit of system' was matched by his attempt to place freedom of individual action and statement in a framework of co-operation and organization. On the one hand were the evils of 'sect', but on the other 'the comparative impotence of unorganized effort'.[3] Chamberlain's enthusiasm for organization as a remedy for chaos in reform politics was an important influence. Writing to Chamberlain about the 'Caucus', he remarked: 'I'm a bit of an individualist myself—but subject to the conditions of practical action, when the time for practical action has arrived.' After all, he pointed out, 'it is well worth remembering that Mill, the great apostle of individualism, was one of the best of party men in the House'.[4] In 1879, in *Burke,* he admits party to be a necessary

[1] Harris, *Auberon Herbert,* p. 223.
[2] Chamberlain to H. Broadhurst, 23 Apr. 1880, Chamberlain MSS.
[3] To Richard Congreve, 8 Jan. 1874, B.M. Add. MSS. 45241, f. 61.
[4] To Chamberlain, 20 Oct. 1878.

evil: 'Party combination is exactly one of those contrivances which, as it might seem, a wise man would accept for working purposes, but about which he would take care to say as little as possible.'[1] In 1882 he observed that Burke, while warning that 'party men' can become narrow and bigoted, did say that duty might necessitate involvement in a party and that it was the evils attendant on the position, rather than the position *per se,* that one had to keep free from. Mill himself, observing this principle, had been able to have a useful career.[2]

We have now to trace the movement of Morley's interest from literary work to politics. In his 1879 study of Burke he can be seen exploring the implications of this movement. Now himself over 40 years of age, he consoles himself with the reflection that it was 'to literature rather than to public affairs' that Burke's ambitions also had turned first and that Burke was 30 'before he approached even the threshold of the arena' of practical politics. Having himself just decided to leave unfinished the history of the French revolution and turn to more practical work, Morley writes:

It must sometimes have occurred to Burke to wonder whether he had made the right choice when he locked away the fragments of his History, and plunged into the torment of party and Parliament. But his interests and aptitudes were too strong and overmastering for him to have been right in doing otherwise. Contact with affairs was an indispensable condition for the full use of his great faculties, in spite of their being less faculties of affairs than of speculation. Public life was the actual field in which to test, and work out, and use with good effect the moral ideas which were Burke's most sincere and genuine interest.[3]

That Morley now wished to extend his own faculties of 'speculation' in this way is indicated in his comment to Chamberlain that 'it is exactly because I hope to become a thoroughly useful political writer that I lean to parliament'.[4]

[1] *Burke,* p. 75.
[2] *F.R.,* Jan. 1882, p. 116.
[3] *Burke,* pp. 28, 302–3. See Appendix, p. 387: 'History'.
[4] To Chamberlain, 3 Jan. 1878.

In 1880 he became editor of the London daily newspaper, the *Pall Mall Gazette*. This marked a further stage in his involvement in practical politics. By turning to a form of journalism that required response to, and comment on, events 'as they arose' day by day, he abandoned his detachment and plunged into the stream of political incident. For a further two years, however, he retained the editorship of the *Fortnightly*, seeking still to preserve a balance between the detachment that gave the comprehensive view and an involvement that allowed close contact with practical reality. For the risk was one which he had foreseen in *On Compromise*, that a daily newspaper tends to 'limit its view to the possibilities of the day' and, 'being most closely affected by the particular', to 'turn its back upon all that is general'.[1] But the compression of his outlook had now become even more pronounced. His writings in the *Fortnightly* itself assumed more and more of the character of *Pall Mall* editorials, and when in October 1882 he gave up the *Fortnightly*, his work there had ceased to have much special significance for him.

He was now tending to use his pen mainly as an instrument of political controversy. His editorship of the *Pall Mall* opened with a campaign to force the Liberal leaders to abide by their declarations of 1879 and withdraw Sir Bartle Frere from the Transvaal. Then Morley made a determined attack on coercion in Ireland and tried to assist Gladstone in resisting pressures to extend coercion.[2] The climax was the campaign against W. E. Forster which preceded, and was widely believed to have helped to effect, Forster's resignation from the Irish Secretaryship. The way in which Morley had become, deliberately, a force in practical politics began to impose some strain on his relationship with Chamberlain. When he attacked the Irish policy of a Government of which Chamberlain was a member, Chamberlain urged him to appreciate that 'you and I are in the same boat—you in the press and I in the Cabinet'. Morley replied that he acted as he did because there was a distinction between Chamberlain as 'practical

[1] *On Compromise*, p. 34. F.R., Apr. 1874, p. 436.
[2] Cf. to Gladstone, 30 Oct. 1880, 30 Apr. 1881, B.M. Add. MSS. 44255, ff. 23, 25.

Minister' and himself as 'spiritual Power'.[1] Such a distinction was becoming less tenable now, however.

In January 1883 a seat fell vacant at Newcastle owing to the illness of Sir Ashton Dilke. Even though the ground had been carefully cultivated here for Morley since at least 1877 and he now enjoyed the support of the local Liberal leader, Robert Spence Watson, Morley's candidature was promoted with some secrecy and in some haste as a precaution against the development of local resentment towards this 'outsider'.[2] Ostrogorski was later to allege that Morley had been the instrument of a conspiracy by 'the Caucus' which disliked the independence of Joseph Cowen, Newcastle's other M.P.[3] But Morley achieved success at last and was elected to Parliament in February 1883.

[1] Chamberlain to Morley, 18 Oct. 1881. Morley to Chamberlain, 21 Oct. 1881.
[2] Cf. Morley to Sir Charles Dilke, 31 Jan. 1883, B.M. Add. MSS. 43895, f. 160.
[3] M. Ostrogorski, *Democracy and the Organization of Political Parties*, I, 1902, pp. 235–6.

9

IRELAND AND IMPERIALISM, 1879-1885

THE two issues which dominated Morley's activity both as writer and as politician between 1879 and 1885 were Ireland and British policy in Africa. It was the Irish question that brought him into a leading position in Liberal politics, and his concern with it became the major preoccupation of his political career. Before 1885 and the crisis over home rule he had made a reputation as the most formidable critic in the press of the coercion of the Irish. He became convinced that the attempt to suppress Irish agitation was futile in that, far from serving as an essential preliminary to the improvement of the condition of Ireland, it only made the situation worse. Force perpetually begat force, and as a result of many decades of coercion acts there seemed now to be an 'unfortunate circle in which Irish affairs are by a disastrous conjunction of circumstances compelled to move'. In the first place, only a vigorous—and, therefore, inevitably for a people in the social condition of the Irish, rough and violent—agitation was ever able to bring Irish grievances to the attention of Parliament. But the English people and Government, disgusted by the violence, detesting social turbulence, and fearing lest a precedent of the use of force to secure concessions might be established, insisted on striking down the agitator at the same time as doing something about the grievances. 'Then comes the vexatious conclusion. The Irish are more provoked by the application of force than they are gratified by the extension of justice. The English are then in turn disgusted by what they consider to be ingratitude.' And so relations spiralled down into ever deeper alienation.[1] Coercion inflamed the Irish and poisoned the atmosphere within which reforms had to operate. Englishmen should appreciate how coercion must appear to the Irish people. To them it was 'the

[1] *P.M.G.*, 21 Oct. 1881.

regular and accepted symbol' of English sympathy, 'not with them, but with those whom justly or not they regard as their oppressors', namely the landlords. Coercion was connected in the Irish mind with a long series of historic incidents, the memory of which caused its reappearance to be felt as a calculated insult and act of deepest enmity.[1]

The main consequence of coercion was, in Morley's opinion, to bring about an increase in disorder—by worsening the Irishman's view of the law and thus making it all the more difficult to instil into him those basic concepts of law and order on which any permanent pacification of Ireland depended, by driving discontent underground and diverting influence and initiative from those who at least preferred to work in the open to Fenians and secret societies with fewer scruples about violent methods, and by removing in the Land League the sole effective barrier to the landlords' efforts to wring arrears of rent out of their tenants.[2] Clearly one side or the other would have to desist first from the use of force and break the vicious circle. Which was it to be?

Morley neither believed that the Irish ought to desist from agitation nor saw any justification for the Government's efforts to force them to desist. He insisted that the English must make the first move because of their responsibility for making Ireland and Irishmen unhappy and turbulent. To the end of his life he maintained that 'all the faults of the Irish character' could be traced to the 'abominable treatment' of Ireland by the English.[3] Furthermore, he was convinced that the Irish agitation was necessary and legitimate in the circumstances, and that the Land League had been the only friend of the Irish tenants and had served them well, in some respects like a trade union. By developing in the Irish peasants a 'habit of self-reliance and self-help', it showed itself to be a 'steadying' and 'conservative' force.[4] In Morley's opinion, the League had done 'downright good work in raising up the tenants

[1] *F.R.*, Apr. 1881, pp. 412-13.
[2] Ibid., pp. 413-14, 407. *P.M.G.*, 5 Jan. 1881. To Chamberlain, 30 Nov. 1881.
[3] J. H. Morgan, *John, Viscount Morley. An Appreciation and Some Reminiscences*, 1924, p. 52. *F.R.*, July 1881, pp. 8-9.
[4] *F.R.*, July 1881, p. 6. *P.M.G.*, 15 Sept. 1881.

against their truly detestable tyrants'.[1] Morley frequently emphasized that the Land League had brought Irish grievances to the attention of the Government and paved the way for the Land Act of 1881.[2] It had helped give the action of Government an organic link with social reality. Morley was obviously influenced by his dislike of any interference with the 'natural play of forces'. Agitation was a natural form of expression of opinion in such circumstances. 'The all-important thing' was 'that arbitrary powers are not to be used to repress that play of antagonistic social forces which is legitimate in England, which ought to remain legitimate in Ireland, and without which we cannot know how to settle the land system on a secure basis'.[3] Interference with natural processes would produce unnatural substitutes such as secret societies.[4] So long as a country lacked a fully democratic government, agitation had a vital role to play.[5]

Thinking about Ireland in this way, Morley aimed in his journalism at persuading his countrymen that their overriding duty and responsibility were to conciliate Ireland and that the first step towards this conciliation must be the abandoning of recourse to coercion.

The use of force against the native peoples of Egypt and southern Africa was equally as abhorrent to Morley, and, apart from a brief and unhappy attempt to support and justify intervention in Egypt in 1882, he consistently opposed interference in their affairs. Again, it was disruption of 'natural' development that he objected to. In 1879, condemning British action against the Zulus, he pleaded with his readers 'to understand that these barbarous peoples, in spite of their barbarism, have a life of their own and a social system of their own, with unwritten laws, usages, and customs, as strong and as binding as ours, constituting a national life less organic than ours, but not any less real or stable'. In it there was 'a law' and 'an order which you cannot replace at a stroke by the order

[1] To Chamberlain, 19 Oct. 1881.
[2] *P.M.G.*, 18 Nov. 1880, 20 Oct. 1881, 23 Feb. 1883.
[3] *P.M.G.*, 25 Jan. 1881.
[4] *P.M.G.*, 20 May 1882.
[5] *P.M.G.*, 23 Feb. 1883.

and the ideas of an advanced society'. 'A "regulated" growth cannot be a natural growth', argued the *Pall Mall Gazette* in 1882. 'Nature will not have her hand forced', and primitive peoples should be left alone to attain civilization 'in a normal way'. 'It is not our business', Morley wrote in 1876, 'to go about throwing confusion into countries that are going through the course of evolution in the regular way.' Thus the Sudan, for example, 'must be left to its own people to work out their own deliverance in their own fashion'. 'Communities do best when left to run their own course, follow their own fashions, be governed according to their own laws, work out their own laws.'[1]

Morley was also very concerned about the possible effects of coercion and imperialism on the health of the community in whose name these policies were carried out. By 1878 the economic depression and the constant fluctuations of public excitement with regard to the Eastern question were making him feel increasingly anxious about the stability of British political life. Thus the rising and falling of wage-rates distracted the working man 'in his domestic, public, or religious interests by restless desires and vague aims' and produced 'that fatal habit of mind, discontent with one's present': 'our population is as yet a long way removed from such practice of self-control as enables them to bear the excitement of these violent fluctuations without detriment.'[2] And then, in an article discussing reactions of popular sentiment to developments in foreign and imperial policy, he warned that, while England was the only state in the Western world to have escape a revolution in its political affairs in the previous twenty years, there were signs that even its stability was in danger, that even it could be 'submitted to one of those great changes'. Imperialism threatened democracy. Being 'a policy of emergencies' which necessitated transfer of authority to the executive and to soldiers and officials, it was 'absolutely and for ever incompatible' with the maintenance of an 'open democracy of free people, such as ours is'.[3] Another

---

[1] *F.R.*, Mar. 1879, pp. 334, 351–2. *P.M.G.*, 10 Aug., 4 Oct., 13 Nov. 1882. To Chamberlain, 28 Jan. 1876. *Hansard*, 3, 294, 1077.

[2] *F.R.*, Oct. 1878, p. 557.

[3] *F.R.*, Sept. 1878, pp. 313–33.

factor to be taken into account was that the 'destruction of capital in military enterprises breeds Socialism'.¹

The coercion of the Irish also had serious implications for the future of freedom in England itself. To those Liberals who supported coercion Morley repeated Burke's warning during the American revolution: 'In order to prove that the Americans had no right to their liberties, we were every day endeavouring to subvert the maxims which preserve the whole spirit of our own. To prove that the Americans ought to be free, we were obliged to depreciate the value of freedom itself.' 'Our fathers paid the penalty then', he reminded his readers; the demoralization of public opinion caused by this 'temporary infusion of arbitrary ideas into the popular mind' made much easier the imposition of repressive measures on English liberty in the 1790s. 'The retribution is not likely to be less rigorously exacted now.'² Morley feared that Gladstone, for instance, would 'never again be able to tell his countrymen that force is no remedy'.³

Initially these two issues had a purely negative significance for Morley. Each threatened the stability and health of the new democracy, on which his attention was primarily fixed. Each was tending to preoccupy politicians and distract them from urgent issues of domestic policy. In 1877 he complained that 'new entanglements' in Egypt 'must quite inevitably tend to throw domestic questions and interests into the background more and more'.⁴ Later he argued that 'each new foreign engagement' was 'a mischievous interruption to our proper business of working out social improvements in our own country'.⁵ 'Let us', he urged, 'spread civilization at home. Let us think of our own Hovas, Bechuanas, fellaheen.'⁶ As for Ireland, it was already crowding out the parliamentary order paper. Were Egypt taken over as well,

---

¹ *Cobden*, II, p. 70.
² *F.R.*, Sept. 1882, pp. 399–400. Cf. *Burke*, p. 114, and *Edmund Burke*, pp. 140–2, 258–9.
³ *F.R.*, Apr. 1881, p. 407.
⁴ To Chamberlain, 11 July 1877.
⁵ *P.M.G.*, 13 Feb. 1883, p. 11, c. 1. *F.R.*, Mar. 1879, p. 329.
⁶ *The Times*, 13 Dec. 1883, p. 6, c. 3.

the working classes might be so indignant at the wasting of Parliament's time that they might favour some 'formidable' remedy.[1] In other words, at this critical stage the new experiment in parliamentary democracy might receive a fatal discredit.

And yet gradually opposition to coercion and imperialism acquired a more positive aspect in Morley's own politics, developing into his preoccupation and distracting him from domestic issues. Why was this?

The disorganization of Radicalism was to Morley one of the most perplexing features of the system within which he had to work as an M.P. from 1883 on. In 1880 Chamberlain, Dilke, and other leading Radicals had entered, and thereafter had to accept a share in the official responsibility for the policies of, an administration dominated by Whigs and moderates. Morley had long been anxious that the Radicals should keep clear of the compromises of parliamentary politics. As early as 1875 he was complaining that one Radical, Trevelyan, had 'got the House of Commons tone about him rather too strong, in discussing politics'.[2] When in 1876 Chamberlain entered the Commons, Morley advised him to take 'an austere, cool, firm, semi-isolated line' and let a party 'gradually cluster round him'.[3] But after 1880 such conduct was no longer possible. The radicals were split, some being in a Government the policies of which others such as Morley might feel it their duty to attack.[4] Morley became increasingly concerned about the position of those Radicals who, by being given appointments outside the Cabinet, suffered the '*clôture* of office' without having any significant voice in the determination of policy.[5] Some Radicals were, he suspected, now being 'corrupted' by the influences of the London official world.[6] Matters were made even worse by the weakness and disunity of the Radicals who did remain 'below the gangway'. Radicalism was now being disintegrated in 'the makeshifts and compromises of office' and

[1] *Hansard*, 3, 284, 1034; 286, 1565–6.
[2] To Chamberlain, 29 Aug. 1875.
[3] To Chamberlain, 5 July 1876.
[4] Cf. *P.M.G.*, 28 Aug. 1880.
[5] Cf. *P.M.G.*, 27 Sept. 1882.
[6] *P.M.G.*, 26 Dec. 1882.

'the endless transactions of political opportunism'; while these other non-governmental Radicals, instead of being 'uncompromising' and testifying 'with unflinching fidelity their devotion to Liberal principle', were 'neutralized' by the muddled, unsystematic condition of their thinking.[1]

By 1883 the disunity and disintegration of Radical activity and thought had become a persistent theme with Morley. In his own campaign at Newcastle he was the candidate of the local Liberal 'caucus' which was by that time strongly opposing the independent attitude of Joseph Cowen, the other M.P. for Newcastle and a well-known Radical. Morley spoke of parliamentary government in Europe as being 'ruined by disintegrating forces' and warned English Radicals not to press the interests of their own 'little groups and individualities' too far: 'The Liberal party had several shades. There were plenty of sections, and quite right, because it contained those men who had independence of mind. But for the purposes of action . . . , it was their business to keep their differences in the background and to unite upon the principles upon which they were all agreed.'[2] Later in the year he wrote that the development of agitation on such issues as 'Sunday closing, Blue Ribbonism, local option', and the Contagious Diseases Acts only 'increases the perils of the situation' by making politics more unstable.[3] He urged delegates to a parliamentary-reform conference in Leeds to unite and co-operate lest they arrive at the French situation of many small groups perpetually quarrelling with one another. They must take care that Radicalism did not degenerate into 'a great number of highly interesting fissiparous and extremely ungenerous and original-minded animalcula'.[4] The problem was that whereas 'the party of Conservatism' was 'solid and coherent by its nature and composition', representing as it did 'a phalanx of interests spontaneously bound together by common hopes and common fears', 'there is not naturally, and there cannot

[1] *P.M.G.*, 27 Sept. 1882, 16 Feb. 1883.
[2] *N.D.C.*, 12 Feb. 1883, p. 3, c. 2; 14 Feb. 1883, p. 3, c. 1; 19 Feb. 1883, p. 3, c. 4.
[3] *Macmillan's Magazine*, June 1883, p. 160.
[4] *The Times*, 18 Oct. 1883, p. 6, c. 1.

be, the same closeness of social or intellectual cohesion' in Liberal and Radical politics.[1]

Chamberlain believed that he had found the answer to this problem. Party organization, the 'caucus' and the National Liberal Federation, seemed to him the best way of imposing order on reform politics and of persuading minority sections to 'keep purely personal preferences in the background' and accept a deferment of their special questions until greater issues were dealt with. He saw the organization as providing an umbrella, under which all the sections could meet and discuss policy and arrive at a sense of common purpose which would make them willing to defer to majority decisions in 'the selection of those measures of reform and progress to which priority shall be given'. In this way could be ended that 'unsatisfactory and anarchical condition of things' in which a seat might be contested by, amongst others, 'a teetotaller, a Tichbornite, an anti-vaccinationist, a Home Ruler, and an anti-Contagious-Diseases-Act candidate', because these sectionalists, 'believing their cause of supreme importance, refuse to sacrifice it for the general good of Liberalism, and attempt, although only representing a minority, to control the action of the whole party'.[2]

Morley and Chamberlain were agreed in their diagnosis of the problems confronting Liberalism and Radicalism. They were not, however, agreed on a remedy. For Morley the primary need remained a bond of thought, of agreed principles and ideas, that could bind together these diverse interests naturally and organically. In 1882 he wrote of Ireland, parliamentary reform, land reform, imperialism, and the power of the State to interfere with the freedom of contract and of minorities, as 'only some of the questions' which 'time and circumstances are pressing upon us'. 'In Education, in Economics, the problems are as many.' There was an urgent need for 'systematic politics', for 'clear and definite principles' to guide men in dealing with these questions; yet there could not be seen in operation any 'system of political or social

[1] *Macmillan's Magazine*, Nov. 1883, p. 76.
[2] *F.R.*, July 1877, pp. 127–9; Nov. 1878, pp. 721 ff. R. S. Watson, *The National Liberal Federation*, 1907, pp. 19–20, 24.

principles'. And, Morley warned, there would have to be 'great schools' of political thought 'before we can make sure of powerful parties'.[1] Organization was not enough.

These factors go far to explain the change in Morley's attitude towards the involvement of Irish and imperial issues in the politics of the day. At first he was simply worried about the effect of coercion and imperialism on the tone of domestic politics, and denounced them as policies in which a true Liberal ought not to be implicated. Anyone who did become so implicated had lost the right to call himself a Liberal. 'The leaders of the party of progress', he declared after the passing of the Coercion Act in 1881, 'have lost their title for a long time to come to talk their old language, or to appeal to the deep and generous commonplaces of law and freedom'. It was impossible to 'have liberalism in England without its application to Ireland'.[2] Gradually the negative became the positive. Opposition to coercion and imperialism began to provide the test of definition of true Liberalism, and concentration on these issues seemed the best way in which Liberals could discover a sense of common purpose. In November 1882 Morley published an article entitled 'Irish Revolution and English Liberalism', in which he presented the Irish question as well suited for the attention of Liberals because it involved fundamental principles of Liberalism. A 'modern Liberal' must oppose the maintenance of the existing land system in Ireland; bureaucratic, centralized administration in Ireland offended against 'a maxim of English Liberalism'; the principles of Liberals would make them favour the extension of the Irish franchise.[3]

So strongly did he now seem to believe that opposition to existing Irish government and policy and to imperialism constituted the test of true Liberalism that he even spoke of a possible disruption of the Liberal party as a consequence of the enforcing of the test. 'The first authentic whisper of permanent occupation,

---
[1] *Studies in Literature*, pp. 346–7. *F.R.*, Apr. 1882, pp. 503–4; Oct. 1882, pp. 520–1.
[2] *F.R.*, Apr. 1881, pp. 407, 418.
[3] *The Nineteenth Century*, Nov. 1882, pp. 647–61.

or the most minute annexation, by England in Egypt, will', the *Pall Mall Gazette* warned on 18 July 1882, 'break the party to pieces'. A few months earlier[1] it had predicted that 'if the administration of the Coercion Act goes on until the end of the session on its present lines, it will produce a far more dangerous schism in the Liberal ranks than was made by the once famous Twenty-fifth Clause [of the 1870 Education Act] eight years ago'. Morley began also to refer to electoral defeat as an acceptable price to pay for firm adherence to principle on these issues. In July 1881 he offered the example of Fox. 'It is true that his political principles did not bring him power, and it may be that a return to them would again exclude his party from office. It would not be the first time that English Liberals have deliberately faced exclusion, rather than abandon a just, generous, and in the long run an inevitable policy of conciliation towards Ireland.' And, quoting Macaulay on how 'for the sake of Ireland' the Whigs 'remained out of office for twenty years', he appealed to their successors to carry on 'the great work' of Irish conciliation and emancipation, 'whatever sacrifice it may involve'.[2] Already one can see developing the frame of mind which was to lead to his taking a large share in giving the Liberal party an Irish policy which inaugurated twenty years of almost uninterrupted exile from office.

Indeed, the disposition to prefer firm adherence to principle at 'whatever sacrifice' to helpless drifting amid 'the endless transactions of political opportunism' was a prominent feature of his political thinking. He found highly admirable the conduct of Fox, who saw a party fall to pieces and suffered almost complete exile from office because he 'upheld the standard of liberal principles', and of Burke, in whose public life 'the most memorable act' was 'his unhesitating abandonment and violent disruption of his party when what he conceived to be the dictates of political wisdom were no longer the guide of their conduct'.[3] As in the early 1880s anti-imperialism and anti-coercion changed from mere opposition to

[1] 14 Mar. 1882.
[2] *F.R.*, July 1881, pp. 1–2.
[3] *F.R.*, Aug. 1879, pp. 194–5; Feb. 1867, p. 138. *Edmund Burke*, p. 27. *Burke*, p. 78.

distracting influences into principles for defining true Liberalism, the way was being prepared for Morley's part in the destruction of the old Liberal party amidst the intensified political confusion after the 1884 Reform Act and its reconstruction on an extension of one of these principles.

What is particularly significant about all this is that Morley now seemed to be turning from domestic policy to external issues to find the substance for a single great question. The reasons for this development may be found in the failure of disestablishment as a cause to satisfy the conditions for such a question. We have seen how Morley was forced to the realization that an agitation for disestablishment could not exercise a binding, cohering influence over Liberal and Radical politics, because it was only one among many sectional reform proposals. Nor could it provide any kind of 'national impulse', as it remained true to its real nature as the expression of the grievances of merely one section. As an issue, it proved to be divisive and sectional, not national and unifying. The lesson to be learned was that the characteristics which Morley looked for in a great question were not easily to be found in domestic, internal issues. Such a question might be more profitably sought in an external issue, one which was literally outside the nation as well as outside the range of competing domestic-reform interests.

In the early 1880s Morley had not entirely abandoned hope of discovering some internal issue that might fill the role of a single great question. In 1882 he began to believe that 'the Land quest[io]n will have to be the next great business'.[1] Hitherto he had been interested in land reform only in what he called 'the limited sense of the legal reformers'—the reform of tenure and 'the emancipation of the land from artificial restrictions' on ownership, such as entails and settlements. Once again, what appealed to him was the kind of reform which meant replacing the 'artificial' by the 'natural'. 'Circumstances are breaking down the present system', he wrote. 'In replacing it by another, the only safe course is to trust to the free working of economic conditions.'

[1] To Chamberlain, 24 Dec. 1882.

Reform should help the man burdened and restricted by 'our present artificial system of settlement', and institute a 'free system' with all the 'immense advantages, economical, social, and moral,' that flow from such a system. But he had to admit that this could not be 'the next great question', as it involved 'numerous and complex issues' and 'innumerable details' which would be confusing.[1] However, in 1882, after reflecting on the great popularity of the writings of Henry George, he saw a possible way of making the land question less 'limited' so that, while still based on the assumption of replacing an artificial by a natural system, it could become the focus of a great popular campaign appealing to urban working men. He reread Mill and found that he, like Henry George and A. R. Wallace, 'saw that the mere legal reformers—the removers of restrictions on transfer—do not touch the root of the matter'. Thus fortified, Morley wrote to Chamberlain:[2]

> The workmen are full of the ideas of Henry George. They are reading his book by thousands of copies. In London 'Nationalisation of the Land' is the one subject that would furnish a base for agitation. Why? Not because the workmen want farms, but because they are beginning to suspect that the reason why they are crammed into lodgings . . . and why if they want a little house of their own they must go to a distant suburb and pay 8/s. a week and rates, is that the landlord and the land grabber screw a rack rent out of their necessities. They feel, too, at last, that it is the immigrants from the country who lower their wages and compete for room in the towns—and this immigration arises from the land system. If I were standing for a metropolitan borough, this is the question that I shd. raise—as the only *really* interesting one now in the air. I presume that someth[in]g of the same sort is going on in the minds of the artisans elsewhere.

The 'most prominent point in my eye' was, he wrote, 'how the town populations could be attracted to the question of land reform'.

For the time being nothing further was done to develop this

---

[1] *P.M.G.*, 27 July 1880, 11 June, 1881 6, 13 Jan. 1882. Cf. *F.R.*, Jan. 1876, pp. 150, 154; Feb. 1876, pp. 304–5.

[2] 24 Dec. 1882, 7 Jan. 1883.

question. Imperialism and Ireland were the preoccupying questions and prevented Morley, at least, from giving much further attention to domestic policy before the end of 1884. And by that time the alliance between Chamberlain and Morley was showing signs of serious strain as a result of the growing divergence between them on imperial and Irish policy.

Even before 1880 there were indications that Morley did not see altogether eye to eye with Chamberlain on imperial issues;[1] but, according to Morley, his first consciousness of a substantial divergence came when he was studying the anti-expansionist principles of Cobden.[2] The Liberal Government's intervention in Egypt in 1882 embarrassed Morley considerably. While feeling 'very uncomfortable about it' and resolving to resist any proposals for occupation and annexation, he at first tried to encourage a positive policy aimed at restoring order and securing for the Egyptians 'a truly national government'.[3] By early August, however, the *Pall Mall*, while still insisting on Britain's duty to restore order before withdrawing, was reminding its readers that 'it is very difficult for a nation to attain self-government under patronage'.[4] As the months wore on and Britain remained in Egypt, the criticism became sharper and Morley began to put some public pressure on Chamberlain. Thus, when in December 1882 *The Times* interpreted a speech by Chamberlain as meaning that he favoured continued occupation of Egypt, the *Pall Mall* issued a warning to him to be more careful henceforth: 'In fact Mr. Chamberlain's previous deliverances make it impossible that he should have taken any other line [than favouring evacuation]. That is the line emphatically demanded by the bulk of those by whom Mr. Chamberlain is supported in the country, and to favour any policy leading, however indirectly, to "annexation, protectorate, or indefinite supervision", would have been to

[1] Cf. Chamberlain to Morley, 25 Dec. 1875. Morley to Chamberlain, 11 July 1877, 16 Oct. 1878.
[2] *Recollections*, I, p. 162.
[3] G. P. Gooch, *Life of Lord Courtney*, 1920, p. 174. *P.M.G.*, 13, 14, 15, 18 July 1882. F.R., July 1882, pp. 119–21.
[4] *P.M.G.*, 10 Aug. 1882.

forfeit their confidence and lose their adhesion.'[1] The Radical leaders were warned of the hold gained over middle- and working-class opinion by the principles of Cobden and Bright.[2] From his first speech in the House of Commons, Morley pursued an independent line on imperial policy, highly critical of the Liberal Government.[3] Not surprisingly, this soon led to further differences between Chamberlain and himself.

In January 1884 Chamberlain, giving a speech at Newcastle in Morley's presence, referred to the Egyptian situation in terms such as the following: 'We have assumed a duty which we cannot neglect. . . . We cannot leave Egypt to anarchy. . . . The task is likely to be more difficult that was supposed. It will take a longer time than was anticipated.' But, when Morley rose to speak briefly after Chamberlain, he revealed a very different attitude. He warned against annexationist ideas in the Liberal party and proclaimed his own intention of joining 'those whether they were few or whether they were many who were for standing by our solemn pledges'.[4] When he made a strong attack in the Commons a month later on the Government's Egyptian policy, Gladstone told him that he agreed privately with most of what he said; and Morley replied that he and Gladstone appeared to be 'the last of the Cobdenites'. He now had little faith in Chamberlain, for he reflected that, were Gladstone to leave the Cabinet, it would be 'straight Jingo'.[5] Throughout 1884 he made vigorous attacks on the imperial policies of the Government.[6] He and Chamberlain were now drifting further and further apart. When in December Chamberlain suggested that he might join the Government, he replied that he would be reluctant to do so 'until the Egyptian abominations are wiped up somehow or other'.[7] It was at this time that Chamberlain was assuring Cape Afrikaaners that 'they

[1] *P.M.G.*, 20 Dec. 1882.
[2] *P.M.G.*, 22, 26 Dec. 1882.
[3] *Hansard*, 3, 277, 423-5; 282, 1650, 2117-28.
[4] *The Times*, 16 Jan. 1884, p. 10, cc. 1, 4.
[5] *Hansard*, 3, 284, 1027-34. Hirst, *Early Life & Letters*, II, p. 193.
[6] *Hansard*, 3, 285, 1710-12. *The Times*, 9 June 1884, p. 8, c. 6; 19 June 1884, p. 6, c. 4; 20 Nov. 1884, p. 6, c. 3. Cf. his letter to Leonard Courtney, 22 Nov. 1884. Gooch, *Life of Courtney*, p. 206.
[7] To Chamberlain, 2 Dec. 1884.

will find the Radical party more sternly Imperial than the most bigotted Tory', and that the Cape politician, Merriman, declared himself after talking with Chamberlain to be 'delighted' to find 'that the Radicals generally do not share the views expressed so ably by Mr. Morley as to the worthlessness of colonies'.[1] Morley soon found himself making this kind of report to Chamberlain: 'I met Ld. Reay yesterday [30 December 1884]. He spoke as if you and I were now wide as the poles asunder. I told him it was news to me, and very disagreeable news.'

The crisis over the relief of Gordon in the Sudan brought renewed conflict between them in February 1885. Morley, under strong pressure from such associates as Frederic Harrison, Leonard Courtney, Sir Wilfrid Lawson, and his chairman at Newcastle, Spence Watson, waged a vigorous public campaign against British involvement in the Sudan.[2] Chamberlain protested, but Morley replied:

if it [the government's policy] points to indefinite operations for the purpose of smashing the Mahdi, then I for one cannot go with it for an hour. . . . As I told you in reply to your scoldings about a certain vote of mine, war in the Soudan is an affair of political conscience with me. I would rather leave the H. of C., and go back to my books again, than have anything to do with such a business.[3]

Chamberlain was particularly concerned lest Morley, in his anti-imperialist zeal, might be led into an 'alliance with the Tories'; for, since Morley was generally looked on as Chamberlain's close ally, his actions were liable to be interpreted as inspired by Chamberlain himself. 'Liberate your soul & preserve your consistency . . . but do not', Chamberlain warned him, 'join with the Tories whose policy is even more hateful than that of the Government.' Chamberlain was most anxious that their own association should not be disrupted: 'There is much common work for us to do in the future.' But Morley did not entirely rule

[1] J. A. Froude to Chamberlain, 1 Dec. 1884, Chamberlain MSS. J. L. Garvin, *The Life of Joseph Chamberlain*, I, 1932, p. 530.
[2] *The Times*, 11 Feb. 1885, p. 10, c. 4. Gooch, *Life of Courtney*, pp. 222–3. P. Corder, *The Life of Robert Spence Watson*, 1914, p. 240.
[3] To Chamberlain, 14 Feb. 1885.

out such a rift, even although saying that it would be 'so odious and intolerable' as to incline him to make his 'bow to the whole business' of politics.[1] A week later, however, he moved an amendment in the House of Commons regretting the Government's decision 'to employ the forces of the Crown for the overthrow of the power of the Mahdi'; but he had framed it so that the Conservatives could not possibly vote for it, and he thereafter insisted that he was prepared to give a vote for conscience only when the Government's existence was not in danger.[2]

Interwoven among these episodes were similar crises concerning the Government's Irish policy when Morley found himself likewise in growing conflict with Chamberlain. It became apparent that Chamberlain had views on Irish policy which he did not wish to discard even although they diverged from the ideas of the man who professed to be his 'spiritual adviser'. As early as 1877 we find Chamberlain regretting Morley's 'half kindness for those rascally Irishmen who are destined to give us a great deal of trouble yet'.[3] The attacks made by the *Pall Mall Gazette* on Forster's coercion policy in the winter of 1881-2 greatly embarrassed Chamberlain, for his close connection with the editor led many people to suppose that he was employing the *Pall Mall* to make the criticisms of his own colleagues which ministerial responsibility forbade him from making publicly in his own name. In fact, his attitude to disorder and coercion was very different from Morley's. 'Anarchy and intimidation must be put down' and 'order must be restored'— such were his principles for dealing with the situation. His arguments were often based on concern for what Morley regarded as the narrow expediency: 'I feel strongly that the immediate necessity & duty of the moment is to support the Executive in the main lines of its policy and not to criticize details'; 'we have to deal with the present and must leave the future to take care of itself.'[4] But Morley tried to make Chamberlain see that his own

---

[1] Chamberlain to Morley, 15 Feb. 1885. Morley to Chamberlain, 16 Feb. 1885.
[2] *Hansard*, 3, 294, 1071-8; 298, 216-18. *The Times*, 2 Apr. 1885, p. 12, c. 1.
[3] Chamberlain to Morley, 3 Oct. 1877.
[4] Chamberlain to Morley, 18 Oct. 1881.

situation must be governed by different considerations, particularly that of preserving consistency and respect as an upholder of Liberal principles. As it was, John Bright had written reminding him that the difficulty of his position stemmed from his having opposed coercion earlier in 1881. Anxious not to be forced to go the whole way towards backing Chamberlain in support of coercion, he first of all pleaded with him to preserve silence on the issue and then asked him to make plain his disagreement with the extreme coercionists. 'We must keep some ground of our own, and this might give it to us.' He thus explained why he did not want to be associated with the support of coercion: 'I don't want to be dished as a democrat for the rest of my natural life. There's the rub.' Chamberlain was 'a practical Minister'; 'but the case of the spiritual Power is different.'[1] Chamberlain then tried to bridge this gap by claiming that even Mill would have approved of coercion under the circumstances and by urging Morley to be less rigid: 'People have short memories; and do not expect even from their spiritual advisers absolute infallibility.'[2] A few weeks of reluctant quiescence culminated in another eruption of conscience in December 1881, when Morley confessed to Chamberlain that privately he took the 'revolutionary view' of the Irish situation, approving of even violent agitation and thinking that 'the hotter they [the Irish] make it for the "garrison" the better'. This was 'the real view of the Irish business'; but, of course, he acknowledged, 'a Minister cannot take that line' because public opinion was not ready for it. He assured Chamberlain that he would try to perceive the Government's difficulties and recognize that 'order must be kept on the principles of the existing system'.[3] The editorial in the *Pall Mall* on 27 December showed him seeking a reconciliation along these lines, insisting on the need to preserve order, but also warning that Liberals would retain a clear conscience only if they also strove to attain a form of government that would 'satisfy Ireland'.

Within a few months Morley's own Liberal conscience was

[1] To Chamberlain, 19, 20, 21 Oct. 1881.
[2] Chamberlain to Morley, 21 Oct. 1881.
[3] To Chamberlain, 5, 9, 19, 29 Dec. 1881.

impelling him to renew his protests against coercion. His campaign for the resignation of Forster from the Irish Secretaryship began in March and ended when Forster did resign early in May 1882. Harcourt said to Chamberlain at the time: 'Your mischievous friend, J. Morley, has done this.' But the *Pall Mall* was really only underlining the realities of the situation for Forster. Chamberlain claimed some years later that the last straw for Forster was really the appointment of Lord Spencer, the new Lord Lieutenant, to a place in the Cabinet, as this gave 'a point to the criticisms of the *Pall Mall* and others'.[1] Nevertheless, it was widely believed that Morley's attacks had been inspired by Chamberlain in order to secure the Irish Office for himself. Chamberlain, showing signs of impatience at Morley's intrusions into the sphere of practical politics, pointed out to him that creating such a belief was the surest way 'to destroy any chance of success which I might otherwise have had'.[2]

In January 1883 the *Pall Mall Gazette* attacked the Irish policy of Lord Spencer and Sir George Trevelyan, although Morley wrote privately that his 'thorough affection' for Trevelyan was keeping him as quiet as was possible 'without absolute stultification of one's self'. Once again, Chamberlain was suspected of inspiring Morley's attacks. Dilke told him that Trevelyan and Spencer believed that he had set Morley against them. Chamberlain denied this, remarking that, on the contrary, he had done all he could to keep Morley 'straight'—'but you know he is "kittle-cattle to drive" '.[3] Once Morley had entered Parliament, Egypt rather than Ireland occupied his attention, but he remained ominously ready to assert his independent views if need should again arise. Thus on 5 June 1885 he declared: 'I cannot help feeling that I have a right to exercise my own judgment [about coercion] as I did in 1881; and as my judgment was not wrong then—as everybody now admits—I am not now prepared to sacrifice my judgment in this matter on the authority of a million statesmen.'[4]

[1] Morley to Gladstone, 10 Aug. 1888, B.M. Add. MSS. 44255, ff. 252–3.
[2] *Recollections*, I, pp. 194–7.
[3] Garvin, *Life of Chamberlain*, I, p. 389. Morley to Sir E. Hamilton, 1 Feb. 1883, B.M. Add. MSS. 48619.
[4] *The Times*, 6 June 1885, p. 12, c. 4.

10

CHAMBERLAIN'S RADICAL CAMPAIGN, 1885

FOR a while after Morley's entry into the Commons Radicals seemed to have found a cause on which they could act in unison—the extension of the franchise. In October 1883, for example, Morley presided at a conference in Leeds on this question and was pleased to note that Radicals and Liberals of widely varying views on other questions had been able to unite in sponsoring this conference.[1] But as the success of this campaign became assured, the question of the form which the activity of Radicals and Liberals was to take after the passing of the Reform Bill began to loom large and ominously unclear. For Morley himself the nature of the final phase of the campaign suggested what the 'next great business' might be—the 'mending or ending' of the House of Lords, which was proving so obstructive with its demands for the simultaneous promotion of a Redistribution Bill. In July 1884 Morley had begun to present this as a great question for working-class voters. Speaking at the Durham miners' gala, he declared that, now that the peers and the Tories had 'flung down the gauntlet', the working men of the country 'would not be slow' to pick it up 'and to hurl defiance in their teeth'. 'Should they', he asked, 'whose forefathers would not endure the tyranny and misgovernment of kings, submit to the oppression and stupidity of peers?' Turning to gesture at 'that great pile', Durham Cathedral, he claimed that, after eight centuries in which it had witnessed many struggles 'between feudalism and humanity, between the privileged few and the toiling multitude', there had now come another such struggle. Victory over the House of Lords would add 'another and a most glorious victory to those achievements of the past'.[2]

[1] *The Times*, 18 Oct. 1883, p. 6, cc. 1–2. [2] *The Times*, 7 July 1884, p. 7, cc. 1–2.

Particularly interesting in this rhetoric is the reference to the past as providing a guide-line to action in the present and future. Concern for continuity had always been a feature of Morley's thinking on society and politics and dominated his belief in progress. This concern influenced his attitude now to the problems of practical politics. In 1887 he was to write that one of the problems of 'modern democracy' was 'how our hopes for the future are to be linked to wise reverence for tradition and the past'.[1] Increasingly from now on, in the new, confused, and uncertain conditions of this 'modern democracy', he seemed to look for guidance to the certainties and lines of progression of the past. His rhetoric would involve an appeal primarily to the emotions and passions that had attached to great issues in the past, safe, tried, and proven areas of agitation. When in his younger days he had claimed for himself and his associates the role of discerning the lines of the future, the emphasis had been on looking ahead, on seeing what issues were likely to come up for urgent attention. But gradually, as his youthful idealism had faded and the unreadiness of political thinking to give effective guidance in emergencies 'as they arose' oppressed him more and more, the emphasis shifted from the lines of the future to the lines of the past. His confidence in the certainty of progress, and the definiteness of his understanding of the form which that progress would assume, diminished, and the concept of progress was replaced by the concept of the obstruction to progress. The work of looking ahead and preparing men for what one discerned on the lines of the future became the work of clearing obstructions on the line immediately in front. The line that had once been discernible stretching far into the future could now be seen stretching only back into the past, and estimates of its future course were made blindly in terms only of where it had already been.

Morley's concern for 'natural' and 'organic' change always made him insist on respect for the 'organic' integrity of the past development of a society. The reformer, he had once written, must appreciate that 'manners, customs, opinions, have old roots which must be sought in a historic past', and must keep in mind

[1] *Studies in Literature*, p. 54.

'the whole series of actual incidents between present and past'.¹ Morley's belief that 'an improved future' could be secured only through 'an unbroken continuation' of the lines of historical development² produced a steadily increasing preoccupation with the past until finally the precedents and modes of thought and action in the past completely dominated his own political attitudes. The lack of a system was also a factor in this, for it is always the function of a system to lay down laws of change which indicate what future development must inevitably be. As system disappeared from Morley's thinking, he found himself—unlike a positivist, for example—unable to feel certain about the future, and so he turned to the past to re-create for himself a sense of certainty about human affairs.

By September 1884 the issue of the power of the Lords was developing into the latest of Morley's great questions. With the Lords depicted in his rhetoric as the enemies of popular rights, legislative improvements, and the free expansion of national life, removal of this obstruction seemed the key that would open the way to certain progress. 'This agitation was ripening the matter for solution', he declared: here was the next great business after the Reform Bill. After a better Commons had been secured, 'the turn of the Lords would come pretty speedily'. Morley therefore urged Gladstone to prefer the creation of peers to a dissolution on the two issues of franchise reform and the Lords. Here was a question which seemed to be spreading itself over the sectionalism of the Liberal party, occupying the attention of the party 'as a whole' and furnishing 'a bond of agreement among all shades and sections' of it. Classes within the nation were also bound up within it. 'It is not one class only which has joined in the cry', Morley claimed; 'not only the poor and the indigent and the discontented', but also 'bankers and merchants and men of great substance'.³ Was this at last the great cause that would unite the

¹ *Rousseau*, II, pp. 125–6.
² Ibid., II, p. 122. *Studies in Literature*, p. 178.
³ *The Times*, 8 Sept. 1884, p. 7, c. 3; 16 Sept. 1884, p. 10, c. 6; 6 Oct. 1884, p. 7, c. 4; 30 Oct. 1884, p. 10, cc. 2–3. To Gladstone, 13 Oct. 1884, B.M. Add. MSS. 44255, ff. 49–50. *Macmillan's Magazine*, Oct. 1884, p. 470.

Liberal party and the nation in the enthusiasm of a 'vivid national impulse'?

Having developed the issue to this extent, and having expressed strong opposition to any compromise by which 'the plain issue that is now before the country, and is now well and firmly grasped' by the Government's supporters might be 'confused and obscured',[1] Morley was naturally extremely displeased by the settlement with the Lords and the consequent abrupt deflation of the feeling against them. He made no secret of his regret at the destruction of an issue that had been thoroughly developed for the attention of the new voters.[2] When 217 Liberal M.P.s went to the Foreign Office on 1 December to hear from Gladstone the terms of the compromise, Morley was one of the Radicals 'conspicuous by their absence'.[3] This affair put further strain on Morley's relations with Chamberlain, who had acquiesced in the settlement from within the Government. He dissociated himself from Chamberlain in his speeches, and warned of the anger of Radicals should they discover 'that their recognized leaders are muzzled by office, and that they can only take part in the government of the country on condition of stifling their opinions'.[4] Chamberlain, in fact, spoke to Morley about 'damping down the House of Lords question'.[5]

For Chamberlain was developing his own, rather different, ideas as to what form the politics of the new democracy should take. Whereas Morley had been thinking of a single great question, Chamberlain wanted a programme. Whereas Morley had been trying to arouse emotions associated with great struggles for reform in the past, Chamberlain was prepared to enter on the unfirm ground of new emotions about new issues. Chamberlain was discerning the lines of the future when he wrote that 'ideas and

---

[1] *The Times*, 27 Sept. 1884, p. 8, c. 3. *Macmillan's Magazine*, Nov. 1884, pp. 71–2.
[2] *The Times*, 20 Nov. 1884, p. 6, c. 3; 26 Nov. 1884, p. 6, cc. 2–3.
[3] *The Times*, 2 Dec. 1884, p. 10, c. 5.
[4] *The Times*, 26 Nov. 1884, p. 6, c. 2; 11 Feb. 1885, p. 10, c. 4. Cf. H. H. Fowler to Morley, 19 Nov. 1884, E. H. Fowler, *The Life of Henry Hartley Fowler, First Viscount Wolverhampton, G.C.S.I.*, 1912, p. 168.
[5] Morley to Chamberlain, 19 Dec. 1884.

wants and claims which have been hitherto ignored in legislation will find a voice in Parliament, and will compel the attention of statesmen'. The 'nature of the domestic legislation of the future' was to be predominantly 'social' and not 'purely political' as in the past.[1] Morley, by contrast, had been offering political reform, and in such a way as to stress its resemblance to reforms of the past. Now, in an endeavour to 'secure some great movement of popular opinion' and to 'excite the passionate fervour which I desire to see among the people', Chamberlain offered a programme of radical reforms.[2]

The passing of the 1884 Reform Bill was seen by Chamberlain as the signal for the final campaign to oust the Whigs from their position of influence in the Liberal party and to establish the ascendancy of the Radicals. Contemporaries could hardly have expected that Morley would greet with anything less than wholehearted enthusiasm the prospect of the triumph of the Radicalism with which he had been so prominently associated since 1873; and Chamberlain naturally assumed that he would enjoy Morley's close co-operation. He wrote to Morley after the first series of speeches outlining his new campaign: 'I hope and believe that you, Dilke and I stand together in this. If we do, we will utterly destroy the Whigs and have a Radical Government before many years are out.'[3] In Morley's reply there was, however, a slight note of caution. He wrote simply that the programme would serve 'to keep the Radicals in good heart and to assure the Whigs that they are no longer the masters of the party'.[4] Chamberlain made considerable efforts to involve Morley in the campaign. In April he fastened on Morley the appearance of implication by using a quotation from *Burke* as a point against the Whigs in a speech.[5] After the resignation of the Liberal Government in June he proposed that a 'Radical junto' consisting of Morley, Dilke, Trevelyan, Shaw-Lefevre, and himself should meet frequently

[1] *The Radical Programme*, 1885, pp. v–vi, 61.
[2] *The Times*, 9 Sept. 1885, p. 6, cc. 2–3.
[3] 2 Feb. 1885.
[4] 3 Feb. 1885.
[5] *The Times*, 29 Apr. 1885, p. 10, c. 1.

in order to discuss policy and concert action. Dilke recorded Morley's attendance at its first meeting on 4 July, and thereafter he seems to have been a regular attender at its weekly meetings.[1] Yet on 30 August Chamberlain considered a further appeal to Morley for co-operation necessary. 'The times are critical', he wrote, 'and everything depends on the General election. I am convinced I am on the right track—the only one worth travelling by a Radical—and I think we shall win.' It is curious that he should have thought that Morley needed reminding of these points at this stage. 'I think it is most desirable', he told Morley, 'that we should have a long talk. . . . I should feel much helped & strengthened by your friendly sympathy & cooperation.'

It was at a meeting presided over by Morley, a month later, that Chamberlain chose to declare his refusal to join any government which excluded his policies from its programme. 'The fact is', he told Morley afterwards, 'that these Whigs & moderate Liberals are only just beginning to find out that we are in earnest.' He made it plain that the 'we' was intended to include Morley by arguing that 'the Whigs must come down' if the Radical leaders 'all' stood aloof from Gladstone's efforts to find a compromise programme, and by then urging Morley 'to emphasize the "declaration" and to accept it' for himself when next he spoke.[2] In the autumn the meetings of the 'junto' appear to have continued, perhaps less regularly, with Morley still attending.[3] Early in October Chamberlain informed Sir William Harcourt that, should the Whig leader Hartington decide on a complete break with the Radicals, Dilke, Morley, and himself would organize their own party and programme.[4] On 26 October he warned Gladstone that 'neither I nor Dilke nor Morley, nor I *think* Lefevre, could honestly join any Government' that did not take

---

[1] J. L. Garvin, *The Life of Joseph Chamberlain*, II, 1933, p. 6. S. Gwynn and G. M. Tuckwell, *The Life of Sir Charles Dilke*, II, 1917, pp. 149, 154-7. F. E. Hamer (ed.), *The Personal Papers of Lord Rendel*, 1931, p. 181.

[2] 26 Sept. 1885.

[3] Gwynn and Tuckwell, *Life of Dilke*, II, p. 218. Lord Eversley, *Gladstone and Ireland*, 1912, p. 280.

[4] Garvin, *Life of Chamberlain*, II, p. 103.

up his local-government policies. 'We are absolutely bound by our declarations, as well as by our recent action, in such a case, to remain outside and bide our time.'[1]

But Chamberlain was assuming a great deal too much about Morley's attitude to his Radical campaign. For Morley had begun to have serious misgivings about that campaign from the point when Chamberlain had invited his audience to 'go back to the origin of things' and realize that 'when our social arrangements first began to shape themselves every man was born into the world with natural rights, with a right to a share in the great inheritance of the community, with a right to a part of the land of his birth'. Alleging that these rights had been stolen or lost or otherwise wrongly alienated, until completely replaced by the institution of private property, Chamberlain demanded that the propertied classes pay 'ransom' for being allowed to continue holding property thus acquired in violation of 'natural rights'.[2] Morley had written at once to give some 'spiritual advice' and warn of the treacherousness of the ground on to which Chamberlain had ventured. The expression 'natural rights' sounded well, he admitted, and had been 'a powerful revolutionary weapon before now'. But it was not 'a true way of putting things—and certainly not the most useful and fertile way'. 'Nature', being 'simply the mastery of the strongest', conferred no rights on man. 'Two savage tribes contend for a tract of land of wh. they are in need for their subsistence: *nature* gave the right to this land to the tribe wh. was strong enough to thrash the other.' While thus demolishing the abstraction of 'nature', he tried also to direct Chamberlain back on to safe utilitarian principles: 'No right is worth a straw apart from the good that it brings: and all claims to rights must depend—not upon nature—but upon the good that the said rights are calculated to bring to the greatest number. General utility, public expediency, the greatest happiness of the greatest number—these are the tests and standards of a right; not the dictate of nature.'[3]

But the complementary relationship between the two men was

[1] Ibid., II, pp. 114–15.
[2] *The Times*, 6 Jan. 1885, p. 7, c. 4.
[3] To Chamberlain, 6 Jan. 1885.

no longer working as it had been meant to work. Morley had for some years been developing an independent role in the practical sphere of politics, and now Chamberlain was producing some political thinking of his own and refusing to take Morley's advice that it was fallacious. Eight days after Morley had written to him Chamberlain declared in a speech that, 'after all, in spite of what political economists tell us, the poor have rights which cannot be safely ignored'. Whereas Morley had told him that it is 'law, institution, custom, that confer right on a man—not nature', Chamberlain denied that 'there are no rights outside the law' and argued that the making of law by majorities is itself an instance of 'the mastery of the strongest', against which he found preferable 'considerations of natural justice and equity'.[1]

Since 1873 Morley had shown himself perpetually concerned about the 'respectability' and 'safeness' of the Radicalism with which he was associated, and his constant warning to Chamberlain was, 'Let's keep ourselves *respectable*'.[2] In particular, he wished to see English Radicalism free from any French associations. He had frequently insisted that English Radicalism was in no way influenced by French Radical thought. Thus in 1868 he offered as proof that in it there was 'no Jacobinism' and 'no revolution' the fact that English Radicals did not refer to abstract rights or make deductions from an *a priori* system.[3] In 1873 he advised Chamberlain that in order to reach the 'respectable middle class', conciliate 'timid friends', and destroy the notion that the Radicals were 'Communists, &c.', they must show that their reform proposals were 'all commended by the fact of their promoting good government, order &c.' and were not 'mere deductions from abstract principles—but sober, sensible, practical plans'.[4] In 1882 the *Pall Mall Gazette* insisted that the Radicals wanted reforms for practical reasons, not 'for the sake of the Rights of Man' or any 'abstract principle'; and Chamberlain's work at the Board of Trade was cited as proof that he was not a 'mischievous theorist' and 'hare-

[1] *The Times*, 15 Jan. 1885, p. 7, cc. 1–2.
[2] Cf. to Chamberlain, 24 Oct. 1873, 14 July, 20, 21, 27 Dec. 1875, 12 Feb. 1876.
[3] *F.R.*, Dec. 1868, pp. 681–93.
[4] To Chamberlain, 17 Aug. 1873.

brained revolutionist' guilty of 'sentimentalism, theorizing, and so forth'.[1]

One can therefore understand Morley's reaction to Chamberlain's talk of 'natural rights'. He later wrote that, having 'never said a word about "Natural Rights" in any piece of practical public business in all my life', he regarded Chamberlain's use of the phrase with 'as much surprise and dismay as if I were this afternoon to meet a Deinotherium shambling down Parliament Street'.[2] He did make some effort, however, to grasp what Chamberlain was trying to say and to allow for his inexperience in the handling of political concepts. Chamberlain asked critics such as Morley 'not to be afraid of words'. 'Because the doctrine of natural rights was abused in the time of the French Revolution do not', he asked, 'ignore the fundamental right which every man holds in common for a chance of decent existence.'[3] And Morley, writing later in the year, did try to discount the significance of the words:

Men often pick up old phrases for new events, even when they are judging events afresh with independent minds. When a politician of the day speaks of natural rights, he uses a loose traditional expression for a view of social equities which has come to him, not from a book, but from a survey of certain existing social facts. Now the phrase, the literary description, is the least significant part of the matter.[4]

Nevertheless, it was clear that Morley could not like the attachment of these particular words to the issue of land reform, an issue which, as he wrote in February 1885, he preferred to discuss in 'utilitarian' and 'positive' terms.[5] He had long been especially afraid of the effect of vague, abstract language in this area. In 1873 he had advised Chamberlain 'to leave the *land* out of the question', because he was afraid that 'such a cry as Free Land' might be 'seized upon and spoiled by reckless and wild people who don't know what they really want—or else who want what it is im-

[1] *P.M.G.*, 6 Jan., 25 Mar. 1882.
[2] *Studies in Literature*, pp. 174-5.
[3] *The Times*, 29 Apr. 1885, p. 10, c. 2.
[4] *Studies in Literature*, p. 120.
[5] *The Times*, 7 Feb. 1885, p. 8, c. 3.

possible from the nature of things that they should ever get'.[1] In 1881 and 1882 the *Pall Mall* warned that, 'when complex matter of this kind comes on to platforms and into party programmes, there is a very obvious danger that politicians may commit themselves to doctrine, whether in the way of advance or obstruction, which they have never honestly worked out'. The drawback to the issue of land reform was that 'men have meant by it very different things' and 'vagueness may do more harm in regard to the Land Question than in any other part of the political field' by 'raising expectations which cannot be prudently satisfied'.[2] It is not surprising that Morley was apprehensive as to the impact of the idea that every man has a 'natural right' to the land.

Caution and moderation became the keynotes of his speeches. In October 1884 he had spoken 'in favour of caution in approaching and preparing measures' and had warned that 'there never was a time when they needed more to be united in all classes and divisions than now'.[3] After the launching of Chamberlain's campaign Morley stressed more than ever the importance of a 'sense of social union and common citizenship' and the danger of the arousing of 'envy', 'jealousy between poor and rich', and 'bitterness of class feeling', from all of which, he alleged, England had hitherto been strikingly free.[4] This was just after Chamberlain had been saying that the landowners represented the violation of the 'natural rights' of all men and that the rich should pay a 'ransom' to society. Morley's great aim now seemed to be to slow down the development of Radical excitement. He would warn against belief in any easy way out of the problems of modern life, and would stress the vital role of patience, caution, and foresight, as well as energy and enthusiasm, in the improvement of society.[5] He deplored the 'excessive hurry and impatience' which he claimed to have observed of late even in 'political friends', and upheld the type of practical reformer 'who without sacrificing a jot of conviction or principle yet has a regard for times and

---

[1] To Chamberlain, 18, 22 Aug. 1873.
[2] *P.M.G.*, 3, 5 Nov. 1881, 13 Jan. 1882.
[3] *The Times*, 6 Oct. 1884, p. 7, c. 4.
[4] *The Times*, 11 Feb. 1885, p. 10, c. 4.
[5] *The Times*, 9 July 1885, p. 10, c. 2.

seasons' and 'measures his actions with a view to his resources'.[1]

Now, it was, in fact, impatience and lack of self-control that Morley most complained about in Chamberlain. Many years later he observed of Chamberlain's Radicalism that it was 'always of the *autoritaire* type, impatient of control and at times frankly belligerent'.[2] In 1875 he had written to Chamberlain about the importance of making their Radicalism respectable, and added this warning: '*it will take time*. You are of the eager sort, and I expect you to be disappointed with the whole business. I rather fear that.'[3] But in 1885 Chamberlain's impatience at having to temper his Radicalism to the requirements of working with Whigs and moderates finally erupted, and Morley found that even he could no longer exercise his control as a 'spiritual adviser' over Chamberlain. After their ways had parted, he was to refer to Chamberlain's display of 'want of wisdom and self-control', and to associate this comment with praise of Hartington, whose own possession of these qualities Morley called 'the strongest bulwark we have against all the strong socialist doctrine I hate'.[4] In other words, Chamberlain's impatient lack of concern for the solidity and stability of the structure which he had set up in the name of Liberal policy had created the danger of the seeping through of 'socialist doctrine'.

Chamberlain, for his part, found Morley excessively cautious and timid. As early as March 1884 he was complaining of the 'folly' displayed in a parliamentary debate by Morley. His 'weakness in the matter', Chamberlain wrote, 'makes me almost hopeless of his future as a politician'. This weakness he summed up as a tendency to be 'swayed by every gust of opinion in the lobbies' and an inability to set aside 'minor considerations in the pursuit of a broad general policy'.[5] In October 1885 he called Morley 'dreadfully timid'.[6]

[1] *The Times*, 23 July 1885, p. 6, c. 4; 6 June 1885, p. 12, c. 3.
[2] Quoted in Sir Almeric Fitzroy, *Memoirs*, 3rd edition, II, n.d., p. 501.
[3] 27 Dec. 1875.
[4] To Gladstone, 27 Dec. 1886, B.M. Add. MSS. 44255, f. 159. M. V. Brett (ed.), *Journals and Letters of Reginald Viscount Esher*, I, 1934, p. 132.
[5] Chamberlain to J. T. Bunce, 20 Mar. 1884, Chamberlain MSS.
[6] Chamberlain to Dilke, 17 Oct. 1885, Chamberlain MSS.

It soon became evident that Morley was reluctant to associate himself fully with Chamberlain's campaign. In June Chamberlain was not certain whether to include Morley in the 'junto', and, although he attended a meeting on 11 July, for instance, he alone of those present did not take part in a deputation to Gladstone on Irish policy and party organization.[1] Chamberlain's letter of 30 August indicates doubts about Morley's commitment to the campaign and suggests that he felt that Morley was not yet extending 'friendly sympathy & cooperation'. Whether they were defeated or not, 'at least', Chamberlain rather pointedly remarked, 'I hope we shall have the consolation of having done all in our power to advance the cause we care for'.

For some years Morley had been predicting that 'the Social Question' was going to emerge very soon into political prominence.[2] But his own ideas on it were far from ready or systematized when in 1885 Chamberlain demanded that domestic legislation be now social rather than political. He recognized that some degree of State interference was called for to deal with social problems that were beyond the control of the individual. The 'regulation of industry' and of 'relations between labour and capital' could not, he conceded, be 'safely left to the unfettered play of individual competition'.[3] In 1880 he had written to an extreme opponent of State interference: 'I am afraid that I do not agree with you as to paternal government. I am no partisan of a policy of incessant meddling with individual freedom, but I do strongly believe that in so populous a society as ours now is, you may well have a certain protection thrown over classes of men and women who are unable to protect themselves.'[4] He could see that some readjustment of Liberal thinking must take place. Liberals needed systematic principles to guide them on the issue of 'limitations on free contract'. There had already been for quite a few years 'incessant

---

[1] Gwynn and Tuckwell, *Life of Dilke*, II, pp. 149, 156–7.
[2] Cf. *P.M.G.*, 26 Dec. 1882, 16 Apr. 1883.
[3] *Cobden*, I, pp. 297–8.
[4] To Auberon Herbert, 28 Apr. 1880, quoted in S. H. Harris, *Auberon Herbert: Crusader for Liberty*, 1943, p. 223.

extension' of State supervision and interference 'in all directions', and Liberal thought had to take account of this.¹

But Morley's own thinking had become rather deeply involved in the development of principles of opposition to State interference as a result of his preoccupation with Irish and imperial questions. As his letter to Chamberlain on 'natural rights' showed, his basic principles remained those of utilitarian expediency and 'the greatest happiness of the greatest number', even though he had admitted some years earlier that these principles no longer offered any 'effective unity' or systematic guidance for practical politicians. No satisfactory attempt had yet been made to relate the 'greatest happiness' principle to a situation in which the 'greatest number' had the vote. Did the multitude know, and did it express through its votes, what its happiness was? How was it possible to distinguish deciding on what seemed socially expedient in a democratic society from mere political opportunism and helpless drifting in the ebbs and currents of popular feeling? Like Comte's 'Good of Humanity', Chamberlain's 'natural rights' could only seem to Morley a 'fantastic decoration' on what were still basically utilitarian principles. And so it did nothing to overcome the problem of adapting utilitarianism to the new democratic situation. Rhetoric was no effective substitute for systematic principles.

There is no evidence that Chamberlain had consulted Morley before producing his Radical programme of 1885. Morley had been preoccupied with Ireland and imperialism and, in domestic affairs, with parliamentary reform. The assumption in their alliance had always been that issues such as disestablishment, secular education, and the reduction of the powers of the House of Lords would be the basis of any Radical campaign in which they engaged. Now, confronted so abruptly with this introduction of the 'Social Question', Morley was confused and unsure of himself. He sought to evade the definite commitment which Chamberlain was demanding of all Liberals for or against his programme. He appeared to be trying to face two ways at once, to be cautious and conciliatory of moderate opinion and yet to

¹ *Studies in Literature*, p. 347. *F.R.*, Apr. 1882, p. 504; Oct. 1882, pp. 520–1.

maintain his association with Chamberlain. In one speech, in February 1885, he expressed the hope 'that no attempt is going to be made from either wing to enforce a narrow, exclusive, and intolerant definition of Liberal principles on the Liberal party'. He argued that the party 'ought to be built on broad foundations', appealed for 'tolerance and concession for the sake of the common object of agreement', and asked the more ardent Liberals to have patience with 'the slow man'.[1] Later in the year he declared that, since, owing to the phenomenon of 'Tory Democracy', the Conservative party was losing its old character, 'the Liberal party will have to do duty for both parties'. There were men in it, he claimed, 'who comprehend true Conservatism combined with true Liberalism'. He then described himself as such a man, significantly identifying himself in this regard with Gladstone, not Chamberlain: 'I am a cautious Whig by temperament, I am a sound Liberal by training, and I am a thorough Radical by observation and experience.'[2]

His speeches at this time show a balanced construction, combining recommendations of caution and moderation with discussion and support of aspects of the Radical programme. But gradually the cautiousness starts to be replaced by harder, clearer attitudes. The balance becomes the same as that which developed in 1873, the occasion when Chamberlain had last produced a Radical programme. The shape into which Morley's desire for caution and control in political action now moulded itself was that of the 'single great question'. We shall see how Morley moved towards commitment to a great question and towards finding in this commitment as intolerant and narrow a definition of Liberal principles as any suggested by Chamberlain.

Although the compromise over the Reform Bill had left Morley temporarily without a single great question to oppose to Chamberlain's programme, he was still obviously anxious to find one. In June 1885, for example, he praised that kind of 'practical reformer' who 'is often content to take one question at once, and shapes his policy with a view to the most fruitful re-

[1] *The Times*, 11 Feb. 1885, p. 10, cc. 3-4.
[2] *The Times*, 17 Sept. 1885, p. 4, c. 1.

sults'. He argued that Radicals should feel especially satisfied just now 'with this way of handling politics', because it was 'this kind of Radicalism, and nothing else', that led to the Reform Act, the achievement of which single measure was, he considered, ample compensation for all other disappointments and postponements in the previous five years.[1] The conflict between the two modes of political agitation is seen clearly in the *Radical Programme* of 1885. Produced as a series of articles in the *Fortnightly Review* and then published in book form with an introduction by Chamberlain, this illustrates very well the 'programme' approach to Radical politics—with its anonymity, the wide range of topics covered, and the way in which Chamberlain's own supervision provides the cohesion.[2] In his introduction Chamberlain linked this attempt 'to compile a definite and practical programme for the Radical Party' with the arrival of 'the time for action' by Radicals; and one of the contributors described the programme as a detailed but 'comprehensive scheme of legislative action upon which the energies of Radicals may be concentrated, and which may form a rallying ground for the party'.[3] But Morley believed that a programme dispersed, rather than concentrated, the energies of Radicals, and, in the tradition of Cobden, preferred a single issue as the means of binding them together. And, embedded in the *Radical Programme*, there was an example of this approach— Morley's own contribution, entitled 'Religious Equality', which dealt with the question of disestablishment in a very self-contained, isolated way as a single issue 'especially fitted' to appeal to working-class voters.[4]

But during the 1885 he turned away from domestic policy issues towards those two essentially external issues which had already for some years been enlarging their significance in his political thinking—Ireland and imperialism.

[1] *The Times*, 6 June 1885, p. 12, c. 3.
[2] Cf. Garvin, *The Life of Joseph Chamberlain*, I, 1932, p. 546.
[3] *The Radical Programme*, 1885, pp. vi, 17, 20.
[4] Ibid., pp. 132-53.

11

THE RIFT WITH CHAMBERLAIN, 1885–1886

IN this new political situation, in which the great difficulty confronting the politician was to discover some insight into the ideas and aims of the working-class electorate, one fact seemed quite certain to Morley: the working men of the country were for peace and against imperialism. This conviction he based, in part, on his interpretation of the electors' verdict in 1880, when, he believed, 'depression of trade and the desire for legislative improvements were both of them secondary in the public mind' to indignation against Beaconsfield's imperial policies.[1] In 1884, speaking in support of the Reform Bill, he asked 'whether there was an audience in England that would respond so earnestly to an appeal for peace as an audience of workmen', 'labourers in the country' as well as 'the artizans in the towns'.[2] An 'unmuzzled' people would see to it that the 'phantom of a sanguinary foreign policy would vanish from their midst'.[3] By April 1885 he was suggesting anti-imperialism as the great Radical cause for the coming elections.[4] Soon the issue had become that which distinguished true from false Liberals, and Morley was placing greater importance on attention to it than on attention to Chamberlain's Radical programme. Progress on domestic reform would not be possible, he warned, so long as a Liberal government was dis-

---

[1] *F.R.*, May 1880, pp. 734–5. *P.M.G.*, 31 Dec. 1880, 4 Oct. 1882. Cf. R. Robinson, J. Gallagher, and A. Denny, *Africa and the Victorians*, 1961, p. 23. And yet in 1878 Morley had written: 'I cannot help thinking that there will soon be a great call for Gladstone: he has always been associated with prosperity, and people will begin to miss their prosperity before long, unless I am mistaken.' To Chamberlain, 16 Oct. 1878.
[2] *Hansard*, 3, 286, 1564.
[3] *The Times*, 20 Nov. 1884, p. 6, c. 3.
[4] *The Times*, 2 Apr. 1885, p. 12, c. 1.

THE RIFT WITH CHAMBERLAIN, 1885-1886   163

posed to involve the country in wars and foreign adventures: 'I am rather surprised in reading election proceedings to find that this is not more often made a point of. It is no use for us to come forward with measures for improving the lot of the poor as long as we are willing to acquiesce in and connive at these wars, the burden of which, depend upon it, falls in the last resort upon the backs of the industrious and the poor.' By this stage Morley was separating himself quite unmistakably and sharply from Chamberlain. The issue that he was now telling the voters was the most important was one that had caused a strong disagreement between the two men in February 1885; and, indeed, he now suggested to the voters that they require their representatives to pursue a policy of peace, 'even at the cost of withstanding their friends in office'. He declared that he hoped to see stronger resistance to jingoism in the new Parliament, 'if the Radicals are what I hope they will be'.[1]

But opposition to imperialism was a purely negative principle. There was nothing positive in it that could serve to concentrate and direct the actions of a reforming government once the imperialistic tendency in British policy had been halted. However, the issue of Irish home rule was looming as a far more substantial and positive preoccupation. The development of Morley's political thinking prior to 1885 had been such as to leave him unprepared for any introduction of 'the Social Question' into domestic politics, but very ready indeed for a major Irish crisis. On the problems of Ireland he had by now acquired, through his journalistic activity, a wide range of systematically developed arguments and principles; and, in particular, conviction of the wrongness of coercion had led to a conviction of the rightness of home rule.

One of the earliest suggestions that Morley was attracted to the idea of home rule for Ireland can be found in a letter of 1877, in which he wrote: 'Is it possible that by conceding some sort of Home Rule, we might be developing in the Irish a new sort of sense of responsibility? Might they not feel on their honour to send good men, and to insist on the good men behaving themselves

[1] *The Times*, 20 Oct. 1885, p. 6, c. 3; 26 Oct. 1885, p. 7, c. 4; 12 Nov. 1885, p. 10, c. 1.

with dignity and sense, if they had a sort of parliament of their own—like a State legislature?'¹ For the next few years he seems to have felt, however, that extensive measures of reform stopping short of home rule might suffice to weaken the demand for that particular reform.² It was not until the campaign against coercion that 'arguments pressed themselves forward which led much further than mere resistance to the policy of coercion', led, in fact, to the conviction that 'the whole system of governing Irel[an]d by Engl[an]d is wrong'.³

Morley came to see that, if the Irish were not going to desist from violent agitation and could not be expected to in the circumstances created by this 'system of governing Ireland by England', neither would the British be prepared to give up the use of force against such agitation. The efforts of the Irish to force their grievances on to the attention of the British Government and Parliament by what were the only really effective means available, violence and turbulent agitation, only made non-Irish opinion the more hostile to them and the readier to coerce them. '. . . the rise of angry and vindictive impatience in England and Scotland against Irish turbulence . . . is perfectly intelligible. When one nation has taken in hand the very unhopeful task of governing another, there is sure to spring up the sentiment of mastery; and if that sense of mastery is defied it is very apt to take the form of blind rage.'⁴ In the early 1880s he tried to make English opinion appreciate the deeper meaning beneath the use of force—that the basic cause of Irish unrest was not the agitation of the Land League and a few revolutionaries but social and economic grievances which the agitation merely dramatized and sought to remedy; that if the landlords were suffering legal wrongs now, the tenants had been suffering moral wrongs for generations; and that the only just course for Englishmen to pursue, in view of their responsibility for 'so evil a state of things', was to 'bear evil-doing', where it could not be struck at by vigorous application of the ordinary

¹ To Chamberlain, 10 Oct. 1877.
² *P.M.G.*, 2 Nov. 1880, 23 Aug., 29 Sept. 1881. *F,R,*. July 1881, pp. 2, 17, 20.
³ *Gladstone*, III, p. 296. To Chamberlain, 19 Dec. 1881.
⁴ *P.M.G.*, 4 June 1881. Cf. to Chamberlain, 19 Oct. 1881. *P.M.G.*, 14 Oct. 1880.

THE RIFT WITH CHAMBERLAIN, 1885-1886   165

legal processes, 'with a sensible patience', and to institute basic economic and political reforms.¹ But his efforts seemed of no avail. In 1872 he had urged Harrison to take 'the measure of the truly special circ[umstance]es of Ireland—wh. needs quite peculiar ways of dealing with it'.² This Englishmen would not do. Their attitude seemed to bear out what he had once written in explanation of English misgovernment of Ireland: 'Inability to realise states of society, of government, of opinion, of maxims of conduct that are not their own, is the common characteristic of an unimaginative people like ourselves.'³ He came to the conclusion that the English were not fitted to rule Ireland, because of their 'want of appreciation of the mind and the working of the imagination of the people of Ireland' and their inability to take into account 'the interests or customs, the peculiar objects and peculiar experiences, of the great majority' of the Irish.⁴

In October 1881 the *Pall Mall Gazette* warned that, if the Irish persisted in agitation, 'Great Britain will have to do nothing less than to frame a wholly new system of government for Ireland'. 'What a task that will be', it continued, 'can be guessed. But, however tremendous the undertaking, it will have to be faced; for it is intolerable, it is even impossible, that we can continue to carry on government in Ireland by a series of spasmodic *coups d'état*.'⁵ The development of Morley's thought towards the home-rule solution as a result of the crisis over coercion can be gauged from an article he wrote for *The Nineteenth Century* in November 1882.⁶ 'There can be very little doubt', he wrote, 'though nobody says very much about it, that in their utter weariness people in England are silently familiarising themselves with the notion that some form of autonomy will have to be devised for Ireland.' He revealed his own interest by discussing details of home rule and by urging the Irish not to abandon their plans but to develop them more

¹ *F.R.*, Apr. 1881, pp. 409-12; July 1881, pp. 6-7. *P.M.G.*, 27 Dec. 1881, 29 Mar. 1882.
² To Harrison, 21 May 1872.
³ *F.R.*, July 1868, p. 109.
⁴ *Hansard*, 3, 306, 951; 315, 1362. *Handbook of Home Rule*, p. 249.
⁵ *P.M.G.*, 17 Oct. 1881.
⁶ pp. 647-59.

thoroughly. It was possible, he wrote, that there was now no other way then home rule 'out of a position that has become intolerable and dangerous', 'that Irish society may have got into such a condition that nothing short of a violent political revolution will bring the long crisis to an end, just as nothing but a Jacobin revolution could have saved France a hundred years ago'. A few months later he wrote of the new administration of Trevelyan and Spencer: 'If they fail—if they cannot carry on without these harsh and discredited methods—it will persuade me at last that this miserable little country will be better by itself. I don't know how Ireland could be unhappier, or England more humiliated.'

'But', he added, 'all that is not yet.'[1] For the next two years he was preoccupied with the questions of imperialism and parliamentary reform. But the seed of the home-rule policy was firmly planted in his mind, ready to germinate when another crisis developed in Irish affairs. By September 1885 such a germination was beginning. Thus on 19 September he wrote to Chamberlain: 'I, for my part, cannot refuse to consider the question of some sort of autonomy.' In his speeches he now asserted that Ireland should be given 'a system of government which would meet her highest claims', such a government 'as should enable order to be restored in that unfortunate country by the hands and will of the people of that country themselves, and by their own leaders' and should utilize 'the national sentiments of Ireland and the desire of the nation to manage its own affairs in its own way'.[2]

Whereas Chamberlain and Dilke reacted to the Irish problem by placing it, along with many other policy issues, under their commodious 'umbrella' of local government reform[3] Morley, who wished to see Ireland detached from the rest of Britain, developed his Irish policy as a single great issue separate from, and requiring priority of attention over, all other questions. When in a speech on 16 September he warned that conservative elements in the

[1] To Sir E. Hamilton, 1 Feb. 1883, B.M. Add. MSS. 48619.
[2] *The Times*, 17 Sept. 1885, p. 4, c. 3; 30 Sept. 1885, p. 6, c. 2; 16 Oct. 1885, p. 7, c. 5; 24 Oct. 1885, p. 10, c. 6.
[3] Cf. *The Times*, 15 Jan. 1885, p. 7, c. 2; 4 June 1885, p. 8, c. 2; 10 June 1885, p. 10, c. 6; 18 June 1885, p. 7, c. 3; 22 July 1885, p. 11, c. 4. *The Radical Programme*, pp. 233–52. J. L. Garvin, *The Life of Joseph Chamberlain*, II, 1933, pp. 7–8.

THE RIFT WITH CHAMBERLAIN, 1885-1886

Liberal party ought to be preserved and that there was a 'source of danger' in great expectations of boons from the new Parliament, he was able to replace his emphasis on moderation and caution with descriptions of this new and definite alternative preoccupation. The Irish question, he warned, might prevent the realization of the hopes which the public were entertaining about the situation after the elections. 'I myself am very much afraid that there is not only a possibility but a probability, and I will say almost a certainty, of these hopes being dashed to the ground.' He described the construction of a new system of government for Ireland as a great post-election task for the whole nation: 'I will not believe that the political genius, the political sagacity, the inventiveness of the great English nation . . . the political faculty which has been the admiration, the wonder, and the envy of the world will fail us in fulfilling the task that is now laid upon us by every consideration of duty and every consideration of interest.'[1]

The balanced construction of Morley's speeches now assumed a somewhat different form. Thus in a speech at Cambridge at the end of September he prefaced a declaration of support for Chamberlain's programme with the observation that, 'until Parliament had made up its mind how it was going to deal with the question of the government of Ireland it was of very little avail for them to make up their minds on other questions'.[2] By October Chamberlain was speaking confidently of a split in the Liberal party over his programme and was assuming that Morley was committed to his side in this division; and yet Morley had now begun to refer to Ireland as the probable cause of any division that might occur among Liberals. On 15 October he described Irish reform as the 'first task and difficulty' for the new Parliament. Once again, before discussing Chamberlain's programme, he provided himself with a guarantee against being obliged to translate such discussion into action: 'It was of no use for any of them to flourish programmes about and promulgate manifestoes so long as that fearful problem [Ireland] remained in the way.' An appeal to Gladstone to frame a scheme for Ireland that would 'leave them in

[1] *The Times*, 17 Sept. 1885, p. 4, cc. 1-3.
[2] *The Times*, 30 Sept. 1885, p. 6, cc. 2-3.

Great Britain free to go on with their own work' was virtually a statement of withdrawal for the time being from Chamberlain's campaign.[1] A week later he spoke of the Liberal leaders as being committed 'to a great change' in Ireland, and his argument that only by effecting such a change could Britain 'recover her control over her own affairs' implied the impracticability for the time being of Chamberlain's programme.[2] One of the central points of Chamberlain's campaign was the necessity for radical reforms as a consequence of the extension of the franchise. By November Morley was even altering this into an argument for concentration on Ireland. Ireland, he said, 'would be first in the order of importance and importunity' because so many more Irishmen now had the vote. 'If they were not going to listen to the wishes and aspirations of the Irish electors they should not have given them the vote.' Thus attention was shifted from the new voters in the rest of the country, whose support Chamberlain was so anxious to secure. According to Morley, the Reform Bill was followed naturally and inevitably by concentration on Irish policy, not on social reform as Chamberlain had been insisting ever since the Bill had been passed: 'It was impossible to his mind for a democratic Chamber, such as the House of Commons would be, professing in all its discussions to appeal to the public voice, not to hear with some assent, and not to resist without great difficulty, the drift of the proposals likely to be made by the Irish members.'[3] By this time Morley was clearly assuming that Ireland would be the great issue after the elections and welcoming the prospect.

The chances of his assumption being proved correct were greatly enhanced by the nature of the election results which left the Parnellite M.P.s exactly filling the gap between Liberals and Conservatives. Chamberlain was determined to minimize the influence of the Parnellites in this situation so that they should not force the Liberals to concentrate on Irish policy to the detriment of his Radical programme; and he therefore argued that the

---

[1] *The Times*, 16 Oct. 1885, p. 7, cc. 5–6.
[2] *The Times*, 24 Oct. 1885, p. 10, c. 6.
[3] *The Times*, 12 Nov. 1885, p. 10, c. 1.

THE RIFT WITH CHAMBERLAIN, 1885-1886   169

Liberals should allow the Conservatives to remain in office, either to discredit themselves by attempting to satisfy the demands of the Irish, whose allies they had appeared to be becoming, or to present with the Liberals a united front against Irish influence. Morley at first proceeded cautiously and continued to be associated with the Radicals. Dilke records a further meeting of the 'junto' of Chamberlain, Morley, Shaw-Lefevre, and himself from 5 to 7 December.[1] To the outside world the alliance appeared intact. Thus on 9 December Reginald Brett wrote to Chamberlain expressing the hope that 'you and Morley will be content to bide your time'.[2] Four days later T. Wemyss Reid, editor of the *Leeds Mercury*, wrote to Herbert Gladstone claiming that a 'clever trap' was being laid 'by the Birmingham trio': 'I have heard on very high authority the outcome of the Chamberlain–Dilke–Morley–consultations . . . The three are resolved to prevent the formation of a Govt. by your father,—of course for their own reasons. They allege, however, that Mr. Gladstone has come to an agreement with Parnell, and that it is to prevent his carrying out a scheme which Mr. Parnell accepts that they are determined to thwart his plans.'[3]

Herbert Gladstone replied to Reid: 'My information is not extensive, but so far as it goes, it quite bears out your own, excepting however, in the case of J. M. Do you feel sure he is a consenting party?'[4] The truth was that Morley was at this time expressing strong disapproval of Dilke's public advocacy of the strategy of leaving the Conservatives in office.[5] On the 14th he told Robert Spence Watson in Newcastle that he would adhere firmly to the line 'that Gladstone and nobody else is our chief'.[6] By the 15th Wemyss Reid had realized his error and now informed Herbert Gladstone 'that Morley entirely disagrees with Dilke and

[1] S. Gwynn and G. M. Tuckwell, *The Life of the Rt. Hon. Sir Charles W. Dilke, Bart., M.P.*, II, 1917, p. 194. Cf. *Recollections*, I, p. 204.
[2] M. V. Brett (ed.), *Journals and Letters of Reginald Viscount Esher*, I, 1934, p. 118.
[3] B.M. Add. MSS. 46041, ff. 65–7.
[4] B.M. Add. MSS. 46041, f. 69.
[5] To Chamberlain, 13 Dec. 1885. Labouchere to H. Gladstone, 30 Dec. [1885], B.M. Add. MSS. 46015, f. 135.
[6] Hirst, *Early Life & Letters*, II, p. 271.

approves altogether of the situation presented' in a letter in which Herbert Gladstone had written that the Liberals could not 'calmly proceed to look on a Tory Government dealing with local government, and to ignore the 86 Irish and their action'.[1] On the same day Morley told Watson that 'much dirty intriguing is going on' and assured him that he would be no party to 'snubbing the Old Man'.[2] Wemyss Reid later claimed that Herbert Gladstone's letter of the 14th, on which the 'Hawarden Kite', Herberts' disclosure of his father's thinking on the Irish crisis, was partly founded, 'had been seen by no one but John Morley'. That Morley may have given some assurance as to his own conduct to those who were organizing the flying of the 'Kite' is suggested by the gloss put on the disclosure by Jeans, London correspondent of the *Leeds Mercury*, to the effect that Gladstone, although strong enough to carry home rule without the Radicals, had 'every reason to expect that some of the most important members of that wing will give him their cordial assistance'.[3]

The rift between Chamberlain and Morley now widened rapidly. On the 15th Chamberlain replied to Morley's complaints about Dilke's speeches with the declaration that 'in principle' Dilke was right. 'I am glad all Radicals do not share Morley's views', he wrote.[4] Morley, however, stated an objection 'to anything that looks like deliberate isolation on personal grounds, at a moment when there is no great *practical* issue that I know of, on which Radicals take a line of their own'. Nevertheless, he continued, he himself had a distinctive 'line' on the Irish question—'and I should stultify myself if I did not express it', although he would do so in such a way as 'to make it clear that I speak for nobody but myself'.[5] Thus Chamberlain and the Radicals were not to stand apart from Gladstone and the Whigs, although the purpose of Chamberlain's campaign had been to emphasize the urgent importance of

---

[1] Viscount Gladstone, *After Thirty Years*, 1929, p. 311. H. Gladstone to Reid, 14 Dec. 1885, B.M. Add. MSS. 46041, ff. 69–74.
[2] Hirst, *Early Life & Letters*, II, pp. 272–3.
[3] Reid to H. Gladstone, 17 Dec. [1885], B.M. Add. MSS. 46041, f. 76. *The Times* 18 Dec. 1885, p. 6, c. 1.
[4] To Morley, 15 Dec. 1885. Garvin, *Life of Chamberlain*, II, p. 134.
[5] To Chamberlain, 16 Dec. 1885.

distinctive Radical proposals on land and local-government reform; yet Morley himself was to take a stand independently from Chamberlain on Irish policy.

On the 21st Chamberlain wrote to Morley: 'I do not think there is the least chance of carrying a separate Parliament in the House or in the country.' But that night, in a speech at Newcastle, Morley revealed himself as committed to support of an attempt to carry such a policy. His was, in fact, the first voice among leading Liberals to be raised in approval of the new departure suggested in Herbert Gladstone's disclosure. He condemned the notion of leaving the Conservatives in office and appealed to Gladstone to prepare a large scheme of self-government for Ireland.[1] Three days later he wrote to Chamberlain explaining that, although Chamberlain might not have liked the speech, the making of it had been 'necessary to my mental peace'. Chamberlain certainly had not liked it. He wrote back accusing Morley of raising 'false hopes by vague generalities' in insisting that imperial unity could be maintained after the granting of home rule. Suggesting that he had 'foreseen for a long time that we were drifting apart', he now remarked: 'I know that I cannot convince you in this matter or change your course.' The fact now had to be faced that, on the most important issue to have arisen since Morley had entered Parliament, 'we are working against each other and not as allies'. The ending of the alliance was to him 'a bitter disappointment'; but end it must, for Chamberlain would soon have to make public his own total opposition to the policy attributed to Gladstone.

A practical man's scorn for the impracticality of a literary man now emerged in Chamberlain's attitude—a sure sign of the breaking up of the complementary relationship. 'I am sick of the vague generalities of John Morley and the *Daily News*', he wrote on the 26th, 'and I am not going to swallow separation with my eyes shut.'[2] He could see two clear alternatives, national councils and total separation; but in between lay this 'hazy idea of Home Rule visible in Morley's speech and Gladstone's assumed intention'.

---

[1] *The Times*, 22 Dec. 1885, p. 6, cc. 3-4.
[2] Garvin, *Life of Chamberlain*, II, p. 145.

Such 'vague language' was in Chamberlain's opinion 'dangerous and mischievous', because home rule would certainly lead to separation, and 'all guarantees and securities, whether for the protection of minorities or for the security of the Empire', would be found to be 'absolutely illusory'. The *Daily News* and Morley and Co.' were leading English Liberals 'to commit themselves in the dark' by their 'indefinite talk about Home Rule'.[1]

On 28 December Morley replied to Chamberlain's accusations. He explained his speech as intended to demonstrate that not all the party agreed on Irish policy with Hartington and Goschen and disagreed with Gladstone—which meant, although he did not say this, that the speech had also displayed Ireland, not Chamberlain's Radicalism, as the dividing factor in the party. He protested against Chamberlain's assumption that their political connection was at an end; but then, after all, Chamberlain had made a similar assumption at the time of the Sudan crisis, and no split had, in fact, occurred. He denied that there was any 'drifting apart': 'I should have thought that we had never worked together more cordially than during the last four months.' On the following day Morley discussed the situation with Henry Labouchere. They agreed that, since Chamberlain would 'commit political suicide' by going against Gladstone, he was most likely in the end to make 'a merit of necessity'. Morley suggested that the argument that 'he is being used by the Whigs, who, having used him, will throw him over', would have 'more influence with him, than anything else'; and he and Labouchere decided to concentrate on this kind of argument.[2]

On 1 January Morley wrote another long letter to Chamberlain urging him not to be too quick to assume 'that our difference is irreconcilable', although, if they did finally differ 'vitally on a vital question', then a severance would have to come. For a few days pleasant personal relations were resumed, but a strong pro-home rule speech by Morley at Chelmsford on the 7th put the

---

[1] Chamberlain to Dilke, 26 Dec. 1885, quoted in Gwynn and Tuckwell, *Life of Dilke*, II, pp. 199–201.
[2] Labouchere to Herbert Gladstone, 30 Dec. [1885], B. M.Add. MSS. 46015, f. 135.

fat once more in the fire. Chamberlain's reaction was very bitter. He described the speech as 'very foolish and mischievous' and showed increasing impatience with the impracticality of a man of letters. Morley, he complained, had talked ' "literary" nonsense (the worst of all) about the Empire etc.' and had not been capable of taking a practical standpoint and 'conciliating the inconsistent conditions of the problem as he states it.'[1] By the 12th Chamberlain was writing that 'John Morley is taking his own line and I look forward to a probable severance of our political relations'. His description of Morley's failings laid great stress on impracticality. Morley, lacking 'any clear idea whatsoever of a practical scheme', had used 'phrases which will be interpreted in various senses' and had raised 'hopes that he cannot fulfil'. 'Morley puts forward conditions', he wrote, 'which in practice will be found absolutely inconsistent', as there was 'no halfway house' between national councils and separation. Sooner or later Morley would have either 'to abandon the idea of Home Rule or to admit the dismemberment of the Empire.'[2] That night Lord Randolph Churchill dined with Chamberlain and found him 'very bitter against John Morley who he said was trying to run alone'. 'They were he said great friends still but would never be political friends again.'[3] Chamberlain was clearly resentful at the attempt by his 'literary' ally to 'run alone' in practical politics.

On the 13th Morley had a conversation with Chamberlain about 'our relations' and found it 'painful indeed, but made easier by simple honesty and sincerity of desire in both of us to preserve good feeling'.[4] Two days later Reginald Brett noted after meeting Chamberlain: 'His soreness in speaking of Morley was unconcealed. "We have made Morley's position", he said, "and now he goes his own way. Well, let it be understood that, though our private friendship remains untouched, in future we act no longer together. I shall make this plain on the first available

[1] Chamberlain to Dilke, 8 Jan. 1886, Chamberlain MSS.
[2] Chamberlain to J. T. Bunce, 12 Jan. 1886, Chamberlain MSS.
[3] Churchill to Lord Salisbury, 13 Jan. 1886, quoted in R. R. James, *Lord Randolph Churchill*, 1959, p. 228.
[4] *Recollections*, I, p. 210.

occasion."'[1] The climax came when on 31 January Gladstone offered Morley the post of Chief Secretary for Ireland in his new Government. Still anxious, it would seem, to work in harness with Chamberlain if at all possible, Morley asked to be given time to consult him. According to Morley, Chamberlain changed colour for an instant, but then said that Morley was now 'bound to accept' the post. Morley did so, but for a few days 'nursed the idea that I might be useful as a buffer between Chamberlain and the Prime Minister'. Dilke, now *hors de combat* on account of his involvement in a divorce scandal, wrote to Morley on 2 February: 'My *one* hope is that you will work—my hope, not for your own sake, but for the sake of Radical principles—as completely with Chamberlain as I did. It is the only way to stand against the overwhelming numbers of the Whig peers.' But it was not to be. Within a short time, Morley later claimed, Chamberlain 'practically dropped' him and henceforward acted towards him coldly and distantly.[2]

As the divergence between Morley and Chamberlain had been developing, the complementary halves of their alliance had been breaking apart. Hitherto Morley had seemed content to bow to Chamberlain's practical judgement. For example, when in August 1873 Chamberlain had resisted his arguments in favour of concentration on one issue as against a programme, he had yielded to Chamberlain's practicality: 'I have come to the conclusion that you are more likely to be right than I, because no one can know as well as you what the Education question can or cannot do among the constituencies. If you think it too weak, it no doubt is so.'[3] Yet, when in 1885 Chamberlain again advanced this kind of practical argument relating to his assessment of a policy's chances 'among the constituencies', Morley rejected it. In the 1870s Morley had not wanted to trespass on his ally's ground. He was the specula-

---

[1] Brett, *Journals and Letters of Esher*, I, p. 120.
[2] *Recollections*, I, pp. 213–16. F. E. Hamer (ed.), *The Personal Papers of Lord Rendel*, 1931, pp. 181–2. Garvin, *Life of Chamberlain*, II, p. 195. Gwynn and Tuckwell, *Life of Dilke*, II, p. 210.
[3] To Chamberlain, 22 Aug. 1873.

tive publicist, and practical politics should be left to Chamberlain.[1] As 'an academic politician at bottom', he was glad to have 'the weaknesses incident to the character' 'set right by a good friend of another type'.[2] And Chamberlain had been prepared to make allowances accordingly, as when he commented on Morley's intention to write a certain article: 'I can see that the Prophet must speak when the afflatus is on him, and I judge you & myself by very different standards.'[3]

After 1880 the relationship between the 'academic' and the 'practical' politician became increasingly one of rivalry rather than of co-operation. According to J. L. Garvin, Chamberlain had a 'straight talk' with Morley in 1884 about his tendency to take a line of his own in practical politics; and Morley wrote a letter to Chamberlain which, as Garvin rightly observes, overwhelmed 'the practical man with academic allusions'.[4] In a speech to the Eighty Club in April 1885 Chamberlain, in his anxiety perhaps to place Morley's recent independence over the Sudan crisis in the right perspective, laid great stress on his being primarily a man of letters. He referred to Morley's 'admirable Life of Burke' and suggested that regret might one day be felt 'that he had ever left the pleasant paths of literature for the thorny road of politics'.[5] When the home-rule crisis came Morley admitted that he was striking out on his own, but only, he insisted, in the realm of opinion, always considered to be his legitimate concern within the alliance. In October 1885 he said that 'if a man takes great pains to form his opinions and to gather accurate knowledge on which to base them, then he is entitled to have a mind of his own.'[6] 'I have thought, read, written about Ireland all my life', he told Chamberlain. 'Here comes a crisis. Am I to be debarred from saying what I think . . .?'[7] But Chamberlain felt that no longer was it simply a matter of Morley's having a mind of his own.

---

[1] Cf., e.g., to Chamberlain, 15 Mar. 1874.
[2] To Chamberlain, 31 Jan. 1876.
[3] 1 Apr. 1876.
[4] *Recollections*, I, p. 159. Garvin, *Life of Chamberlain*, I, pp. 519–20.
[5] *The Times*, 29 Apr. 1885, p. 10, c. 1.
[6] *The Times*, 20 Oct. 1885, p. 6, c. 3.
[7] *Recollections*, I, p. 207.

Morley was also now taking a practical course of his own that was independent of, and indeed very adversely affected, Chamberlain's own practical course. Chamberlain had once found a sense of personal completion in his association with this 'academic' politician. But now he seemed to want to remind Morley of the superiority of his own practical powers. According to Morley, Chamberlain told him bluntly: 'If you go into the Cabinet without me, you will have me against you, and I shall smash you.'[1] This was, of course, only the reverse of that extreme and rather crude literariness with which Morley had answered Chamberlain during their quarrel in 1884.

Morley had not, however, struck out entirely on his own in practical politics. In fact, it soon became apparent that he had transferred his allegiance and the services of his abilities as a man of ideas to another great practical politician, one whom he considered more reliable and a greater stabilizing influence than Chamberlain.

The importance in the new political circumstances of strong, stabilizing leadership was a theme very much in Morley's mind at this time. Thus, in December 1886 he expressed the hope that the Marquis of Hartington would not finally sever himself from the Liberal party by joining a Conservative Cabinet. Reginald Brett reported to Hartington what Morley's feelings were on this: 'it would leave the Liberal Party, and consequently the destinies of the country, in the hands of those in whom he has no confidence. He said there was no one in public life with whom he so often agreed, and under whom he would sooner serve, than yourself. "I look upon him as the strongest bulwark we have against all the strong socialist doctrine I hate,"' he said.[2] 'He contributes elements', Morley told Gladstone, 'wh. some day or other, in face of Chamberlain's proved want of wisdom and self-control, we shall sorely need.'[3]

The problem was, of course, what kind of leadership was to

---

[1] Ibid., I, pp. 211–12. Hamer, *Personal Papers of Lord Rendel*, p. 181.
[2] Brett, *Journals and Letters of Esher*, I, pp. 131–2. To Spencer, 27 Dec. 1886.
[3] To Gladstone, 27 Dec. 1886, B.M. Add. MSS. 44255, f. 159.

succeed that of Gladstone. For the time being it was on the authority of Gladstone, associated with concentration on the great cause of Irish home rule, that Morley relied for order and control in the politics of democracy. In the early 1880s, when he first wrote of how solid a bulwark the leadership of such a man as Gladstone could be against the perils and difficulties of popular government, the process which was to culminate in his abandonment of Chamberlain for Gladstone can be seen beginning. The editorial in the *Pall Mall Gazette* for 10 November 1882 is especially significant in this regard. It argued that, in place of that 'instability of popular government' which results from 'the reckless wilfulness with which masses of men, both passionate and ignorant, insist upon imposing their views upon the Ministers whom they create', there had developed in Britain an enormous reverence for and trust in Gladstone, a disposition to regard his character 'as a guarantee for the soundness of his policy', and a willingness to accept from him policies or actions which were not generally understood or even which offended his supporters, just because it was Gladstone who was responsible. In these attitudes, declared the *Pall Mall*, and 'in the forbearance which is content for a time to accept a postponement of its most cherished aspirations if their leader says it is necessary, we have a feature of English democracy which deserves to be considered as one of the best and most truly conservative forces of our time'. Indeed, 'it provides a guarantee for the stability of government and for some degree of continuity of administration for which no Constitutional arrangements can provide a substitute'.

In February 1886 Morley wrote expressing anxiety about the instability and excitability of democracy as 'abundantly shown during the last five years by a variety of unfortunate public adventures'. The 'highly increased molecular activity' which democracy sets up seemed to have weakened 'the stability of national temperament', and now there were grave fears as to whether 'firm and stable government' would continue.[1] It was with such thoughts and fears in his mind that Morley looked to the remedy defined by the *Pall Mall Gazette* in 1882. When Chamberlain

[1] *Studies in Literature*, pp. 106–8.

offered to the new voters new policies and sought to arouse and excite them with slogans strange in the English experience and of dangerous consequence in the experiences of other countries, Morley preferred that they should have that 'guarantee' of stability and continuity, the leadership of Gladstone, and counted on their once more being 'content for a time to accept a postponement of [their] most cherished aspirations if their leader says it is necessary'.

There was a very close resemblance between the ideas of Gladstone and Morley as to the form which Liberal policy should take. Gladstone was well known for his 'one idea at a time faculty', and only in concentration on a single great cause had he seemed able since at least 1867 to envisage the introduction of order into reform politics.[1] In 1885 gradually, as with Morley, anxiety about the new Radicalism became associated with the idea that Ireland might become a great preoccupying issue, might act on all other issues 'like the sun on a fire in the grate', 'shoulder aside everything else', and, by throwing 'into the background those minor points of difference about the schools and small holdings which threaten to drive the Whigs into the arms of the Tories or into retirement', 'unite us all'.[2] And when Gladstone began placing 'the reconstruction of government in Ireland' in the forefront of his programme, Morley's response was enthusiastic.[3] The composition of Gladstone's election manifesto had at first seemed 'extremely odious' to Morley, because it was 'so vague, wordy, indefinite'.[4] But the development of a commitment in Gladstone to one great cause in particular transformed the situation.

Why was it that Gladstone turned to Morley to shoulder with himself the principal responsibility for preparing and expounding the home-rule policy? The reason is to be found partly in the

[1] Cf. J. L. Hammond, *Gladstone and the Irish Nation*, 1938, p. 64. *Gladstone*, II, pp. 479, 481, 502-3.

[2] S. Childers, *The Life and Correspondence of the Right Hon. Hugh C. E. Childers*, II, 1901, p. 234. A. L. Thorold, *The Life of Henry Labouchere*, 1913, p. 239. Garvin, *Life of Chamberlain*, II, p. 113. Hirst, *Early Life & Letters*, II, p. 263.

[3] *The Times*, 5 Nov. 1885, p. 12, c. 1; 12 Nov. 1885, p. 10, c. 1; 16 Oct. 1885, p. 7, c. 5.

[4] To Chamberlain, 19 Sept. 1885.

THE RIFT WITH CHAMBERLAIN, 1885-1886   179

difficulties of Gladstone's position. At an age when most politicians have long since sought retirement, Gladstone had before him the task, first of devising a radical new departure in the constitutional arrangements of the nation, and then of having this accepted by an unprepared and divided Liberal party and an equally unprepared public opinion. For this task he was bound to value very highly the assistance of one such as Morley, who shared his own 'one idea at a time faculty' and readiness to accept total concentration on a single issue, who had 'thought, read, written about Ireland' for many years, and who had mastered the arguments in favour of home rule as well as many of the difficult and complex problems associated with the devising of a scheme. Gladstone's awareness of Morley as a man whom he could turn to and depend on in a crisis of this kind did not suddenly emerge towards the end of 1885, but had been gradually developing since at least 1880. Thus in October 1880 Morley had been close enough to Gladstone to feel justified in writing to him describing his own work in the press 'resisting the cry for coercion' and 'making public opinion about Ireland more generous, candid, and impartial', and thanking Gladstone for his approval of this.[1] Two months later Gladstone, when at a dinner party with Morley, took him aside and revealed to him the Government's coercion proposals.[2] In 1882, when resisting demands for a renewal of coercion, Gladstone complained of being 'almost alone in his view in the Cabinet';[3] but at the same time he also showed himself aware that the editor of the *Pall Mall Gazette* was a strong advocate of views similar to his own on Irish and imperial policy. In November 1880, after Morley had written to him, Gladstone had told Lord Granville that the few private communications which he had made to the press had been 'mostly to Mr. J. Morley with whose handiwork, considering his difficulties, I am a good deal struck'. In April 1881, when the Duke of Argyll declared his intention of resigning over the Irish Land Bill, Gladstone, wanting some non-official explanation to appear in the press, thought at once of the *Pall Mall Gazette*.

[1] To Gladstone, 30 Oct. 1880, B.M. Add. MSS. 44255, f. 23.
[2] Morley to Chamberlain, 31 Dec. 1880.
[3] Quoted in Viscount Gladstone, *After Thirty Years*, 1929, p. 273.

And a year later, when W. E. Forster made a statement in the Commons which gave the impression that the Government had made up its mind to renew the Coercion Act, Gladstone 'caused a word to be conveyed to the P[all] M[all] G[azette] in the sense that the impression as to Forster's meaning is quite erroneous'.[1] When the crisis of December 1885 came Morley was foremost, indeed practically alone, among prominent Liberals in declaring his approval of Gladstone's alleged intentions in Irish policy; and then, having taken this stand, he went to Gladstone and offered to write editorials for the *Daily News* 'turning' it in the direction of support for Gladstone if Gladstone would tell him 'what was in his mind'. 'He told me,' Morley later disclosed, 'and I wrote three. I was in the middle of the fourth, when a note came from the G.O.M. asking me to call. I went and he offered me the Irish Secretaryship. I was very much surprised.'[2] In fact, at this stage Morley was more advanced and more definite in his views on the home-rule policy than Gladstone himself. Letters which passed between them on 2 February 1886 in connection with Morley's appointment show that Morley was conscious of this and that Gladstone acknowledged it. Morley's letter was full of clear, firm observations on points of detail, whereas Gladstone's merely contained such statements as these: 'It would be too much to say I have a design to propose an Irish Legislative body: for I do not sufficiently see my way as to what it wd. be reasonable to recommend to the Cabinet, the Queen, & Parliament . . . my mind is quite open . . .'[3]

For Gladstone, Morley soon became much more than a political ally. He became one of Gladstone's closest friends in the remaining years of Gladstone's life. In 1888 Stuart Rendel told Morley of a visit to Gladstone at Hawarden: 'The way in which he spoke of you went to my heart. "I love John Morley" he wound up, and then again "I *love* John Morley".'[4] In 1890 Gladstone told Morley:

[1] Gladstone to Granville, 1 Nov. 1880, 5 Apr. 1881, 29 Mar. 1882, quoted in A. Ramm (ed.), *The Political Correspondence of Mr. Gladstone and Lord Granville 1876–1886*, I, Oxford, 1962, pp. 214, 252, 352.
[2] J. Saxon Mills, *Sir Edward Cook, K.B.E. A Biography*, 1921, pp. 49–50.
[3] B. M. Add. MSS. 44255, ff. 54–7.
[4] Rendel to Morley, 18 Sept. 1888, Harcourt MSS.

'It is not indeed the common lot of man to make serious additions to the friendships which so greatly help us in this pilgrimage, after seventy-six years old; but I rejoice to think that in your case it has been accomplished for me.'[1] In his diary for 8 October 1892 he called Morley 'about the best stay I have'; and a few months later he told Morley that 'you continue to be as you have been all along a prop & a main prop to me'.[2] And Morley, for his part, found a great personal satisfaction in the friendship, referring to it in later years as 'the deepest & happiest experience of his life'.[3] The significance of his transference of allegiance from Chamberlain to Gladstone can be fully understood only if this friendship is taken into account, for it too developed as the complementary kind of relationship that Morley always seemed particularly anxious to find. He was later to tell Andrew Carnegie that 'men like you and Mr. G. are of the right and only healthy sort'.[4] This meant that Gladstone seemed extroverted, a man of action and decision, free, unlike Morley, from debilitating moods of morbid, introspective meditation and from excessive self-consciousness. This was the type of character with which Morley longed to identify himself. From the very first the attraction of Gladstone to Morley was 'his simplicity' and his 'freedom from small egotism and self-consciousness'.[5] Gladstone seemed the 'purest' and 'simplest' figure of the age.[6] Morley's relationship with him developed in a tension of opposites, with Gladstone reacting against those characteristics which Morley so feared in himself and with Morley appreciating the justness of Gladstone's rebukes, but seeming unable to change his attitude. In a conversation once, when Morley produced a 'favourite proposition' that *Measure for Measure* was 'one of the most modern' of

[1] Gladstone to Morley, 30 Dec. 1890, quoted in *Gladstone*, III, p. 458.
[2] *Gladstone*, III, p. 499. Gladstone to Morley, 17 Jan. 1893, B.M. Add. MSS. 44257, f. 77.
[3] Undated memo. of conversation between Morley and Mrs. Mary Drew, Gladstone's daughter, on 19 Nov. 1920, B.M. Add. MSS. 46240, f. 138. Cf. Morley to Mrs. Catherine Gladstone, 18 May 1899, B.M. Add. MSS. 46226, f. 268. Morley to Harrison, 26 May 1898.
[4] To Carnegie, 28 Dec. 1903.
[5] To Harrison, 16 Feb. 1876.
[6] To Harrison, 26 Nov. 1888.

Shakespeare's plays because of its profound analysis of character in 'moral catastrophe' and because of 'the deep irony of our modern time in it all', he found that Gladstone did not 'care at all for this sort of criticism'. Morley then reflected that Gladstone was 'too healthy, too objective, too simple for all the complexities of morbid analysis' and that he knew 'not the very rudiment of *Weltschmerz*'.[1] On another occasion, puzzling Gladstone by another favourite saying, 'that Love of Truth is more often than we think only a fine name for Temper', he reminded himself that 'Mr. G. has a thorough dislike for anything that has a cynical or sardonic flavour about it.'[2]

Even in Gladstone's lifetime Morley was tending to idealize his character.[3] He developed an extremely protective attitude towards him, just as he had towards Chamberlain in the 1870s. He tried to shelter him from unpleasantness, to preserve his serenity, to comfort and encourage him. He would constantly assure him that his 'splendid work' would be successful and that passing clouds were only transient difficulties.[4] Sir Philip Magnus has alleged that Gladstone overvalued Morley because Morley 'tended to say smooth things to him and to give him the support and comfort which he liked', and has detected in Morley's letters to Gladstone an occasional 'sycophantic note'.[5] Perhaps it would be more accurate to say that Gladstone correctly estimated Morley's value in relation to his own needs.

[1] *Recollections*, I, p. 288. *Gladstone*, III, pp. 424–5.
[2] *Gladstone*, III, p. 472.
[3] Cf. to Harrison, 26 Nov. 1888.
[4] Cf. to Gladstone, 28 Dec. 1889, 27 Dec. 1890, B.M. Add. MSS. 44256, ff. 39, 99–100.
[5] P. Magnus, *Gladstone. A Biography*, 1954, p. 381.

12

THE HOME-RULE ISSUE

THE main concern of Morley's politics for at least the next ten years was to be the policy of home rule for Ireland, and it would therefore be worth while at this stage to summarize the systematic theory or philosophy of home rule which he himself evolved and expounded.

In the first place, he believed that the improvement of Ireland could come only through the free play of forces. 'I have faith in mankind, placed under free institutions', he wrote.[1] Out of this freedom would evolve an organic order: 'In a few years men learn to reason. The extreme violence of opinions subsides. Hostile theories correct each other, the scattered elements of truth cease to contend and begin to coalesce, and at length a system of justice and order is educed out of the chaos. That is a process which we expect and believe, in the light of the history of other nations and our own, will go on in Ireland.'[2] A 'liberal Catholicism', he argued, 'would be sure to spring up and become powerful, if a free play of forces were allowed by Home Rule, as it would be allowed.'[3] Rule by aliens stifled any such natural development. In support of home rule he quoted from Mill's *Representative Government*: 'It is an inherent condition of human affairs that no intention, however sincere, of protecting the interests of others can make it safe or salutary to tie up their own hands. Still more obviously true is it, that by their own hands only can any positive and durable improvement of their circumstances in life be worked out.'[4] Even benevolence practised by English Liberals was not an acceptable substitute. Thus when in 1890 Harcourt suggested that the Liberal party should

---

[1] To Gladstone, 8 Aug. 1889, B.M. Add. MSS. 44256, ff. 28–9.
[2] *The Times*, 29 June 1886, p. 6, c. 4.
[3] To Gladstone, 30 Aug. 1889, B.M. Add. MSS. 44256, f. 35.
[4] *Handbook of Home Rule*, pp. 250–1.

confine itself for the time being to seeking an Irish policy 'conformable to that which a properly constituted and wisely conducted Home Rule Parliament would secure for Ireland', and firmly founded 'upon really Liberal principles of Irish administration and legislation', Morley pointed out that these two aspects were irreconcilable. 'I'll be hanged if I know', he wrote, 'what really Liberal principles of Irish legislation and administration are.' For, whereas in England to be a Liberal was to oppose denominational education, such an attitude could scarcely be applied in the very different conditions of Ireland. 'English Liberals', unlike an Irish home-rule Parliament, would not 'take a stand in favour of endowing Catholic colleges'.[1]

Secondly, he maintained that it was not possible to achieve a stable settlement by limiting the scope of free institutions to that of local government, the 'autonomy of gas and sewage'.[2] Ireland needed strong central government. Local-government reform on its own would only make the governmental system 'a hundred times weaker' by having popularly elected local bodies dominated by the nationalists, but still controlled by an alien central executive which the nationalists would spend most of their time opposing and harassing.[3] Thirdly, he insisted that the establishment of a home-rule Government was essential for any satisfactory settlement of Ireland's social and economic problems. Ireland could not be improved without certain drastic social changes, such as the transference of population from congested areas, which would be very upsetting and unpopular. Only an Irish Government, elected by and responsible to the Irish people, would have sufficient authority for the carrying through of such changes. Here was exemplified 'the impotence of England to do for Ireland the good which Ireland might do for herself'. Any plan to displace population from the west coast of Ireland would be practicable only 'if carried out by an Irish authority, backed by the solid weight of Irish opinion', for 'any exertion of compulsory power by a British Minister would raise the whole countryside in squalid insurrection,

[1] Harcourt to Morley, 23 Dec. 1890. Morley to Harcourt, 26 Dec. 1890.
[2] *The Times*, 9 June 1886, p. 6, c. 4.
[3] *Hansard*, 4, 55, 502–7. *The Times*, 8 Jan. 1886, p. 6, c. 2; 12 July 1886, p. 8, c. 2; 1 Oct. 1888, p. 10, c. 3.

government would become impossible, and the work of transplantation would end in ghastly failure'. There was thus a fundamental 'relation between self-government and agrarian discontent, misery, and backwardness'. The congested districts needed twenty-five to fifty years of 'skilful, patient, vigilant, persistent attention', which only those could give who enjoyed 'the confidence of the Irish people' and 'whose whole character, interest, and reputation are bound up in bringing about an improvement'.[1] Similar arguments applied to land purchase. He warned that 'no scheme will be workable or safe which is not backed by local authorities, who, in turn, are backed by a central Government resting upon the public opinion of the country'. Morley believed the conversion of tenants into owners to be 'indispensable'. But this could be accomplished only if the purchaser's annuity were very low, and 'you cannot make the annuity low, unless you have the advantage of British credit', which 'is only safe on condition of a large political settlement'. This was because 'an Irish Parliament, or Irish central authority, could alone compel fulfilment of obligation'. Home rule was 'a means of interposing between the Irish tenant and the British State an authority interested enough and strong enough to cause the bargain to be kept'. It would be wrong, he argued, to make the Irish peasantry stand 'directly face to face with the British State', for, if a tenant defaulted in such a situation, it would be 'utter folly and infatuation for the British Government to attempt to enforce the remedies'; 'only a native Government and a national Government, with all the force of Irish opinion behind it', could 'secure a strict enforcement of the law'. This problem of compelling fulfilment of obligation was at the root of the matter, for he dreaded the prospect of continual renewals of coercion by the British Government in order to make a rebellious Irish peasantry pay its debts. 'One of the great arguments for H.R.', he wrote, 'is that without a strong Irish govt., every pound advanced or guaranteed for the operation of purchase, is an extra nail in the coffin of amicable connexions between Engl[an]d & Irel[an]d.'[2]

[1] *Handbook of Home Rule*, pp. 257–8. *Hansard*, 3, 343, 1938.
[2] To Spencer, 30 Oct. 1888, 17 Jan. 1890. J. L. Garvin, *The Life of Joseph Chamberlain*, II, 1933, p. 286. *Hansard*, 3, 310, 910–11; 343, 1935–6. *Handbook of Home Rule*, p. 258. *The Times*, 26 Nov. 1887, p. 7, c. 3.

Fourthly, home rule would detach Irish domestic politics from the British political system; and this had come to seem a very desirable objective. Only thus could Ireland's very distinctive problems and conditions be taken fully into account on their own merits in policy-making. Morley would argue that England, Scotland, and Wales, 'which are healthy and normal', needed different institutions and different treatment from Ireland, 'which is in a very peculiar and abnormal state'.[1] But it was difficult, so long as Ireland remained within a unified British political system, to prevent the special ways of dealing with this 'peculiar' state from being seen, and very often feared and opposed, as precedents for the rest of the United Kingdom. On one occasion Morley tried to explain to the Commons that, while there was great social distress in England, too, 'these miseries are not due, as far as I know, to causes which the Legislature could, and admits that it ought to, prevent'. What 'constitutes the peculiarity of Irish wrongs and Irish grievances' is 'that you have there a gross moral wrong'.[2] We shall see how in Newcastle Morley came under strong pressure from local socialists 'to lift up your voice in favour of the working men of this country as you have done for Ireland'. Ireland appeared to be introducing dangerous distractions and cross-currents into British politics.

Related to this was the objection that stable, continuous government of Ireland was rendered impossible by the way in which Irish problems and issues were caught up in non-Irish politics. Decisions on them were too often made not on the merits but 'with reference to the accidents of party antagonism at home'. The English did not look at 'the facts of Irish society as they are in themselves', but judged Irish questions through the medium of party calculation and class and religious prejudice. In conducting the government of Ireland politicians elected by and responsible to a non-Irish electorate naturally tended to 'look over the heads of the people of Ireland, and to consider mainly what will be thought by the ignorant public in England'.[3] Thus in 1898 Morley

---

[1] *The Times*, 21 June 1886, p. 7, cc. 4–5.
[2] *Hansard*, 3, 316, 327.
[3] *F.R.*, Jan. 1882, pp. 126–7; Feb. 1882, p. 269. *Handbook of Home Rule*, p. 252.

was to attribute the Unionist Cabinet's refusal to act further on the question of a Catholic University to the opposition of the party whips and leading politicians such as Chamberlain who had an eye to 'elections, and the divisions that the project would be likely to set up in the constituencies'. 'So there is one proof more', he was to say, 'how unfit is England to govern Ireland.'[1] Furthermore, British government of Ireland lacked continuity, coherence, and stability because of the frequent changes of government in London and of the changes of policy both as a result of this and as a result of movements of opinion within the non-Irish parties. Ireland was 'the shuttlecock of English parties', whose vacillating policies—'a chaos of alternate hesitancies and precipitancies, of desperate expedients and dilapidated prophecies'—fatally weakened Irish government.[2] Irish disrespect for the law was, Morley argued, scarcely to be wondered at when the question of whether coercive legislation 'is to be operative or not, whether it is to be called into life or left dormant and dead, is dependent on the political changes at Westminster'. He therefore advocated home rule as the means of withdrawing Irish government from 'the ebb and flow of Party victories in Great Britain'.[3]

Another aspect of the situation which he deplored was the way in which Ireland was used as the 'cockpit in which English factions choose to fight out their battles'. It seemed to him that 'unfortunate Ireland' was 'only too well fitted, too exactly fitted, to be the cockpit' for the struggles of the non-Irish parties. Orators delighted in using Irish issues for the display of 'all the grand common-places of their art', such as ' "Law and order" on the one side, "Reconciliation of the people" and "Freedom of a nation" on the other'. He made this attack on those who used the Irish question as a distraction and diversion: 'the man who hates change in England, the man who distrusts the look of present things and dreads the future, the man whose great object is to stem the democratic tide and to save his cherished inequalities and

---

[1] To Harcourt, 18, 24 Nov. 1898.
[2] *Cobden*, I, p. 360. *Hansard*, 3, 304, 1274.
[3] *Hansard*, 4, 23, 784–5; 11, 652.

privileges, delights with his whole heart in keeping as long as he can, and for ever if he can, the two great political hosts of this country eternally clashing in the Irish ditch.'[1]

And yet Morley himself was to be one of those who consciously and even with considerable relief and enthusiasm contributed to the choosing of Ireland as the arena for the conflict of parties in this period. His voice was among the loudest in insisting that Ireland be established as *the* dividing factor in party politics, *the* great issue of political controversy and debate. A typical utterance was this declaration in 1889: 'From this moment henceforth there is only one distinction among politicians in England, and that is, the distinction between Coercionists and Anti-Coercionists. I accept at present no other distinction.'[2] For the home-rule policy assumed a significance wider than that of being a solution of the Irish problem; it became also a great cause to preoccupy the Liberal party and the electorate of England, Scotland, and Wales, and as such it came to possess totally different characteristics which account for a striking ambiguity in Morley's presentation and utilization of it. Morley, and many other prominent Liberals, seemed to regard the preoccupation of the electorate and of the political parties with Irish policy after 1885 as by no means an unwelcome development. In Morley's case at least the explanation for this can be found in the way in which the Irish question now acquired, in his political thinking and practice, those characteristics which he had previously hoped to see develop in single great issues of domestic politics.

In December 1885 the crucial problem was the interpretation of the results of the general election. There had really been three separate verdicts in the election: from the boroughs, a clear swing to the Conservatives; from the counties, an unmistakable pronouncement by the new voters in favour of Chamberlain's programme; and from Ireland, strong approval of the home-rule objectives of Parnell and his party. Morley proceeded now to claim that the great result of the election was the verdict of the

[1] *Hansard*, 4, 16, 1838. *The Times*, 22 Sept. 1891, p. 5, c. 4.
[2] *The Times*, 14 Feb. 1889, p. 6, c. 2.

Irish for home rule and to minimize the significance of the changes in the rest of the country, where it was obvious that, in so far as the Liberals had made gains, Chamberlain was entitled to a great deal of the credit. One of the main difficulties for Liberal thinkers in this period was to decide how the principle of 'the greatest happiness of the greatest number' related to the expression of the opinion of 'the greatest number' through the mechanisms of parliamentary democracy. Chamberlain himself had, in fact, made frequent reference to the principle on connection with his campaign in 1885.[1] His agrarian programme had produced a striking manifestation of popular opinion in the counties. But, as Labouchere observed, there had not been any 'urban cow', any effective counterpart of 'three acres and a cow' in the towns and cities. Even Chamberlain seemed unable to think of anything more exciting for the urban masses than disestablishment and educational reform. In September 1885 Morley had said to Hartington about Chamberlain's policy of 'Free Schools': 'What else have we to offer to the towns?'[2] But this period was seeing the rapid growth of the influence of socialism over British political thinking. The politics of 'the greatest number' and 'the people's wants' were entering on uncertain and perhaps dangerous ground. In Ireland, however, the greatest number had delivered a clear verdict, and one that involved nationalism and the aspiration towards self-government. For Liberals such as Morley and Gladstone this was firm and well-tested ground. Concentration on the Irish situation, furthermore, meant that they could appear to be accepting a democratic verdict while they were, in fact, continuing to evade the implications of democracy in the greater part of the United Kingdom.

In his speeches Morley now ignored the results of the elections everywhere except in Ireland, although the verdict of the newly enfranchised agricultural labourers had been as clear and decisive as that of the Irish. Thus on 21 December 1885 he referred exclusively to the Irish results. If the Irish wanted self-government, as they said that they did, then they should be given it. 'Is the

[1] Cf. Garvin, *Life of Chamberlain*, I, pp. 384, 550; II, p. 123.
[2] To Chamberlain, 3 Sept. 1885.

enormous and imposing majority that Mr. Parnell has obtained in Ireland to count for nothing? If it is to count for nothing, what becomes of our theories of representative government?' It would now be disastrous, he argued, to disappoint the Irish after their hopes had been raised so high. At first he tried to claim that the election campaign even in England had been mainly about Ireland. Had not Gladstone 'from first to last' placed the Irish question 'in the most prominent place' in his speeches? 'The question was raised, the issue was stated, and the attitude of the party was described again and again, and in speech after speech, by Mr. Gladstone in Mid Lothian.' If some Liberals had not appreciated this, there had been a misunderstanding on their part. Gladstone had invited people to vote Liberal so that the party could settle the Irish problem, and to that work it would therefore now turn.[1] But Morley soon abandoned this argument, knowing full well, as he was later to admit in his *Life of Gladstone*, that during the elections 'there was nothing like general concentration on the Irish prospect' and that most 'British electors were thinking mainly of promised agrarian boons, fair trade, the church in danger, or some other of their own domestic affairs'.[2] By early January 1886 he was denouncing 'this moonshine about a mandate' and declaring that 330 Liberal M.P.s could not be expected to sit still and do nothing, 'as though they had never heard of the Irish question before in all their lives', because they had no 'mandate' on it. 'We have got a mandate', he argued, 'and I know of no other'—although Chamberlain at this time was insisting that several distinct promises emanating from his own section had alone saved the party from electoral disaster. The mandate was simply that they should apply liberal principles to 'any emergency that may arise'. He then reverted to his claim that the great consequence of the elections had been the return of eighty-six Parnellite M.P.s. He condemned the 'kind of legerdemain that I think induces some of our friends and all our opponents to reduce to nothing the importance' and 'to whittle away the meaning of that great demonstration of Irish opinion'. It now appeared from his

---

[1] *The Times*, 22 Dec. 1885, p. 6, cc. 3-4.
[2] *Gladstone*, III, p. 232.

arguments that in any event the elections had been futile everywhere except in Ireland, since he alleged that only Irish home rule could restore to the House of Commons 'the power of being able to carry out the will and wishes of those who elect its members'. This meant that the complexities of English politics could be ignored entirely: 'It is no use for us in Essex or in Northumberland and Durham to return a majority to Parliament, for that majority finds itself powerless.' In other words, if there was any meaning in the votes of the English democracy, he was absolving himself for the time being from the duty of finding out what it was and of facing up to its implications.[1]

More and more he tended to look back before the elections to the Reform Act itself and to claim that concentration on the policy of home rule for Ireland was a natural sequel to that measure and a perfect expression of its true spirit and meaning. Chamberlain had said that the Reform Bill had been passed under pressure from the people because they looked for social reforms from a reformed Parliament. But Morley now associated the extension of the franchise with the issue of justice for Ireland. Home rule, he claimed, was the type of reform for which the Reform Bill had been passed. Indeed, Chamberlain's very arguments about the consequences of extending the franchise were produced in support of this claim. In 1888 Morley referred to Chamberlain as having gone 'up and down the country saying eloquent things about natural rights, about people who did not toil nor spin', and about 'ransom', and then, 'when a few Irish peasants took the lesson to heart', 'turned round and said they were anarchists and robbers'.[2] In February 1886 he spoke thus in his constituency about the new Parliament; 'Here, for the first time, was the voice of the English democracy able to make itself heard. Was it to be endured and was it to be thought of that the first message from the English democracy to their fellow subjects in Ireland was to be the old sanguinary impotent message [of coercion]?' Is it credible, he went on, 'that this great city of Newcastle, which has before now, for

[1] *The Times*, 8 Jan. 1886, p. 6, c. 1.
[2] *The Times*, 1 Oct. 1888, p. 10, c. 1.

30 or 40 years, so often lifted up its voice on behalf of justice and freedom, is going to say now that Ireland shall be plunged into this system?'[1]

The politics of home rule were the politics of democracy. 'It is hopeless', he said, 'for a country like our own and a Government like our own, resting upon a popular basis, and appealing in every hour of its existence to popular principles . . . to attempt to treat the Irish vote as given in the last election in Ireland as if it were of no matter and no account.'[2] It would be wrong to continue to govern Ireland 'in disregard of all the sentiments and wishes of the majority of those who live in it'.[3] As for the wishes of the majority of those who lived in England, his interpretation was of this kind: 'I reflect that the franchise has now been given to the working people of England, and they, with their plain, simple, and honest ideas, have now got power in their own hands. If anybody tells me they will assent to the proposition that one of the three kingdoms is to be perpetually governed by this exceptional law, I think he is desperately mistaken.'[4] By 1892 he was even claiming that the new democracy had turned to the Irish question in 1886 of its own accord and choice. It was 'a striking thing and a most encouraging thing', he then said, 'for those who look at the hearts and motives of voters' 'to think that the first great cause to which the British democracy put its hand after getting the vote', the 'cause which first won [its] hearts and obtained [its] thorough support', was 'an unselfish cause, the cause of Ireland', 'in which the British democracy for itself might seem to have so little to gain'.[5]

It was, of course, absurd to suggest that there had been any voluntary turning to preoccupation with Ireland by the new electorate or by a majority of its representatives in 1886. It seemed as if Morley had grown so accustomed by 1892 to emphasizing the significance of the demands of the new Irish voters that they

---

[1] *The Times*, 9 Feb. 1886, p. 7, c. 3.
[2] *The Times*, 22 Apr. 1886, p. 6, c. 3.
[3] *The Times*, 1 May 1886, p. 9, c. 2.
[4] *The Times*, 30 Oct. 1889, p. 6, c. 5.
[5] *The Times*, 5 May 1892, p. 6, c. 3; 6 July 1892, p. 11, c. 5.

had come to represent for him the whole of the British democracy. But his remarks on the nature of the concentration on Irish policy do show us very clearly what made him welcome it in the political circumstances of the time. It was, he said, 'an unselfish cause', an issue in which the new voters had 'so little to gain'. In other words, it had nothing to do with class interests, with 'socialism' and the extortion of 'ransom' from one class by another. Instead, it unified the nation by focusing its attention on an issue outside its own class divisions. Morley was later to admit that he had believed that no division of political parties along class lines could possibly 'follow upon a difference of opinion as to what was the best form of government for Ireland'.[1] This was why he now became so insistent that 'H.R. remains & must remain the dividing line'.[2] The differences between the parties had seemed to be growing blurred in 1885, with Churchill's 'Tory Democracy' suggesting the possibility of an accelerating competition in social reform promises for the working class. But now Morley and others could find in the Irish controversy a means of re-establishing a firm distinction between the parties with the Tories once more depictable as wicked enemies of the people. Thus in a speech in November 1886, when condemning the 'Tory programme of reform' and trying to expose its alleged insincerity, he evidently began to feel himself to be on unfirm ground, for he soon terminated this part of his speech with this remark: 'There is one subject at any rate upon which I feel that there will be a gulf profound as the Serbonian Bog between us and the Government . . . Ireland.'[3] On another occasion he found in condemnation of the 'pure, unadulterated Toryism' of the Irish policy of Balfour a way of diverting attention from the confusion in domestic policy: 'They may bring in what Bills they like for England and Scotland, but Ireland they are governing as the darkest and blackest old Tories would have governed it. The Tory party is going down the incline.' 'Can it be said', he than asked concerning coercion, 'that this does away with the necessity for the

---

[1] *The Times*, 5 Feb. 1896, p. 7, c. 1.
[2] To Haldane, 29 Jan. 1888, Haldane MSS. 5903, f. 77.
[3] *The Times*, 4 Nov. 1886, p. 6, c. 6.

Liberal party?' The Irish policy was proof, he would say, of 'the wickedness of Toryism'.[1]

We must turn next to examine what significance Morley saw the concentration on the home-rule policy as having for the development of the Liberal party.

[1] *The Times*, 21 Apr. 1888, p. 12, c. 2; 8 Oct. 1890, p. 4, c. 5.

13
THE LIBERAL PARTY AND THE HOME-RULE PREOCCUPATION

A REMARKABLE feature of Morley's speeches after December 1885 is the absence of any strong note of indignation or regret concerning the emergence of the Irish obstacle to the realization of Chamberlain's radical aims. He had been unable to accept Chamberlain's programme of radical reforms as a sound and safe vehicle for political action. In 1882 he had written that the lack of a 'body of systematic political thought at work in our own day' was most unfortunate because 'the perplexities of to-day are as embarrassing as any in our history, and they may prove even more dangerous'.[1] By 1886 this lack had still not been made good, and Morley significantly referred to it again in a review of Sir Henry Maine's *Popular Government* in February 1886. The work of government had now, he observed, to be carried on under new parliamentary conditions; but, 'in meeting this prospect, we have the aid neither of strong and systematic political schools, nor powerful and coherent political parties'. In democratic politics a disturbing tendency to disorganization was becoming apparent. Democracy seemed too unstable and fluid, too easily swayed and excited; the great problem in connection with it was the achievement of 'firm and stable government'.[2]

In this situation concentration on a single great issue, such as home rule, seemed to offer the best chance of firmness and coherence in politics. Because political principles were still not sufficiently organized and systematized to provide a firm basis for a programme of reforms, only concentration on a single issue —which, as we have seen, was for Morley a substitute for possession of a system—could provide coherence and a 'spirit of system'.

---
[1] *Studies in Literature*, pp. 346–7. F.R., Oct. 1882, pp. 520–1.
[2] *Studies in Literature*, pp. 106–7.

At this time Morley was especially outspoken in his condemnation of 'programme' politics. For example, in November 1886 he pointed out that the National Liberal Federation had turned away from that kind of politics which consisted of attempts to 'break out of hand and develop all kinds of monstrous and intolerable articles and political programmes'. The Liberals of the N.L.F. were 'reasonable, prudent, moderate, sober' men, he said, who had no 'chimerical schemes' in their programme and 'no single new article' except the dominant one of home rule.[1] Two years later he wrote that he still doubted 'whether time is ripe for new party programmes'. The party should concentrate on demonstrating the quality of its Liberalism 'from time to time on given measures or proposals', and for the time being 'H.R. remains & must remain the dividing line'.[2] In a speech in December 1889, referring to 'constant talk of a programme', he recalled how Bright used to say 'that he distrusted programmes' and 'that long programmes were like the 39 Articles, which had a good deal more articles than religion'. Reform, he argued, was much better if accomplished as one 'single right thing' at a time, for, 'however moderate be its area, every single right thing is sure to lead to the doing of a great number of unforeseen right things'.[3]

Morley was conscious of his own age as being one of great confusion and instability in thinking on institutions and property. In *On Compromise* he had written of how, in an age of transition in the bases of thought, the 'work of destruction' was 'done impalpably, indirectly, almost silently and as if by unseen hands' and filled those 'who dwell in the tower of ancient faiths' with 'constant apprehension' and 'misgiving'.[4] Now, in the political sphere, the emphasis was again on the unseen, uncomprehended nature of the changes. He would speak of a 'feeling that the country is engaged in a process of transformation the full scope and purport of which few of us can yet pretend to realize', and would write of how 'considerable changes' were, 'quietly and un-

---

[1] *The Times*, 4 Nov. 1886, p. 6, c. 6.
[2] To Haldane, 29 Jan. 1888, Haldane MSS. 5903, f. 77.
[3] *The Times*, 10 Dec. 1889, p. 6, c. 6.
[4] pp. 36–7. *F.R.*, Apr. 1874, p. 437.

seen, overtaking the parliamentary systems'.[1] In the great political issues that were now emerging into prominence, particularly those which concerned the role of the State in regard to social welfare and the regulation of the economy, Liberals such as Morley felt insecure and full of 'constant apprehension'. Morley was to show himself to be perpetually afraid of hidden hazards and dangerous complexities. He often referred to the great difficulties that would be involved in State intervention in these areas: 'You must know where you are going. You must look all round. You must try and gauge a measure, and every effect of what is proposed.'[2] It was obvious that Chamberlain had failed to convince Morley that he knew where he was going. Now, of such proposals as the Eight Hours Bill he would say: 'When they were steering their way through those tortuous and obscure economic currents it was well to go slow and not fast, or else they would find that while they had been going ahead rapidly they had run the great ship of State upon a most dangerous sandbank.'[3] The home-rule preoccupation, as we shall see, had the great merit from this point of view of forcing politicians to 'go slow' whether they wanted to or not.

The confusion of which Liberals were conscious was not merely external. Within the party there remained a great variety of competing sections and 'fads', interests and pressures, each demanding priority of attention, each regarded by its adherents as constituting the truest expression of liberalism.[4] The great Irish policy came to provide a bulwark against this internal confusion as well. Morley and others were able to use it to supply a simple, clear-cut definition of Liberalism. Its particular advantage for this purpose was that it was an external issue not sponsored by any of the groups within the party and therefore did not offend against the claims by each of these groups to represent a truer, more important

[1] *The Times*, 5 Apr. 1888, p. 7, c. 1. F. W. Hirst, *In the Golden Days*, 1947, p. 160.
[2] *The Times*, 3 Dec. 1895, p. 6, c. 3.
[3] *The Times*, 5 Feb. 1896, p. 7, c. 2.
[4] Cf. the 1888 report of the Council of the N.L.F., quoted in R. S. Watson, *The National Liberal Federation*, 1907, pp. 101–2. Cf. also M. Ostrogorski, *Democracy and the Organization of Political Parties*, I, 1902, p. 315.

application of liberal principles than any other group. Morley's remark that, should the party 'cease to be faithful to its own convictions and stanch to its own professions', it would be destroyed raised again the great problem of defining exactly what these were. But Morley was now able to offer a simple test: 'on the great question that is now before the country the Liberal party . . . is stanch to those principles and faithful to its convictions'.[1] The home-rule policy was referred to by him as proof that 'Liberalism is no empty word' but 'a living principle' and 'a living faith', still expressing 'the highest hopes, aspirations, and convictions of mankind'. Here was the test of true Liberalism: 'Liberals who are not in earnest in this great reform in the government of Ireland, depend upon it, are not very much in earnest about the other reforms either. . . . What would Liberalism be worth, what Liberal would be worth his salt if he sat down and folded his arms in perfect contentment under a system of permanent coercion for Ireland?'[2] Thus adherence to this one policy was made to serve as a token of commitment of a Liberal kind on 'the other reforms'.

It will be noted how often the definition involved a reference back to previous struggles. By the end of 1885 Liberals seemed no longer to have a clear, agreed understanding as to what made them all Liberals or what they ought to be doing together in politics. However, Morley saw in the Irish issue a means of reawakening feelings which had inspired Liberals in common causes in the past.[3] After so many years of confusion Liberals were now told that an Irish settlement was their 'first duty'[4] and that they could carry out this duty in the manner in which the great Liberal reforms of the past had been achieved. Morley helped to draw their minds away from the confusion and danger of the present and future to the certain triumphs of the past. In advocating home rule he himself believed that he was discerning 'the lines of the future', appreciating 'the forces at work in modern politics' so as 'to

[1] *The Times*, 4 Nov. 1886, pp. 6–7.
[2] *The Times*, 7 Nov. 1889, p. 10, c. 4; 30 Jan. 1890, p. 7, c. 1; 5 May 1892, p. 6, c. 3.
[3] For examples, cf. *Hansard*, 3, 308, 344, and *The Times*, 8 Jan. 1886, p. 6, c. 1.
[4] *The Times*, 1 Dec. 1886, p. 7, c. 3.

foresee the path along which we shall move'.[1] But, in so far as the concentration on home rule was the product of a turning away from trying to discern the 'forces at work' in the 'modern politics' of the *whole* British democracy, we can see why there was this backward-looking aspect to it as a policy for the preoccupation of the country. The kind of emotion which Morley sought to arouse in his promotion of it can be gauged from his commendation of it as based on 'considerations of sobriety, of reason, and of justice, as fully as any change that any of the forefathers of our constitution worked for and fought for', and from these arguments against stopping short of home rule: 'It was not in this way that our forefathers made constitutional reform. Our forefathers did not say, Let us constitute a limited Monarchy. What they said was, in very plain English, "Let us prevent the King from taking our money.". . .'[2]

'Depend upon it,' he would insist, 'we are fighting the old battle of oppression on the one side and freedom on the other';[3] and his rhetoric would be concentrated on arousing emotions appropriate to this theme. Of coercion he declared: 'this is the kind of Government against which our fathers rose, which they would not endure, and in consequence of which . . . it was that that movement for the Reform Bill of 1832 received its strongest, its most powerful impetus.' In 1891 he said to an audience of working men that it was 'the same battle now against democracy', the coercionists being those 'who used to say that you, all of you, and all your fellow-workers in the villages, were unfit to have the franchise'.[4] Thus the Irish policy gave Liberalism a *raison d'être* by reviving, concentrating, and focalizing in itself the incidents and emotions of great struggles in which Liberalism had triumphed in the past. The Liberals, not knowing how to fight the battles of the present and future, such as those to which Chamberlain had pointed the way, were to fight the battles of the past over again instead. In 1873 Morley had written: 'True statesmanship lies in

---

[1] *Handbook of Home Rule*, p. 261.
[2] *The Times*, 5 Apr. 1888, p. 7, c. 1; 30 Oct. 1889, p. 7, c. 1.
[3] *The Times*, 7 Nov. 1889, p. 10, c. 4.
[4] *The Times*, 8 Oct. 1890, p. 4, c. 5; 14 Jan. 1891, p. 10, c. 3.

right discernment of the progressive forces of a given society, in strenuous development of them, and in courageous reliance upon them.'[1] Now his own statesmanship consisted only in discerning, developing, and relying upon what had been the progressive impulses and forces in England in the past.

The Irish policy, as advocated and presented by Morley, offered to the Liberal party other lines of solution to problems that had long beset it. For example, it enforced within the party and in the nation what Bagehot had termed a 'polity of discussion'. The argument, employed by Morley and numerous other Liberals after 1885, that Ireland constituted a great obstruction and that nothing could be done in the area of domestic reform until after it had been removed by the concession of home rule, served to effect a divorce between discussion and action in domestic policy, to stave off the necessity for decision, and to keep the sectional reform interests in order by assuring them that commitment to action on their behalf was as yet impossible because of this obstruction.

In 1877 Goldwin Smith had written in the *Fortnightly Review* of 'misgivings in Liberal breasts' at 'the restless and resistless might of the main current which is sweeping away with unprecedented and ever-increasing rapidity all the dams and barriers of the past'. There was, he asserted, cause for great anxiety about the urgency with which 'the great problems of the future' were thronging 'upon us, and the failure of all provisional arrangements to stave off the necessity of solving them'.[2] In the great Irish obstruction was to appear a new 'dam and barrier' and just such a 'provisional arrangement' as Smith described. Morley found that it enabled him to continue, as in 1885, to associate discussion of, and expressions of enthusiasm for, domestic reform with the proviso that unfortunately no action was yet possible on it. For example, here is his reply in 1887 to a demand by Chamberlain that the Liberals 'sink the Irish question' and 'get on with religious equality, local boards, and so forth'; 'We would like nothing better than to get

---

[1] *National Education*, p. 71. F.R., Sept. 1873, p. 314.
[2] F.R., July 1877, pp. 4–5.

on with these great questions. But . . . the position of Ireland will not let us come to deal with our own affairs. . . . Disestablishment and liquor reform and free schools we are all in favour of, and when we have rid ourselves of the Irish question we shall devote ourselves to these great and important issues. Nobody is more for that than I am. . . .' A few years later he asked an audience not to believe that Ireland 'is the only question that interests the Liberal party'. 'Far from that.' There were labour questions, for instance; but they knew very well that the next election 'will not turn upon these questions, but will turn, and must turn, and'—he admitted significantly in view of his own difficulties at Newcastle with regard to labour questions—'I for one am not sorry that it must turn upon the government of Ireland'. At times, in election campaigns particularly, even discussion was prevented if it might appear to be a prelude to action. In 1892 he told an audience that he would have liked to discuss with them 'some of the many questions that more directly come home to English audiences': 'I should have liked to argue them with you. . . . But, gentlemen—and this is the text of the sermon I am preaching to you to-night—Parliament will never be able to tackle these great questions until . . . you have left Irishmen free to do their own business in their own country.'[1]

Presented in this way, the Irish problem enabled Morley to preserve a faith in progress, even though he himself could not now see how or where to advance, because it represented the concept of history as progress with interruptions and obstructions. By arguing that Ireland obstructed progress and action on all other questions, he could cast off the burden of confusion and indecision and find in the Irish question the scapegoat for lack of progress in domestic reform. Morley spoke of how in 1880 Liberals had been hoping to carry through many reforms. 'The locomotive and the train were waiting and the line seemed clear, but the Irish pointsman shunted the train on to a siding from which they had not yet extricated themselves, and from which they would not extricate themselves unless they accepted the policy which he pressed upon

[1] *The Times*, 3 Oct. 1887, p. 8, c. 2; 8 Oct. 1890, p. 4, c. 3; 31 Mar. 1892, p. 10, c. 4.

them.'[1] This suggested that progress remained certain and that the cause of the breakdown was external and mechanical, not the subjective factors of fear, indecision, and doubt in Liberal politics.

The value of the Irish obstruction for many Liberals lay in the fact that, unlike indecision, it could be made to appear as an obstruction for which they themselves were not responsible. Thus Morley rejected Chamberlain's allegation that the home-rule policy has been 'sprung upon' the country as a device for ensuring the shelving of all other questions. 'I think', he said, 'Home Rule came upon us by reason of circumstances, events, and conjunctures which no statesman could have avoided, and that has been plain to everybody who has closely watched politics since 1880.'[2] He was able to attribute to the Irish obstruction a state of affairs in which, after all the effort and trouble of securing Reform Acts, they still found themselves 'impotent to bring up any of those arrears of legislation' which they had 'so long been deploring'.[3]

Another feature of the great Irish policy was the way in which it acted as a substitute for system. Morley presented it as all-embracing, 'not only the cause of Ireland' but 'the cause of justice, the cause of improvement, the cause of progress, and the cause of advance in our own island as well'.[4] It imposed order on politics by subordinating all other questions to itself. On one occasion Morley asked: 'While we are talking about Ireland, are there no English and Scottish questions waiting?' The audience cheered, whereupon Morley drew this conclusion: 'you have to ask yourselves as sensible men whether you are going to persist in a system of government in Ireland . . . which has robbed and which is now robbing you of the control over your own affairs and questions'.[5] Thus all issues in British politics were made to appear bound up with and dependent on this single question. It offered a solution to the problem of fixing priority of attention for reform questions. It imposed a temporary order on the multitude of

---

[1] *The Times*, 25 June 1892, p. 10, c. 5.
[2] *The Times*, 3 Oct. 1887, p. 8, c. 2.
[3] *The Times*, 12 Feb. 1887, p. 12, c. 1.
[4] *The Times*, 19 Apr. 1888, p. 6, c. 3.
[5] *The Times*, 12 Feb. 1886, p. 10, c. 6.

THE HOME-RULE PREOCCUPATION 203

sectional reform interests. The frequency with which Morley and other Liberals emphasized its being 'the first question' shows this aspect clearly. Morley would direct this argument at the sectionalist advocates of reforms. The Irish question was 'the first duty of England—the first duty of Great Britain—the first duty of Englishmen and Scotchmen'. So long as 'Ireland blocks the way', there was no point in agitating for other reforms.[1]

A semblance of coherence and system was introduced into Liberal politics by the exploitation of the Irish issue as a 'focalizing' question. Because it was the key to further progress on all other questions, they were 'focalized' or comprehended within it. In 1873 Gladstone, oppressed by the variety and confusion of reform questions, craved one particular issue that might, if 'worked into certain shapes', 'help to mould the rest, at least for the time'.[2] Such an issue was home rule now. As an issue external to the special reform interests of Liberals, it performed the same 'moulding' and disciplining function as Chamberlain had looked for in the machinery of party organization.[3] In *On Compromise* Morley had condemned party as the means of carrying out 'the general consensus of the whole' because this usually had the result that 'men who care very strongly about anything are to surrender that and the hope of it, for the sake of succeeding in something about which they care very little or not at all'.[4] And yet he became aware that this, as the typical attitude of the sectionalist, had its dangers and that an urgent need did exist to bring 'A. and B.', 'each riding a hobby of his own', to co-operate in a sense of common interest.[5] The solution was to substitute for party organization a single great external question by which the adherents to all the competing internal reform issues might be persuaded to come together and work for a cause in which none of them had any direct interest at all. The argument of the home-rule policy was that each section would serve its own true interests best by concentrating for a time

[1] *The Times*, 1 Dec. 1886, p. 7, c. 3; 10 Oct. 1888, p. 12, c. 1; 31 Mar. 1887, p. 10, c. 1; 12 Feb. 1887, p. 12, c. 1; 22 Apr. 1887, p. 10, c. 6.
[2] *Gladstone*, II, p. 479.
[3] Cf. *F.R.*, July 1877, p. 127.
[4] p. 20. *F.R.*, Apr. 1874, p. 431.
[5] Cf. *F.R.*, Sept. 1876, p. 404.

on the common task of clearing the Irish obstruction out of the way. Thus in February 1886 Morley told those who wanted parliament to get on with 'its own proper work', 'with measures' of which the country had 'heard so much during the last three months for ameliorating the condition of the English people', that they should for that very reason support the home-rule policy.[1] In 1887 he told London Liberals that only when home rule had been conceded would attention to other reforms be possible, and added: 'it is because of this that we are here to-night to ask you to help us'.[2] The emphasis was on inducing Liberals to do what their leaders had been finding increasing difficulty hitherto in persuading them to do: work with other Liberals. For example, in 1887 he asked Liberals in the West of England to 'raise up your voices with the others' and 'join hands with them' in order to be set free to secure the domestic reforms which they wanted.[3] In 1889 he urged his own constituents, many of whom were impatient for labour reforms, to join in the protest against the coercion of the Irish because 'in making the protest' they would be 'rendering a great service' not only to Ireland but 'to all those other causes which are waiting for the settlement of this question'.[4]

This argument was much favoured by Gladstone. Speaking of the licensing question, he once said: 'to those who are desirous of its settlement . . . [and] the settlement of . . . other subjects . . . , the more you desire your own particular subject to be dealt with so much the more is the need for the speedy solution of the great matter which *alike* impedes *them all*—namely, the sound adjustment of the Irish question.' Ireland, according to Gladstone, was 'that subject to which, not only in despite of our own special preferences, but for the sake of our special preferences, we must direct our supreme attention'. His comment on regional interests sums up very well this view of the significance of concentrating on Ireland: 'the interests of each part of the country will be most solidly provided for by putting forward boldly *that*

---

[1] *The Times*, 9 Feb. 1886, p. 7, c. 4.
[2] *The Times*, 12 Jan. 1887, p. 7, c. 2.
[3] *The Times*, 3 Oct. 1887, p. 8, cc. 1–2.
[4] *The Times*, 5 Feb. 1889, p. 10, c. 4.

great interest of the whole which is so much concentrated in the Irish question.'[1]

Morley, it will be recalled, had seen the *Fortnightly Review* during his editorship as 'a sort of substitute for a philosophic synthesis', and 'a provisional rallying-point for efforts the most divergent'. Now the home-rule policy was filling a similar role in the realm of politics, concentrating on itself the many divergent reform interests and rallying reformers to work together in devotion to itself. This single great issue was now a corner-stone, holding all together. Other questions were thought of not in a direct connection with one another but in relation to this central 'rallying-point'. As Gladstone put it, 'Ireland is first and last in the thoughts of everybody; and so it must be, for English questions are guided and governed by Irish motives.'[2] Thus Morley now repeatedly opposed making disestablishment into a major issue because of the complicating effect which it could have on the Irish policy.[3] Morley's own speeches indicate that he welcomed the Irish question as a provisional substitute for system, bringing order into a confused situation. On one occasion, after referring to 'the great question' and describing how he said to himself every day, 'Keep your eye on Ireland', he contrasted this kind of politics with 'the squabbles and intrigues and recriminations of politicians'.[4] In a speech late in 1886, after claiming that there was a trend towards 'degraded politics' 'in which, instead of great parties upon broad convictions, we shall see little factions, shifting combinations, existing for some paltry convenience of the hour', he promised that the Liberals and their home-rule crusade would 'have something to do with the dispelling' of this trend.[5]

Concentration on the Irish policy was welcomed because it presented a form of relief from the disunity, confusion, and drift that had characterized the history of the Liberal party between

---

[1] *The Times*, 18 Mar. 1887, p. 10, c. 1; 20 Oct. 1887, p. 6, cc. 2–3; 25 Mar. 1890, p. 10, c. 1; 2 Nov. 1888, p. 7, c. 6. My emphasis.

[2] *The Times*, 2 July 1888, p. 7, c. 1.

[3] Cf. to Harcourt, 18 Nov. 1886, 2 Oct. 1898; to Gladstone, 2 June 1891, B.M. Add. MSS. 44256, ff. 147–8.

[4] *The Times*, 7 July 1887, p. 7, c. 2.

[5] *The Times*, 4 Nov. 1886, p. 6, c. 6.

1873 and 1885. 'Our position is perfectly clear', Morley would now say; 'we are standing with our foot upon a rock.'[1] In 1886 he told the National Liberal Federation that he rejoiced in the fact that 'there has been a greater unanimity of opinion upon the great central question of the hour than there has been on any question since that of the franchise'—a particular reminder of the chaos during 1885. The party, he continually remarked, had 'never been more united, more firm, more compact'.[2]

The Irish preoccupation also offered a respite from the difficult and perilous work of deciding on domestic policy. Morley would often turn from the confusion in that sphere to focus his attention on the Irish question. For example, in 1888 he began a speech by observing that Liberalism had reached a 'very critical moment' because of changes in attitudes to institutions, such as property. Somehow, he said, 'in these changes that are going on and that lie before us', a solid, sober Liberalism must be made to prevail. Then he turned to the home-rule policy: 'They [those who fear change] may say . . . "Ah, but you are for a great change in the constitution of Ireland." Yes, I am . . . That change in the constitution of Ireland for which we are now fighting . . . is a change commended by considerations of sobriety, of reason, and of justice. . . .'[3] In another speech, in 1889, the relief was obvious when, after referring to social reform and to the difficulties to be encountered in that area of policy, he was able to continue thus: 'Now, turning to Ireland, which I find is the one thing the people of England want to hear talked about. . .'[4] On Ireland at least he felt that he could be sure that he was on firm ground, in contact with what was unambiguously 'right'. 'Depend upon it,' he said, 'if a man is sent to prison for three months with every circumstance of shame and humiliation because he says "Three cheers for the Plan of Campaign", because he gives bread to starving peasants, do not doubt which side is right, and which side is wrong. Right and wrong are in the nature of things—laws of

---

[1] *The Times*, 3 Oct. 1887, p. 8, c. 1.
[2] *The Times*, 4 Nov. 1886, p. 6, c. 3; 13 Dec. 1888, p. 12, c. 4.
[3] *The Times*, 5 Apr. 1888, p. 7, c. 1.
[4] *The Times*, 14 Feb. 1889, p. 6, c. 2.

right and wrong are graven on the tables of experience and of history.'[1] To have this conviction was of obvious importance to one who wished to be guided by principles of 'right and wrong' that arose out of 'the nature of things'.

Home rule was a policy which, even though in 1886 it had torn the party asunder and precipitated a very serious schism, nevertheless thereafter caused its adherents to feel pleased that they were so united and harmonious in their views. Defeat and division came to seem far less significant to Morley and many other Liberals than the feeling of being 'right' and on firm ground. On 21 December 1885, urging Liberals to address themselves to the great Irish question, Morley warned them that the task would be a long one and would, 'perhaps, destroy a great party', and then said that, nevertheless, they had a duty to undertake it.[2] What was important for him now was that the Liberals should have a 'fixed' line and no longer be 'weak' and 'wavering'. In February 1886 he declared: 'it is better to fail in such an attempt as we are about to make than never to make that attempt at all. We may fail, this Ministry may fail . . . we may fall soon, we may be a short Government; but I hope . . . we shall not be a weak or a wavering Government. The line will be fixed upon, has been fixed upon.'[3] In 1879 he had written that Burke, for the sake of a great cause, not only 'deliberately broke his party in pieces' but also 'broke away from the friendships of a life'. Even this sacrifice Morley himself was now prepared to make. As he insisted on placing his concern for the reconstruction of Irish government before the perpetuation of the alliance between himself and Chamberlain, their friendship came to an abrupt and bitter end; and Chamberlain said that it was 'Fox and Burke over again'.[4]

Henceforward Morley displayed a remarkable indifference to arguments that the home-rule policy should be dropped or changed or supplemented because it was proving unpopular;

---

[1] *The Times*, 7 Nov. 1889, p. 10, c. 4.
[2] *The Times*, 22 Dec. 1885, p. 6, c. 4.
[3] *The Times*, 9 Feb. 1886, p. 7, c. 4.
[4] *Recollections*, I, p. 204. *Burke*, p. 78.

concentration on it seemed worth while quite apart from any consideration of its electoral appeal or of the chances of achieving the objective. After the defeat of the Home Rule Bill in 1886, Morley said: 'Whether in office or out of office, we are not going to let the flag go down. Whether in office or out of office, we can never abandon the cause...' In subsequent years his perpetual theme was that the Liberals would fight to win justice for Ireland 'at whatever cost to ourselves'. He would remind his fellow Liberals that Cobden had never been 'frightened out of a political conviction by the fact that an accidental Parliamentary majority was against him; he never thought he must be wrong because a particular general election had gone the other way'. Morley would admit that 'we are in the wilderness', but then would say: 'There are worse places ... than the wilderness. We would rather be in the wilderness with a good conscience and a great cause, than we would be among the flesh-pots of Egypt.' Electoral considerations seemed to be almost irrelevant: 'whatever constituencies may do, the course of men like us is clear.' Again and again the defiant phrase, 'whatever may happen', appeared in his speeches. On one occasion he even went so far as to say of the claim 'that the country is quite sick of hearing about Ireland'; 'I do not care whether it is or not.' He took a similar attitude in letters to colleagues, declaring that he would adhere to his own views 'whatever the British elector may say', and urging that the party should continue working for home rule, even if 'not in the expectation of victory at the election'.[1]

It was as if he had come to the conclusion that, in the continuing absence of systematic principles to guide politicians among the perilous currents of democratic politics, it was safer to commit one's activity totally to a single great cause and to follow wherever this might lead than to base activity on the pursuit of electoral success.

There was a marked ambiguity in Morley's attitude to the great

---

[1] *The Times*, 9 June 1886, p. 6, c. 2; 7 Apr. 1887, p. 6, c. 4; 16 May 1887, p. 7, c. 1; 8 June 1888, p. 10, cc. 1, 3; 13 Dec. 1888, p. 12, c. 4; 5 Feb. 1889, p. 10, c. 2. To Harcourt, 30 July 1887, 21 Dec. 1890.

Irish 'obstruction'. At times it seemed that he did not want an early settlement of the question so as to have this allegedly frustrating and disliked obstruction removed, but would be pleased to see it remain for many years to come. The concentration on the Irish policy provided at least a temporary relief from many of the difficulties confronting Liberalism at the time, and Morley's public lamentations over this barrier to progress in domestic reform were in striking contrast to his exploitation of the advantages which its existence seemed to him to confer on his thinking and practice as a Liberal.

14

MORLEY AND THE MAINTENANCE OF THE GREAT IRISH POLICY

IT was in such a situation, with many Liberals finding both merit and advantage in concentration on this single issue, that Morley attained a position of great prominence in the party leadership. From his having thought and written about policies of conciliating Ireland in all their implications over a long period, no one was better fitted than he was to expound the new policy. Many years earlier he had argued that 'in times of distraction' the advantage lies with 'the party that knows its own aims most definitely'.[1] Morley's own total commitment to this single issue now tended to give him this kind of authority. In the *Recollections* he comments on a remark by Lord Acton that his importance in 1886 was, if anything, 'excessive': 'The secret was quite simple. In moments like this it is the men who know their own mind that are important even to excess.'[2]

Morley's determination in the early 1880s to maintain an independent and consistent position on the coercion issue now paid a useful dividend. With many of the other Gladstonians, including Harcourt, Spencer, and Gladstone himself, almost inextricably compromised by previous policy and utterances, Morley's association with the new policy had great value, for against him at least charges of inconsistency and shameless reversal of attitude were not easily brought. Leading Conservatives—Balfour, Churchill, Salisbury—acknowledged that he was 'a Home-Ruler by conviction', could 'base upon his public performances a claim to sincerity in connection with this question', and was the only statesman with 'a right to propose a Home Rule Bill'.[3] The other leaders,

[1] *Rousseau*, II, p. 135.   [2] I, p. 218.
[3] K. Young, *Arthur James Balfour*, 1963, p. 94. *Hansard*, 3, 304, 1339 (Churchill). G. W. E. Russell (ed.), *Malcolm MacColl Memoirs and Correspondence*, 1914, p. 281 (Salisbury).

embarrassed by the sudden reversal, could be attacked with long lists of statements made before 1886 against Irish nationalism and home rule. A burden of inconsistency and unpreparedness lay heavy on many of these men; it did not lie on Morley. As he wrote later, he had 'a firmer record on the policy';[1] and he exploited this asset to the full. In 1887, replying to attempts by the Conservative Government to use the precedent of 1882 to justify their own coercion, he pointed out that he himself had not then been in the Commons and added 'I hope that if I had been I should have objected to a great many clauses of that Act'.[2] In 1888 he reminded the House that 'I had nothing to do with the administration of the Coercion Act of Lord Spencer, and I spoke against the Coercion Act of Mr. Forster's time in season and out of season'. 'Against me', he claimed, 'no *tu quoque* arguments' were possible, for 'I detested the system of coercion when my own friends supported it, and I detest it now'.[3]

Far from resenting this ostentatious detachment, Morley's colleagues showed much appreciation of its value for the Liberal party's commitment to home rule. For example, Harcourt at first found Morley's advanced views on the Irish question most inconvenient. Having himself been a leading coercionist and bitter foe of the Irish nationalists, he did not want the party to be prematurely committed to a home-rule policy, and wrote to Gladstone when the Government of 1886 was being formed imploring him, on account of Morley's views on Ireland, to give Morley any post but that of Irish Secretary.[4] But, once the policy had been taken up, he found these same views an invaluable asset. As Morley later observed, Harcourt's conversion to home rule was extremely rapid.[5] Indeed, he was never to be a convinced home-ruler, but had decided to follow Gladstone rather than jeopardize his own political future. Morley's genuine and long-prepared convictions on the question became for Harcourt and others essential as a cover for their own inconsistency and lack of

[1] *Recollections*, I, p. 218.
[2] *Hansard*, 3, 314, 817.
[3] *Hansard*, 3, 329, 1783; 331, 1127. Cf. *Hansard*, 4, 23, 782.
[4] A. G. Gardiner, *The Life of Sir William Harcourt*, I, 1923, pp. 563-4.
[5] *Recollections*, II, p. 12.

conviction. Thus Harcourt in July 1886, trying to disprove allegations that there had been some deception of his colleagues by Gladstone as to his Irish policy when his Government was formed, exploited the advanced nature of Morley's views, even though these had so alarmed him at the time: 'The very fact that Mr. Morley was made Chief Secretary for Ireland was sufficient evidence' of the lack of secrecy about Gladstone's intentions, 'for everybody knew perfectly well that Mr. John Morley was an avowed Home Ruler'.[1] In 1889 Lord Spencer, the one-time coercionist Lord Lieutenant, who had changed policies in 1886 with equal suddenness although with far more conviction, made this assertion: 'It was often said that Liberals had turned round suddenly on the Irish question and taken the constituencies by storm, and that there had been no preparation for the change. But long before the majority of the Liberal party were in favour of it Mr. John Morley was a staunch supporter of Home Rule.'[2]

In short, from the process of reshaping Liberal politics on the mould of the single great issue of home rule Morley emerged as one of the most important members of the party's leadership. In December 1886 H. H. Fowler, congratulating him on 'the brilliant success of this year', wrote: 'Twelve months ago you were below the gangway, now you are one of the foremost, most popular, most trusted leaders of the Party . . . I doubt whether our political history has any parallel for so swift, so sure, so well-deserved a rise. The future of the Liberal party will . . . be coloured, influenced, controlled by you.'[3] A few months later Harcourt, when denying suggestions by Chamberlain that 'Morley's friends in the lobbies & in the Press' were intriguing to secure for him the deputy leadership, added: 'That J. Morley has many friends and admirers who look forward to his eventually taking the first place in the Liberal Party I have no doubt is perfectly true & seems to me quite natural.'[4] When in November

---

[1] *The Times*, 12 July 1886, p. 10, c. 5. Cf. *Gladstone*, III, p. 296.

[2] *The Times*, 7 Feb. 1889, p. 6, c. 3.

[3] E. H. Fowler, *The Life of Henry Hartley Fowler, First Viscount Wolverhampton*, 1912, pp. 212–13.

[4] Chamberlain to Harcourt, 28 Feb. 1887; Harcourt to Chamberlain, 1 Mar. 1887, Chamberlain MSS.

1890 Morley suggested to Schnadhorst, the great Liberal organizer, that the Parnell crisis meant the end of Gladstone's career and hence the collapse of the party, Schnadhorst replied: 'They won't break up, they will rally to you, and by that I mean you personally.'[1]

But Morley was not so sure. He was always conscious of a certain fragility in his position. Thus in 1892 he remarked: '... Mr. Gladstone is very old. ... There is an old Indian idea that when a great chief dies, his friends and horses and dogs should be buried with him. So it must be with us!'[2] This corner of experience, this single question, into which he had retreated through an inability to arrive at a comprehensive understanding of the whole, could be seen, not as the microcosm or substitute for system into which he tried to turn it, but as a prison within which he was becoming ever more inescapably immured. Once he was committed to the great Irish policy, he was a prisoner of the logic of 'single-great-issue' politics which dictated that he should become less and less capable of surviving in any other kind of politics. There was accuracy as well as spite in Jesse Collings's comment on Morley: 'In his political future he has nothing but Ireland to rely on & it is a poor mouse that has but one hole. If Ireland & Gladstone drops where is Morley.'[3] In 1893 Haldane said that Morley 'had ruined himself by want of sympathy with everything but Home Rule'. Morley seemed to him to have become 'too much associated with the Irish question to the exclusion of others', whereas a party leader must be able to co-ordinate and view widely.[4]

Among the Liberal leaders Morley's was perhaps the predominant influence against any tendencies to undermine or disintegrate the Irish policy. He frequently declared that, so long as they had this 'great principle' as a focus for their activity, Liberals would be unwise to inquire too closely into points of detail, for that would

[1] *Recollections*, I, p. 257.
[2] H. G. Hutchinson (ed.), *Private Diaries of the Rt. Hon. Sir Algernon West*, 1922, pp. 95-6.
[3] Collings to Chamberlain, 4 Nov. 1891, Chamberlain MSS.
[4] Hutchinson, *Diaries of West*, p. 110. [Lord Haldane], *Richard Burdon Haldane. An Autobiography*, 1929, pp. 96, 156.

once again bring complexity and confusion into their politics. After 1885 the Irish policy furnished the systematic principle that held together the politics of Gladstonian Liberalism. Analysis and criticism of detail are the disintegrators of any system of thought, as the positivists, for example, realized. Morley found the 'spirit of system' in the Irish policy and refused to tolerate its destruction through controversy over detail.[1]

In fact, the Liberal leaders dared not publish a detailed scheme of home rule after 1886 for fear that the resulting 'niggling arguments' over its provisions would be ruinous both to the unity of the party and to the integrity of the policy that gave it that unity. If Gladstone did frame a Bill, Morley said in 1887, the consequence would be that every word in it, 'from the first word of the preamble to the last word of the definition clause, would have been made a pretext' for a host of 'objections, difficulties, and crotchets'.[2] As it was, whenever the leaders themselves sat down to consider the details of a scheme, serious differences among them were revealed.[3] In particular, they could not agree on two questions of detail—the exclusion of the Irish M.P.s from the Imperial Parliament after the concession of home rule, and land policy. On these Morley took an extreme stand against compromise which illustrates very well his obsession with system.

Morley argued that only the complete exclusion of the Irish members would make home rule meaningful, and for as long as he could he insisted on it as the *sine qua non* of any scheme. 'I am for no plan of Thorough [i.e. home rule],' he told Chamberlain in January 1886, 'unless it involves the disappearance of the Irish members from our House. If that be not possible, I would almost try to muddle and potter on.'[4] 'The more I think of it,' he wrote in April 1886, 'the more convinced I am of the folly of allowing 103, or 40, or any other number of Irish members, to come swooping down on our parliament, fitfully and at their own pleasure or

[1] *The Times*, 26 Oct. 1887, p. 10, c. 2; 7 Nov. 1889, p. 10, c. 4; 21 June 1892, p. 12, c. 2.
[2] *The Times*, 26 Oct. 1887, p. 10, c. 1.
[3] Cf. Morley on these differences in *The Times*, 10 Dec. 1889, p. 6, c. 4. see F. S. L. Lyons, *The Fall of Parnell 1890–91*, 1960, pp. 105–8.
[4] To Chamberlain, 1 Jan. 1886.

caprice, to spoil our business.'¹ He made into a central feature of his case for home rule the argument that 'there is no power on earth that can prevent the Irish members in such circumstances from being in the future Parliament what they were in the past, and what to some extent they are in the present, the arbiters and the masters of English policy, of English legislative business, and of the rise and fall of British Administrations'.² But his colleagues did not view the problem in quite so 'thorough' a way, and Morley's differences with them and their inability to decide what sort of retention they wanted made this question a constant disintegrating element within the great home-rule policy.³

As for land policy, Morley's colleagues found particular difficulty in accepting his insistence on the necessity for accompanying or preceding home rule with a land settlement. It seemed to Morley that the Irish land system was Britain's responsibility and ought to be reformed by Britain before Ireland was handed over to the Irish to govern.⁴ 'We say that there is an obligation of honour', he wrote, 'and next we say that H. Rule would never work if the Irish Parliament were left with the landlords on their hands.'⁵ For he could see that, if the land question remained unsettled, the new Irish Government might oppress the landlords and impose harsh terms on them, thus provoking the imperial Government to intervene. In 1882 he had asked whether the English would be prepared to see the landlords sent 'flying for their lives, with bag and baggage'. Land, being the question that

¹ To Gladstone, 13 Apr. 1886, B.M. Add. MSS. 44255, ff. 72–3.
² *The Times*, 22 Apr. 1886, p. 6, c. 4; 8 Jan. 1886, p. 6, c. 1.
³ For Morley's views on this question and disagreements with colleagues, see to Gladstone, 13 Apr., 3, 5, 8 May 1886, 30 May, 7 June 1887, B.M. Add. MSS. 44255, ff. 72, 81, 83–4, 205–6, 209. Labouchere to Chamberlain, 1 May 1886, Chamberlain to Labouchere, 2 May 1886, Chamberlain to Harcourt, and Dilke to Chamberlain, 5 May 1886, Chamberlain MSS. Labouchere to H. Gladstone, [3 May 1886], B.M. Add. MSS. 46016, f. 13. J. L. Garvin, *The Life of Joseph Chamberlain*, II, 1933, pp. 287–8. Harcourt to Gladstone, 27 May 1887, Harcourt to Spencer, 25 Oct. 1889, Harcourt MSS. Morley to Spencer 28 May 1887, 28 July 1891, Spencer MSS. *Gladstone*, III, p. 386. *The Times*, 26 Sept. 1887, p. 8, c. 1; 20 June 1892, p. 11, c. 6; 1 July 1892, p. 9, c. 2; 4 July 1892, p. 6, c. 4. Fowler, *Life of H. H. Fowler*, p. 235. *Recollections*, I, pp. 294–5. To Rosebery, 28 May 1887.
⁴ *The Times*, 22 June 1886, p. 11, c. 3. *Gladstone*, III, p. 301.
⁵ To Harcourt, 29 Aug. 1886.

interested the Irish more than all other questions put together, could not be excluded from the control of an Irish Government; yet could the Irish be expected 'to handle the interests of those whom they regard as their hereditary tyrants and most cruel oppressors with the respect for property and interests that is exacted by public opinion in this country'? The conclusion was that 'some form of equitable expropriation must precede any effectual form of Home Rule.'[1] And so, when he himself was helping in the preparation of a Home Rule Bill, he insisted that it be accompanied by a land-purchase scheme 'to prevent tenants from confiscating the property of their landlords'.[2] After 1886 he continued to argue 'against H.R. unaccompanied by Purchase'.[3] As he told Gladstone,[4] he believed that 'the Home Rule question cannot be well settled, so long as the Land question is unsettled'. Home rule was intended to provide 'a means of gradually putting an end to the social alienation which is the curse of Ireland'; but if on 'the very threshold of the new parliament' this 'great object of discord and quarrel' were to present itself, Ireland would at once see a 'furious and envenomed fight between landlords and tenants'. He acknowledged 'a political motive' of creating for a home-rule Ireland a conservative class of landowners 'interested in the maintenance of order' and with 'some reason . . . to rally round the institutions of the country.'[5] This would inaugurate a home-rule system on a stable basis, whereas instability would ensue if an Irish Parliament had to deal with a question 'touching so many interests, raising so many passions, and having such deep and bitter roots in old historic memories'.[6] It would be a 'door for agitation'; the land war and the political war must be ended together.[7]

[1] *The Nineteenth Century*, Nov. 1882, pp. 654–5.
[2] *The Times*, 8 Jan. 1886, p. 6, c. 1. To Gladstone, 2 Feb. 1886. B.M. Add. MSS. 44255, ff. 54, 56. *Gladstone*, III, p. 301.
[3] To Harcourt, 5, 12 Oct. 1890. Marquess of Crewe, *Lord Rosebery*, I, 1931, p. 303. *The Times*, 14 Jan. 1891, p. 10, c. 4.
[4] 19 Aug. 1886, 1 Jan. 1887, B.M. Add. MSS. 44255, ff. 111, 171–2.
[5] *Hansard*, 3, 306, 946.
[6] *The Times*, 26 Sept. 1887, p. 8, c. 1.
[7] *The Times*, 1 Oct. 1888, p. 10, c. 3. To Gladstone, 13 Nov. 1890, B.M. Add. MSS. 44256, f. 64. *Recollections*, I, p. 252.

But Morley's colleagues, apart from Lord Spencer, had not liked the association of land purchase with the Home Rule Bill in 1886, and he had thereafter to fight against a strong inclination on their part to drop the idea.[1] What they particularly objected to —and feared electorally—was the proposed employment of the credit of the British taxpayer.[2] Another source of difficulty was the attempt by Balfour to settle the land question 'without reference', as Morley put it, 'to the satisfaction of the demand for autonomy', because Morley had long insisted that the two questions could not 'be considered and handled apart from one another' and that it was impossible to deal with the land 'on principles and by machinery independent of the political question'.[3] He would incline at one moment, under pressure from the Irish and from his own colleagues, towards supporting and accepting Balfour's measures as helping to clear the way for a safe home-rule settlement; and then at the next, remembering that these bills were intended as substitutes for home rule, would condemn them for not being associated with measures of political conciliation. Furthermore, while telling the Liberal party that land purchase must accompany or precede home rule, he also had to tell the Unionists that home rule ought to accompany or follow land purchase. The different stances required for these arguments led to considerable confusion.[4]

Thus the Irish policy was in constant danger of losing its coherence through the examination and discussion of detail. It is not surprising that Morley, who had seen previous single issues, that

[1] Cf. *Gladstone*, III, pp. 301, 324. Gardiner, *Harcourt*, II, pp. 7–8. To Spencer, 30 Oct. 1888; to Harcourt, 5, 12, 27 Oct. 1890.

[2] Cf. *The Times*, 12 July 1886, p. 8, c. 2. To Harcourt, 28, 30 July 1887; to Spencer, 20 Mar., 30 July 1887, 29, 30 Oct. 1888; to Gladstone, 1 Aug. 1887, B.M. Add. MSS. 44255, ff. 215–16. Gladstone to Spencer, 4 Aug. 1887, Spencer MSS.

[3] To Chamberlain, 3 Feb. 1886.

[4] Cf. *Hansard*, 3, 310, 910–11; 314, 296–7; 330, 1745–51; 331, 471; 343, 1927–38; 352, 404–5, 750–61; 354, 446. *The Times*, 26 Sept. 1887, p. 8, c. 1; 26 Nov. 1887, p. 7, c. 3; 5 Apr. 1888, p. 7, c. 4; 30 Jan. 1890, p. 7, c. 2; 24 Apr. 1890, p. 6, c. 4. To Harcourt, 24 Dec. 1889. To Gladstone, 28 Oct. 1888, 2 Apr., 13 Nov. 1890, B.M. Add. MSS. 44255, ff. 277–8; 44256, ff. 44, 64. To Ripon, 18 Nov. 1888, B.M. Add. MSS. 43541, f. 45. To Spencer, 17 Nov. 1888, 17 Jan, 1890. Sir E. Grey to Haldane, 8 Nov. 1890, Haldane MSS. 5903, ff. 173–4.

were intended for the concentration of Liberals' political action, disintegrated by compromise and difficulties over detail, should have urged Liberals to debate the principle of home rule, but refuse to 'argue all these details ... about the retention of the Irish members, about the separate treatment of Ulster, about the control of law and order'.[1]

This was the danger from within. But there was also a danger from without, from those Liberals who resented and wished to end the concentration of the party's policy and action on this one question. The first challenge of this kind came from those who continued to call themselves Liberals in regard to general policy, but were Unionists with regard to Ireland and, repudiating Gladstone's leadership, opposed both the form of his Irish policy and the way in which it monopolized political attention.

Morley was anxious to force the dissentient Liberals into acknowledging home rule as the dividing issue in party politics. The Conservatives, rallying around the cry of 'Constitution and Empire in danger', seemed to be as pleased as were the Gladstonian Liberals to be doing battle on the field of Irish politics; but the independent existence of Chamberlain and his followers was a perpetual reminder that there was an alternative to this kind of politics. Morley was confident that the dissentients would soon feel compelled by their abhorrence of Tory coercion to return to the fold. In June 1886 he asked them: 'Is Ireland to be governed by a method of which they entirely disapprove, and is England to be governed by a party whose principles and maxims they themselves repudiate?'[2] 'It seems to me', he wrote to Gladstone on 19 July, 'that it would be wiser to leave them alone, until new circumstances at no remote date drive them to vote against their Tory confederates.'[3]

The developments of December 1886 gave hope that these expectations would be fulfilled. The resignation of Lord Randolph Churchill from the Conservative Government made it much less certain that there would be any strong pressure within it for

---

[1] *The Times*, 7 July 1887, p. 7, c. 3.
[2] *Hansard*, 3, 306, 937. *The Times*, 9 June 1886, p. 6, c. 2.
[3] B.M. Add. MSS. 44255, f. 102.

attention to domestic reform. It was widely believed that now the Government would turn much more whole-heartedly to a coercionist Irish policy. Before the stranglehold of the Irish question closed on British politics, Chamberlain was determined to make an effort to undermine the home-rule basis of the Gladstonian party, and made overtures for the reunifying of the Liberals.

Morley himself saw the possibility that the Gladstonians might 'patch up with J. Chamberlain on basis of Land, plus Local Councils: Home Rule to be left open for consideration: Mr. Parnell to agree to give time for said consideration, his security being the presence of Mr. Gladstone at the helm'.[1] But he approached the proposed negotiations with caution and suspicion. On the one hand, he believed that they were unnecessary and that the Liberals should simply wait for the consequences of Churchill's resignation to 'hasten on the Irish question, by breaking up both sets of Unionists'. 'If we stand firm', he had written earlier in December with regard to the prospect of a coercionist policy, 'events will divide that camp very speedily.'[2] On the other hand, he feared that interference with this process, in the form of negotiations, would be more likely to disintegrate the Gladstonian party than to break up the Unionists.

He was particularly worried about the lack of firmness in his own colleagues. He was aware that in the Liberal leadership he was rather isolated in the 'thoroughness' and the uncompromising quality of his views on the home-rule policy. In the *Recollections*[3] he remarks that he played so important a role in the party during this period because he was firm and 'thorough' and 'had a watchful eye on men tempted to be back-sliders'. In his opinion most of his colleagues in January 1887 were potential 'back-sliders'. In telling friends on 23 December that he himself would stand to his guns he added the qualification, 'whatever you hear about other people'.[4] Chamberlain, in fact, was already aware of this distinction and had on occasions aimed at isolating Morley as much as possible by

---

[1] To Harcourt, 24 Dec. 1886.
[2] To Spencer, 27 Dec. 1886. To Harcourt, 10 Dec. 1886.
[3] I, p. 218.
[4] G. P. Gooch, *Life of Lord Courtney*, 1920, p. 271.

exploiting it.¹ Now his strategy was to try to separate Morley from his colleagues and deal with the latter only. On 26 December he told Harcourt that the men whom he would like to see at the conference table were 'you Herschell & Fowler as the three conspicuous Gladstonians who have done nothing to embitter the differences which have arisen & have shown moderation & fairness throughout.'² But the opponents of 'surrender' to Chamberlain knew that they could rely on Morley. On 31 December Arnold Morley wrote to Gladstone about H. H. Fowler: 'I fear from his speeches that he is inclined perhaps to sacrifice too much for the sake of reconciliation. John Morley, whose presence is most important, would of course stand firm.'³

Reluctantly Morley agreed to join the delegation to the 'Round Table' conference. On 3 January 1887 he wrote:

Herschell is weak on the question, Fowler is weaker, and Harcourt is apt to fly off at a tangent. If Chamb^n captures them at any point, he will be able to denounce me as stubborn, &c. &c.⁴

Herschell is so D-d conciliatory; and Fowler (according to Spencer) has some very flabby opinions. If I am left in minority of one on important points (which is a conceivable issue, in spite of your [Harcourt's] well-known love for 'Justice to Ireland'), it would be a moral triumph for J. Chamberlain.⁵

Three days later he was reported as worried 'that he might be overweighted if Harcourt & Herschell at all inclined' towards conciliating Chamberlain by 'departure from principle'.⁶ When the conference began Morley adopted a strongly uncompromising attitude. 'To my mind', Harcourt was soon telling him, 'the least hopeful part of our business consists in your incurable inveteracy against J.C. I believe it to be unjust.'⁷ But Morley, still relying on coercion to make Chamberlain feel uncomfortable 'in the Tory

---

¹ Cf., e.g., Chamberlain to Labouchere, 2 May 1886, Chamberlain MSS.
² Chamberlain MSS.
³ B.M. Add. MSS. 44253, f. 52.
⁴ To Spencer.
⁵ To Harcourt.
⁶ Arnold Morley to Gladstone, 6 Jan. 1887, B.M. Add. MSS. 44253, f. 55.
⁷ 19 Jan. 1887.

camp',[1] was concerned at the 'Round Table' only to increase the difficulties of Chamberlain's position. On 6 January he wrote to Harcourt that he was 'sorry to hear that J. Chamberlain is so well satisfied', and reminded him that their aim must be to 'drive or draw J. Chamberlain up to the Leeds resolution[2] before we break up' and 'at the close of the conference leave him thoroughly worsted'. Harcourt, horrified at this revelation of the frame of mind in which Morley was approaching the negotiations, replied on the 7th: 'I do not at all concur in your desire that anyone shall be "thoroughly worsted" in our conference. On the contrary I desire that everyone shall have the best of it. This is of the essence of a "compromise" as you will find if you attentively study a philosophical work on that subject which I always keep by my bedside.' But, a month later, writing to Lord Ripon,[3] Morley claimed that the conference had been justified 'by the fact of the disgust and suspicion about J.C. wh. has now entered the minds of his allies'. 'What we have done has forced J.C. to show his hand, while we are exactly where we were.' Chamberlain had made concessions which would have the effect of widening the gap between himself and Hartington, and 'I don't think we shd. have screwed him up to this point, without the temptation of the Round Table. He will carry off not one single scrap of substance from us.'

Morley's attitude was obviously influenced by the personal consequences of the disruption of his complementary relationship with Chamberlain. At the beginning of 1886, as we have seen, Chamberlain reacted bitterly against Morley's 'taking his own line' and 'trying to run alone' by scorning him as devoid of practical talents.[4] Thereafter Morley, who had previously been so appreciative of Chamberlain's possession of these talents and so conscious of his own weaknesses in that regard, and who was now

[1] To Harcourt, 18 Jan. 1887.
[2] Of the N.L.F. conference of Nov. 1886 pledging the party to work for home rule. *The Times*, 4 Nov. 1886, p. 6, c. 2.
[3] 7 Feb. 1887, B.M. Add. MSS. 43541, ff. 18–19.
[4] See above, pp. 171–2.

trying to fill both halves of the relationship by himself, seemed perpetually apprehensive that Chamberlain might be engaged in carrying out his threat to 'smash' him and might be exerting his great practical powers to outwit Morley and triumph over him so as to demonstrate his impotence as a mere academic or 'literary' politician. In 1886 a threat by Morley to resign should Gladstone give way to Chamberlain on the issue of the retention of Irish M.P.s was checked by the thought of 'the triumph that this [his resignation] would be' to Chamberlain.[1] At the 'Round Table' conference he took a 'rather cynical view' of Chamberlain as a cunning schemer and 'a very *adroit* and tenacious player'.[2] In the *Life of Gladstone* Chamberlain was to be depicted as making his political calculations at this time out of an 'instinct of party management'.[3] It was as if, once the complementary relationship had ended and Morley's 'spiritual' influence over Chamberlain had been removed, Morley refused to believe that Chamberlain could now possibly be influenced by considerations of principle. All that was left was the 'adroit player' of the political game. And Chamberlain took exactly the opposite line. It was a pity, he would say, that Morley had ever left the sphere of literature, where he might have shone still brighter, for a sphere in which he could never succeed.[4] In 1895 he wrote concerning Morley's defeat at Newcastle: 'Alas, poor Morley! I confess I was sorry for Harcourt but I shed no tears over the philosopher in politics.'[5] In other words, Morley's rebuff was no more than he deserved for daring to 'run alone' in practical politics.

Morley became obsessed with the idea that Chamberlain's great aim was to force him to 'surrender'. In April 1886 he said that the only kind of agreement in which Chamberlain was interested was one involving 'surrender by us at every point'.[6]

---

[1] Labouchere to H. Gladstone (probably mid-Mar. or May 1886), B.M. Add. MSS. 46016, f. 13.
[2] To Spencer, 27 Dec. 1886.
[3] III, p. 295.
[4] Cf. Garvin, *Chamberlain*, II, pp. 364, 491–2.
[5] Chamberlain to James, 18 July 1895, Lord Askwith, *Lord James of Hereford*, 1930, p. 240.
[6] To Gladstone, 19 Apr. 1886, B.M. Add. MSS. 44255, ff. 74–5.

'Chamberlain', he claimed, 'wants us to go down on our knees, and this cannot be done for the money.'¹ In 1887 his attitude was unchanged. 'Joe means to come back with flying colours or not at all', he would warn; 'the slightest concession will be taken to mean abject surrender.'² Yet these ultra-practical motives which he attributed to Chamberlain were, in fact, his own when contemplating the strategy of negotiation for reunion. It seemed that, in order to prove that he himself was capable of being a 'practical power', he imitated what he saw as practical in Chamberlain's conduct and adopted an extreme and exaggerated practicality, refusing concessions and trying to lure Chamberlain into an appearance of 'abject surrender'. Indeed, his behaviour was very like that which he had once described in Robespierre, a 'doctrinaire' in politics who, according to Morley, was 'really moved' in causing the downfall of Danton 'by nothing more than his invariable dread of being left behind, of finding himself on the weaker side, of not seeming practical and political enough.'³

Morley seemed to believe that, where principles were at stake, compromise was wrong; this, after all, had been one of the themes of his own book *On Compromise*. Negotiations in a mood of conciliatoriness were both dangerous and unnecessary. One may compare his behaviour in 1886–7 with his reaction to Harcourt's questioning of the Irish policy in 1891. 'I stand firm', he was then to declare, 'and positively decline to meet him (outside the H. of C.) until Mr. G. and other colleagues have settled whether we are to take the line of the N'castle speech,⁴ or that of his letters [to Morley].' 'I understand', he added, 'that the result of my obduracy is highly salutary on him.'⁵ Throughout his career Morley sought firmness in his political thought and practice. Concessions and compromises would undermine such firmness,

¹ Labouchere to Chamberlain, 1 May 1886, Chamberlain MSS.
² To Ripon, 14 Mar. 1887, B.M. Add. MSS. 43541, f. 20. To Spencer, 28 May 1887.
³ F.R., Sept. 1876, p. 343. *Critical Miscellanies*, I, p. 94.
⁴ A speech in which Morley pledged the Liberals to a continuing commitment to home rule.
⁵ To Spencer, 21 Jan. 1891.

and therefore he opposed those who tried to bring them about.

Moreover, in 1887 Morley's uncompromising attitude accurately reflected the views of important sections of the party. In part, he represented their views; in part, he acted as he did because he was under pressure from them; and in part also, he was able to use their insistence on firmness as an excuse for opposition to concession and as a means of covering his own feelings about the matter. One advocate of firmness with whom he was in constant contact was Lord Ripon. On 17 January Ripon wrote to him: 'I hope you are holding firm in your conferences with Chamberlain & Trevelyan . . . Liberal reunion is a very good thing, but adherence to principle is much better. I have complete confidence in you but I cannot say so much for your colleagues.' Two weeks later he urged Morley to 'bear in mind that it is not impossible, in attempting to heal one breach, to produce another', and drew his attention to 'the strong feeling' against the conference of Alfred Illingworth and 'the great body of W. Riding Liberals who were, at the last Election, the heartiest supporters whom Mr. Gladstone had in England'. 'Personally', Ripon added, 'I should care very little if the round table were, as Illingworth said, to be "put up for sale".'[1] It was these letters which elicited from Morley his assurances, already quoted, as to the firmness of his attitude at the conference. His own letters contain numerous references to Liberals whose views he alleged obliged him to oppose concession. In October 1886 it was 'our friends in Yorkshire, Durham, and Northumb^d' who 'are all very strong on the point that we must not show any excess of eagerness to meet' the dissentient Liberals.[2] In January 1887 he warned Harcourt that, since 'the chances are 10 to 1 against *modus vivendi*, and then we shall want all our friends', it would be wrong to 'damp their ardour in the meanwhile'. Such was the ardour of these friends, he insisted, that the negotiators had either to leave Chamberlain 'thoroughly worsted' or face 'a worse split in the party than any yet'. 'Be sure of that', he added. 'Arnold Morley told me yesterday [5 January] that they

---

[1] Ripon to Morley, 17 Jan., 4 Feb. 1887, B.M. Add. MSS. 43 541, ff. 10–11, 16–17. See also Granville to Gladstone, 13 Jan. 1887, B.M. Add. MSS. 44, 180, f. 5.

[2] To Gladstone, 28 Oct. 1886. B.M. Add. MSS. 44255, f. 126.

had many remonstrants at Parliament Street.'¹ By March he was advising Harcourt to ignore Chamberlain in his speeches, because any mention of him threatened the harmony of the party which had regarded the conference 'with such restless distrust and suspicion'.²

The views of the Irish were also a major consideration in his mind. In July 1886 he had urged Gladstone to resign rather than meet Parliament again, as he considered it impossible to 'frame a policy that would rally any considerable section of Unionist Liberals, which would not at the same time alienate the Irish party'. Before the conference began he wrote to Gladstone to warn him that Parnell was 'uneasy as to negotiations' and extracted from him a firm assurance that there was 'no occasion' for Parnell's uneasiness and that 'Home Rule is still the first order of the day'.³ As for the idea of leaving home rule open for consideration with Parnell's accepting this on the security of Gladstone's continued leadership, Morley discovered that it was out of the question because of 'Parnell's "hurry" lest Mr. G. should die, and his determination to make the most of him while he can'.⁴

Once the conference had begun Chamberlain became immersed in the details of home-rule policy and in discussing what form that policy should take. At Birmingham on 29 January he broke away to reassert his belief that the measures 'for which we were fighting in 1885 are as important as ever—they are more urgent than ever', and that Ireland should be dealt with in the broad context of 'the interests and the wishes of the greater nation of which Ireland is only a part'.⁵ This speech so angered Morley that he called for the termination of the conference.⁶ Although it dragged on a little longer, the end came with Chamberlain's letter to the *Baptist* in 25 February. In this he condemned the

[1] To Harcourt, 3, 6 Jan. 1887. Cf. Arnold Morley to Gladstone, 17 Dec. 1886, 6 Jan. 1887, B.M. Add. MSS. 44253, ff. 46, 55.

[2] 7 Mar. 1887.

[3] To Gladstone, 19 July 1886, B.M. Add. MSS. 44255, f. 101. To Harcourt, 4 Jan. 1887.

[4] M. V. Brett (ed.), *Journals and Letters of Reginald Viscount Esher*, I, 1934, p. 133.

[5] *The Times*, 31 Jan. 1887, p. 10, cc. 1–2.

[6] Gardiner, *Harcourt*, II, p. 31. Arnold Morley to Gladstone, 4 Feb. 1887, B.M. Add. MSS. 44253, f. 66.

postponing of attention to the needs of the 32 million people living in the rest of the country until the wishes of the three million Irish had been satisfied. 'The issue of the Round Table Conference' he declared, 'will decide much more than the Irish question. It will decide the immediate future of the Liberal party and whether or no all Liberal reform is to be indefinitely adjourned.'[1] But Morley had defined the purpose of the conference as to 'drive or draw' Chamberlain up to the Leeds resolution committing the party to home rule. What Chamberlain now did was to break out of this trap and confront Liberals in the country with an alternative kind of debate, a debate on whether they preferred concentration on this one question or attention to domestic reform. According to Harcourt, a settlement was very near and was frustrated only by Morley's speeches, which irritated Chamberlain and provoked the *Baptist* letter.[2] As all Morley's speeches at the time stressed the theme of concentrating on securing home rule, the nature of the conflict between the two men is obvious.[3]

In April 1887 Morley said that, when Chamberlain started making hostile statements outside the conference room, it was no longer possible to 'hope that our co-operation would be marked by that spirit of mutual trust and reciprocal confidence which were essential to the transaction of such a piece of business'.[4] Morley's letters to his colleagues suggest that his own contribution to the creation of this spirit was very small. He left no doubt that he felt not the slightest trust in Chamberlain who, he alleged, was ruled by 'egotism, irascibility, and perversity'.[5] Nor, as we have seen, did he at any time believe in the negotiations. Chamberlain came close to describing Morley's attitude when he referred to Liberals who thought that 'no concession whatever should be made to the Liberal Unionists, because, they say, if we are only left severely alone we shall all sneak back one after another to the fold without making any condition whatsoever'.[6] Indeed, in 1888

---

[1] Garvin, *Chamberlain*, II, p. 292.
[2] *Recollections*, I, p. 297.
[3] e.g. *The Times*, 12 Feb. 1887, p. 12, cc. 1-3.
[4] *The Times*, 21 Apr. 1887, p. 11, c. 2.
[5] To Harcourt, 18 Jan. 1887.
[6] *The Times*, 14 Mar. 1887, p. 10, c. 2.

Morley was still waiting for Chamberlain, 'unless he is utterly changed', to feel so uncomfortable in 'the party of "gentlemen" ' that he would 'have to leave'.[1]

After the breakdown of the conference Ireland became hardened as the issue of party strife. The dissentient Liberals were obliged either, like Trevelyan, to make their peace with a Liberal party obsessed with home rule or, like Chamberlain, to move towards association with the Conservatives in non-Irish as well as Irish policy. The challenge from Chamberlain and his supporters had been warded off with comparative ease because of the fact that they did happen to oppose home rule as a solution to the Irish problem and were therefore vulnerable to efforts to 'group' them on that particular issue within a situation of consensus by the two main parties to let it dominate politics. More dangerous were those who, accepting home rule as a policy for Ireland, worked from within the party against the exclusive and all-absorbing nature of the party's attention to that policy.

[1] To Gladstone, 28 Mar. 1888, B.M. Add. MSS. 44256, f. 237.

15

COERCION

AMONG those who followed Gladstone and favoured home rule as a solution to Ireland's problems resentment at the concentration of the party's efforts on that one policy gradually developed. In October 1886 H. H. Fowler warned Morley not to assume when considering 'the currents which are at present influencing the party' that 'the rigid attitude' of certain Liberals 'predominates'. There was 'another current', associated with Liberals in the constituencies who did not like being separated from other Liberals merely because of a difference on this one question.[1] Two sources of unrest became of particular concern to Morley himself—the arguments advanced from within the leadership by Sir William Harcourt in favour of widening the programme and the efforts of Radicals and Socialists in Morley's own constituency of Newcastle to stir up resentment among working men against his preoccupation with Irish policy.

Harcourt had for a long time made little attempt to disguise his annoyance at Liberal attention to the problems of Ireland. In 1885 he wanted the Cabinet to take a line which he described as 'No Home Rule, no coercion, no remedial legislation, no Ireland at all'.[2] Morley had to acknowledge in 1887 that 'Harcourt was never a Home Ruler'.[3] From his days at the Home Office, Harcourt had become known as one of the Liberal leaders least sympathetic towards the Irish Nationalists. When the Liberals initiated their alliance with the Irish, Harcourt's distaste was unaltered, although less publicly avowed. Morley was aware of this, as he

---

[1] E. H. Fowler, *The Life of Henry Hartley Fowler, First Viscount Wolverhampton*, 1912, pp. 210–11.

[2] S. Gwynn and G. M. Tuckwell, *The Life of the Rt. Hon. Sir Charles W. Dilke*, II, 1917, p. 132.

[3] Ibid., II, p. 267.

was also of Harcourt's belief that it was wrong for the 'party of progress' thus to coop itself up within a single policy. In November 1886 Harcourt told Morley that '9 people out of 10 think Ireland a bore' and 'would gladly turn to something else', and suggested instead a bolder programme of Radical reform at home.[1] For the next year or so he refrained from developing this theme, but by early 1888 his impatience began to become publicly apparent. In a speech in February of that year he referred to the naturalness of a division between a party of progress and a party of Conservatism, but emphasized how wide must be the area covered by the former if it was to justify its existence.[2] The implication was plain. The Liberal party as a party of progress was stultifying itself by its concentration on a single issue and ran the risk of being superseded in a system the natural development in which was the formation of parties on the two broad tendencies.

It was not long before Harcourt was telling Morley that he was having doubts as to whether he would not have done better to have resigned with Chamberlain in 1886, because then Gladstone could not have continued with the Home Rule Bill 'and the whole situation would have been different'.[3] In October 1889 he declared that home rule, while 'a great, and the first, chapter in the volume of Liberal policy', was not the whole of it. It had been right, he said, to concentrate at first 'almost exclusively' on home rule; but now 'it is time that we should bring forward and ripen other great questions which belong to the Liberal creed'. He then suggested that it was playing the Tories' game to concentrate on home rule. The Liberals' enemies, such as London landlords, had been hoping 'that the question of Home Rule was going to crush out all other questions; that it would enable them to get rid of all other reforms'. In fact, he argued, these reforms, if included in the party's programme, would 'help to carry Home Rule, and Home Rule will help to carry those other things'. 'Reforms mutually propel one another.' He urged the party to spend more time on other questions which were 'good in themselves, as Home

[1] Harcourt to Morley, 20 Nov. 1886.
[2] *The Times*, 8 Feb. 1888, p. 10, cc. 1–2.
[3] J. L. Garvin, *The Life of Joseph Chamberlain*, II, 1933, p. 196.

Rule is good in itself,' and then 'they will all come together'.[1]

Harcourt was challenging Morley's home-rule politics in their fundamentals. Six days after delivering this speech he wrote to Morley pointing out that the Liberals were not likely to gain support if they told-non-Irish voters 'that the Irish are to have what they want first and that that is our present care and the poor Britishers will be considered afterwards and their secondary claims accommodated to the Irish requirements when these are satisfied'. 'I don't see', he remarked, 'that we shall gain much by representing ourselves as looking only to the Irish case and postponing the consideration of British interests.'[2] But, on the same day, Morley told an audience at Bristol that there could be no proper attention to anything else until Ireland was settled.[3] On 6 November he rejected the allegation that England was 'sick of the Irish question' and used Harcourt's point that there were 'other questions waiting at the door' as an additional justification for concentrating on securing home rule as quickly as possible.[4] The time for attending to these other questions would, he kept on saying, be 'as soon as the Irish question is cleared away'.[5]

In Morley's own constituency resentment and impatience concerning the Irish preoccupation also began to appear. Working men were urged by labour and Socialist speakers to insist that their own questions be given priority even over home rule.[6] Notable among these speakers was the Radical agitator, R. B. Cunninghame Graham. He would, for example, ask the working men of Newcastle 'what (unless they are Irishmen) they expect to gain from a party of which Mr. Morley is the leader [sic]'. When Morley stated his opposition to eight-hours legislation, Graham wrote that this was a 'heartless and cruel' attitude, which proved that 'Ireland has pushed Great Britain out of his sight' and that 'the whole inhabitants of England and Scotland might starve, and Mr.

---

[1] *The Times*, 24 Oct. 1889, p. 10, cc. 5–6.
[2] Harcourt to Morley, 29 Oct. 1889.
[3] *The Times*, 30 Oct. 1889, pp. 6–7.
[4] *The Times*, 7 Nov. 1889, p. 10, cc. 3–4.
[5] *The Times*, 20 Nov. 1889, p. 9, c. 6.
[6] See, e.g., *N.D.C.*, 24 Oct. 1888, p. 5, c. 3; 11 Feb. 1889, p. 5, c. 6.

Morley would, turning over the pages of some narrow doctrinaire sheet, such as the *Daily News*, remark on the paucity of news from Kerry'. Graham paid particular attention to Newcastle, and his message to labour there was that 'far too much importance had been given to the question of Home Rule for Ireland, as it was not, in his opinion, a question which affected the great body of the working men of England and Scotland'.[1]

Morley attempted to answer these challenges in various ways. For instance, he tried through his own statements to fasten on to his party the appearance of an irrevocable and total commitment to working for home rule until it was achieved. In 1886, immediately after the defeat of the Home Rule Bill, he announced that 'we will do nothing and we will take no course that will show a trace or a shadow of doubt or misgiving as to the policy on which we have embarked'. The party could 'never abandon the cause'.[2] Again and again he laid stress on the duration of the commitment. The Leeds resolution of November 1886, was, he asserted, proof that the Irish question would 'engross the attention and the political interest of the Liberal party until the question is settled, and settled in our sense'. He fastened the commitment on to his colleagues by announcing in advance discredit for anyone who would repudiate it: 'I cannot imagine any one interfering in a great transaction of this kind who should venture to accept a great proposal and then should be willing for any consideration whatever to back out of it.'[3]

The alliance with the Irish also helped to make the Liberals appear completely committed. For example, the declared purpose of his visit to Ireland early in 1888 for a series of speeches and demonstrations—to make the Irish 'understand that the Liberal party mean to stand to their guns'[4]—had the additional consequence of making it more difficult and dishonourable for the party to take any other course. When he spoke in Dublin he referred to his

[1] *N.D.C.*, 15 Feb. 1889, p. 5, c. 1, 27 Apr. 1889, p. 4, c. 6; 22 Nov. 1890, p. 5, c. 3.
[2] *The Times*, 9 June 1886, p. 6, c. 2.
[3] *The Times*, 12 Feb. 1887, p. 12, c. 2; 7 July 1887, p. 7, c. 1.
[4] To Gladstone, 28 Jan. 1888, B.M. Add. MSS. 44255, f. 237.

colleagues, including Harcourt, as committed to the cause, and pledged the party not to 'abate one jot of heart or hope in the struggle in which we are embarked'.[1] He often warned the Liberals that only their firm commitment to home rule kept the Irish from relapsing into unconstitutional and violent conduct.[2]

But for all the problems involved in maintaining the Irish policy it was the campaign against coercion which seemed to offer the most effective remedy. Morley and other Liberal leaders greeted with obvious relief the chance at the beginning of 1887 to transfer attention to this aspect of the Irish issue. For coercion, unlike home rule, made the issue appear clear cut and uncomplicated. Telling Harcourt that they 'must fight Coercion, unaccompanied by remedial measures with tooth and claw', Morley remarked that recent evictions of Irish tenants had been 'a blessing, as reducing the system to its naked elements'.[3] So attracted was he to the idea of concentrating on this aspect that he began declaring himself to be 'most favourable to the view that we might well widen our basis, so as to comprehend all who resist Coercion as a policy, even if they do not accept so full a measure of conciliation as we think wise'.[4] The campaign against coercion enabled discussion on home rule to be confined to the general principles, and the details of a home-rule scheme were no longer at the forefront of political controversy. In May 1887 Morley made clear the significance of this change when he said that the business of the party was now not to produce a detailed scheme of home rule but 'to examine the Coercion Bill line by line and to watch it with unsleeping vigilance'.[5] In September he spoke of how matters now stood between the two sections of Liberals:

We have one point, and one point only. Whether they [the dissentients] agree more or less with a scheme for Home Rule is not now the question. The question is whether they are in favour of an arbitrary and violent

[1] *The Times*, 3 Feb. 1888, p. 10, c. 5; 4 Feb. 1888, p. 8, c. 4.
[2] Cf. *The Times*, 21 Apr. 1887, p. 11, c. 4; 3 Feb. 1888, p. 10, cc. 4–5. Cf. also to Gladstone, 13 Nov. 1887, B.M. Add. MSS. 44255, ff. 227–8.
[3] To Harcourt, 18 Jan. 1887.
[4] To Gladstone, 10 Apr. 1887, B.M. Add. MSS. 44255, f. 192.
[5] *The Times*, 26 May 1887, p. 7, cc. 1–2.

system of government in Ireland. . . . We have now entered upon a new chapter. Affairs in Ireland within the last two, three, or four months have taken a new departure. Let us leave the old controversy . . . till the time comes when we can discuss it fruitfully.¹

A few days later he said: 'The immediate controversy of the moment does not turn upon the scheme of Home Rule . . . The question of the moment is not the Home Rule Bill, but coercion and the administration of coercion.'² Against the disintegrating effect of discussion of detail he made this appeal: 'Do not be turned aside by this or that point as to the retention of Irish members, or as to land purchase, or anything else. Keep your eye fixed upon this main issue—is coercion to go on; is coercion to be the last word of the people of England to the people of Ireland?'³

A great advantage of this 'new departure' was that it appealed even to Harcourt. Before long he was urging Morley to 'take great pains to impress' on Gladstone 'the expediency of concentrating the batteries as much as possible on the practicable breach of Coercion and as little as possible on Home Rule'. 'This I think is the capital tactic of the moment', he wrote. In reply Morley reported that Gladstone 'proposed to go exactly on your line and mine—i.e. to say little about H.R., and to show up present misgovernment'.⁴

The controversy over coercion offered the best means of dramatizing and keeping alive the Irish question in the minds of the English people. Thus, in January 1887 Lord Ripon suggested to Morley that, if the details of evictions were laid before the English public, strong feelings of indignation would be aroused that would be useful 'from a Party point of view'.⁵ In 1891 Harcourt summed up the expediency of concentration on coercion in this way: 'the success that we have achieved has been a good deal more from the opposition to Coercion than from the advocacy of

[1] *The Times*, 26 Sept. 1887, p. 8, c. 1.
[2] *The Times*, 3 Oct. 1887, p. 8, c. 1.
[3] *The Times*, 20 Aug. 1888, p. 10, c. 3.
[4] Harcourt to Morley, 8 Oct. 1887. Morley to Harcourt, 13 Oct. 1887.
[5] 17 Jan. 1887, B.M. Add. MSS. 43541, f. 10.

Home Rule. The British people care a good deal more about the *wrongs* than about the *rights* of the Irish.'[1]

For there were two great drawbacks that the Liberals had to overcome before they could successfully wage a campaign on behalf of the Irish. The first was that to which the *Pall Mall Gazette* drew attention in 1880 when it referred to the ignorance and apathy of the English about the problems of Ireland. 'Nobody in England or Scotland', it complained, 'feels about Ireland with the keenness, the energy, the intensity with which hundreds of thousands of them feel about temperance, about slavery, even about the county franchise or the House of Lords.'[2] In 1888 Morley commented: 'Considering the pressure of daily life upon all, he could easily see how great affairs transacted at a distance might sink into a second place.'[3] But emphasis on the details of coercion could help people to 'feel about Ireland'. Thus, in response to a claim by Harcourt in late 1886 that '9 people out of 10 think Ireland a bore' and 'are sick of the subject and would gladly turn to something else if they could safely do so', Morley wrote: '*My notion* . . . is that the business next January, as it was last, will be *Coercion*. That blessed word will give a new shape to the kaleidoscope and all the present talk will prove to be perfectly idle.'[4]

But secondly, before sympathy for oppressed and coerced Irishmen could be aroused in England, English prejudice against the Irish had to be countered. Furthermore, there was the danger at the time of this prejudice being increased by Irish unruliness and violence. At the end of 1886 Morley urged Parnell to moderate the 'plan of campaign' because of its effect on non-Irish opinion.[5] Harcourt was worried that the allegation against the Liberals of 'complicity in agrarian confiscation and general anarchy and plunder' might be 'likely to be a telling and mischievous ground of attack'. 'I think we must carry ourselves very circumspectly to

[1] Harcourt to Morley, 3 Jan. 1891.
[2] *P.M.G.*, 20 Sept. 1880.
[3] *The Times*, 30 June 1888, p. 9, c. 5.
[4] Harcourt to Morley, 20 Nov. 1886; Morley to Harcourt, 25 Nov. 1886.
[5] Cf. Morley to Gladstone, 7 Dec. 1886; Gladstone to Morley, 8 Dec. 1886, B.M. Add. MSS. 44255, ff. 135–6, 139. *Gladstone*, III, p. 371.

keep out of its reach', he warned Morley.¹ In 1888 the crisis caused by the articles in *The Times* on 'Parnellism and Crime' was regarded by Morley as 'a horrid nuisance for us', and he tried to dissuade Parnell from bringing an action: 'Apart from the issue of the business, it diverts the public mind from Coercion. . . . the *Times* will be sure to insist on bringing in all the agrarian murders &c. This bloody story would go on for days, and for days the public mind would be saturated with the very part of the Irish question wh. it is our interest to minimise.'²

Morley's speeches reveal increasingly frequent recourse to a way of presenting the Irish situation which offered a solution to both these problems. Not only did it avoid the necessity of basing the case on trying to arouse the sympathy of Englishmen for Irishmen, but it also had the positive effect of making Englishmen 'feel about Ireland' nevertheless. In 1887 Morley set the keynote of this approach when he said to the National Liberal Federation: 'we ought to feel, everyone of us in this hall, and in every town in England, that an infraction of the fair constitutional right of the poorest peasant in Galway or Mayo is an infraction of your right and mine.'³ The method of arousing this feeling was to work on the Englishman's fear and imagination in order to develop in him sympathy for himself. The Englishman was asked how he would like coercion in England rather than how he liked its being employed in Ireland. In April 1887 Morley gave this advice to London Liberals on how to conduct the campaign against coercion: 'I should like you, in your arguments with your neighbours upon this Bill, to ask them, and to ask one another, how you would endure a measure of this kind applied in England.'⁴ He himself frequently invited his audiences to imagine how such a measure could affect their own lives. For example, in a speech at Norwich he said: 'Let them [the Government] bring in a Bill giving to a couple of county justices, because there had been some poaching in the district, power to summon half the labourers and farmers

---

¹ Harcourt to Morley, 9 Dec. 1886.
² To Ripon, 10, 13 July 1888, B.M. Add. MSS. 43541, ff. 51–3.
³ *The Times*, 21 Apr. 1887, p. 11, c. 3.
⁴ *The Times*, 7 Apr. 1887, p. 6, c. 3.

from the country side and ask them in private where they were on such a night and what they were going and whether they knew what so-and-so was doing. ('Shame.') That was the nature of this Bill.'[1]

In particular, he employed this kind of appeal to interest the working class in the Irish cause and thereby attach them both to it and to the Liberal party who had adopted it. It was obvious that home rule was not in itself an issue likely to appeal to English working men. 'The masses care very little about Ireland,' Labouchere once observed; 'justice to Ireland does not arouse their enthusiasm, unless it be wrapped up in what they regard as justice to themselves.'[2] He meant by this that the home-rule policy ought to be wrapped up between attractive proposals of radical domestic reform. But the coercion controversy enabled the Irish question itself to be presented to the working class in terms of 'justice to themselves'. Morley found in it a way of giving working men the impression that the Irish struggle was also their own; and he did this by developing through it two kinds of reference—to past and to future.

In his discussions of the implications of coercion he would refer back to the old battles over 'conspiracy', the right to combine, and other trade-union causes. This dramatized the Irish question for working men, provided a point of identification in it for them, encouraged them to think about politics in terms of re-fighting old battles rather than entering on new contests involving socialistic reform demands, and gave the politician the sense of knowing where he was with the working class because he could use arguments that were known to have appealed to them in the past while at the same time arousing emotions now regarded as safe by most Liberals.[3] Thus in an address to the London Liberal and Radical Union in March 1887 Morley incorporated in an attack on coercion this comment: 'There are, I am sure, in this Council

---

[1] *The Times*, 26 May 1887, p. 7, c. 2.
[2] Labouchere to H. Gladstone, 9 July [1886], B.M. Add. MSS. 46016, f. 98.
[3] On the appeal of the coercion issue to working men, see also L. P. Curtis, Jr., *Coercion and Conciliation in Ireland 1880–1892—A Study in Conservative Unionism*, Princeton and London, 1963, pp. 260–1, and J. L. Hammond, *Gladstone and the Irish Nation*, 1938, pp. 569–75.

many members of trade unions, who can remember, as I can, the struggle to get the legality of trade combinations recognized. They will remember the extraordinary difficulty and delicacy of the questions connected with inciting to conspiracy and intimidation. Those questions are to be decided in Ireland by two resident magistrates.'[1] At Norwich in May 1887 he sought to reawaken against coercion emotions associated with former labour struggles: 'Let the Government bring in a Bill re-enacting all the old harsh bad laws against trade unions; let them bring in a Bill giving to a couple of county justices the power of inflicting six months' imprisonment with hard labour on a number of labourers who had met on the village green and combined to ask for a lower rent for their allotments.' ('Shame.')[2] On another occasion he described the imprisoning of Irish M.P.s and then said to his audience: 'We look back—some of you I daresay can remember it—with shame and disgust to the days when Ernest Jones and the Chartists were lowered to the level of ordinary criminals for political offences.'[3]

Secondly, he seemed to be trying to arouse fears that the same methods as were being used in Ireland might soon be extended to the rest of the United Kingdom, particularly in connection with an attack on trade unionism. Since the rights of trade unions were still far from settled and the country was on the verge of a major new era of trade-union expansion and industrial conflict, the emotional basis for a positive response to such a mode of presenting the coercion issue must have been fairly easily discernible. In a speech in London early in 1887 Morley warned his audience that 'in operation the [coercion] Bill will exceedingly affect the principles of trade unionism', and asked them to 'think of the Lord Mayor having it in his power to suppress a trade union and to declare it an illegal combination because he thought it fatal to law and order and to the maintenance of the Administration'. At this a voice, as significant as the voices that cried 'Shame' during his speech at Norwich, exclaimed 'Let them try it on'.[4] Agricultural trade

---

[1] *The Times*, 31 Mar. 1887, p. 10, c. 1.
[2] *The Times*, 26 May 1887, p. 7, c. 2.
[3] *The Times*, 8 June 1888, p. 10, c. 3.
[4] *The Times*, 7 Apr. 1887, p. 6, cc. 3-4.

unionism was in an especially uncertain stage of development, and at Norwich Morley sought to establish a connection between the coercion of the Irish peasants when they tried to organize and the problems of the English farm labourers. 'He did not know', he said, 'whether they had trade unions in Norwich ('Yes'), but he maintained that this Bill was a deliberate attempt to introduce by statute some of the old pieces of Judge-made law.'[1]

In these various ways Morley tried to present the Irish issue as involving interests and principles with which his English audiences could feel familiar in terms of their own situation. The Liberals, in preoccupying themselves with the problems of the Irish, were not turning their backs on the problems of the working people of England, but, on the contrary, were revealing themselves as the truest exponents of the basic principles of the British working-class movement. The Conservatives were seeking, according to Morley, 'to put down these combinations for which they had fought in England, and which were as fully needed in Ireland as they were ever needed in England'.[2] Combination 'has made men of you', he told an audience of Durham miners in 1889; the Liberals, he went on, were fighting the Government over their Irish policy because 'the Government are doing in Ireland exactly towards the tenant combinations as in the bad old days the laws and those who were then the makers of the laws endeavoured to do towards people like yourselves'.[3]

The Irish question would remain the predominating issue in British politics only if the public were kept diverted by it and interested in it. This is, no doubt, why we so often find Morley celebrating yet another 'new departure' in connection with it and assuring his audiences that the Irish question was 'taking a new shape' and 'very rapidly moving on a new turn'.[4] But why was it that Morley continued to see such great need for the concentration

[1] *The Times*, 26 May 1887, p. 7, c. 3.
[2] Ibid.
[3] *The Times*, 8 July 1889, p. 7, c. 6.
[4] *The Times*, 14 Feb. 1889, p. 6, c. 2.

of the activity of his party and the political feelings of the whole country on this one issue? In the next chapter we shall examine further the significance of the Irish policy as an 'umbrella' over political activity and discussion and see the reasons for Morley's disinclination to favour its removal from that position.

16

THE SEARCH FOR NEW LIBERAL POLICY, 1886-1890

THE great Irish policy concentrated the energies of Liberals within itself, furnishing them with a reason for temporarily deferring decision and action on other questions. However, it also functioned as an umbrella covering the disorganized variety of these other questions while Liberals continued to debate in the hope of evolving some order among them. It is clear that Morley had turned away from the area of social reform in 1885 because he considered that the country could not yet safely be allowed to concentrate on this type of policy. More time was needed for the evolution of principles to guide practice. Until that evolution had occurred, discussion must be divorced from action.

The Irish question can be seen in Morley's politics as helping to establish what Bagehot had called a 'polity of discussion'. The 'faddists' who had been harassing the Liberal leaders for so long could go on arguing and debating and trying to win people over to their particular causes, but they could now be told that there was no possibility for the time being of commitment or action by the Liberal party on any of these causes.

Morley's characteristic response to demands for action was to call for the fullest, freest discussion of the issues involved. We shall see, for example, how he was under constant pressure from Radicals and Socialists in Newcastle to commit himself on labour reform. At the end of 1889 he agreed to discuss these demands with a deputation of Socialists. After this meeting he told Newcastle Liberals that he had foreseen that the Reform Acts would be followed 'by new demands of all kinds on the part of the new electors'. Liberals must take account of the 'great ferment upon social questions of the utmost difficulty' which was developing in the public mind. They should not try to stifle the new ideas, but should adopt the strategy 'of inviting those who advocate' them to come forward to fair and free discussion'. The way to prevent unwise extensions of State activity and to enable people to reach 'sound and solid conclusions' on social problems was to allow 'time to discuss the arguments over and thresh out the question'.[1] 'Discussion', he often insisted, 'is the very salt of a wholesome democracy.'[2] One demand which particularly vexed him was that for the legal enforcement of an eight-hour working day, and on this he would say: 'let them give the democracy time; let it hear the arguments, and they would find out that it would come to a right and sound conclusion in this question. He only asked that the question should be argued and not rushed.'[3] On one occasion he remarked that 'we cannot hear too constantly, too articulately, too clearly the voice of our working population'. 'What is important', he said, '—and our democracy is a farce if we do not recognise and act upon it—is that we should hear what they have to say, and that they should have the opportunity, a full opportunity, of delivering their voice in places where that voice is most sure to be heard.'[4]

Walter Bagehot, writing after the 1867 Reform Act, had maintained that no harm can come to society so long as men are merely talking about great issues. 'If you want to stop instant and immediate action', he wrote in *Physics and Politics*, 'always make it a condition that the action shall not begin till a considerable number of persons have talked over it, and have agreed on it.' For, once such a debate has begun among people of 'different temperaments, different ideas, and different educations', one has 'an almost infallible security that nothing, or almost nothing, will be done with excessive rapidity'. There will be objections and counter-objections, 'and so in the end nothing will probably be done, or at least only the minimum which is plainly urgent'. For the purpose of preventing hasty action there was, Bagehot wrote, 'no device like a polity of discussion'.[5]

[1] *The Times*, 6 Nov. 1889, p. 10, c. 2.
[2] *The Times*, 31 Jan. 1890, p. 7, c. 2.
[3] *The Times*, 8 Nov. 1890, p. 9, c. 2.
[4] *The Times*, 2 Oct. 1891, p. 10, c. 1.
[5] W. Bagehot, *Physics and Politics*, 1906, pp. 192–4.

The great Irish policy after 1885 seemed from Morley's presentation of it to be designed to secure the establishment of such a 'polity of discussion' by enforcing a severance between discussion and the possibility of translating it into action. Morley's speeches illustrate this in their two-part construction. A first part would consist of a discussion of issues of domestic policy and an acceptance of their importance. But the second would in effect cancel out the first by raising the objection that nothing could be done about these until after home rule had been conceded to Ireland. Thus Morley could talk about domestic policy and give his approval to various proposals, but what he appeared to be giving with one hand he was taking away with the other, and discussion was not to be affected by the 'desire to act promptly'. It was said to be rendered by the Irish preoccupation 'more or less impractical'. 'It is idle', Morley would say, 'for us to start forth'—that is, move into action—'on our voyage of social reform in Great Britain so long as the deck of the ship of State is cumbered and loaded with the Irish question.' Ireland made Parliament 'impotent' to deal with domestic policy, and stopped 'all effectual discussion upon measures of social progress for our teeming and toiling population at home'.[1]

Temporarily it was only the second half of Morley's speeches, the pretext of an enforced deferment of action on everything except Irish policy, that provided order and a 'spirit of system' in his politics. But it was obvious that for the Liberal party as a whole the benefits that accrued from concentration on home rule could be of only very limited duration. Before long, if home rule were not achieved, the policy would have to be discarded or relegated. Morley's reply to Liberals impatient to press on with other reforms that their very impatience was an added reason for whole-hearted devotion to the work of securing Irish home rule may have helped to keep the party in order temporarily, but it was a wasting argument, since it depended for its effectiveness on rapid progress towards an early achievement of the goal. From Morley's point

[1] *The Times*, 12 Feb. 1887, p. 12, c. 1; 30 Jan. 1890, p. 7, c. 1; 22 Sept. 1891, p. 5, cc. 3-4.

of view, therefore, it was of great importance that beneath the umbrella of the Irish policy Liberals should be striving to discover order and agreement in their ideas and in their planning for action. To this work Morley himself devoted considerable time and thought, although of course, the retention of the Irish policy in first place remained the overriding consideration. He hoped, it would seem, that, when eventually the Irish umbrella was removed, strong, coherent principles and policies would be found to have developed beneath its shade. In 1888 he told an audience: 'Nothing can be done until the first question before us is disposed of. When that question is out of the way then we will deal with the others. Meanwhile those other questions are ripening, you are pressing them into the minds of one another, they are making their way into the minds of members of Parliament . . . .'[1] In 1889 he referred to other questions that were 'slowly ripening'.[2] In particular, there was the necessity of finding reform policies that would arouse, but arouse safely, the enthusiasm of the working class.

Morley at this time gives the impression of one groping in darkness on strange ground in search of a new point of contact with the world of labour to replace that supplied by the Irish issue. In February 1889 Beatrice Potter wrote after a long talk with him: 'He was preparing for an interview at Newcastle, and was full of the eight hours' movement and other social questions. In his speeches he asserts that the social question is the one thing to live for . . . And yet he has evidently never thought about social questions; he does not know even the ABC of labour problems.'[3] In 1891 Morley spoke of 'the vast, dim world of manual labour': 'We want to know what ideas are working in the minds of the labouring classes; we want to examine them; we want to give them time to ripen; we want to see whether there are among them demands that legislation can meet and can deal with.'[4] Sometimes, in hope rather than in confident knowledge, he would

[1] *The Times*, 9 Oct. 1888, p. 6, c. 5.
[2] *The Times*, 7 Dec. 1889, p. 6, c. 4.
[3] B. Webb, *My Apprenticeship*, 1929, p. 306.
[4] *The Times*, 22 Sept. 1891, p. 5, c. 2.

make suggestions as to what these might be. Thus in a speech in 1889 he described possible reforms in connection with land, taxation, and electoral procedure, and declared: 'Unless I am wrong the working men of England and other classes besides the working men will take these questions up . . . .'[1] The incorporation of the 'other classes' is significant as showing that the right kind of issue remained what he had insisted on in the early 1870s, an issue that did not appeal to or make the working class a factor by itself in politics.

He began cautiously to develop various questions in order to discover whether they were yet ready to become the focus of political action. For example, he appeared after 1887 to take great interest in local government reform, and even spoke of it, in a manner reminiscent of Chamberlain's Radical campaign in 1885, as a possible umbrella to cover other reforms, his argument being that it would be far less 'mischievous and dangerous' for local authorities to make experiments in the way of social reform than for the State to do so.[2] Another question which he began to explore was temperance and licensing reform. As yet he had to admit that, while he believed that ratepayers should control the issue of liquor licences, he did 'not know whether opinion in England is ripe for such a provision as that', and, he warned, 'you must not go in advance of the general opinion'.[3] But his comments on the temperance issue in general showed that he was attracted to it as a possible single great question of domestic reform.[4] Before long he was calling the temperance movement the greatest, most deep-seated moral movement since anti-slavery.[5] In 1889 he said of 'local option': 'It is perfectly idle to go on saying in general terms that you are for trusting the people and yet decline, as the Government has hitherto declined, to trust the people in a particular

---

[1] *The Times*, 23 Jan. 1889, p. 10, c. 2.
[2] *The Times*, 5 Apr. 1888, p. 7, cc. 2-3; 20 Aug. 1888, p. 10, c. 1; 20 Nov. 1889, p. 10, c. 1; 21 Nov. 1890, p. 10, c. 2. 4 Aug. 1891, p. 8, cc. 1-2; 22 Sept. 1891, p. 5, c. 3. *Hansard*, 3, 344, 348-9.
[3] *The Times*, 5 Apr. 1888, p. 7, c. 2.
[4] Cf., e.g., to Harcourt, 9 June 1888. *The Times*, 20 Aug. 1888, p. 10, c. 1; 5 Feb. 1889, p. 10, c. 1.
[5] *The Times*, 20 Nov. 1889, p. 10, c. 1.

question in which they . . . have shown themselves interested beyond almost any other question in the whole field of social reform.'[1] A year later he told the N.L.F. that temperance was 'perhaps the most important' cause of all, and declared: 'I am fervently convinced of its urgency and its necessity.'[2] This isolation of a single issue and its presentation as the first in importance and as the test of sincere concern for democratic reform are characteristic of Morley and show how he was trying to develop some order in Liberal ideas on domestic policy.

At this time Morley's interest in working out the future pattern of Liberal policy was being stimulated by two particular influences. The first of these came from a group of younger Liberals—of whom R. B. Haldane, Asquith, and Edward Grey were the most prominent—with whom he became associated in the late 1880s. These men appeared to be as anxious as he was himself to counter tendencies in the party towards 'dangerous' Radicalism. In 1889 they organized themselves into a group which, wrote Haldane, 'should gain the confidence of the public by its constructive propositions, and which should by means of these not only attain a position from which to criticise with the utmost frankness & firmness the people with whose names we were at present being labelled, i.e. Labouchere & Company, but at the same time, while perfectly loyal to our front bench, stimulate it to really lead the party'. As Haldane saw it, there was a vacuum in domestic policy with 'neither Mr. G. nor any one else' having 'an idea to broach'. They must act at once 'to prevent Laby & Co. stepping in to fill the gap' and taking over the party by default.[3]

In these men we can recognize the developing 'Liberal Imperialist' section of the party. At this stage, however, imperialism was not the cause of division between them and Morley that it was later to become. Indeed, when the group was formed, Haldane wrote concerning Lord Rosebery: 'I find myself at one with him

---

[1] *The Times*, 10 Dec. 1889, p. 6, c. 5.
[2] *The Times*, 21 Nov. 1890, p. 10, c. 2.
[3] D. Sommer, *Haldane of Cloan. His Life and Times 1856–1928*, 1960, pp. 76–7. Haldane to R. Ferguson, 4 Nov. 1889, Haldane MSS. 5903, ff. 139–40.

on his Imperial policy. He is going in a few days to advocate a programme of regular Colonial Conferences and to this even a Morleyite like myself can wish God speed!'[1] The link between them and Morley was forged mainly by the progressive-élitist aspect of Morley's political philosophy, for this both attracted them to him as a guide in political conduct and attracted him to them as a possible realization of the ideal described by him in *On Compromise*. According to Asquith's biographers, Morley was 'uncritically accepted and whole-heartedly admired by the young Liberal group' as 'a mentor, a sponsor, in matters political a guide, philosopher, and friend'.[2] *On Compromise* made a deep impression on them, obviously in its aspect of a treatise of élitist conduct, written for young men who were told that they were 'holders of a trust' and that the progress of society depended on their initiative. Winston Churchill was later to describe it as having been 'for many years a guide to Liberal youth'.[3] G. M. Trevelyan tells us that 'Morley's clear-cut and limpid intellect had a great fascination' for the young Edward Grey, 'not on political questions alone'. *On Compromise* and Morley's French studies became a part 'of Grey's spiritual being'.[4] In 1890 Haldane wrote of having spent an evening with 'not the John Morley of the H of Commons—but the old John Morley of Compromise', the man 'to whom one looks up as a leader'.[5]

Morley's relations with these younger Liberals were at their closest from 1889 to about 1895. In September 1889 we find him advising Haldane—very much in the style of the 'Morley of Compromise'—as to how 'a man with a future, like you', ought to conduct himself in politics. He warned Haldane not to 'disable himself for future occasions by premature committals' on policy issues. Then he added: 'I hope we shall stand together.'[6] Two

[1] Sommer, *Haldane of Cloan*, p. 77.
[2] J. A. Spender and C. Asquith, *Life of Herbert Henry Asquith, Lord Oxford and Asquith*, I, 1932, p. 70.
[3] W. S. Churchill, *Great Contemporaries*, 1938, p. 99.
[4] G. M. Trevelyan, *Grey of Fallodon Being the Life of Sir Edward Grey Afterwards Viscount Grey of Fallodon*, 1937, p. 33.
[5] Haldane to his sister, 30 Oct. 1890, Haldane MSS. 6010, f. 77.
[6] T. Haldane, 5 Sept. 1889, Haldane MSS. 5903, f. 132.

months later Haldane was writing that the young Liberals were going to 'look to J.M. & Fowler on the front bench as those with whom we are informally but in substance in touch'; and on 13 November Morley held the dinner at which the group was brought into being.[1] He seems to have tried to have dinner meetings regularly. Early in 1890 he wrote to Haldane: 'When will you and Asquith come to dine here—Feb. 6, 7, 8, or possibly 10. Then I'll get the others.'[2] It soon became apparent that, if Morley was to be the group's 'spiritual adviser', Rosebery was the man whom they aimed to make practical leader.[3] Morley himself was, as we shall see, to prefer Rosebery as leader in 1894. He tried hard to keep the group in existence and to promote the claims of its members within the party. Thus in August 1891 he urged Asquith to come to Newcastle to support Gladstone at the meeting of the National Liberal Federation and told him that he had been 'cracking up our matchless band of young men.'[4] When a year later he felt concern about the electoral problems of the party, he told Asquith: 'Much, and very much, depends on three or four of us standing firm together.'[5] Finally, when Asquith and Acland were appointed to the Cabinet in 1892, they thanked Morley on behalf of the group 'for your loyal and strenuous efforts on our behalf'.[6]

These younger Liberals stimulated Morley to begin organizing his thinking on domestic policy. On 12 November 1889 Haldane wrote to his sister: 'We are—a number of us—at work trying to set the Gladstonians in the H. of C. on their legs in the matter of a home programme. Asquith & I have been at work on it, and we dine at John Morleys & with Grey & others tomorrow to define our lines.'[7] The effect of this is evident from the important speech on 'Liberalism and Social Reform' which Morley gave at the

[1] Haldane to Ferguson, 4 Nov. 1889, and to his sister Elizabeth, 12 Nov. 1889, Haldane MSS. 5903, f. 140, and 6010, f. 45. Sommer, *Haldane of Cloan*, p. 77.
[2] 24 Jan. 1890, Haldane MSS. 5903, f. 148.
[3] Cf. Morley to Rosebery, 27 Jan. 1890, Rosebery MSS.
[4] To Asquith, 13 Aug. 1891, Asquith MSS. Dep. 9, f. 1. Cf. *Recollections*, I, p. 323.
[5] 16 Aug. 1892, Asquith MSS, Dep. 9, f. 17.
[6] *Recollections*, I, p. 324. For Morley's very close relations with Asquith at this time, see also ibid., I, pp. 369–76; II, p. 45.
[7] Haldane MSS. 6010, f. 45.

Eighty Club a week later.[1] The most recent historian of Fabianism uses this speech to illustrate the extent to which leading Liberals were now being influenced by new thinking on social reform.[2] In the speech Morley admitted that the desire of the new voters for such reform was now much clearer than it had been in 1885, and proceeded to outline a programme of measures including the 'free breakfast table', free education, and free meals in schools. As Professor McBriar points out, Haldane did later make some decidedly exaggerated claims about the extent of Fabian influence over Morley at this time.[3] Elizabeth Haldane later recalled that Morley was 'drawing up a political programme' in the late 1880s and that in connection with this Haldane had tried to arrange a meeting between him and Sidney Webb.[4] From a letter written by Morley to Harcourt only a month after the Eighty Club speech it appears that not only Morley but Gladstone himself did meet Webb at this time, and that their opinion of him was the reverse of favourable. 'Sydney [sic] Webb is an ass', wrote Morley, '—but a clever ass—and a horrid bore. He knows no more of working men than I know of Hampshire peasants. Don't let him bore you. He half killed Mr. G, with his long yarns.'[5] Morley was later to tell Haldane: 'The Fabians interest and stimulate and suggest—but they are loose, superficial, crude, and impertinent.'[6] The younger Liberals had brought Morley into contact with the new social radicalism, and, even if he could not agree with the Fabians, he did at least seem prepared for a while to think seriously about the work of effecting a reconciliation between Liberalism and these new trends of thought.

Morley's dislike of Sidney Webb is not surprising in view of his considerable antagonism to London intellectual Radicalism in general. But, in fact, Morley's own attitude to the distinctive social

[1] *The Times*, 20 Nov. 1889, p. 10, cc. 1–2.
[2] A. M. McBriar, *Fabian Socialism and English Politics 1884–1918*, Cambridge, 1962, pp. 240–1.
[3] Ibid., p. 241, fn. 2.
[4] E. S. Haldane, *From One Century to Another. Reminiscences*, 1937, p. 106.
[5] Morley to Harcourt, 26 Dec. 1889.
[6] 28 Sept. 1891, Haldane MSS. 5903, f. 190.

NEW LIBERAL POLICY 1886-1890 249

and political conditions of London did have an important influence over his political thinking at this time. London provided the second stimulus to his efforts to work out new principles for Liberal domestic policy.

London always had a particular fascination for Morley. He seemed above all to resent the fact that he had been impelled to go there in order to earn his living and yet had never been able to find in it a proper community to which to attach himself. In his letters London is described constantly in phrases such as 'the vortex', 'this chaotic monster of a city', and 'so cold and *unhomeish*'.[1] London seemed a magnet drawing to itself able young men from the provinces.[2] But, once they were there, London seemed to drain them of vitality. Someone who was 'a clever workman and a citizen' in a provincial town would there become just 'one more atom' in a 'huge, overgrown, and unwieldy community'.[3] Morley often describes intellectuals in London as sterile and impotent. Their ideas seemed to him to suffer from lack of contact with practical reality. 'London academic radicals' were 'full of good ideas and good will, but it ends in mere fuss'.[4] To Morley there was always something odd and unnatural and unhealthy about life in London.

In the late 1880s London was significant for him principally because he feared and disliked what he saw happening in politics there. The politics of London presented a challenge as a microcosm of all that was potentially most dangerous for Liberalism. Morley believed that it was urgently necessary that the unhealthy elements in London Radicalism should be extinguished or at least countered and prevented from becoming contagious. The 'healthy' Liberalism of the provinces, of Scotland, and of Wales must be enabled to predominate.

The home-rule crisis seemed to Morley to have drawn the line of distinction in Liberal politics between London and the rest of the country even more sharply. According to Morley, Liberals in

---

[1] To Harrison, 11 Apr. 1875. To Chamberlain, 20 Dec. 1875, 10 July 1876.
[2] Cf. *Modern Characteristics*, pp. 4–5. *Critical Miscellanies*, III, pp. 2–3. *F.R.*, Nov., 1876, pp. 632–3.
[3] *Critical Miscellanies*, III, p. 3.
[4] To Chamberlain, 28 Nov. 1876.

the North of England, and in Scotland and Wales, staunchly supported the strategy of concentrating on the home-rule policy, but London Liberals were 'very anxious that we should have some other immediate aim of policy before us, besides Ireland'.[1] He now became very worried both about the Radicals and also about the working men in London, and often contrasted them with their 'sound', 'sober' provincial counterparts. 'This strike epidemic', he wrote in 1889, 'is almost confined to London. In the provinces the men have asked reasonable advances, and have got them.'[2] 'The working people of the North of England' seemed to 'take a different view of their interests from the view taken by the working people of London'.[3] As for London Radicalism, he was telling London audiences as early as September 1885 that he had 'heard some very bad things' about it and that it did not have a 'straightforward and practical complexion'.[4] By contrast, it was 'the solid, serious, reflective Liberalism of the North-East of England' to which he looked 'most confidently for the safe progress of the fortunes of our country'.[5] In 1890 he explained to the National Liberal Federation that it was the enormous population of London which caused the Radicals there to be impatient about social reform; but he warned that this impatience needed checking by 'the greater deliberateness, if I may say so the steadfastness, of provincial Radicalism'.[6]

'Provincial' though his Liberalism was, Morley refused to neglect or ignore London, for in its very distinctiveness lay a challenge that could not safely be turned down by the Liberals. Asa Briggs has observed that 'In all parts of the country it was recognized during the 1880s and '90s that London politics "counted", congenial or uncongenial though they might be held to be. When writers in periodicals wished to talk of the "politics of the future", as they often did, they looked closely and carefully

[1] *The Times*, 12 July 1886, p. 8, c. 2. To Gladstone, 15 Nov., 7 Dec. 1886, B.M. Add. MSS. 44255, ff. 129, 133.
[2] To Harcourt, 26 Dec. 1889.
[3] *The Times*, 5 May 1892, p. 6, c.3.
[4] *The Times*, 17 Sept. 1885, p. 4, c. 2.
[5] *The Times*, 5 Apr. 1888, p. 7, c. 1.
[6] *The Times*, 21 Nov. 1890, p. 10, c. 1.

at the politics of London.'[1] London seemed to have advanced furthest towards the politics of class war in which middle-class Liberalism would have no place. In 1887 Morley remarked that in London there were on the one hand Socialist demonstrations and 'licence' and yet on the other 'the Tories have a predominance of five to one' over the Liberals.[2] The inclination of Londoners to vote Conservative appears to have been very much on his mind during this period.[3] And it was in connection with London politics that he saw most clearly the relationship between the survival of the Liberal party and the survival of an independent middle class. He was at this time putting great stress on the desirability of shaping Liberal policy with regard to the interests of 'a class for whom I have, at least, as much sympathy as I have for the working men—the struggling lower middle class', 'a class whose life is one of hard, bitter, incessant struggle for bare subsistence'. He advocated reform of taxation and landholding that would help the small tradesman and shopkeeper, a type of citizen 'too good for us to allow him to be lost sight of'.[4] It may have been his campaign for Westminster in 1880 that first aroused his interest in the political position of the London shopkeepers.[5] His later interest is evident in a letter which he wrote to Chamberlain in 1888. In this, sinking for the moment his differences with Chamberlain over Ireland in face of the new dangers for Liberalism and the middle class, and writing that 'unless I misread your hopes for the future, the picture will not be much more agreeable to you than it is to me', he deplored 'the anarchic follies of the London Radicals' as 'playing the Tory game to a marvel'; in other words, driving the middle class away from Liberalism. 'We cannot win, without accession of strength from the London constituencies and that strength will never come so long as these blatant democrats persist in frightening the small shopkeeper. . . .' In December 1889, writing to Harcourt on 'our prospects in London', he argued

[1] A. Briggs, *Victorian Cities*, 1963, pp. 341–2.
[2] *The Times*, 26 Oct. 1887, p. 10, c. 1.
[3] Cf. *N.D.C.*, 4 Feb. 1889, p. 5, c. 3.
[4] *The Times*, 5 Apr. 1888, p. 7, c. 3; 13 Dec. 1888, p. 12, c. 5; 23 Jan. 1889, p. 10, c. 2.
[5] Cf. *F.R.*, May 1880, p. 729.

that the strikes taking place at that time 'won't be likely to draw the small shopkeeper towards Radicalism'.[1]

The challenge presented by London after 1885 to a politician such as Morley was this: the infection of class politics, which threatened to destroy Liberalism, must be checked at its source, London must be purged, and a healthy, 'sober', provincial-style Liberalism be encouraged there instead. Morley responded to this challenge and became a prominent protagonist in the struggle in London between the Liberals and the socialistic, 'anarchic' Radicals. In 1892 he even thought of standing for the London County Council, and of thus following in the path of Rosebery, whom he praised for having 'abundantly shown how well you know that London ought not to be left out of Liberal account'.[2] In January 1887, presiding at the inaugural meeting of the London Liberal Radical Union, Morley declared that the Liberal party proposed to make 'a good, stout, deadlift effort to bring London into line with the Liberalism of the rest of England, and to add the enormous contribution of the influence of London to the great stream which flows with such volume, with such steadiness, and with such force in Scotland, in Ireland, in Wales; aye, and in the greater part of England itself'.[3] He spoke frequently at meetings in London, in the hope, as he put it, of promoting 'a good understanding between the Radicalism of the provinces and the Radicalism of London'.

It was the great Irish policy which Morley first of all tried to use to bridge the gulf. In April 1887 he offered the campaign against coercion to the Liberals and Radicals of the south of London as an issue to 'bring South London and other parts of London back again to the Liberal flag.' In October 1887 he appealed to Londoners to 'join with us in the north and join with the people of Scotland' to see that justice was done to Ireland.[4] However, he came to recognize that the vastness and dispersiveness of London

[1] To Chamberlain, 8 Feb. 1888. To Harcourt, 26 Dec. 1889.
[2] Arnold Morley to Gladstone, 5 Feb. 1892, B.M. Add. MSS. 44254, ff. 181–2. *Recollections*, I, p. 313.
[3] *The Times*, 12 Jan. 1887, p. 7, cc. 1–2.
[4] *The Times*, 31 Mar. 1887, p. 10, c. 1; 7 Apr. 1887, p. 6, c. 1; 3 Oct. 1887, p. 8, c. 1.

life did pose a special problem. In *Cobden* he had written that London 'is no centre for the kind of agitation' represented by the Anti-Corn Law League. 'In London there is no effective unity; interests are too varied and dispersive; zeal loses its directness and edge amid the distracting play of so many miscellaneous social and intellectual elements.'[1] Perhaps 'dispersive' programmes best suited the character of London; and perhaps the relevant question about London politics was not whether they were to be organized around a programme or a single issue but what the programme was to contain and promise. There was a danger that, if the Liberals continued to insist on their single great issue with its strong 'provincial' and 'Celtic Fringe' flavour, Londoners, not understanding this kind of politics, might succumb to the Socialist programmes as the only examples of the other kind holding the field. After a year of trying to persuade London Radicals to concentrate on the Irish question, Morley himself set to work to devise a Liberal programme for London that would take account of the social evils which Socialists condemned, but would guide into safer channels the search for remedies for them. In December 1888 in a speech at Clerkenwell he outlined what he thereafter called his 'Clerkenwell programme'—including taxation of ground landlords for expenditure on public improvements, and the ending of the leasehold system. Discussing London's problems such as high rents, bad sanitation, and 'sweating', he said: 'I do not wonder at the impatience and anger of our Socialist friends. Let me be frank. I think them wrong. . . .' He warned against excessive reliance for social improvement on legislation. 'London', he believed, 'will not be attacked by politics alone or first.' Repeatedly he insisted that what he was advocating was 'not Jacobinism', 'not cupidity', 'not teaching the working classes to covet what is not theirs'. 'In nothing that I have said', he declared, 'do I mean to promise you the millennium': politics could not 'mitigate the tribulations and the chances and changes of human life'.[2] Subsequent speeches in London developed these themes and this kind

[1] *Cobden*, I, pp. 143-4. Cf. N. McCord, *The Anti-Corn Law League 1838-1846*, 1958, pp. 17, 44, 48, 75-7.
[2] *The Times*, 13 Dec. 1888, p. 12, cc. 4-5. *Recollections*, I, p. 313.

of programme. In 1890 he explained to the National Liberal Federation why he had thus deviated into 'programme' politics: 'An enormous population such as that of London must present problems of its own. It is natural that men with alert minds, with their hearts set on fire by the wrong, the suffering, the misery they see around them . . . should be impatient and should press on with what they believe to be practicable remedies.' But he himself had tried in his Clerkenwell 'programme' to define 'the needs of London and the direction to which we should look to meet those needs'.[1]

These, then, were the principal influences that were encouraging Morley to develop his thinking on Liberal policy. But hardly had the process of reconstruction begun before two crises abruptly halted his cautious groping forward into the new areas of policy and drove him back, more of a prisoner than ever, into the confines of the single great policy.

The first of these was the development of an agitation for the enforcement by law of a maximum working day of eight hours. Morley was to encounter this in his own constituency of Newcastle, and when, in his fear of being prematurely committed to inadequately worked out policies of State intervention, he fell back on an extreme Cobdenite *laissez-faire* position, his reputation with the labour movement was dealt a blow from which it never completely recovered.

The second was the Parnell divorce crisis of 1890–1. By threatening to remove the Irish 'umbrella' while beneath it Liberal thinking and planning remained disorganized and incoherent, this crisis led Morley to concentrate on repairing the defences and shoring up the Irish policy.

[1] *The Times*, 21 Nov. 1890, p. 10, c. 1.

17

TWO CRISES:
THE EIGHT-HOUR DAY AND
THE PARNELL DIVORCE

IN his thinking on social and economic reform Morley was obsessed by a fear of interfering with what he considered 'natural' processes. He would argue that, while 'a political leap in the dark', such as home rule, was unlikely to do the country much harm, 'when they touched the vital organs of national life—industry, trade, commerce—a leap in the dark might land them not merely in a mistake but in catastrophe and ruin'.[1] Those who had 'panaceas' were wrong, because 'they begin by taking society to pieces', and 'society, we may be quite sure, will not let itself be taken to pieces'. His faith in a natural, and therefore inevitable, progress, lingered on. 'Humanity', he would say, 'is always opening new ways out for itself.'[2] Social policy should be based, he believed, on the development of the 'spontaneous qualities of human nature', on encouraging and enabling 'the individual man to train himself in temperance, in self-reliance, in energy, in sympathy, in sense of duty to his neighbours'.[3]

Morley's speeches on social policy betrayed his uneasiness and uncertainty in this area. He was obviously acutely conscious of how vague and unfixed as yet the governing principles were, especially with regard to the crucial question of the proper limits of State intervention; and, after making tentative advances into this strange new territory, he would recoil as he encountered complications and unfirm ground. For example, we find him in a speech in 1889 circling doubtfully around the question of national

---

[1] *The Times*, 8 Nov. 1890, p. 9, c. 2.
[2] *The Times*, 20 Nov. 1889, p. 10, c. 3.
[3] *The Times*, 10 Dec. 1889, p. 6, c. 6; 24 Apr. 1890, p. 6, c. 4.

insurance and old-age pensions without arriving at any firm conclusion. He found many difficulties, and yet he had to admit that, in view of the fact that 45 per cent of those who attained the age of sixty were or had been paupers, 'I cannot conceive any subject more worthy of the attention of the Legislature'. But what could the legislature safely do about it? Somehow they had to discover 'how to provide against poverty without injuring society at large, without weakening the springs of responsible action' in individuals.[1] Six months later he told a deputation that he could not yet say whether he was in favour of national insurance, but he was doing his best 'to form an opinion' and was 'considering the subject, which I regard as one of the most serious that can engage the attention of people interested in the state of society'. A speech to the Newcastle Liberal Club the next day shows how the lack of fixed lines, such as he could find in the Irish question, worried him. He stressed the importance for the country's future of 'the accuracy with which the limits of State interference are traced' and of whether 'the dividing line between what ought to be done and what could be wisely and well done by the State on the one hand, or by voluntary effort on the other, is efficiently drawn and efficiently guarded and preserved'.[2] It was characteristic of him that the one firm 'dividing line' to which he did resort was that between England and Ireland, as when he claimed that in Ireland 'a gross moral wrong' inflicted by the British Government justified State interference, whereas in England social distress was 'not due, as far as I know, to causes which the Legislature could, and admits that it ought to, prevent'.[3]

At this time there emerged one particular issue involving State interference in economic life which Morley felt impelled to contest: the issue of whether or not a maximum working day of eight hours should be enforced by law. His opposition to this demand constituted a serious set-back to his efforts to bring his thinking as a Liberal into line with the aspirations of the working class. H. W.

[1] *The Times*, 23 Apr. 1889, p. 8, c. 2.
[2] *The Times*, 5 Nov. 1889, p. 10, c. 5; 6 Nov. 1889, p. 10, c. 2.
[3] *Hansard*, 3, 316, 327.

Massingham later wrote of this as a turning-point in Morley's career: 'Was it not the business of the humanitarian thinker to open the road from Manchester Liberalism to the social Liberalism of the 'nineties? Morley had a great opportunity'—and he chose instead to look back.[1]

He decided to take a firm stand against Eight Hours Bills because he saw in them the forerunners of a kind of legislation which he feared and which he wanted to prevent from becoming commonplace and generally accepted. It was at this point that he determined to oppose the further encroachment of what he once referred to as 'the strong socialist doctrine I hate'. Once again he seized upon the 'practical application' of a general principle 'to a special case then and there before us' and placed on it the whole burden of a complex situation. In 1892 he told Harcourt that he would 'have no part nor lot in any governm^t that brings in 8 hours' bills', because these would pave the way for a series of 'labour questions' which 'will undoubtedly follow'.[2] The Eight Hours Bill, he said, 'marks the appearance of new principles, right or wrong, of a most far-reaching kind'. The division on it in the Commons in 1892, when it received the support of some prominent politicians, might prove to represent 'a new departure for good or for evil, to point to a new distribution of political force, and to be a memorable landmark in the history and the aims, the structure and the composition, of English political parties'.[3]

Morley's great objection to eight-hours legislation was that it would lead to dangerous interference with the free working of natural economic processes. It would mean 'thrusting an Act of Parliament like a ramrod into all the delicate and complex machinery of British industry'. An Eight Hours Bill for miners, for example, would impose uniform regulations on an industry characterized by great diversity of local and natural conditions. He argued that it would be wrong to 'enable the Legislature, which is ignorant of these things, which is biased in these things—to give

---

[1] H. J. Massingham (ed.), *H.W.M. A Selection from the Writings of H. W. Massingham*, 1925, pp. 25–6. See also Additional Note on p. 270.
[2] To Harcourt, 26 Mar. 1892.
[3] *The Times*, 31 Mar. 1892, p. 10, cc. 4–5.

the Legislature the power of saying how many hours a day a man shall or shall not work'. Eight-hours legislation was dangerous as interference with 'the vital organs of national life—industry, trade, commerce'. Even trade unionism, as part of the system of natural adjustment of interests in industrial life, was threatened, for a precedent might be established for the regulation of wages by Parliament. Morley warned trade unionists: 'If they only got into the habit of substituting legislation for their own free and manly organization the effect would be, and it must be, to damage their trade unions.' He insisted that the only right and proper way to secure a limitation of working hours—of which he fully approved so long as it was obtained in this way—was through 'voluntary action' on the part of unionists and negotiations with employers. Such negotiations could be relied on to reveal whether a reduction of working hours was compatible with the 'larger interests at stake'.[1]

Morley believed that free and open discussion 'under the greatest possible variety of circumstances' would be 'the best means of expressing to the working men of this country the entire fallacy and delusiveness of this proposal'. When it was 'fully explained the workmen will bring it to a sharp end'.[2] Hence his indignation against politicians, especially his own colleagues, who seemed to him to be giving way to the labour agitation for opportunistic, electoral reasons without allowing this time for discussion and explanation and without even themselves being convinced of the need for such legislation. In 1890 Haldane wrote that 'John Morley has made a bargain with me that he & I are to continue to fight out the eight hours question at any risk, not because of the pros & cons, so much as because of the wrong reasons which are making politicians yield'.[3] In a speech a week after Haldane wrote this Morley warned of the great danger of a 'leap in the dark', and made this appeal to other politicians: 'let them give the democracy

[1] *The Times*, 22 Sept. 1891, p. 5, c. 2; 31 Mar. 1892, p. 10, c. 4; 20 Nov. 1889, p. 10, c. 3; 8 Nov. 1890, p. 9, c. 2; 23 Apr. 1889, p. 8, c. 2; 8 July 1889, p. 7, c. 5; 5 July 1892, p. 10, c. 3; 4 Feb. 1889, p. 7, c. 4; 21 Nov. 1890, p. 10, c. 2; 5 Feb. 1889, p. 10, c. 1.

[2] *Hansard*, 3, 337, 730. To Spencer, 8 Sept. 1890.

[3] Haldane to his sister Elizabeth, 30 Oct. 1890, Haldane MSS. 6010, f. 77.

EIGHT-HOUR DAY AND PARNELL DIVORCE 259

time. . . . He only asked that the question should be argued and not rushed.'[1] After a division in the Commons on the question in March 1892 he wrote very bitterly: 'That has taken place which I apprehended. The Labour party—that is, the most headstrong and unscrupulous and shallow of those who speak for labour—has captured the Liberal party. Even worse—the Liberal party, on our bench at any rate, has surrendered *sans phrase*, without a word of explanation or vindication.' In a speech shortly afterwards he deplored his colleagues' hastiness. Such a proposal 'at all events, demands full, fair, and abundant discussion' 'at close quarters'. This 'would have cleared up the issues, dark and intricate, which are involved in this important question' and 'would have brought the economic bearings and the philanthropic aspects to a focus'; yet the House had divided after a very brief debate, and some leading politicians had seen fit to support a proposal so inadequately discussed.[2]

Morley clearly hoped that discussion and debate would expose and intensify disagreements on the details of the question which he knew to exist among working men and Radicals. He often pointed to such disagreements as an excuse for his own refusal to support Eight Hours Bills.[3] In addition, the delay that 'abundant discussion' would impose would allow the natural adjustments and operations of economic life to extinguish the agitation.[4]

Whereas most of his colleagues either came out in support of eight-hours legislation or else contrived to conceal their lack of sympathy by equivocation or evasion, Morley frequently and unequivocally stated his firm refusal to vote for any such legislation; and it was this outspokenness, together with the powerful armoury of arguments which he employed, that concentrated on himself the indignation and enmity of those Socialists who sought

[1] *The Times*, 8 Nov. 1890, p. 9, c. 2.
[2] To Harcourt, 26 Mar. 1892. *The Times*, 31 Mar. 1892, p. 10, cc. 4–5.
[3] See. e.g., to Harcourt, 2 June 1891. *The Times*, 5 Feb. 1889, p. 10, c. 1; 5 July 1892, p. 10, c. 3. Hansard, 3, 337, 731. A. G. Gardiner. *The Life of Sir William Harcourt*, II, 1923, p. 171. A. M. McBriar, *Fabian Socialism and English Politics 1884–1918*, Cambridge, 1962, pp. 243–4. H. Pelling, *The Origins of the Labour Party 1880–1900*, 1954, p. 98.
[4] Cf. to Harcourt, 11 Sept., 22 Oct. 1891.

an issue that might produce a revolt of working men from the Liberal party. But such a development bore the seeds of danger for Morley's own electoral position in Newcastle.

In January 1889 three Labour candidates, demanding 'justice for their class', were elected to the Newcastle School Board.[1] Beatrice Potter spoke to Morley soon after and found him 'anxious about the socialists at Newcastle. Up till now he has treated them with indifference, not to say contempt; but they mustered two thousand votes at the last School Board election, and Morley began to take them seriously'.[2] On 2 February he wrote to Harcourt: 'The Socialists threaten to give me some trouble about their 8 hours bill. I shall point blank and at all costs refuse to vote for it, and they can do as they please.' That day he was interviewed by a deputation from the Newcastle branch of the Social Democratic Federation, among whom were the three successful candidates, and he gave them exactly this refusal. He stood firm against their threats to create 'a little divide within the Liberal camp' by running a Labour candidate against himself at the next election. 'If the end of all this is that I am ejected from this seat, it won't kill me at all,' he nonchalantly replied. 'I shall be able to earn my living comfortably.'[3] When he addressed a public meeting in Newcastle a few days later the excited state of feeling in the constituency was very evident. A reference to having had 'the pleasure of three hours' wrestling with certain friends and constituents of mine' was greeted with hisses and cries of 'No' and 'Enemies' from the audience. When he urged working men to recognize that a shorter working day meant lower wages, there was uproar. But he insisted that he would not vote for any Eight Hours Bill, even though the Socialists had dropped 'a hint that there might be electoral contingencies.'[4]

A vigorous agitation on the eight-hours question now developed in Newcastle, and the involvement in this of hostility to Morley became increasingly strong. In April 1889 Morley was

[1] For this election, see *N.D.C.*, 7–17 Jan. 1889.
[2] B. Webb, *My Apprenticeship*, 1929, p. 306.
[3] *N.D.C.*, 4 Feb. 1889, pp. 4–5. *The Times*, 4 Feb. 1889, p. 7, c. 4.
[4] *The Times*, 5 Feb. 1889, p. 10, c. 1.

EIGHT-HOUR DAY AND PARNELL DIVORCE 261

about to address a meeting of the Newcastle Liberal Association, when J. Laidler, one of the Socialists on the School Board, rose to move an expression of regret that Morley could not 'see his way to support the demand of the working classes in seeking to better their social condition'. He warned that Labour might have 'to take a step to Mr. Morley's detriment' and 'to try to replace their senior member by someone who would support their views'. The motion received only three votes. Morley then denied that there was any inconsistency between his expressions of concern for social improvement and his refusal to support the eight-hours proposal. He believed that 'a Parliamentary Eight Hours Bill extending to all forms of industry and labour would not better the condition of the working classes'. As for the threats regarding the next election, his reply was: 'Let them'. He would rather lose his seat than give way to this demand.[1] In May 1889 a newly formed Newcastle Labour Electoral Organization commenced an agitation with the double theme of attacking Morley's views on the eight-hours question and of promoting the idea of independent Labour candidatures.[2] However, Morley told the Commons in June that, in spite of this, 'I have nothing to fear from my constituents'. He was convinced that they were nearly all behind him on the issue.[3] A series of reversals for Labour candidatess in municipal elections later in the year put him in an increasingly confident frame of mind, and when in November another deputation of Socialists waited on him to ascertain his views on various questions 'in view of the approaching general election', they found him as firm as ever against that 'most mischievous, impractical proposal', an Eight Hours Bill. He told Harcourt that he now believed that the working men of Newcastle 'hate and despise' the Socialists.[4]

Meanwhile, from outside Newcastle attention was beginning to be focused on the situation there by prominent Socialists and Radicals, notably R. B. Cunninghame Graham, who became an outspoken critic of Morley. For example, after the interview in

[1] *N.D.C.*, 25 Apr. 1889, p. 4, c. 5. *The Times*, 25 Apr. 1889, p. 10, c. 4.
[2] *N.D.C.*, 8 May 1889, p. 8, c. 3; 9 May 1889, p. 8, c. 4; 11 May 1889, p. 5, c. 3.
[3] *Hansard*, 3, 337, 730.
[4] *The Times*, 5 Nov. 1889, p. 10, cc. 4–6. To Harcourt, 9 Nov. 1889.

February 1889 he told Newcastle working men that 'I certainly never thought Mr. Morley a Democrat; far from it', and that they had nothing to gain from Morley or his party. In November he interpreted Morley's answers to the deputation as meaning: 'In the coming class war I am on the side of the rich, the sweater, and the capital monger.' Graham urged Socialists to appeal to working men 'to oppose Mr. Morley at the next general election, on the ground that he is a thorough bourgeois and opposed to the working classes'.[1] In March 1890 Graham's wife met a group of 'Labour' critics of Morley and was told by them that, while they thought that they could count on 2,000 votes, they were not certain whether to run a Labour candidate or to use these votes as a bargaining counter between Liberal and Conservative. 'If only one thousand Socialists voted at the election one of the members would be turned out.' There was a chance, therefore, that the Liberal 'caucus' might persuade Morley to modify his opposition to the demands of 'Labour'.[2] Morley was still not particularly worried. In September 1890 he wrote that the eight-hours agitation, although a 'nuisance', would die out before long, as it was based on a 'delusion'. It was only 'the rabid little clique of Socialists' in Newcastle that was causing trouble.[3] At the beginning of November Labour candidates were soundly defeated in municipal elections, and Morley wrote elatedly: 'We are in high spirits at Newcastle: they pricked the labour bubble there on Saturday with a vengeance.' He now considered that he was vindicated in having 'let the Socialists know that I'm their enemy, or rather not their friend'.[4]

Morley was thus finding that a most unwelcome light was being directed on to his views on labour and social questions. The constant attacks and criticisms, and the notoriety which his opposition to eight-hours legislation was gaining him, forced him

---

[1] *N.D.C.*, 15 Feb. 1889, p. 5, c. 1; 27 Apr. 1889, p. 4. c. 6; 28 May 1889, p. 4, cc. 5–6; 7 Nov. 1889, p. 8, c. 2; 19 Nov. 1889, p. 4, c. 5.
[2] *N.D.C.*, 3 Mar. 1890, p. 8, c. 3.
[3] To Harcourt, 5 Sept. 1890.
[4] *N.D.C.*, 3 Nov. 1890, p. 4, c. 6. To Harcourt, 2 Nov. 1890.

to take up a defensive position, besieged within principles that seemed to represent complete negativism in social policy and mere obstruction to the achievement of social reform. And then at the end of 1890 a blow was struck at the Irish policy itself on which his politics had been based since 1885.

Morley was 'much overwhelmed and depressed' by the Parnell divorce crisis.[1] At first he had believed that the affair, though 'hateful', would 'pretty quickly recede into the background' and that Parnell would 'continue to lead—with the fullest support both from his colleagues and from the Irish constituencies'.[2] But he soon became aware of 'the angry currents [of opinion] running against Parnell's continued leadership' in the Liberal party, and after the National Liberal Federation meeting at Sheffield on 21 November 1890 he realized that Parnell's retirement was 'absolutely inevitable' if the home-rule cause was to be saved in Great Britain in view of 'the volume of hostile judgment and obstinate intention'.[3] Parnell had to be repudiated, or else the whole Irish policy would collapse. Morley knew that the Liberal party had to think of the non-Irish electorate, and he urged Parnell to recognize that, so far as it was concerned, the affair was 'much more than a storm in a teacup' and that, 'if he set British feeling at defiance and brazened it out, it would be ruin to home rule at the election'. At first Morley counted on Parnell's yielding to pressure and retiring voluntarily for a time to resume the leadership later on. But Parnell would not follow this course, and, probably because of deliberate evasiveness on Parnell's part, Morley was unable to deliver Gladstone's letter about the leadership to him before the Irish party re-elected him leader. Now the Liberals would be obliged to force the Irish to choose between Parnell and the alliance and would therefore receive the blame for the split that this would cause in the Irish camp.[4]

On at least three counts—Parnell's personal conduct, the role

[1] F. E. Hamer (ed.), *The Personal Papers of Lord Rendel*, 1931, p. 26. J. L. Garvin, *The Life of Joseph Chamberlain*, II, 1933, pp. 407–8.
[2] To Gladstone, 17 Nov. 1890, B.M. Add. MSS. 44256, ff. 72–3.
[3] *Recollections*, I, pp. 256–7. *Gladstone*, III, p. 433. To Spencer, 1 Dec. 1890.
[4] *Gladstone*, III, pp. 434–41, 453. *Recollections*, I pp. 258–61. Hamer, *Papers of Lord Rendel*, pp. 26–7.

of the Church, and the development of factions in the Irish nationalist movement—the divorce crisis seriously set back the home-rule cause in England by increasing anti-Irish feeling. Morley was extremely despondent about its future. On 21 December he noted as one consequence of the crisis: 'Vague, general, presumptive, and indirect discredit—but a most effectual discredit—of Home Rule policy and its English authors, in the mind of a decisive margin in the British Constituencies.' He told Chamberlain that it was 'a fatal blow to the present Gladstonian party; he thought it would lead to a reconsideration of the whole situation'. To Gladstone he remarked that 'the effect on the Liberal party would be to cause the weaker and more detached margin to separate itself wholly, on the ground that no settlement could be come to with the Irish at present'. After talking with Morley at this time, Sir Henry James wrote: 'Nobody could be more despondent over the prospects of the Liberal party than Morley was. He thought Home Rule indefinitely postponed, and with Mr. Gladstone and Parnell away, or even with the latter discredited, no settlement of a Home Rule scheme could be expected.'[1]

But soon Morley was displaying a renewed determination to uphold home rule as the great commitment of the Liberal party. 'For myself, win or lose, I will fight it out,' he told a Newcastle audience in January 1891. 'When the obscuring smoke of the present strife in Ireland has rolled away . . . let Irishmen know that they will see the beacon of friendship and sympathy still burning clear on the English shore.'[2] Morley and many of his colleagues realized that domestic policy remained in a condition of great confusion and unreadiness and that the Irish policy remained indispensable as a cohering and ordering influence. There was a great danger that the flood of sectionalist reform demands which the Irish policy had been holding back might now burst through and overwhelm the party. The Liberal leaders were always very conscious of the strength of the sectionalists' feelings,

---

[1] 'Memo on Irish Affairs', B.M. Add. MSS. 44256, f. 97. Garvin, *Chamberlain*, II, pp. 407–8. Hamer, *Papers of Lord Rendel*, pp. 87–8. Lord Askwith, *Lord James of Hereford*, 1930, p. 222.

[2] *The Times*, 14 Jan. 1891, p. 10, cc. 1–4.

exemplified in this statement by W. S. Caine at a temperance meeting in 1887: 'I believe it will not be very long before, somehow or another, we shall get the Irish question settled. We must then take care that ours comes next. We have been shunted a little too often, and we must take care that we are not shunted any more.'[1] In December 1890 Morley urged Gladstone not to call a meeting of the party until he had made up his own mind on future policy. To offer a *tabula rasa* at such a meeting would be fatal, he warned, for 'every other man in the room would hurry to scribble his own notions thereon'. The position of the party was too critical 'for exposure to the wayward blasts that would be likely to spring up in a party meeting.'[2]

Towards the end of December 1890 Gladstone suggested that, in order 'to keep the party well together in England' and to give it 'reparative strength', some expansion of policy might be advisable.[3] Morley then drew up a list of various reforms that might be incorporated into a wider programme—'direct popular veto', Irish local government, Welsh disestablishment, 'one man one vote', and 'a labourers' programme', including parish councils, the abolition of the plural vote for Poor Law Guardians, relaxation of restrictions on outdoor relief for the aged poor, and compulsory acquisition of land for small holdings by local authorities. But his comments on these reforms show the dilemma of the Liberal leaders. On the one hand, the special interests had to be satisfied. Welsh disestablishment 'must be kept well to the front', and local option 'would undoubtedly put heart into the Temperance people. They are, no doubt, on our side, as it is. But the Irish business will chill them, and they need to be stirred up by warm and active interest in their own question.' But, on the other hand, the mystery of the urban voters remained. 'The boroughs (other than Metropolitan)'—a significant exception—'*want nothing*, except Free Schools', although 'they have views about the H. of L., religious equality, &c.' And his remarks on each of the questions that he

[1] J. Newton, *W. S. Caine, M.P. A Biography*, 1907, p. 179.
[2] To Gladstone, 31 Dec. 1890, B.M. Add. MSS. 44256, f. 104.
[3] Gladstone to Morley, 23 Dec. 1890, *Gladstone*, III, p. 437. Gladstone to Ripon, 29 Dec. 1890, L. Wolf, *Life of the First Marquess of Ripon K.G., P.C., G.C.S.I., D.C.L., Etc.*, II, 1921, p. 198.

thought could be included in a Liberal programme show his consciousness of their inadequacy and the absence of systematic binding principles to give such a programme unity:

> Good, as far as it goes. . . . S. Buxton and other London members assure me that Temperance is very ill fitted to rouse or please *London*, and I quite believe it. . . . Not much use . . . this [Welsh disestablishment] would provoke the Scotch Disestablishers. Also, it is a complex question which would rouse in its course all the strength of the English Church . . . there is no rally in it . . . not by itself adequate [one man, one vote] . . . there is no fight in these things [Lords and religious equality] . . .[1]

Morley's doubts about the possibility of constructing a coherent, unifying programme clearly remained as strong as ever. It is not surprising, therefore, that, since no issue of domestic policy was attractive or substantial enough to be developed as a single great question, he soon returned to the home-rule policy. On 31 December 1890 he wrote to Harcourt that, while 'we must have a wider programme when the time comes', 'the time has not yet come'. To Gladstone he wrote that he thought 'One Man One Vote' 'rather too narrow', but that they had better not try to construct a wider programme for the time being: 'by and bye we should add other questions—notably Temperance and Village politics. But not just at this moment,—among many other reasons for this, that it would embolden Parnell to tell Ireland that we were throwing over H.R., and that he foresaw this.' The Irish question must still be the governing factor, and they ought to wait until it had again 'taken a definite form'. Only then would the Liberals 'know where we are'. He urged 'a Fabian policy as to enlarging the programme'. Any addition should be delayed 'long enough to take off the look—which it would certainly wear to-day—of having been screwed out of us by our Irish troubles'. But, in any event, nothing as yet seemed to him to be 'ripe for action beyond electoral reform'.[2]

---

[1] Memo. on a letter from Gladstone to Arnold Morley, 26 Dec. 1890, enclosed in Arnold Morley to Harcourt, 30 Dec. 1890, Harcourt MSS.

[2] 31 Dec. 1890, 2 Jan. 1891, B.M. Add. MSS. 44256, ff. 103–4, 107.

But within the party's leadership there was a different opinion —that they should 'get rid altogether of Home Rule' and 'push forward English & Scotch questions'.[1] This was, predictably, the opinion of Harcourt. In this crisis he saw a chance at last of ending the alliance with the Irish and the concentration on Irish policy. On 19 December 1890 he suggested to Morley that home rule was now 'by the force of events relegated to the dim and distant future'.[2] He even went so far as to declare that the concentration on Ireland, as on any 'external' issue—and he instanced the wars against revolutionary and Napoleonic France—had been of advantage primarily to the Tories. But, just as after 1815 'the domestic questions overcame' the Tories, so they 'will have to face them now with J. C[hamberlain] and [Leonard] Courtney to prod them'. And yet on the same day Morley told Harcourt that only 'the use of strong H.R. language in England by men like you' could prevent what Morley was clearly most concerned about, 'a general rally to Parnell' in Ireland. On the 21st Morley wrote a memorandum in favour of carrying on the home-rule campaign so as 'to save something of what we have gained at such great cost, by convincing the Irish that for once an English party is thoroughly to be relied upon'. The preservation of the Irish alliance must be the Liberals' primary objective, and in this respect 'the postponement of H.R. in our programme for an indefinite time, means the sharp alienation of Ireland from our party, for another parliament at the very least'. He followed this up on the 26th by reminding Harcourt that, were the Liberals to state publicly that they no longer regarded home rule as '*actual*', the Irish would rally to Parnell because his claim that 'Mr. G. seized the divorce as a pretext for getting rid of H.R.' would seem justified. '*Item,* we should at once lose the Irish vote in Great Britain.'

This correspondence reveals to what extent Morley had become the prisoner of his one great question, unable to think of anything else except in terms of its relationship to Ireland. Harcourt himself

---

[1] As reported by Arnold Morley to Gladstone, 30 Dec. 1890, 1 Jan. 1891, B.M. Add. MSS. 44254, ff. 65, 67.

[2] This correspondence is quoted from the Harcourt MSS. Extensive extracts from it are given in Gardiner, *Harcourt*, II, Chap. VI.

now accused Morley of seeing things 'too exclusively from the Irish standpoint'. Surely, he wrote, Morley was not 'incapable of any statesmanship which lies outside the four corners of that distressful and squalid island and . . . incapable of any eyes or any heart except for a handful of two or three millions of distracted Irish'. He expressed confidence, therefore, that soon 'things will present themselves more in their real proportions' and that for Morley other questions 'quite as important and quite as far-reaching will arise'. As the Liberal party existed in order to achieve 'good for the country at large', it should not be more or less indefinitely confined within the one policy. 'Like the kingdom of Heaven the Liberal Party is a house of many mansions. It is a party of progress and if its advance is checked by insuperable obstacles in one direction it will not dash itself to pieces like a foolish bird, but will go on and prosper in another.'[1]

But whereas to Harcourt the Irish question was just one room in a very large 'house', to Morley the Irish problem constituted an 'insuperable obstacle' which prevented progress in all other directions. For him the home-rule policy represented the key that alone could give access to Harcourt's 'many mansions'.

Between 1891 and 1894 Liberal policy wavered irresolutely between the two types of strategy advocated by Morley and Harcourt. Although there was a mounting desire for escape from the Irish commitment, it was apparent that this impatience could not yet overcome certain formidable obstacles in the path of such an escape. Morley himself laid great stress on the moral obligation resting on the party to stand by the Irish and their cause, especially after it had virtually forced the Irish to repudiate their leader for the sake of the Liberal alliance; and he would warn of the consequences for order in Ireland if the Liberals were now to drop home rule and deprive the Irish people of their hope of national emancipation through a constitutional movement. As for the internal condition of the Liberal party, he continued to emphasize the importance of Gladstone's leadership, even though it was providing direction only on Irish policy. When in January 1891

[1] Harcourt to Morley, 6 Jan. 1891.

Harcourt urged that Gladstone should be persuaded to turn his attention as party leader to other questions, Morley's reply admitted that the confinement within the Irish preoccupation was an inescapable aspect of Gladstone's leadership: 'His sun may still set in glory, even if H.R. falls into utter discredit; but not if he attempts to touch other questions. He does not understand them, nor the sentiment that makes them important with our people.'[1] When Gladstone asked Morley in May 1892 what office he would like, Morley replied that he thought that he should return to the Irish Office. 'Yes. . . . I think so,' said Gladstone. 'The truth is that we're both chained to the oar; I am chained to the oar; you are chained.'[2]

The Irish question had them in its grip. The events of 1886 had completely remodelled the Liberal party in the image of the home-rule policy. If the party were now to attempt to break out of this new mould, might not the result be fragmentation and disintegration in Liberal politics? Lord Spencer put the situation as it appeared to people such as himself and Morley in a letter to Harcourt in 1893. He referred to 'the Irish measure, for which alone some of us continue in Politics, and which we put before every other measure which has to be brought forward in Parliament. I know that you take the exactly opposite view to this but the Liberal Party as it now exists was formed on these lines and those who have thrown themselves in with the Liberals cannot work in a different direction.'[3]

In 1886 the Liberal party was reconstructed in the shape and spirit of a great mid-nineteenth century reform crusade, such as the campaign for the repeal of the Corn Laws. But the essential characteristic of such movements had been that they had specified, limited aims, and that each organization formed was strictly provisional and 'destined to come to an end with the triumph of the particular cause which had called it into life'.[4] This type of political action was clearly not appropriate for one of the two main

[1] To Harcourt, 5 Jan. 1891.
[2] *Gladstone*, III, p. 491.
[3] 6 Jan. 1893, Harcourt MSS.
[4] M. Ostrogorski, *Democracy and the Organization of Political Parties*, I, 1902, pp. 132–3.

parliamentary parties. Concentration on the home-rule policy provided only a very temporary basis for Liberalism; but there was no sign yet of the emergence of a permanent basis. It is scarcely surprising that numerous Liberal politicians, including Morley, feared anarchy as the only alternative to continuing preoccupation with Ireland.

ADDITIONAL NOTE

Page 257, n. 1. The younger Liberals were also somewhat disappointed. See R. Munro Ferguson to Rosebery, 20 Sept. [1889], Rosebery MSS., Box 14: 'Ireland is less to the fore while the relations of labour & capital are what is to puzzle us. There is no leader in the party who has shown himself fit to define a policy thru these difficulties ahead. John Morley is the best & safest in the Commons but he is too theoretical, they say. I am sure that for a perfect politician he *shows* himself too much influenced by his likes & dislikes.'

18
THE COLLAPSE OF THE GREAT IRISH POLICY, 1891–1894

THE crisis of 1890–1 had so weakened the foundations of the great Irish policy that the search for some replacement for it, some new *raison d'être* and cohering principle for the party which had become so closely identified with it, would obviously have to be much more urgently prosecuted. In August 1891 Morley appealed to Rosebery to expound 'a practicable socialism' so that he could influence the outcome of 'all our talk about social reform'.[1] As for himself, the definite conclusion to which he seemed to be trying to bring this 'talk' was another single great question. On 18 March 1891 he spoke in the Commons in support of a Welsh local veto bill, and, after observing that 'we are all talking, some of us rather vaguely, about social reform', proceeded to present 'the Drink question' as the most definite and important kind of social reform. He claimed that the growth of a demand for local polls on liquor licensing was a logical consequence of the extensions of the franchise. Temperance was 'by far the greatest and the deepest moral movement in this country since the anti-slavery agitation'. All other practical projects of social reform 'taken together would not', he maintained, 'do half as much for improving the material prosperity of the country and the well-being of our countrymen as the progress of the temperance cause'.[2] In all this we can see Morley's characteristic employment of a single issue for the purpose of imposing order on the great diversity of reform questions. Liberals were advised that if they all concentrated on working for this one reform they would do far more good than if they tried to attend to all their questions at once.

A month later he supported a proposal for a large reduction in

[1] *Recollections*, I, p. 313.   [2] *Hansard*, 3, 351, 1336–40.

the number of public houses in England and for local authorities to have extended powers to control the issue of licenses and the hours of opening. Again he asserted that the development of opinion on social reform since 1885 had taken the form of the development of this one question. It embodied the political spirit of the new democracy:

The reduction of the franchise and the redistribution of political power have been followed by louder and louder voices in favour of the kind of control which we are advocating. . . . The more clearly you hear the popular voice, the more loud and distinct is that voice in favour of legislation of this kind . . . this tide of opinion is certain to go on and swell . . . the more clearly you gather the popular voice, the more distinctly you perceive the determination of the people to get the powers to protect themselves against what is admitted now on all sides to be the greatest curse that can afflict a community.

Here was the great, concentrating, focalizing issue of social reform for the democracy: 'in democratic countries temperance and social reformers will not be content, and rightly, until some means have been adopted . . . for giving to localities a direct and effective voice in the matter.'[1] In his speeches Morley would now maintain that temperance reform 'would probably be worth all other social reforms put together'.[2] As he began to become absorbed in this question, he appeared increasingly impatient with his involvement in the Irish policy. Thus on 6 September 1891 he wrote to Lord Spencer: 'What a blessing it will be, or would be, if we could get heartily to work at questions of this kind, and escape from the tangled business of Ireland. However, neither for you nor me is that possible.'

When the National Liberal Federation met at Newcastle in October 1891 it shrank from the as yet extremely invidious task of selecting a single issue of domestic policy on to which the efforts of Liberals could be concentrated. The home-rule policy itself was now too weak, however, to hold back the flood of reform demands. The Federation gave way to the special interests, incorporating their reform proposals into a vast 'omnibus' pro-

[1] *Hansard*, 3, 352, 1652–62.
[2] *The Times*, 4 Aug. 1891, p. 8, c. 3.

THE GREAT IRISH POLICY 1891-1894   273

gramme. When Morley addressed the conference, he made it clear, first, that Ireland remained for him the great commitment to action, and, secondly, that in domestic policy he would favour a single issue rather than a programme. However, he appreciated that for the time being the mode of action preferred by the party rank and file was a programme, and he sought to find some principle of coherence and unity for the very miscellaneous collection of items that constituted the 'Newcastle Programme'. He offered 'the principle of privilege': 'The question which divides a Liberal from a Tory is the question of privilege. The Tory is the man who wants to maintain privilege, and the Liberals are the men who stand up for equality. These questions which divide Liberal from Tory, these questions of privilege, are questions that are awaiting us.'[1]

We have seen how after 1885 Morley developed the Irish issue in such a way as to make it appear that a firm dividing-line had been re-established between the parties. Now some other means had to be discovered of defining the difference between Liberals and Tories and of continuing to have the Liberals acknowledged as the agents of progress and reform. The question that seems most to have concerned Morley was how to retain working-class support for and belief in Liberalism. His speeches showed him worried about the possibility that the new ideas and aspirations of the working class might be thought to require new modes of political action, that Liberalism might be considered to have been rendered irrelevant by their emergence. He would insist that 'those hopes and those aspirations will be best met in small things and in great by the triumph, by the acceptance of Liberal principles'.[2] In 1890 he tried to assure delegates to the National Liberal Federation that in regard to the new social aspirations 'the Liberal party alone possess the principles, the maxims, and the instruments, the thought and feeling, which will enable them to deal with those aspirations and to see that they are properly carried out'.[3]

[1] *The Times*, 2 Oct. 1891, p. 9, c. 6; p. 10, c. 1.
[2] *The Times*, 30 Oct. 1889, p. 7, c. 1.
[3] *The Times*, 21 Nov. 1890, p. 10, c. 1.

Nevertheless, he continued to argue that the party was committed to making a Home Rule Bill its first great work on attaining office again; but a much more defensive note was now apparent in his references to the Irish policy. Thus in November 1891, speaking after the conference which produced the 'Newcastle Programme', he said: 'They say that we now put the Irish question in the background. I am not going to put it in the background to-night; and I never will put it in the background.'[1] In February 1892 he declared that, because Ireland 'does block the way of our own reforms', it must come first 'in spite of all which they may say'.[2] He now had to admit that it was not only Liberal Unionists who were saying, 'Do not you think you could now shelve Ireland for a bit?': 'some who are not exactly dissentient Liberals, but in whom their enthusiasm for social reforms overrides other considerations, hint in more or less vague terms something of the same kind.'[3]

He now had to warn his party frequently to keep in mind that 'we Liberals have entered into a solemn engagement with Ireland'. They were bound 'by every consideration of honour and of policy to redeem that engagement'.[4] Furthermore, there was the added moral responsibility resulting from the Liberals' veto on Parnell:

history would present no more abject or contemptible spectacle than the Liberal party would present if, after having in December, 1890, induced the bulk of the Irish members, and, so far as we knew, the bulk of the Irish constituencies, to undergo one of the very sharpest sacrifices that ever man or constituency were asked to undergo, for the sake of maintaining an honest and staunch alliance with the English Liberal party—if that party were now falsely to break its bargain and throw over those allies.[5]

He even went so far as to threaten that, if the home-rule policy were shelved, there would be a further schism in the party. For

---

[1] *The Times*, 28 Nov. 1891, p. 10, c. 3.
[2] *The Times*, 25 Feb. 1892, p. 11, c. 3.
[3] *The Times*, 5 May 1892, p. 6, cc. 2–3.
[4] *The Times*, 14 Jan. 1891, p. 10, c. 4; 22 Sept. 1891, p. 5, c. 3.
[5] *The Times*, 5 May 1892, p. 6, c. 3.

example, in August 1891 he declared, 'without any fear of contradiction from any one who knows the actual state and opinion of our party that Home Rule has, at any rate, effected such a lodgment that any slackness or indefinite delay' in regard to it 'would be instantly followed by a wider and more formidable and more abiding split within the ranks of the Liberal party than that which rent us asunder in 1886'. In May 1892 he repeated that such a split would occur 'if any attempt should be made to, what is called shelve Ireland'.[1]

These were desperate words, but then by 1892 Morley's own political position did seem to be becoming desperate. To those whose task it was to plan and supervise the party's electoral strategy his determined insistence on the maintenance of the great Irish commitment and his equally determined opposition to proposals for labour legislation were growing into something of an embarrassment. Thus in September 1890 Arnold Morley, the Chief Whip, wrote to Gladstone warning that, although John Morley was 'very strong against the demand for Legislative Eight hours—even in the case of miners', the Liberal leaders should not take up too uncompromising a stand on such questions and appear concerned only to help Ireland. For in that case this 'very large & important class affected' by labour issues might feel 'persuaded that their special interests ought to outweigh any consideration of the claims of Ireland in the votes they will be called upon to give', and they would vote for other than Liberal candidates.[2] This revulsion against Morley's type of Liberal politics was indeed what seemed now to be happening in his own constituency of Newcastle.

The agitation on the eight-hours question continued to grow in Newcastle. Towards the end of 1891 a Legal Eight Hours League was set up, and two large demonstrations were held in support of the cause. At these sentiments hostile to Morley were expressed.[3] Agitators continued to combine criticisms of his

[1] *The Times*, 4 Aug. 1891, p. 8, c. 3; 5 May 1892, p. 6, c. 3.
[2] 24 Sept. 1890, B.M. Add. MSS. 44254, ff. 34–5.
[3] *N.D.C.*, 5 Jan. 1891, p. 5, c. 6; 7 Sept. 1891, p. 5, cc. 2–5; 14 Sept. 1891, Supplement, p. 2, c. 6; 26 Sept. 1891, p. 5, c. 2; 3 Oct. 1891, p. 8, c. 4; 28 Oct. 1891, p. 5, c. 5; 18 Nov. 1891, p. 5, c. 4.

position on the eight-hours question with condemnations of his preoccupation with Ireland. In February 1891 Maltman Barry, the Tory radical, 'appealed to the working men of Newcastle to see that their representative gave his attention first to their interests, and next to Ireland': 'Mr. Morley ought to be the representative of Newcastle, and not of Tipperary.'[1] Cunninghame Graham was making a similar appeal.[2] A movement to secure Morley's defeat at the next general election began to grow. In September 1891 two large meetings heard John Burns, Keir Hardie, Graham, and Robert Blatchford call for action by the forces of labour against him. Hardie, for instance, promised that, 'if the men of Newcastle selected one of their number' to stand against Morley, numerous 'labour leaders' would 'come down to Newcastle and financially and by voice and effort render every assistance they could'.[3] 'John Burns & Co. threaten to fight me at Newcastle', wrote Morley after this. But 'they won't make me budge one inch about their ridiculous Eight Hours', even if the result was to 'let a Tory in'.[4]

When the election campaign arrived in June 1892, the Liberal candidates, Morley and Craig, who were the sitting Members, did not have to face the opposition of a Labour candidate. The promotion of an independent Labour candidature was attempted but made little headway and was finally abandoned for lack of time and candidate.[5] On 1 July a meeting organized by a local 'Labour party', the Eight Hours League, and the S.D.F. decided to declare support for the Conservative candidate, Hamond. Two days later a manifesto was issued in the name of the Labour party, asking working men to vote for Hamond because 'Mr. Morley has on every opportunity since he became a member of Parliament opposed the restriction of the hours of labour by legal enactment, recommending the barbarous and inhuman methods of a strike to obtain a shortening of the day's toil'. It added: 'we

[1] N.D.C., 16 Feb. 1891, p. 5, c. 5.
[2] N.D.C., 21 Sept. 1891, p. 4, c. 6; 3 Oct. 1891, Supplement, p. 4, c. 2.
[3] N.D.C., 7 Sept. 1891, p. 5, cc. 2–5; 10 Sept. 1891, p. 5, cc. 3–4.
[4] To Harcourt, 11 Sept. 1891.
[5] N.D.C., 22 June 1892, p. 5, c. 2; 28 June 1892, p. 5, c. 3; 29 June 1892, p. 5, c. 2; 30 June 1892, Supplement, p. 4, c. 6.

wish to impress upon you that if Mr. Morley is returned, he will be a Cabinet Minister, and will be in a position to block any bill dealing with the shortening of the hours of labour.'[1]

The result of the election was a severe blow to Liberalism in Newcastle. Morley was relegated to second place by Hamond, and Craig finished bottom of the poll. Morley claimed that the result was caused not by the eight-hours agitation but by the drink question: 'the publicans worked like heroes [on behalf of Hamond], and the workmen do not like the notion of Sunday Closing.' Hamond himself had 'fought mainly on Fair Trade'. Nevertheless, he had to confess that 'the result is to me shattering and humiliating'.[2]

The question now arose of what action Newcastle Labour should take when Morley had to seek re-election after appointment to the new Liberal Government. On 15 July Keir Hardie, P. Curran, and Cunninghame Graham spoke out strongly in favour of working for Morley's defeat by a Conservative. Hardie declared that 'the best stroke the labour party could do would be to defeat Mr. Morley' whose ideas were 'antagonistic to the new ideas which were beginning to find vent amongst the common people'. Curran said that, 'since the death of Mr. Bradlaugh Mr. Morley was the most powerful exponent of individualism in the country'. Morley was only 'a reformer so far as Individualism was concerned', but opposed 'every reform useful to the community of working men'. Graham called Morley more dangerous to Labour than even 'the most reactionary Tory' and attacked his complete lack of 'sympathy with all the new movements, either ethical, political, or social, which had been springing up in Great Britain during the past ten or twelve years'.[3]

But the working men of Newcastle did not all share this antagonism to Morley. There was, in fact, a sizeable section which supported him and which was now to rally to his defence.

[1] N.D.C., 2 July 1892, p. 5, c. 1; 4 July 1892, p. 5, cc. 3-4.
[2] To Gladstone, 9 July 1892, B.M. Add. MSS. 44256, f. 213.
[3] N.D.C., 16 July 1892, p. 8, cc. 3-4. *The Times*, 16 July 1892, p. 9, c. 1. Not all Radicals or Socialists supported this extreme opposition to Morley. The Fabians condemned it. Cf. N.D.C., 4 July 1892, p. 6, c. 3; 5 July 1892, p. 5, c. 5. A. M. McBriar, *Fabian Socialism and English Politics 1884-1918*, Cambridge, 1962, p. 247.

Throughout Morley's career in Newcastle the local Irish seem to have been a strong, well-organized electoral force. In 1883 there were claimed to be at least 3,000 of them.[1] The second election of 1892 in Newcastle saw a direct clash between the advocates of independent Labour political action who wanted all working men, irrespective of national origin, to put first the interests of their class and those Irishmen who insisted on giving priority to the interests of their nation. In his speech at Newcastle on 15 July, Keir Hardie complained bitterly of the existence 'in every industrial community in Great Britain' of 'a solid body of Irishmen who had voluntarily given up their rights of citizenship on every question save that of Home Rule'. Cunninghame Graham warned that Irish opposition to Labour candidatures, if persisted in, 'will end in provoking retaliation among British workmen which will take the form of opposition to Home Rule'.[2] But throughout the second campaign there were frequent reports of demonstrations by Irishmen at Labour meetings.

On 31 July Charles Diamond, M.P. for North Monaghan, told a meeting of Newcastle Irish that they must vote for Morley 'for the sake of Home Rule and the national interests'.[3] Keir Hardie replied by warning that, 'if the cause of labour was going to be endangered by the unbending opposition of the Irish party, it might become necessary for the Labour party to play the game of retaliation, and prove to the Irish party that, much as they desired to see Home Rule passed, they also desired, and much more desired . . . to see reforms which would benefit Irishmen equally with Englishmen and Scotchmen take their proper place in the Parliamentary programme of what was called the party of progress'.[4] But the Irish appeared undeterred by such threats. They reminded Hardie that, 'without the two millions of Irish residents in Great Britain, of whom one million five hundred thousand were labourers, no labour movement could progress'.[5] Michael

[1] Cf. F. E. Hamer (ed.), *The Personal Papers of Lord Rendel*, 1931, pp. 221-2.
[2] *N.D.C.*, 16 July 1892, p. 8, cc. 3-5. *The Times*, 16 July 1892, p. 9, c. 1.
[3] *N.D.C.*, 2 Aug. 1892, p. 4, c. 6.
[4] *N.D.C.*, 3 Aug. 1892, p. 5, cc. 2-3.
[5] *N.D.C.*, 15 Aug. 1892, p. 5, c. 3.

Davitt himself believed this contest important enough to warrant his intervention. Campaigning on behalf of Morley, he warned that those who helped' the enemies of Ireland' to defeat him 'would be striking a dangerous blow at the labour cause in England': 'Whilst there were 70 Irish Nationalist votes at Westminster ready to be cast, whenever the opportunity presented itself, for the advancement of the labouring classes of Great Britain, he would not be answerable for the manner in which these votes would be cast if a section of the working men of Newcastle voted against Mr. Morley.'[1] Morley continued to refuse to vote for an Eight Hours Bill, and, when the Conservative candidate promised to support such a Bill for miners and in noxious trades, the local Labour leaders decided to call on working men to vote for him.[2] In his campaigning Morley sought to persuade the working men of Newcastle that their interests were as much involved in the success of the home-rule agitation as were the interests of Ireland, because, until home rule was conceded, the House of Commons was 'nothing less than paralysed for British purposes'. He, too, warned of the need of British labour to be sure of Irish support for its own causes.[3]

The result of the election was something of an anticlimax after all this. Morley won it very comfortably. One cannot say for certain that the massive Irish intervention on his behalf was the deciding factor, but in the campaign itself the main feature had undoubtedly been this great rallying of the Irish to the man who had, after all, become since the first election Chief Secretary for Ireland pledged to help bring in a new Home Rule Bill. Morley now confidently asserted that 'they do not really care much for the 8 hours question here: it is only a *drapeau* for a small clique of vanity and spite'.[4] But he could do this only because the election was so clearly on the Irish question. The first election was really

[1] *N.D.C.*, 20 Aug. 1892, p. 5, cc. 3-4; 22 Aug. 1892, p. 6, c. 4. For Davitt's intervention and a brief account of this election see T. W. Moody, 'Michael Davitt and the British Labour Movement 1882-1906', *Transactions of the Royal Historical Society*, 5th Series, vol. 3, p. 70.
[2] *N.D.C.*, 22 Aug. 1892, pp. 4, 5, 8; 23 Aug. 1892, p. 6. *Recollections*, I, p. 326.
[3] *N.D.C.*, 24 Aug. 1892, p. 8, cc. 3-4; 25 Aug. 1892, p. 5, c. 2.
[4] To Gladstone, 23 Aug. 1892, B.M. Add. MSS. 44256, f. 235.

much more significant, as 1895 was to prove, for then, with the Irish policy in ruins, the Newcastle voters completed the process which that election had begun and finally ejected Morley from the seat. Morley had only his commitment to the Irish cause to protect him now, and, except in the special circumstances of the second election in 1892, that was not enough.

The over-all result of the 1892 general election was as disappointing to Morley as was his own initial set-back at Newcastle. The Liberals were again the largest party in the House of Commons, but had failed to gain an absolute majority. They would have to govern in dependence on the Irish vote. On 16 August 1892 Leonard Courtney wrote: 'John Morley makes no secret of his vexation not only in his own case but at the final result for the party. A victory without power! A Government established but too weak to get through their first work.'[1] But, just as Morley assured Gladstone with regard to the first election at Newcastle that 'Ireland had nothing to do with the result', so he blamed factors other than the concentration on Irish policy for the Liberals' unsatisfactory national performance. Above all, he blamed the 1891 deviation into programme. 'The truth is', he told Harcourt, 'we have moved much too fast and too far towards the Extreme Left in every subject at once—and quiet sensible folk don't like it.'[2]

Other Liberal leaders, including even Gladstone, saw the situation rather differently. Harcourt commented on Morley's letter: 'I don't agree with him *generally;* if he had confined his remark to *Ireland* I should agree—It is as Mr. G. observes the radicalism of the British programme which has alone saved us from absolute defeat.'[3] By now enthusiasm for the Irish policy among Morley's colleagues and in the party was disappearing rapidly. There was a mood of deepening frustration and impatience in the Liberal ranks. During 1893 Morley showed himself to be acutely conscious

---

[1] G. P. Gooch, *Life of Lord Courtney*, 1920, p. 296. Cf. Morley to Spencer, 19 July 1892.

[2] To Gladstone, 9 July 1892, B.M. Add. MSS. 44256, f. 213. To Harcourt, 14 July 1892.

[3] Harcourt to Spencer, 18 July 1892, Spencer MSS.

THE GREAT IRISH POLICY 1891-1894   281

of the effect which the laborious progress of the Home Rule Bill through the Commons was having. In June he warned Gladstone and Sir Algernon West that there was 'a marked restiveness springing up, not merely among the martyrs in the House, but among even such faithful men as my own friends in Northumberland and elsewhere in the north'.[1] He admitted to 'the consciousness that my colleagues and my party look upon me, quite wrongly, as it happens, as the real cause of their being plunged in this dismal bog'.[2]

In his devotion to the home-rule cause Morley felt himself becoming increasingly isolated within the Liberal leadership. In December 1892 Lord Acton visited him and found him 'very low and unhappy' because 'there never was a Government as insincere; they none of them cared for Home Rule but he, Asquith, and Mr. Gladstone'. Morley gloomily predicted that, once Gladstone had gone, 'with Rosebery Prime Minister and Sir William Harcourt Leader in the House of Commons, there would be the spectacle of a Home Rule Government with neither Leader keen about it'.[3] Harcourt left his resentment at the continued concentration on home rule in no doubt. At Cabinet meetings, whenever the Home Rule Bill was under discussion, he and Rosebery would occupy an 'ostentatious position apart from the rest' on what they called 'the English Bench', and Harcourt was apparently pleased to note how 'nervous and uneasy' this would make Morley and Spencer.[4] Morley would try to safeguard the future by making public pledges to the Irish that the Liberal party would never desert them in their struggle for home rule, and Rosebery would protest against such attempts 'to bind the Liberal party to Home Rule for ever'.[5]

Even Gladstone caused Morley concern. His description of Morley as 'a main prop to me' sums up the relationship between them very accurately, for Morley found himself having to work

[1] To Gladstone, 21 June 1893, B.M. Add. MSS. 44257, f. 116. H. G. Hutchinson (ed.), *Private Diaries of the Rt. Hon. Sir Algernon West, G.C.B.*, 1922, p. 169.
[2] *Recollections*, I, p. 356.
[3] Hutchinson, *Diaries of Sir Algernon West*, p. 93.
[4] Ibid., p. 82. A. G. Gardiner, *The Life of Sir William Harcourt*, II, 1923, p. 219.
[5] Hutchinson, *Diaries of Sir Algernon West*, p. 153.

more and more strenuously to counteract the consequences of Gladstone's advancing age. Gladstone's growing tendency to procrastinate worried Morley. Time was of the essence, he believed: another Home Rule Bill must be presented while Gladstone still led the party. When in 1891 Gladstone had suggested that the next Liberal Government should postpone a Home Rule Bill for two years, Morley had been aghast: 'A man to be looking at $81\frac{1}{2}$ to his fourth premiership, and to speak of postponing his great measure of policy for a couple of years!' ' . . . the postponement of H.R. for two years! At his age!' 'Mr. G. can hardly be in Office in 1894 at eighty-five years of age.'[1] When the Liberals entered office in 1892, Morley was anxious to start work on the Bill as soon as possible, but Gladstone was slow and reluctant. He proposed to Spencer and Morley that consideration of a scheme be deferred until the next year, but they would not hear of such a delay, and work began in November 1892. Morley was very impatient, saying that 'the Cabinet must meet again in December, so that the Bill may be practically settled by Christmas'. When on 4 December a Cabinet was held, but discussion was entirely on Uganda, Morley was very angry with Gladstone for thus getting side-tracked. Gladstone, he complained, 'did not care to bother himself over Home Rule'.[2] This was only a short while after Morley had written to Gladstone: 'I am uncommonly well pleased to think of you as at work on the great task. It will encourage and inspire other people.'[3]

The struggle to devise and promote a second Home Rule Bill seemed to Morley like a fight against time before the arrival of the catastrophe threatened by Gladstone's declining powers. In December 1892 he remarked to Sir Algernon West that 'Mr. Gladstone was getting old and could not last'. A difficult session with Harcourt over the details of the Bill would cause Morley to sigh, 'Oh! my dear West, Mr. Gladstone is very old.'[4] Morley

---

[1] *Recollections*, I, pp. 278–9. To Spencer, 28 July 1891. Hamer, *Papers of Lord Rendel*, p. 80.
[2] Hutchinson, *Diaries of Sir Algernon West*, pp. 71–2.
[3] 16 Nov. 1892, B.M. Add. MSS. 44257, f. 41.
[4] Hutchinson, *Diaries of Sir Algernon West*, pp. 93, 95–6.

later admitted that he found Gladstone very trying on occasions during this period. He and his assistants would labour for many hours on the Bill, and then Gladstone, speaking in the House, would make his own amendments on the spur of the moment 'with little thought of outlying consequences' such as the effect on the very sensitive Irish.[1]

Privately worried about the impatience in the party, Morley remained in public defiant and unyielding. At Newcastle in August 1893 he repeated his threat that, 'if we Liberals were to play tricks with the Irish question, if we were to break loose from our own pledges, from our own promises, to Ireland', there would be 'a worse and more dangerous split in our party than that which took place in 1885'.[2]

But time had at last run out for the great Irish policy. From the point when, on the Home Rule Bill having been sent to the Lords and there overwhelmingly rejected, the Government decided not to appeal to the country on the issue of this rejection, it could obviously no longer function as the great cohering, concentrating, and defining policy of British Liberalism. The Liberals now had to acknowledge that they could make no further progress with the home-rule policy so long as they insisted on dealing with it exclusively in and by itself. Morley admitted that home rule could not by its own force surmount the barrier of the Lords' veto, because it was not a reform 'eagerly desired by the bulk of the voters' and because the Lords in rejecting it did not 'really resist the will of the British constituencies'.[3] This meant that he and other Liberals were faced with the critical necessity of adopting a completely new perspective on policy. Ireland was no longer the great obstruction which explained all. It was only a fragment of policy, progress on which was controlled by the existence of a greater obstruction, the Lords' veto, that must itself be viewed by Liberals within the wider context of the problem of finding

[1] Cf. Ibid., p. 151. *Recollections*, I, pp. 359–67.
[2] *The Times*, 28 Aug. 1893, p. 10, c. 4.
[3] To Harcourt, 21 Sept. 1894. *The Times*, 10 Dec. 1897, p. 6, c. 1; 24 Mar. 1898, p. 6, c. 2.

policies that would arouse the enthusiasm of the mass of British voters. Home rule was now to be achieved only through the acceptance of it by Conservatives, as in 1922, or through the extra force of popularity gained from policies of social reform which, after 1909, enabled the Liberals to break down the barrier of the Lords.

19

THE CHANGE OF LIBERAL LEADERSHIP, 1894

THE second great blow to the Irish policy was the retirement of Gladstone early in 1894. When Gladstone decided to resign because of disagreement with his colleagues over the naval estimates, Morley, clinging desperately to his belief that Gladstone could maintain the Irish policy in its pre-eminent position, spent several hours with him 'wrestling with all my might', as Morley put it, to make him change his mind. Finally, on 2 February 1894 he addressed a long letter to Gladstone, pleading with him for the sake of Ireland not to resign yet or in such a manner:

You are the only Englishman who has ever struck the imagination of the Irish—whether the Irish at home, or the Irish of the dispersion—: you have become the centre of their admiration, their trust and confidence, and their warm affection. Perhaps in the recesses of their minds, they may not expect that you will carry a H.R. Bill. But at this hour it is not a question of a bill, but of a man. The Irish want you to be there. They want you to stand by them before the world, to carry their flag for them, so long as ever your right arm has strength enough to uphold it. If you leave now, they will discern no reason. The Irish are a suspicious people—no wonder, considering the many sorry turns that for centuries men and fate have played with them. They will undoubtedly suspect, in the absence of some specific cause, more obviously and urgently pressing to-day than it was six months ago, that the reason alleged is not the true reason. The secret of your objection to the naval policy is sure to ooze out. Suspicion will wax hotter. The Irish will not believe that a question of half a dozen warships or a few millions of money more or less, could have induced you to step down from the highest undertaking of your whole life. I dread to think of the effect in Ireland. I have closely watched the working of the rumour of the last eight and forty hours. If the rumour comes true, there will first be a shock of panic; then there will be a violent storm of anger; then there will be sullen clouds of settled resentment, which will go far to undo and to blot out the work of eight years of strenuous and noble endeavour, both on your own part and on the part of a great host of less illustrious, but not less faithful men.[1]

But it was in vain. Gladstone held firmly to his decision, and Morley talked of 'the coming catastrophe'. 'Never again can I know such blackness of days as now,' he told Gladstone. 'Public life has lost its highest attraction, for I have not much hope of seeing great causes advance in my time—in face of all the mischievous forces that seem destined to dominate this country for a good many years to come.'[2] At first he thought of accompanying Gladstone into retirement, and then he went through a period of agonizing indecision as to whether or not to leave the Irish Office for some other Cabinet post. The cause of his dilemma is obvious. So long as Gladstone retained the premiership, the Irish Secretary was one of the most powerful men in the Cabinet. But the power was that of Gladstone's 'main prop'. Without Gladstone Morley would be isolated, thrust away into a small corner, in a job entailing frequent absences from the centre of power. No longer would he have a voice in the determination of over-all priorities in policy. Yet he knew that his own commitment and 'pledge of honour' to the Irish cause were as strong as Gladstone's. On 11 February 1894 he wrote to Gladstone: 'It may be that I, for one, have sold my political soul for the sake of Ireland, and it may be that I am selling it too cheap. But a month on Irish soil only deepends the feeling engendered by a good many other months— that for me [at] least that business is paramount.'[3] However, on 22 February he told Sir Algernon West that, while he was insisting that home rule should remain in the forefront after Gladstone's departure, he himself would stay at the Irish Office for another three months only.[4] For enticing alternatives were being dangled before him. Lewis Harcourt offered the Exchequer should Morley

[1] B.M. Add. MSS. 44257, ff. 150–2.
[2] To Gladstone, 25 Feb., 1, 25 Mar. 1894, B.M. Add. MSS. 44257, ff. 160–3.
[3] B.M. Add. MSS. 44257, f. 158.
[4] H. G. Hutchinson (ed.), *Private Diaries of the Rt. Hon. Sir Algernon West, G.C.B.*, 1922, p. 281.

help to bring about Sir William Harcourt's succession to the premiership, and tried to appease Morley's Irish conscience by suggesting to him that his promotion to the Exchequer would be 'a clear gain for the cause of Home Rule, and the Irish would be quite sharp enough to see it'. According to Lewis Harcourt, Morley was flattered and pleased by the offer.[1]

Morley was also strongly moved by the thought of the Foreign Office. According to J. A. Spender, Morley in later years made 'no secret of the fact' that he had desired this office and was aggrieved at being denied it.[2] This was the post that Gladstone most wished him to have, believing that he was very 'well fitted' for it.[3] It seems very likely that the prospect of going to the Foreign Office influenced Morley in supporting Rosebery for the premiership. In October 1893 Asquith, angling for such support for Rosebery, had hinted to Morley that he 'might take the F.O. if R. became head of Government, as it would never do to have both Premier and F.O. in the H. of L.'[4] Certainly, when Lord Kimberley was given the Foreign Office by Rosebery, Morley complained at having been 'tricked' 'over the Foreign Secretary being in the Lords'. He agreed to remain at the Irish Office, but petulantly laid down the most stringent conditions about not being 'asked to take part in any un-Irish debate, nor to make one single speech in the country'. 'I will lock myself fast in the Irish back-kitchen,' he declared.[5] The Irish policy had indeed shrunk from its Gladstonian status as an all-embracing substitute for a system in Liberal politics. Now even to Morley it seemed like a prison.

In the crisis over the succession to Gladstone, Morley played an important role. There was never any question of Morley himself being in the running. He had become too exclusively identified

[1] Ibid., p. 277. *Recollections*, II, p. 16. R. R. James, *Rosebery. A Biography of Archibald Philip, Fifth Earl of Rosebery*, 1963, pp. 308, 312.
[2] J. A. Spender, *Life, Journalism and Politics*, I, 1927, pp. 57, 132. Cf. J. H. Morgan, *John, Viscount Morley. An Appreciation and Some Reminiscences*, 1924, p. 70.
[3] James, *Rosebery*, p. 237. C. Mallet, *Herbert Gladstone. A Memoir*, 1932, p. 149.
[4] *Recollections*, I, p. 376.
[5] Ibid., II, pp. 17–20. A. G. Gardiner, *The Life of Sir William Harcourt*, II, 1923, p. 269. James, *Rosebery*, pp. 320–34.

with the Irish policy for the party to desire his leadership once its enthusiasm for that policy had in large part evaporated. It was clear that the choice must lie between the two occupants of the 'English bench'. As regards Irish policy Morley had as little to expect from the one as from the other, but in the sharp divergence that had already begun to appear between Harcourt and Rosebery on imperial policy Morley's sympathy with Harcourt was never in any doubt. Nevertheless, it was to Rosebery that he gave his preference in 1894. And this preference was important, because Morley still retained much influence in the party as, more than any other man, the custodian of the Gladstonian legacy. Asquith observed in January 1894 that Harcourt was impossible for Prime Minister because Morley would not serve under him and Morley's inclusion was 'essential to the existence of a Liberal Government.'[1] In part, of course, this was because it was a minority Government, dependent on the Irish, who would be sure to regard the simultaneous departures of Gladstone and Morley as conclusive proof of the Liberals' abandonment of home rule. The result would be a great reinforcement of the position of the anti-Liberal Parnellites and the probable overthrow of the Government. But the other reason is indicated in a remark by Regineld Brett in 1891 that any Liberal Government of which Morley did not approve would from the first be 'viewed with suspicion by the Stalwarts'.[2] Clearly, Morley's threats of a split in the party should the home-rule policy be abandoned were not unrelated to the reality of his own position in it. The more conservative elements in the party—those who, for example, had supported his uncompromising attitude at the Round Table Conference of 1887—had, justifiably, come to regard him as one of the principal influences within the party leadership against the advance of 'socialist doctrine'. Thus Stuart Rendel, the wealthy manufacturer and close friend of Gladstone, who had been in 1886 one of the most 'rigid' opponents of reconciliation with Chamberlain,[3] was to tell Morley in 1895

---

[1] Hutchinson, *Diaries of Sir Algernon West*, p. 242.
[2] M. V. Brett (ed.), *Journals and Letters of Reginald Viscount Esher*, I, 1934, p. 154.
[3] Cf. E. H. Fowler, *The Life of Henry Hartley Fowler, First Viscount Wolverhampton, G.C.S.I.*, 1912, p. 210.

that his value as a man 'untainted with empiricism' would be recognized as soon as 'the present fit of socialism' ended.¹ The question that we must now ask is why Morley used this influence in favour of a man who was, after all, shortly to become the leader of the imperialistic wing of the party.

As early as 1887 Morley had reacted with horror to a suggestion by Rosebery that Harcourt would probably be the next Liberal Prime Minister.² In 1891 Morley told Reginald Brett that he was in 'doubt whether he could ever serve with Harcourt, as his view and H.'s on Ireland diverged widely'.³ As we have seen, Harcourt opposed the concentration on Ireland and demanded a return to attention to domestic reform. But by 1893 Rosebery was clearly adopting much the same point of view. In 1894, therefore, Morley's choice was confined to deciding which of the two was likely to prove the safer practitioner of this non-Gladstonian type of leadership. And in this regard the most significant point is his long-standing distrust of Harcourt as an opportunist—or, as Rendel put it, an 'empiricist'. His writings, especially *On Compromise,* show his fear of opportunistic, 'merely' practical politicians who are undisciplined by any considerations of principle and therefore easily swayed by transient emotions and pressures. He had tried to provide a 'spiritual' control over Chamberlain's political practice, but then had helped to destroy Chamberlain's influence in the party when he had rejected that control. After 1885 the danger remained that, so long as Liberalism lacked a firm underlying set of principles, politicians such as Harcourt could not be easily restrained from adopting any policy whatsoever that seemed expedient and popular.

When Morley first met Harcourt in 1876, he had some very harsh things to say about him. He was 'flashy' and 'a plain and palpable impostor', and the fact that such a man had nevertheless become 'a political success' was enough, Morley said, to 'make me foreswear all politics'.⁴ The *Fortnightly Review* attacked Harcourt

[1] F. E. Hamer (ed.), *The Personal Papers of Lord Rendel,* 1931, p. 126.
[2] The Marquess of Crewe, *Lord Rosebery,* I, 1931, p. 303.
[3] Brett, *Journals and Letters of Viscount Esher,* I, p. 151.
[4] To Chamberlain, 24 Apr. 1876.

at this time as a typical House of Commons politician in his contempt for people with 'political ideas and reasoned principles'.[1] Four years later the *Pall Mall Gazette*, under Morley's editorship, expressed anxiety about the future of the Liberal party in the hands of this 'man of first-rate power acting under the influence of a very active ambition and rather second-rate principles'. Harcourt possessed energy in abundance, but it was very uncertainly controlled and directed, because he was not 'bound by any potent intellectual or moral tie' to the Liberal party. Consequently 'both friends and foes see in him at once a great power and a great peril'.[2]

In view of all this Morley's extremely close personal friendship and political co-operation with Harcourt may seem surprising. But the friendship may well be an example of Morley's tendency to associate with men of 'another type'; and, as for the political alliance, one may see Harcourt as replacing Chamberlain in the role of the very able practical politician over whom Morley would seek to exercise 'spiritual' control. Morley's reservations about Harcourt do not seem to have changed. Early in 1891 he confided in Chamberlain, and it was Harcourt's opportunism, not their differences on Irish policy, which proved to be even then uppermost in his mind. He complained that Harcourt still had 'his characteristic qualities' of 'sufficient unto the day, etc.', and that his policy was 'always dictated by the exigencies of the hour without regard to the future'. For this reason and because Harcourt seemed 'ready to swallow anything', even 'the pranks of Labouchere and the men below the gangway', he 'looked forward with the greatest apprehension to the time when they might be in a majority'.[3] This linking of Harcourt with Labouchere, then regarded as an extreme and undisciplined Radical, is significant in view of the fact that Morley's young Liberal protégés who admired Rosebery and made Harcourt into their *bête noire* were also particularly concerned to counter Labouchere's influence in the party. The two were linked quite often, in fact. In 1893 Sir

[1] *F.R.*, Feb. 1876, pp. 305–6.
[2] *P.M.G.*, 22 July 1880.
[3] J. L. Garvin, *The Life of Joseph Chamberlain*, II, 1933, pp. 488–9.

Charles Dilke wrote of 'a league between Harcourt and Labouchere against the Rosebery—Asquith combination'; and in March 1894 Morley interpreted Labouchere's amendment attacking the House of Lords, moved on the Address just after Rosebery had become Prime Minister, as 'a demonstration in favour of Harcourt against the new premier'.[1] There is not much evidence of personal contact, let alone 'league', between Harcourt and Labouchere, but Labouchere had for a long time been using arguments remarkably similar to those advanced by Harcourt in favour of substituting attention to domestic reform for concentration on Irish policy. Morley himself at one stage believed that Harcourt was 'laying himself out to get the Radical vote'.[2] He warned Harcourt that the kind of Radicalism which Labouchere represented was 'loose, inaccurate, and shallow';[3] but by 1892 he was finding fault with Harcourt for having surrendered to the 'headstrong and unscrupulous and shallow' agitators for the Eight Hours Bill.[4]

Rosebery was a very different proposition. To understand why it was that Morley preferred Rosebery to Harcourt in 1894 we have to consider the changes that had occurred in the élitism which was always so important an aspect of his Liberalism. We have already remarked on the idealistic élitism characteristic of Morley's early political writings, notably *On Compromise*. His prescription then for the discovery of the 'best men' was allied closely with the 'liberty' principle. The field should be left 'open to all comers' so that a leader can emerge who inspires in other men 'the loyalty springing from a rational conviction' that 'he is the best man they can find'. Thus 'the most truly valuable element in representative government theoretically is that it opens the widest and most numerous channels for the access of ability to places of power'.[5] In the same way, in the area of policy he had

---

[1] S. Gwynn and G. M. Tuckwell, *The Life of the Rt. Hon. Sir Charles W. Dilke, Bart, M.P.*, II, 1917, p. 287. *Recollections*, II, p. 22.
[2] Hamer, *Papers of Lord Rendel*, p. 182.
[3] To Harcourt, 2 Jan. 1891.
[4] To Harcourt, 26 Mar. 1892.
[5] *F.R.*, Sept. 1868, pp. 329–31; July 1870, p. 9; Aug. 1873, pp. 239–41, 246. *On Compromise*, pp. 280–2.

looked to free discussion and promulgation of 'new ideas' as the means of finding 'the surest and quickest road' to social improvement. He was as unwilling to impose strong leadership as he was to impose artificial system on political ideas. But, as we have seen, in the emergency of 1885 he looked for some means of creating a provisional 'spirit of system' in Liberal politics. Another aspect of his reaction to that crisis is to be found in his changed attitude towards the problem of Liberal leadership. Rather than persist in keeping the field 'open to all comers' and searching for those who *ought* to be the ruling élite, he tended now to grasp at *existing* authority in leadership—Gladstone, and the Whig aristocracy.

In the moment of emergency the Whig aristocrats appealed to Morley as men with minds trained by 'the habits and tradition of public affairs and great duties'.[1] Some years before, he had written that those men fight the political battle at most advantage who inherit 'a family tradition of exalted courage and generous public spirit' and in whom a preference for 'the larger interests' comes instinctively 'as a matter of prejudice, instead of being acquired as a matter of reason'. However, he also argued at this time that 'the question of titular aristocracy is not touched by this consideration, because titular aristocracies have always postponed the larger interests to the narrow interests of their order'.[2] But in 1886 certain 'titular' aristocrats, even though deserted by most of their order, chose to remain in the Liberal party with Gladstone. Here indeed was a 'prejudice' for 'the larger interests'; and, as Morley had learned from his reading of Burke, the advantage of 'prejudice' is that it makes a man's duty 'a part of his nature' and does not leave him 'hesitating in the moment of decision, sceptical, puzzled, and unresolved'.[3] It is not surprising that Morley, himself perpetually paralysed in 'the moment of decision' by consideration of the claims of reason, should after 1885 have looked to such men for the only already established source of authority in leadership, apart, of course, from Gladstone himself.

Gladstone's authority was unique. For the succession to him

[1] To Minto, 24 Jan. 1908, I.O.L. MSS. Eur. D. 573/3, f. 26.
[2] *F.R.*, Aug. 1870, p. 165.
[3] Cf. above. p. 65.

Morley had clearly begun looking in the direction of the Whigs well before 1894. When in December 1886 the possibility emerged of Hartington's joining a Unionist Government, Morley wrote: 'I am bound to say, that in view of the remoter future of the Liberal party, I should regret the severance of Hart[ingto]n. He contributes elements wh. some day or other, in face of Chamberlain's proved want of wisdom and self-control, we shall sorely need.'[1] It is worth quoting again what Reginald Brett reported to Hartington at this time. According to Brett,

John Morley, whom I saw some days ago, hoped you would refuse on the ground that were you to join Lord Salisbury, it would leave the Liberal Party, and consequently the destinies of the country, in the hands of those in whom he has no confidence. He said there was no one in public life with whom he so often agreed, and under whom he would sooner serve, than yourself. 'I look upon him as the strongest bulwark we have against all the strong socialist doctrine I hate" he said.[2]

In 1891, writing about Gladstone's health, which, he said, gave him 'uneasiness' and 'melancholy thoughts', Morley remarked: 'I wish I could think that Hartington and James would one day be in line with us again.'[3] In later years he admitted that he had 'always had a soft place in my heart for the patrician Whigs', and even sought to indentify himself with them. 'I am as cautious a Whig as any Elliot, Russell, or Grey, that was ever born', he assured Lord Minto in 1906.[4] In 1912 King George V pleased him immensely by saying that 'he looked upon him as the only representative of the old Whigs left in the Cabinet'.[5]

After 1885 Morley established very close personal and political relations with several of the Whigs who still remained in the party —Lord Ripon, for instance,[6] and Lord Spencer, whom Morley

[1] To Gladstone, 27 Dec. 1886, B.M. Add. MSS. 44255, f. 159. To Spencer, 27 Dec. 1886.
[2] 31 Dec. 1886, Brett, *Journals and Letters of Viscount Esher*, pp. 131–2.
[3] To Spencer, 2 Sept. 1891.
[4] To Minto, 1 Oct. 1908, 30 Nov. 1906, I.O.L. MSS. Eur. D. 573/3, f. 296; /1, f. 259.
[5] Sir A. Fitzroy, *Memoirs*, 3rd edition, II, n.d., p. 494.
[6] Cf. L. Wolf, *Life of the First Marquess of Ripon K.G., P.C., G.C.S.I., D.C.L.*,

called 'the very finest type of what the old patrician system of this country could produce'.[1] But above all there was Rosebery. Morley was later to describe Rosebery as the 'most natural-born leader' that he had ever met.[2] The two men became very close friends, and it was obvious well before 1894 that Morley was inclining strongly towards the idea of Rosebery's having the Liberal succession.[3] The turning-point seems to have come in 1891. Early in that year, after his dispute with Harcourt, Morley seemed very depressed, weighed down, obviously, by thoughts of what the next Liberal Government would be like if led by such an opportunist. He told Goschen that 'I see a hundred quackeries in front of us'; and, when Goschen humorously predicted a time when 'we shall have to intervene to protect Morley against his own men'. Morley replied: 'We'll form a party of order, like Cicero's *boni*, and all go down together. . . '[4] Rosebery now began to seem to him the one leader who might be able to save the party in its non-Irish, post-Gladstonian future. In August 1891 he visited Rosebery and urged him to undertake a 'mission': 'Make yourself the exponent and the leader of a practicable socialism.' In other words, Rosebery was to be that bulwark against wild, impracticable 'socialist doctrine' and Laboucherean Radicalism that Morley had once seen Hartington as being and that Harcourt was failing to be. 'Your mission is clear,' Morley insisted. ' . . . what is important is that the Liberal party should keep as well as it can on the high level of principle on which Mr. Gladstone has always spoken for it.'[5]

Morley's decision to support Rosebery in 1894 was undoubtedly influenced in part by personal ambition. But one must also view it in the context of his long-standing preference for Whig aristocrats over Radical opportunists. He was aware that the great Irish policy

---

Etc., II, 1921, p. 181: 'It is possible that Morley's Whiggism, as Sir Sidney Low once ingeniously diagnosed it, awoke an instinctive affinity between the two men.'

[1] To Minto, 19 Aug., 27 Sept. 1910, I.O.L. MSS. Eur. D. 573/5, ff. 137-8, 156-7.
[2] In conversation with Harold Laski in 1922. M. D. Howe (ed.), *Homes-Laski Letters* . . . , I, 1953, p. 415.
[3] Cf. *Recollections*, I, pp. 311-14, 368, 376.
[4] Ibid., I, pp. 270-1.
[5] Ibid., I, pp. 311-19.

could no longer hold sway over the action of the party. The question was therefore which leader would be safer for a party once more concerned with domestic reform policy. The decision in favour of Rosebery had been preparing itself for a considerable time.

But even with Rosebery Morley was to be disappointed. In October 1894 Morley wrote: 'I urge Rosebery to take Collectivism boldly by the throat.' And then he added despairingly: 'But I'm sure he won't.'[1] By 1900 Morley was referring to a statement by Rosebery as 'characteristic—that is to say, it is slippery, selfish, and with no firm political substance in it', and declaring that 'a leader of this sort will do well enough for a party without principles'.[2]

[1] To Carnegie, 21 Oct. 1894.
[2] To Spencer, 25 Sept. 1900.

20
PROBLEMS OF LIBERAL POLICY, 1894–1898

THE retirement of Gladstone and his replacement by a man who cared little about Ireland made no difference to Morley's insistence on the supreme importance of the Irish cause in Liberal politics. Once again Ireland was the absorbing preoccupation of his political activity, the great theme of his speeches. He told his audiences that 'the battle must still be fought'. The torch which Gladstone kindled 'glows with light and must be handed on, and I hope and believe that that torch . . . will not be extinguished because he has retired'. He admitted that it was 'very inconvenient and very tiresome that poor Ireland should be constantly stalking across the path of English reform', but his argument still was that there could be no progress with English reform 'unless we have been true to our own principles in respect to Ireland'. The real reason for his continuation of this theme is apparent in his association of complaints about the competition of reform demands for priority with the remark that 'of the many demands that are made upon us the claim of Ireland to our active attention and our energetic friendship is most necessary'. Ireland was still the central, comprehensive policy for Liberalism. In it were involved 'our own deepest party principles and most solemn party pledges'. He renewed his threat that any abandonment or subordination of the home-rule policy would 'break up this Government, shatter it from without and within', and 'make a dangerous dissension in the Liberal party like that which was made in 1886'. Such a split must be avoided because it would 'put indefinitely back all the most serious British reforms which you and I have at heart'.[1]

Privately, in his mood of sulkiness after he had been denied the

[1] *The Times*, 22 May 1894, p. 11, cc. 1–3.

chance to break out from his own confinement in the Irish 'back-kitchen', he was much less solicitous about these 'British reforms'. 'I shall stand by your side, whenever you want me in the field of foreign policy,' he told Harcourt. 'Otherwise, I mean to attend to my own business in this little island [Ireland], and leave the politics of your adjacent island to other people, who may do whatever platform duty they are inclined to.'[1] To a friend he wrote on setting off for Ireland of 'leaving the unimportant island for the important one'.[2] He professed complete indifference to the attitudes of his colleagues, and hence, not surprisingly, his own isolation in the Cabinet grew ever more marked. By June 1894 he was saying that 'he supposed he was the only person remaining in the Cabinet who sincerely believed in Home Rule'.[3] In a letter to Spencer on 8 January 1895 he urged a certain policy 'with all the force at my command—which under the view now taken of Irish affairs by most of the cabinet is, no doubt, not very great'. But, if he attempted to act on his own, his colleagues would reveal a strong disinclination to let him fasten the home-rule commitment on them any longer.[4] On occasions they would seriously embarrass him by their attempts to disengage themselves from this commitment.

Almost as soon as he became Prime Minister, Rosebery declared that home rule could not be conceded until there was a majority for it in England, since that country was 'the predominant member of the Three Kingdoms'. The Home Rule Bill of 1893 had received the support of a majority of the House of Commons, but only a minority of English M.P.s. Morley had then described as 'intolerable', 'astounding', and 'unconstitutional' the claim 'that no Bill should pass which has not got an English majority'. This would mean, he said, that, even if there were majorities for a certain proposal in Scotland, Wales, and Ireland, 'unless an English majority is on the same side, then the rest of the United Kingdom has to count for nothing!' This 'notion of England as a dictator in

[1] 21 Sept. 1894.
[2] To Carnegie, 23 Sept. 1894.
[3] J. L. Garvin, *The Life of Joseph Chamberlain*, II, 1933, p. 599.
[4] Cf., for example, Harcourt to Rosebery, 28 Jan. 1895, Harcourt MSS.

the United Kingdom' destroyed the principle of a united Parliament in which 'each member, each division of the United Kingdom, is to be counted for just as much whether the member comes from Cork or from Newcastle, whether he comes from Donegal or from Dorset; one man is to count for just the same as another'.[1]

But what Morley either failed to see or refused to admit was that the idea of the need for an English majority was a very natural reaction after an era in which he himself had been among the foremost in insisting on the subordinating and deferring of all non-Irish reforms to the satisfying of the demands of the Irish. If England was to be 'a dictator' now, had not Morley helped to set up Ireland as just such a dictator after 1885, and had he not placed Ireland on the one side and England, Scotland, and Wales on the other and found in the problems of the former an excuse for doing nothing about the problems of the latter? What the 'predominant-member' argument now represented was the feeling among Liberals that they must try to re-establish contact with the moods and desires of the English electorate.

Morley was henceforth obviously well aware of the danger of an identification of the Liberal party with the 'dictatorship' of Ireland. In the 1895 election campaign he sought to place the burden of unreasonableness on the Unionists' use of the 'predominant-member' argument:

it seems to me that 'Unionist' is a very curious name for a party which takes the four divisions of nationality in the United Kingdom, and uses the predominance of one of the four to thwart, to baffle, and to frustrate the legislative requirements of the other three. . . . I do not think that the National or Unionist party starts under very impartial auspices when it begins by putting one nation—viz., the English nation—against the other three, and tells the other three, once for all, that there is no hope for any want of theirs.[2]

But by substituting 'Liberal party' for 'Unionist party' and 'Ireland' for 'English nation' in this we can, in fact, find a re-

---

[1] *The Times*, 28 Aug. 1893, p. 10, cc. 1–2; 9 Nov. 1893, p. 4, c. 2.
[2] *The Times*, 5 July 1895, p. 10, c. 1; 16 July 1895, p. 10, c. 6.

markably accurate commentary on the nature of Morley's own politics after 1885 and on the reason why they had become so unpopular by 1894.

For Morley as Irish Secretary the maintenance of the Irish policy now became a wearisome and frustrating business. He had to deal with the extremely sensitive Irish Nationalist M.P.s under the most inauspicious circumstances. The basis of his own position on the Irish question was undermined by the impracticability for the time being of any further action on home rule. Whereas previously his work as Irish Secretary had been primarily concerned with meeting the wishes of the Irish representatives by preparing the Home Rule Bills, he had now indefinitely to administer a policy that must stop short of those wishes and operate within the very structure which he and they had for long so roundly condemned as unable to provide any satisfactory solution for Ireland's problems. He himself was now very conscious of the difficulty of this position. In a debate on Irish small holdings in April 1894 he remarked that 'I often think that it is a striking instance of the irony of fate that I, who am one of those who strongly believe that Ireland is entitled to the conduct of her own affairs, yet on account of the exigencies of the Office which I have the honour to bear, it should fall to my lot day by day and almost hour by hour to interfere in reference to Irish affairs and to decide matters of this kind'.[1]

Hitherto Morley had not been an 'ordinary' Irish Secretary. His preoccupation with the working out of Home Rule Bills had invested his administration of Irish affairs with an appearance of transitoriness and an excuse for not being judged by the normal standards. According to the Irish Nationalist leader, T. M. Healy, Morley's reply to a complaint in 1886 that he had appointed a Unionist to an Irish office was that he was 'engaged on the task of trying to enable us to manage our own affairs, which should silence all minor criticism'.[2] But now that defence was gone and he was subjected to the full blast of 'minor criticism'. One grave

[1] *Hansard*, 4, 25, 411.
[2] T. M. Healy, *Letters and Leaders of My Day*, II, 1928, p. 384.

disadvantage of being an 'ordinary' Irish Secretary was that he was obliged to enforce the law, even although he had often attacked both its source and its nature. He was naturally determined not to resort to coercion. For he could see how this would complete the destruction of his own position. When in late 1892 there was a dynamite outrage in Dublin, he wrote that he feared that this 'may incline people to tighten the bonds, and for that task they may deem the Tories better fitted than Liberals'.[1] But there were numerous possibilities of embarrassment even in the keeping of order on the basis of the existing law. As Morley realized, this was work for a man who did not believe in self-government for the Irish, and for himself to be performing it tended to weaken the special nature of his attitude towards Ireland. It was a dilemma which he had described very accurately some years before. In 1881 he had told Chamberlain that, while 'privately' he took 'the revolutionary view' that 'the hotter they [the Irish] make it for the "garrison" the better', he recognized that 'a Minister cannot take that line'. Until the constituencies accepted home rule, 'order must be kept on the principles of the existing system', even though one felt that it was wrong.[2] Now he himself was minister, faced with the burden of maintaining the Liberal-Irish alliance and yet also enforcing the law against disorder. He realized that unrest in Ireland could 'easily land me in heavy embarrassments, with consequences reaching far in the relations between English Liberals and Irish Nationalists'.[3] He had to plead with the Irish to understand that he could not 'govern the country without law at all', but they accused him of behaving in the same way as Balfour.[4]

Desperately Morley strove to preserve some special ground between the Irish and the Liberals. He had tried, as far as possible, since he had come to office in 1892 to appear to be governing Ireland as a 'Home Rule' Secretary. Thus he wrote of an Irish

[1] To Gladstone, 25 Dec. 1892, B.M. Add. MSS. 44257, f. 65.
[2] To Chamberlain, 5, 9, 19 Dec. 1881.
[3] To Gladstone, 23 Aug. 1894, B.M. Add. MSS. 44257, ff. 171-2.
[4] Cf. Healy, *Letters and Leaders*, II, p. 400. *Recollections*, I, pp. 355-6; II, pp. 45-6. Hansard, 4, 25, 1950.

military appointment: 'I turned it well over, and came to the conclusion that we must have an Irishman, on H.R. principles.'[1] He tried to base his administration on 'the warm sympathy of the population, and the active support of the political leaders, local as well as parliamentary', and went to great lengths to secure the co-operation of these leaders.[2] He also tried to secure some modest land reforms, and so that his term of office might not be completely barren of achievement he made considerable efforts to win Unionist backing for these. But his Evicted Tenants Bill of 1894 was rejected by the Lords, and a Land Bill of 1895 was lost in the general collapse of Government business.[3] Morley's efforts to escape from the Irish 'back-kitchen' in March 1894 can be easily understood in the light of this unhappy and barren record.

The Liberals' position with regard to other areas of policy was by now equally unhappy. The removal of the Irish 'umbrella' exposed once more the abiding structure of the party—a coalition of many and various reform interests, all competing clamorously for priority of attention. In May 1894 Morley had to warn Liberals that their enemies were exultantly claiming 'that we were being torn to pieces by a disruption of interests—that the Welshmen, the Scotchmen, the Irishmen, the London men, the Labour men were all tugging at us and would together destroy us'. Admitting that 'amongst the various interests which this Government represents there is a rivalry for priority', he denied that this rivalry was disrupting the party. But he nevertheless implored those who were working to secure attention to their own particular reform proposals to keep in mind that 'there is one common interest', the retention in office of a Liberal Government. He asked the Government's 'impatient friends' not to turn against it because it would

---

[1] To Campbell-Bannerman, 9 Jan. 1893, B.M. Add. MSS. 41223, f. 13.
[2] To Gladstone, 19 June 1893, B.M. Add. MSS. 44257, ff. 114-15. *Hansard*, 4, 23, 781-2. *Recollections*, I, pp. 278, 287, 358-9, 372. Healy, *Letters and Leaders*, II, pp. 382-6, 411.
[3] Cf. Garvin, *Chamberlain*, II, p. 600. *Recollections*, I, pp. 347-52. To Chamberlain, 29 July 1894. *Hansard*, 4, 9, 1892-1904; 10, 1458-60; 23, 866-75, 922; 27, 430-5; 28, 362, 1391; 30, 488; 31, 295-320; 32, 735-44. *The Times*, 31 Jan. 1895, p. 6, c. 2.

not 'give a place or priority to any one of these various competitive measures'. They should acknowledge that it alone 'must decide this question of priority', for only the Liberal leaders could have a comprehensive view of how all the pieces fitted or could fit together. 'They know the ground, they know all the considerations which ought to settle whether one Bill shall go before another.'[1] Repeatedly he would plead for 'all the union we can command' in 'the camp of reformers' and ask for acceptance of the principle that the party's objectives must be promoted 'in the way, and at the season which, in the opinion of those who are responsible, will be most conducive to their success'.[2]

But did the Liberal leaders, in fact, possess such a comprehensive view? Did their liberal beliefs have any of that desperately needed 'spirit of system' which the Irish policy had contributed for a period? The absence of it was obvious and went far to explain the failure of the method employed in 1891 for uniting the party, the adoption of a wide programme. As Morley had long argued, without a 'spirit of system' a programme was mere anarchy, a list of reforms no more than a list of elements of friction. Some Liberal leaders believed that it might be possible to find another single question, this time in domestic policy, that would fill the role so admirably performed by home rule after 1885. Gladstone and Rosebery saw a campaign against the House of Lords as exploitable in this way. But Morley did not. 'The plain truth is', he wrote, 'that we can do nothing with the H. of L. unless they really resist the will of the British constituencies—and this they are not now doing.'[3]

For his part Morley continued to concentrate on Irish policy; but his presentation of it was now even less associated with any considerations of electoral popularity. The old mood of regarding electoral defeat as of small significance in comparison with consistent adherence to a firm principle re-emerged. Even at the beginning of the Liberals' term in office he had professed this kind of indifference to the prospect of failure, as when he wrote: 'If we

[1] *The Times*, 22 May 1894, p. 11, c. 1.
[2] *The Times*, 28 June 1894, p. 6, c. 4; 5 July 1895, p. 10, c. 4.
[3] To Harcourt, 21 Sept. 1894.

founder, which is only too probable, at least let us go down with honour.'[1] A year later he was referring to the home-rule commitment as an issue compared with consistency on which 'it is of little concern what becomes of parties or of individuals'.[2] Early in 1894 he declared that Ireland 'is my polestar of honour, even if I were to know that I am driving straight on to failure'.[3] After Rosebery's 'predominant-Member' statement he assured the House of Commons that 'we are as men of honour bound' to the home-rule policy: 'Whatever our fortunes may be, whatever may happen at elections, there are those among us who will never cease to adhere to that policy.'[4] In 1895 he argued that parties and politicians were ruined, not by being put in a minority and ejected from office at elections, but by having 'shallow and inconstant convictions'. Nor was it only to the Irish policy that he then applied such arguments. He spoke in similar terms of the Local Option Bill as a measure by which, 'stand or fall, we abide':

But, they say, 'We are afraid you won't find that a very popular measure.' Popular or not we stand by that measure. . . . I am not in favour of going about with a thermometer and a wind gauge to these great meetings, to set the sails to every passing breeze.
. . . There are worse things in the world than being beaten. If you are beaten in what you know or believe to be a righteous cause which will uplift the condition of the people of the country to which you belong, never mind whether you are beaten or not.[5]

By 1895 almost the entire Liberal leadership seemed infected with his mood. Once more there was among them a craving for the opportunity to purge and to reconstruct, and for the justification for renewed inaction and non-commitment on reform priorities, that would be given by an electoral defeat. Harcourt said in 1894 that 'the fate of the present Government and the issue of the next Election are temporary incidents which I view

[1] To Harcourt, 17 July 1892.
[2] *The Times*, 28 Aug. 1893, p. 10, c. 4.
[3] *Recollections*, II, p. 8.
[4] *Hansard*, 4, 22, 180.
[5] *The Times*, 31 Jan. 1895, p. 7, c. 3; 5 July 1895, p. 10, cc. 2-4; 9 July 1895, p. II, c. 3. See also Morley to Rosebery, 16 Apr. 1894.

with philosophic indifference'.[1] In January 1895 Haldane commented: 'Rot has set in; there is no hope now but to be beaten and then to reconstruct a new party.'[2] In March Morley reported to Gladstone that Harcourt was 'privately protesting all the time that the sooner the ship went to pieces, the better alike for officers and for crew'.[3] 'I can't help feeling that defeat may be good for us,' wrote Herbert Gladstone at this time. 'We are plagued with obstinate faddists who are too strong for the leaders, and except for Ireland I could wish to get rid of them through defeat.'[4] The elections in 1895 found the leadership reduced to a state of total confusion, with each leader riding off on his own hobby-horse.

Morley himself had no cause for complaint that the electors had not taken him at his word. He appeared before the voters of Newcastle with an attitude of frank indifference to the prospect of defeat, with a record of three years of almost exclusive preoccupation with Ireland very infrequently interrupted by visits to his constituents, and with a programme dominated by the impracticable policy of home rule. The voters not surprisingly responded by depriving him of his seat. Once again he had hopefully appealed to the Newcastle Irish for support, assuring them that, even if, 'amidst all the cries that were now making the air resound' in 'the hubbub of a general election' which tended to 'mix up small issues and small questions with great ones', Ireland did not appear most prominent, it nevertheless did remain 'the most important question that Englishmen had to consider' and 'the battle-field of the English parties'.[5] But this can scarcely have endeared him to his non-Irish constituents; and, as for the Irish themselves, they manifested a waning enthusiasm for the Liberal alliance and a certain resentment over some of Morley's actions at the Irish Office.[6] Furthermore, the Newcastle Liberals had angered local Labour organizations by giving their second nomination to the

---

[1] Quoted in R. R. James, *Rosebery. A Biography of Archibald Philip, Fifth Earl of Rosebery*, 1963, p. 345.
[2] Quoted in B. Webb, *Our Partnership*, 1928, p. 121.
[3] 8 Mar. 1895, B.M. Add. MSS. 44257, f. 179.
[4] C. Mallet, *Herbert Gladstone A Memoir*, 1932, p. 156.
[5] *The Times*, 13 July 1895, p. 14, cc. 3–4.
[6] Cf. *N.D.C.*, 8 July 1895, p. 5, c. 2; 11 July 1895, p. 8, c. 2.

former M.P., Craig, rather than to Arthur Henderson, after Morley had agreed to stand with Henderson.¹ An independent Labour candidate entered the field and took 2,300 votes that probably tipped the balance against Morley.

After the defeat of 1895 the idea the Liberal party might well soon be replaced by some new party of progress, founded on a different but more solid and coherent basis, was bound to loom larger in men's minds. 'The disappearance of Mr. Gladstone closed a chapter in party history', Morley wrote in July 1895. Now the Liberals would be 'driven to reconsider their whole position' and to undertake a 'truly formidable' work of reconstruction, as to which Morley's comment was that 'I don't see who are to undertake it, nor on what basis it is to proceed'.² Indeed, in 1894 he had suggested that the party might lose its *raison d'être* when the politics of clearing away obstructions gave way to the politics of social and labour reform: 'I dare say the day may come—it may come sooner than some think—when the Liberal party will be transformed or superseded by some new party; but before the working population of this country have their destinies in their own hands, as they will assuredly do within a measurable distance of time, there is enough ground to be cleared which only the Liberal party is capable of clearing.'³

What Morley and other Liberals seemed most to fear was that the division between political parties might come to coincide with the social division between the working and the propertied classes. In a speech early in 1896 Morley expressed his regret at hearing it said 'in Scotland, and constantly in England', that 'the division of parties now had become to a very considerable extent also a division of classes', so that, 'with comparatively few exceptions, the wealthy and the great were on one side' and 'the numbers were on the other side'. He 'was no revolutionary, and he regretted

¹ Cf. R. S. Watson, *The National Liberal Federation From Its Commencement to the General Election of 1906*, 1907, p. 125. P. Corder, *The Life of Robert Spence Watson*, 1914, pp. 255–6. P. P. Poirier, *The Advent of the Labour Party*, 1958, p. 197.

² To Bryce, 23 July 1895. To Spencer, 28 July 1895. To Ripon, 28 July 1895, B.M. Add. MSS. 43541, f. 80.

³ *The Times*, 22 May 1894, p. 11, c. 5.

such a division'. In particular, he was sorry that 'those who belonged to the wealthy and the aristocratic class should have turned their backs, many of them, upon their old principles and upon their old friends'. There 'was nothing he deplored more than that there should be anything like a severance between class and class'. What must be fostered was a sense of unity, of being 'all Scotchmen, Englishmen, and Irishmen', 'all concerned in the commonwealth' and 'in making the State of which we were all citizens a strong and powerful State'.[1] In a letter to Morley in 1898 his friend and one-time Cabinet colleague, H. H. Fowler, predicted 'the disruption of the Liberal party and the ultimate division of parties into the Haves and Have-nots'.[2] A month after he had received this letter Morley appealed in a speech for support for every movement that 'helps to soften the violence of social contrasts and averts that very evil state of society which the world has seen before now, and may see again, when the relations between rich and poor are mainly or entirely relations of controversy, quarrel, and dispute, and when these disputes and controversies control the main field of political action'.[3]

What followed from this was the necessity of keeping the field of political action as clear as possible of questions involving State interference in social and economic life. We have already seen how Morley had been opposing since the late 1880s any legislation that would involve the fixing by Parliament of wages or hours of work. He now widened his opposition. When a great dispute broke out in the engineering industry in 1897, he said that the issues at stake in it must not be permitted to become the material of political controversy: 'These are not party questions. They go far wider and deeper than the questions that divide parties'[4]—the questions, that is, that Morley believed *ought* to divide parties. In 1892, in a speech advocating that the provision of welfare benefits be attended to in the main by friendly societies and not by the State, he had concluded by expressing the hope

[1] *The Times*, 5 Feb. 1896, p. 7, cc. 1–2.
[2] E. H. Fowler, *The Life of Henry Hartley Fowler, First Viscount Wolverhampton, G.C.S.I.*, 1912, p. 439.
[3] *The Times*, 14 Feb. 1898, p. 12, c. 3.
[4] *The Times*, 10 Dec. 1897, p. 6, c. 2.

that 'the matters on which he had spoken would never be allowed to become the subjects of party politics'.[1] In 1895, speaking on the problems of poverty and hardship in old age, he warned that 'this is not a party question' and added that 'I hope it will not be made a party or political question'.[2] In 1899 he rebuked Unionist politicians for having chosen, 'with a recklessness for which they are now paying and for which they will have to go on paying the penalty', to make 'this particular matter of provision for old age a party and an electioneering cry'. This was 'playing with fire'.[3]

Conscious as he was, however, of the growing sentiment that politics ought to be about social reform, he endeavoured to present such issues as temperance reform as examples of this kind of politics, and claim that, because of their willingness to act on these issues, the Liberals were making a positive response to this sentiment. In 1898 he said: 'They say that we are not a party of social reform. In my judgment there is no part of the area of social reform *which is within the reach of legislation* so important as temperance reform.'[4] Always there was this qualification.

On most issues of social and economic reform, however, Morley now appeared to have retreated into an attitude of doctrinaire opposition to State intervention. He argued that it was 'absurd' and 'perilous to thrust Acts of Parliament . . . like the steam ram-rod into the delicate machinery of commercial undertakings'. Working men should 'reflect very carefully whether Acts of Parliament are the things which they may look to—rude, rough instruments like Acts of Parliament . . . to better their condition with such dangers around them' as the threat of foreign competition.[5] 'Beware of any State action which artificially disturbs the basis of work and wages', was his constant warning. No statesman could 'insure steady work and good wages', for there were 'great economic tides and currents flowing which were beyond the control of any statesman, Government, or community'. These 'great economic events are not capable of

[1] *The Times*, 8 Feb. 1892, p. 12, cc. 1–3.
[2] *The Times*, 5 July 1895, p. 10, c. 2.
[3] *The Times*, 26 May 1899, p. 6, cc. 2–3.
[4] *The Times*, 24 Mar. 1898, p. 6, c. 1. My italics.
[5] *The Times*, 3 Dec. 1895, p. 6, c. 3.

being arrested, and only in a very moderate degree of being directed, by any action which a Legislature can take'.[1]

He opposed any scheme that would entail the direct provision by the State of benefits for sections of the community, as this would promote the idea that Government could be used as the tool of sectional or class interests. The Unionist Government's proposals for helping farmers by assuming part of their rate burden and for subsidizing West Indian sugar-producers seemed to him dangerous precedents of 'distributing public money for the purposes of a single class' or section. 'How far are you going to allow this to take you?' he asked. 'If you are going to give grants to help profits, how far are you off from giving grants in favour of aiding wages?' He warned taxpayers that the end of this process would be 'national workshops to which anybody has a right to go and receive money out of your pockets'.[2]

So disturbed was he by these trends and so anxious was he to remove such questions from 'the main field of political action' that he argued for the greatest possible dismantling of the power of the State and the reorganization of government in smaller, local units. His argument was that, because locally elected bodies 'understand local necessities', 'they are better able to try experiments without possible mischievous results', and that therefore 'you may safely intrust to local bodies powers which would be mischievous and dangerous in the hands of the central Government'. In municipalities the area of government was small enough for those governed to be able to exercise effective control over 'all the dangers, risks, and wastes' for which State action allowed scope. If social reform was to become the main area of political action, then this was the level at which it ought to be tried: 'in such matters, for example, as housing of the poor and so forth, depend upon it the proper machinery through which to carry out these operations is municipal and not Parliamentary.' In the municipalities 'the people who are interested, who will have to pay the rates,

---

[1] *The Times*, 8 Feb. 1892, p. 12, c. 3; 30 May 1895, p. 7, c. 3; 5 Feb. 1896, p. 7, c. 2; 12 Nov. 1896, p. 10, c. 2.
[2] *The Times*, 18 June 1896, p. 6, c. 1; 11 Nov. 1896, p. 8, c. 2; 18 Jan. 1897, p. 9, c. 2; 28 Jan. 1898, p. 4, c. 2.

who may be interfered with', could then retain control over the extension of social reform. Parliament was 'a long way off, was overloaded with work, and was necessarily mechanical in much of its operations, the results of which were apt to be uniform and unelastic'.[1]

As antagonism to State interference became the leading aspect of his attitude to political and social questions, it was increasingly apparent that Morley did after all possess a system of political principles which was forming the basis for his political practice. This was Cobdenism. We have seen how, after writing the *Life of Cobden,* he had dismissed Cobden's principles as inadequate and irrelevant to contemporary conditions and not now fitted to be a 'system of political or social principles, connected with one another, bearing with united pressure in a common direction, and shedding light now on one, now on another, of the problems which circumstances bring up in turn for practical solution'.[2] The system which he had then been seeking was to be one of progress, a guide for reform and change, and Cobdenism was not by that time commonly regarded as such a system. But increasingly, as the failure of the attempt to evolve new principles to guide Liberal action in domestic policy became evident, Cobdenism re-emerged as the only firm foundation that Morley had yet discovered for his political thinking. Even in 1887 he could tell the Cobden Club that Cobden's principles could still be 'the starting point from which to commence and to work out social reform'.[3] Forced on to the defensive and unable to find any satisfactory set of principles for positive political action, he rested his politics on that creed which defined the conditions of social stability and welfare in negative terms of absence of political interference in 'natural' economic and social processes. In particular, his resistance to eight-hours legislation involved his advancing fundamental

---

[1] *The Times,* 20 Nov. 1889, p. 10, c. 1; 21 Nov. 1890, p. 10, c. 2; 23 May 1892, p. 7, c. 2; 7 Feb. 1896, p. 7, cc. 4–5; 19 Feb. 1896, p. 10, c. 6; 12 Nov. 1896, p. 10, c. 2.
[2] *F.R.,* Apr. 1882, p. 503.
[3] *The Times,* 16 May 1887, p. 7, cc. 2–3.

Cobdenite arguments;[1] and from that point the Cobdenite influence rapidly expanded over his whole thinking. In 1898 he wrote to the *Westminster Gazette* to point out that in politics he was a 'resolute Cobdenite'.[2]

Of course, the aspect of his Cobdenism which was most obvious to public opinion by that time was his extreme anti-imperialism; but this was, as we shall see in the next chapter, closely related to his general thinking on the role of the State in national life and the danger of the involvement of class conflict in politics.

[1] Cobden's views on 'parliamentary regulation of labour' became Morley's. Cf. *Cobden*, I, pp. 298-9.
[2] W. Harris, *J. A. Spender*, 1946, pp. 89-90.

21

IMPERIALISM AND LIBERALISM, 1896-1902

MORLEY regarded imperialism and an interventionist foreign policy as examples of harmful interference by the State in natural social and economic conditions. As far as the countries against which such policies were directed were concerned, the argument is obvious; but he also regarded imperialism and interventionism as having the effect of increasing the power and activity of the State in England itself and of causing it to introduce artificial disorganizing factors into social and economic development. Thus one can see from his speeches and writings between 1899 and 1903 that it was the enormous expenditure involved which particularly worried him about the new imperialism, because he feared the effect on economic life and social stability of the means which the State would have to employ to find the necessary additional revenue.[1] The sudden increase in State expenditure as the result of the South African War seemed to him to open the flood-gates for the use of the State's revenue-raising power to effect great changes in the economic and social structure of the country. This is F. W. Hirst's account of Morley's mood late in 1899: 'He is depressed about national expenditure. He fears, when bad times come, that we shall have not retrenchment but "nefarious attacks on property and reversions to Fair Trade".'[2] What he meant was that there were these two highly dangerous methods of meeting increased expenditure at a time when the economy was not expanding. By 'attacks on property' he meant the redistribution of incomes through taxation. In 1901 he attacked the budget of that year as

[1] Cf. *The Times*, 18 Jan. 1899, p. 6, cc. 2, 4. To Harcourt, 24, 27 Feb. 1899, 2 Apr. 1902. To Carnegie, 26 Feb., 5 Apr. 1901, 14 Mar. 1903. *Hansard*, 4, 94, 1075-89. F. W. Hirst, *In the Golden Days*, 1947, pp. 192, 213-14.

[2] Hirst, *In the Golden Days*, p. 192.

having initiated this tendency. He pointed out that, since in 1874 the newly enfranchised urban masses had refused to accept Gladstone's policy of abolishing the income tax, there had been 'a steady systematic growth of direct taxation and a steady, systematic fall of indirect taxation' until, under the impact of irresponsible imperialism and expansionism, the point had been reached where 'at the pace at which we are now going in reference to the income tax a claim—an irresistible claim—will be set up and maintained for a readjustment of the income tax and a reconstruction of it'. An ungraduated income tax had only limited scope for expansion. But readjustment would involve taxing some people more heavily than others, and this, according to Morley, would be difficult to reconcile with 'maxims of public equity'. Furthermore, the fact of the Government's taking such action would introduce questions of class distinction into politics. This would lead to 'trouble of the most serious kind'. Morley now cursed the setting of the income tax 'on its legs' by Gladstone in 1853, for, by thus 'giving a C[hancellor] of Exchequer a reservoir out of which he could draw with ease and certainty whatever was asked for', Gladstone had 'furnished not only the means, but a *direct incentive* to that policy of expenditure which it was the great object of his life to check'.[1]

The alternative method of raising extra revenue was through tariffs and indirect taxes. Throughout his career Morley was a staunch opponent of interference by the State with trade. Tariff reform would not only dislocate natural economic processes; it would also undermine the foundations of social order and stability. Morley argued that it was no coincidence that Great Britain, 'the great free trade country of Europe', was 'the one great country of Western Europe which since 1846 has never known even a shadow of a civil convulsion'. In his campaign against tariff reform he associated with protection such phenomena as social distress, as in England before 1846, political corruption, as in the United States, and political unrest, as on the Continent.[2] And it

[1] *Hansard*, 4, 94, 1085–9. To Harcourt, 16 May 1901. See also *The Times*, 6 June 1901, p. 7, c. 5.
[2] *Hansard*, 4, 129, 634, 644. *The Times*, 4 Nov. 1903, p. 10, c. 1.

was the increase in State expenditure which threatened to be the Trojan horse that would admit those scourges. In 1901 Morley declared that

> if the Government went on with this increasing expenditure our financial system would have to be readjusted, and it would be impossible to go on resting it upon the basis of a comparatively small number of income-taxpayers, and . . . ultimately somebody or other (certainly not he) would propose some of those methods for replenishing the Exchequer which would impair the system of free trade to which we owed our present prosperity.[1]

When in 1909 a Liberal free-trade Government decided that increased expenditure on armaments and on social welfare would have to be met out of increased taxes, Morley wrote that behind the budget 'hangs the spectre of Tariff Reform', for the taxpaying public '*may* say that, if this is the best that can be done under Free Trade, they'll try something else'.[2] It was towards action in this area of policy that his own political ambitions began to move. In 1899, when discussing with him the future of the party, F. W. Hirst came to the conclusion that Morley 'would lean towards the Exchequer'. 'I hope so,' Hirst added. 'He has the imagination and the courage needed. . . . As Chancellor he would be able to put in some sledge-hammer blows at the bloated armament estimates.'[3] In the last months of 1905 Morley made it plain that it was the Exchequer that he wanted in the new Liberal government.[4] Although he did not receive it, he continued to look upon 'the Expenditure of the country' as 'the most formidable of our standing problems'.[5]

The greatest political danger, as he saw it, was that the increase in national expenditure might be made popular and acceptable in the eyes of the majority of electors, while the minority would

[1] *The Times*, 6 June 1901, p. 7, c. 5.
[2] To Minto, 7, 23 Apr. 1909, I.O.L. MSS. Eur. D. 573/4, ff. 74, 90.
[3] Hirst, *In the Golden Days*, p. 176.
[4] Cf. [Lord Haldane], *Richard Burdon Haldane. An Autobiography*, 1929, p. 97. Haldane to Knollys, 19 Oct. 1905 (draft), Haldane MSS. 5906, f. 222. M. V. Brett (ed.), *Journals and Letters of Reginald Viscount Esher*, II, 1934, pp. 121–2.
[5] To Minto, 2 Dec. 1909, I.O.L. MSS. Eur. D. 573/4, f. 252.

be left to bear the extra taxation burden. He sought therefore to encourage the belief that increased expenditure, far from being a means of enhanced social well-being, was antagonistic to the achievement of this. 'Suppose they were interested in housing or pensions, or even in temperance,' he said to an audience in 1903; '—whatever subject of social reform they chanced to be interested in, they might depend upon it they would find themselves checkmated when the time came by the bad financial position in which they would find the country standing.'[1] He would argue that, if the country remained in 'its present mood of financial indifference, of financial slackness', the 'expenditure due to Imperialism and militarism would ruin the country'.[2] If the country desired social reform, it 'would have to return to the old catchwords, "Peace and retrenchment" ': 'They could have no social reform without expenditure of public money. What they required, therefore, was a reduction of public expenditure.'[3] In other words, there would have to be a compensating reduction in other areas of public expenditure. A strict limit must be placed on the amount of money taken by the Government from the people in taxes, and priorities between, say, military expenditure on the one hand and housing and old-age pensions on the other must be fixed within that limit. There must be no idea of a bottomless reservoir of tax revenue.

Morley had long been worried that the power of committing the country to large and expensive policies at home and abroad rested with that section of the community, the working-class voters, 'which, under the present system of national taxation, will pay least towards their cost'.[4] In 1902 he said that 'I cannot conceive a country in a more absolutely perilous position than a country in which a great host of electors are to dictate a policy, and then are not to pay for that policy. . . . this nation is in an indescribable peril if all voters are to vote for war whenever they like, or for anything else, and yet have no sense of responsibility.'[5]

---

[1] *The Times*, 16 Apr. 1903, p. 4, c. 2.
[2] *The Times*, 5 Nov. 1901, p. 8, c. 5.
[3] *The Times*, 24 Oct. 1905, p. 6, c. 3.
[4] *P.M.G.*, 4 Oct. 1882. To Chamberlain, 23 Nov. 1876.
[5] *The Times*, 9 June 1902, p.13, c. 3.

He warned working-class voters that they would suffer in the end because 'the burden of taxation, however spread and however disguised, at last comes heaviest on the shoulders of the industrial community'.[1] In other words, the interests of the taxed employing class and the non-taxpaying working people were identical fundamentally. He was obviously extremely concerned that the operation of the tax system might accentuate class differences and produce 'nefarious attacks on property'. He would claim that 'so closely connected and related were all the members, parts and motions of the body politic, that they might be sure that every tax in the long run, and more or less, was a disadvantage to everybody; and however ingeniously they might endeavour to adjust the burden yet the wear and tear of it in the last resort found its way to the wage-earning classes, and all taxes reacted on the condition of the whole people'.[2] He welcomed an increase in indirect taxation in 1902, since this would lead to 'the working man finding out that in supporting the war, he has been as great a fool as other people'.[3]

Popular imperialism was the root of the evil. 'I want you to see where your policy of military adventure . . . has brought you to,' he said to an audience in 1903. 'You are fixed with an increase of taxation which will stand and grip you.'[4] It was necessary, therefore, to make imperialism appear as unattractive as possible to the mass electorate; and Morley repeatedly argued that imperialism was antagonistic to social progress. This brought him into conflict with Rosebery and those younger Liberals with whom he had been so closely associated some years earlier, for they were now looking to imperialism as a systematic concept that would provide the foundation for a programme of Liberal reform. Morley, on the other hand, wanted to effect a complete separation between imperialism and the politics of social reform. Thus in a speech in 1900 he tried to establish a clear dividing-line:

Had they thought of the relations between Imperialism and social re-

[1] *The Times*, 8 Feb. 1892, p. 12, cc. 1–3.
[2] *The Times*, 6 June 1901, p. 7, c. 5.
[3] *The Times*, 9 June 1902, p. 13, c. 3. To Harcourt, 2 Apr. 1902.
[4] *The Times*, 14 Apr. 1903, p. 8, c. 2.

form? Could we continue this process of territorial expansion with our increasing Budgets? What we wanted was resolute and sustained attention to strengthening our industrial position . . . if he were to choose between the Socialist and the Militarist, with all his random aims, his profusion of the national resources, his disregard for the rights and feelings of other people, he himself declared he considered the Socialist's standards were higher and their [sic] means were no less wise.[1]

The high cost of imperialism threatened to compel the adoption by politicians of taxation as a revenue-raising device on such a scale as to constitute a grave danger to the social stability and economic prosperity of the nation. It would mean, Morley warned his audiences, 'starving those causes, those movements, those reforms upon which the new generation has its chance and only chance of being a better, stronger generation than that which is now going before it'.[2] Nor was it only money that was being squandered. There was also the distraction of political attention, the absorption of politicians' energies. He argued that, 'so long as Imperialism is placed first and foremost, is placed in such a position as to attract to itself the interest, the force, the intellect of statesmen and of the public whom statesmen are supposed to lead', 'reform in any large or serious sense, reform of the arrangements and institutions of this country becomes impossible'. Indeed, 'the withdrawal of public interest, the direction of public excitement into wrong channels, . . . made all talk of social reform complete moonshine. So long as their most prominent men in the Government and out of the Government had their whole minds concentrated on what was called this new policy they would be no better off.'[3]

But have we not already encountered this kind of argument in Morley's career? Certainly, it bears a very striking resemblance to what he said after 1885 about the relationship of the Irish 'obstruc-

[1] *The Times*, 11 June 1900, p. 3, c. 3. Cf. also *The Times*, 24 Oct. 1905, p. 6, c. 3. R. W. Perks saw this speech as 'Morley's bid for the socialist vote as a counter poise to Liberal Imperialism.' Perks to Rosebery, 14 June 1900, Rosebery MSS. Box 39.
[2] *The Times*, 14 Apr. 1903, p. 8, c. 2.
[3] *The Times*, 20 Jan. 1899, p. 10, c. 4; 26 May 1899, p. 6, c. 3.

tion' to the possibilities of advance in domestic reform. While there can be no doubt that Morley felt deeply concerned over the implications of imperialism for the social, political, and economic life of the country, as he had also felt concerned over the implications of denying self-government to the Irish, we must also ask whether he showed the same disposition to welcome public preoccupation with the issue of imperialism as he had shown with regard to the Irish question. In other words, were the characteristics of his anti-imperialism after 1895 those of a successor in his political thinking to the great Irish preoccupation?

Even after the defeat of 1895 Ireland appeared to remain for a time Morley's great interest in politics. It was as the Liberal opposition's chief spokesman on Irish affairs that he intended to re-enter Parliament.[1] His friends supported him in this view of his role in political life. Stuart Rendel assured him that, because 'Ireland would remain', his position could not be prejudiced 'by mere lapse of time and by new men and matter'.[2] In July 1895 Gladstone advised him that he should not be in any haste to return to Parliament, but should wait until 'the moment Irish affairs come on to the horizon', when the importance of his being once more in active politics would be at once apparent.[3] And in the meantime he set to work, with Gladstone's encouragement, on a different method of promoting the Irish cause—a book on it, which he thought of calling 'Ireland and England: a Chapter in the History of Ten Years'.[4]

He had to acknowledge that the home-rule policy had lost most if its efficacy both as a cohering force in Liberal politics and also as an influence against the emergence of class division as the predominant characteristic of national politics. In 1896, in the speech in which he expressed concern about the development of a concidence between class and party divisions, he also said that

[1] F. E. Hamer (ed), *The Personal Papers of Lord Rendel*, 1931, p. 125.
[2] Ibid., p. 126.
[3] Morley to Carnegie, 29 July 1895.
[4] Cf. to Gladstone, 1 Aug., 26 Sept. 1895, 23 Jan., 5 Sept., 5 Oct., 24 Nov. 1896, B.M. Add. MSS. 44257, ff. 190, 193, 198, 215-6, 221, 225. To Carnegie, 29 July, 2, 6 Aug. 1895, 22 Sept. 1896, 3 Jan., 22 Nov., 24 Dec. 1897. A proof-copy of this book is in the Morley Library, Ashburne Hall, Manchester.

concentration on the home-rule controversy ought to have prevented this. He had never, he said, 'been able to see why that division [along class lines] should follow upon a difference of opinion as to what was the best form of government for Ireland'. What, then, had gone wrong? All that he could conclude was that the home-rule issue had been imposed on politics too late, 'that before the new Home Rule policy was launched there must have been latent differences underneath' which were now coming to the surface.[1]

As for the Liberal party, he had to confess in September 1895 that in the area of Irish policy 'I'm afraid I don't see anything but *accidents* for us to look to'—'and that', he admitted, 'is not a very satisfactory foundation for a party to rest upon.'[2] His colleagues had no intention of using it as a foundation at all. By the end of 1895 he was having to try to explain away their omission of Ireland from their speeches and to reprove them for thereby making 'our opponents' 'jubilant'.[3] In 1896 he complained that Harcourt 'knows and cares as much about Ireland as he does for the north pole' and would gladly see a 'Tory-Irish alliance'.[4] In 1898 he protested against declarations made by Sir Edward Grey and other Liberals in opposition to 'taking office dependent on the Irish vote'. This, he said, implied 'a return to the old way of governing Ireland by a tacit or open understanding between the two English parties united against the Irish party'.[5] His efforts to revive the issue of the Union met with no success. For example, early in 1897 he suggested that involved in the report of a commission on Irish finances was 'a most important aspect' of 'the great controversy of the time, which has produced one of the most striking party disruptions in our history'. The Irish finances could not be discussed 'without direct and constant reference to the policy and instruments of the Union', and if the Liberals could 'get the Doctrine of separate entity firmly established', 'we shall have gone a good many leagues on the H.R. journey'. But

[1] *The Times*, 5 Feb. 1896, p. 7, c. 1.
[2] To Spencer, 26 Sept. 1895.
[3] *The Times*, 3 Dec. 1895, p. 6, c. 3.
[4] To Spencer, 19 Aug. 1896.
[5] To Haldane, 26 Aug. 1898, Haldane MSS. 5904, ff. 153-4.

Harcourt and H. H. Fowler contended that the question ought to be kept 'outside Home Rule' and that their arguments on it ought to assume the Union; and Morley finally agreed to take this line 'so as to rope in the Unionist Irish'. He therefore said in a speech that 'I think this particular controversy ought to stand clear of Home Rule', adding: 'You will not think, I hope, that I am backing out of Home Rule.'[1] The disintegration of the home-rule policy was obviously at an advanced stage when Morley's colleagues were obliging him to assume the Union in his discussion of Irish affairs.

The mood of the Irish also forced Morley on to the defensive, for they showed an embarrassing readiness to accept from the Unionist Government measures short of home rule. Morley found the special relationship between Irish Nationalists and the Liberal party crumbling in his grasp. He tried to defend the Irish against 'a certain feeling of dissatisfaction, or at all events of perplexity, in our party upon the action which the Irish parties are now taking'.[2] After the Irish had accepted local government reforms in 1898, he admitted that it would now be 'foolish to hide' the fact 'that the particular chapter in the relations of the Liberal party to Ireland which opened in 1886 may be approaching its last page'. The Irish were 'not bound because of any of our party ties to reject what they regard as a boon'.[3]

A disposition to admit defeat and abandon the apparently hopeless struggle gathered strength in his mind. He wrote that 'the Irish stone has rolled down to the bottom of the hill once more' and that therefore 'I don't feel that I have much more to do in politics'. 'The Irish business has miscarried, and I only care in a secondary degree for other things.'[4] But for Harcourt's persuasion he would

---

[1] To Harcourt, 29 Oct. 1896, 4, 11 Jan. 1897. Harcourt to Morley, 10, 13 Jan. 1897. Morley to Fowler, 30 Dec. 1896, quoted in E. H. Fowler, *The Life of Henry Hartley Fowler, First Viscount Wolverhampton, G.C.S.I.*, 1912, p. 418. To Lord Welby, 20 Dec. 1896, Welby MSS., Lind. Dep. 24/3/3/3, f. 266. *The Times*, 18 Jan. 1897, p. 9, cc. 2–3.

[2] *The Times*, 22 Feb. 1897, p. 10, c. 2.

[3] *The Times*, 24 Mar. 1898, p. 6, c. 2; 23 June 1898, p. 10, c. 4; 20 Jan. 1899, p. 10, c. 5.

[4] To Gladstone, 23 Jan. 1896, B.M. Add. MSS. 44257, f. 196. To Spencer, 13 Feb. 1896.

probably have retired permanently from parliamentary politics.[1] Reluctantly he accepted nomination for a Scottish seat, the Montrose Burghs, and was returned early in 1896. He tried for a time to convince himself and his colleagues that 'the Irish question will pretty soon come to life again', very probably at the next election.[2] But imperialism seemed to him to have had the effect of making the English people indifferent to the rights of the 'oppressed Irish'.[3] In 1899 he told F. W. Hirst that, although Ireland remained the one subject that really interested him, 'I shall be dead before it comes up again'.[4] So bitterly did he feel that his own career had reached a dead end that he began complaining of having 'wasted ten years on Ireland'.[5]

Morley's involvement in the Irish question had moved from the practical to the literary sphere, but even his attempt to achieve something there was a failure. Having spent two and a half years on his 'Irish book' and having completed it early in 1898, he decided not to publish it, principally because friends advised him that 'the time was not propitious' and because he feared that the typical reaction to it would be the query, 'Why have you taken so much trouble to tell us what we knew all about before?' 'Why tell the dreary yarn over again?'[6] The Irish policy was now just a 'dreary yarn'; and it was partly in order to fill this vacuum that Morley turned the materials of the 'Irish book', the fragments and details of a policy now seeming drained of all vitality, into materials for the commemoration of a great personality—Gladstone.[7]

But a new political issue seemed to be emerging that might take the place of Ireland—imperialism. As we have seen, even in 1885

[1] To Harcourt, 27 Nov. 1895.
[2] To Harcourt, 6 Jan. 1898. To Spencer, 15 June 1898.
[3] Cf. to Spencer, 18 Oct. 1898.
[4] Hirst, *In the Golden Days*, p. 188.
[5] To Campbell-Bannerman, 6 Dec. 1901, B.M. Add. MSS. 41223, f. 75.
[6] To Gladstone, 26, 31 Oct., 25 Dec. 1897, B.M. Add. MSS. 44257, ff. 229–34. To Carnegie, 11 Jan., 2 Oct. 1898. To Mrs. Drew, 1, 4, 27 Mar. 1898, B.M. Add. MSS. 46240, ff. 18–23. H. G. Hutchinson (ed.), *Private Diaries of the Rt. Hon. Sir Algernon West, G.C.B.*, 1922, p. 348.
[7] For the connection between the 'Irish book' and the *Life of Gladstone*, cf. Viscount Gladstone, *After Thirty Years*, 1929, p. 24.

anti-imperialism had been for Morley the possible alternative to home rule as an issue that might preoccupy the new electorate. Morley's own interest in imperialism showed signs of reviving after the Parnell crisis.[1] There appeared to be a direct connection between such a revival and any set-back to the Irish policy. In May 1891 he wrote a series of letters to Harcourt, saying, on the one hand, that 'I have lost all interest in the H. of C., even in the Irish bog where I am constrained to dwell', and, on the other, that a question of imperial policy 're-kindles the holy fires in my bosom which blazed so mightily against Bartle Frere a dozen years ago'; declaring that 'I shall have done with the H. of C. the first moment after the Irish question is *really settled* once for all', and then adding, 'unless I wait until the British occupation of Egypt is brought to an end, also'.[2] Late in 1892 Sir Algernon West talked with Morley when he was facing up to the question of the nature of his politics after the Home Rule Bill had been rejected by the House of Lords. At this time there was much controversy in the Cabinet over British policy with regard to Uganda. When Morley remarked that the Cabinet 'would be out on Uganda', West pointed out that 'that would imperil Ireland'. 'No,' Morley replied, 'as Irish Home Rule passing is impossible. The Lords would not pass it, and he would definitely say "Good-bye" to the Cabinet rather than occupy or remain in Uganda.' When he said that he wanted to resign on the issue, Gladstone was surprised and indignant, and reminded him of his 'personal responsibility as Chief Secretary for the Home Rule policy of the government' and that 'it would be ridiculous for him to resign on a side issue'. Nevertheless, when in January 1893 West asked him whether it was 'worth while to throw up Home Rule' over such an issue, Morley persisted in saying that he would not agree to allowing Cromer to have an additional regiment in Egypt, even if the break-up of the Government were to ensue from such an attitude.[3]

[1] Cf. *Hansard*, 3, 350, 1442–5. S. Gwynn and G. M. Tuckwell, *The Life of the Rt. Hon. Sir Charles W. Dilke, Bart.*, M.P., II, 1917, p. 253.

[2] To Harcourt, 18, 28, 31 May 1891.

[3] Hutchinson, *Diaries of Sir Algernon West*, pp. 70, 124. Hirst, *In the Golden Days*, p. 171.

Morley believed that there was an element of continuity in the transfer of interest from home rule to anti-imperialism. Denial of self-government to Ireland had become bound up in the larger issue of imperialism, just as national education had been subsumed in the cause of disestablishment:

Unionists, in resisting the new Liberal policy for Ireland, were naturally forced to make their appeal to all the feelings and opinions bound up with concentration, imperial Parliament, imperial unity, and determined mastery in the hands of 'the predominant partner'. Conservative reaction had set in during the general election of [1885] . . . What precipitated this reaction in the direction of Imperialism was the proposal of Home Rule, and the arguments and temper in which its antagonists found their most effective resort.[1]

But, if maintenance of the Union and then imperialism were the issues within which the expression of basic conservative attitudes became concentrated, so did anti-imperialism develop for Morley the same characteristics in relation to his Liberal thought and practice as had previously been found in the home-rule policy. His statements give the impression that he was conscious that he was now turning to the next single great question. In January 1896, after the Jameson Raid, he declared: 'A new scene has opened. New subjects have come up for discussion, and a new leaf seems as if it were about to be turned over in the great volume of our national destinies.'[2]

He was attracted to the issue of anti-imperialism in part because he sensed in it a means of providing once again simple, clear-cut definitions of liberal principles and of giving to the Liberal party firm and distinctive ground of its own. This was one reason for his impatience with the Liberal imperialists. He believed that, far from providing Liberalism with a new creed, as they thought that they were doing, they were working for the disappearance of the Liberal party as a distinctive force in politics by the way in which they endorsed and even tried to outdo the new imperialism of the Unionists. A party could survive only if based on principles

---

[1] *Miscellanies Fourth Series*, pp. 272–3.
[2] *The Times*, 31 Jan. 1896, p. 6, c. 4.

acknowledged to be peculiarly its own. Ruin lay through imitative electoral opportunism. At the apparent full tide of popular imperialism he urged Liberals to hold firm to their convictions and principles and not be swept away as the result of considering 'the fortunes of the party at this particular hour' or 'the fate of this or that electoral campaign'.[1] While it was natural for Liberals to 'be inclined to revise old maxims and readjust their mariner's compass', they must be careful to 'stick to the polar star' of principle. Otherwise they would be wafted out of their course and driven into dangerous harbours 'by the passing gusts and squalls'. He offered this description of the conditions essential to the survival of Liberalism: 'the Liberal party will only be useful as an instrument of human progress so long as they walk persistently and steadfastly in the path of these watchwords—peace, economy, and reform. If the Liberal party abandon that path, what will they be but a body without a soul?' The party, he said, must stand firm on distinctive principles and not be 'of the nature of the chameleon'.[2] Indeed, in his struggle to make the party anti-imperialist Morley saw himself as fighting for its very survival. In June 1900 he implored Liberals not to 'discard party catchwords and party impulses', for the country must have 'an effective party system' and in order to survive within this system the Liberal party needed to have 'clear views, distinct opinions, firm fidelity to principles broad, sound and established'. Liberal imperialism, however, was scarcely distinguishable from Tory imperialism. He gave this warning: 'the day when the Liberal party forsook its old principles of peace, economy, and reform the Liberal party would have to disband and to disappear. Who would take its place? The Socialists would take its place.'[3]

In relation to the threat of independent political action by labour, at least, anti-imperialism did seem to have value in the struggle for the survival of Liberalism. Like the issue of opposition to Irish coercion, it temporarily overlaid the trend towards the reconstruction of party politics along the lines of class division by

[1] *The Times*, 25 Mar. 1898, p. 12, c. 1.
[2] *The Times*, 18 Jan. 1899, p. 6, cc. 1–3.
[3] *The Times*, 11 June 1900, p. 3, c. 3.

effecting a *rapprochement* between Morley and Labour leaders that for a time obscured their differences on social policy. Morley had appreciated almost at once the scope for this kind of development of the issue. At the beginning of 1896, when he was so worried about the appearance of class division in politics, he hailed the controversy over imperialism as a 'new departure' and urged working men to take an interest in it, because 'the cause of peace is the cause of progress' and 'no body of men are so much interested in the cause of peace as the working classes of this country'.[1] By 1900 Beatrice Webb was writing that 'Leonard Courtney and John Morley are acclaimed as the only honest politicians by the recognized Labour leaders, who have one and all gone pro-Boer'.[2] Keir Hardie, who had been so strong an opponent of Morley in Newcastle, now argued for an alliance between Labour and such Liberals as Morley.[3] J. B. Glasier, another former opponent of Morley, now thought that Morley stood 'for much that [was] essential to a socialist state and international peace'.[4] All this seems to have suggested to Morley the possibility of a permanent alliance on this basis. In June 1902 he said that he was 'glad to think' that during the previous three years all the 'working men representatives' in the Commons had opposed 'militarism and Imperialist policy'.[5] In a speech in April 1903 his method of dealing with 'the labour question' was to claim 'that when he spoke of peace he touched the main tap root of the wellbeing of labour' and that when in 1899 he 'protested against a certain war, he was then advocating the cause of labour in its broadest and deepest shape'.

The interests of labour were [he said] involved in peace more than the interests of any other portion of the community. . . . To those who said he did not care sufficiently for labour questions he replied that it was war which produced unsteadiness in labour and which, after a flush

[1] *The Times*, 31 Jan. 1896, pp. 6–7.
[2] B. Webb, *Our Partnership*, 1948, p. 200.
[3] P. P. Poirier, *The Advent of the Labour Party*, 1958, p. 125. F. Bealey and H. Pelling, *Labour and Politics 1900–1906. A History of the Labour Representation Committee*, 1958, p. 60.
[4] Poirier, *Advent of the Labour Party*, p. 110.
[5] *The Times*, 9 June 1902, p. 13, c. 3.

of prosperity, left them worse off than before. In support of that view he quoted from a speech of Mr. Barnes, Labour candidate for the Blackfriars division of Glasgow, to the effect that one of the most important questions upon which the forces of labour should be applied was the preservation of peace among the nations. That was his own doctrine, too. It was the pure milk of the word of progress.[1]

Anti-imperialism resembled the Irish policy also in Morley's use of it to define Liberalism in terms of historical continuity and precedent. Morley was anxious to preserve as much as possible of a link with the Liberalism of the past. He said that, while his colleagues 'represent new currents of opinion', 'I stick to the old ones'. He refused to be 'untrue to all the lessons I have ever learned from the great Ministers of political wisdom', notably Gladstone.[2] It was in particular the Gladstonian past of Liberalism that he wanted to see continuing to influence the practice of Liberals. When in 1898 he undertook the task of writing the official biography of Gladstone, he wrote: 'I really do not know that I can perform a better service to the party.'[3] On the other hand, the Liberal imperialists, whom he regarded as 'anti-Gladstonians',[4] felt 'cold shivers' at the very thought of his writing the biography,[5] and suspected that the work might become the basis for a crusade against imperialism and against them.[6] Indeed, Morley told Hirst that he wanted it to be 'apostolic' because 'of late years we have had no politics except Jingoism'; but 'the doctrine' was to be 'well larded with personal and other attractions, so that it will slip easily down the public gullet'.[7]

Another feature of anti-imperialism was that, in contrast to the confusions and perplexities surrounding domestic policy, it seemed to involve a clear-cut case of 'right' against 'wrong'

---

[1] *The Times*, 16 Apr. 1903, p. 4, c. 2.
[2] To Spencer, 2 Dec. 1898. *The Times*, 18 Jan. 1899, p. 6, cc. 1–2.
[3] *The Times*, 18 Nov. 1898, p. 6, c. 4.
[4] To Bryce, 26 Sept. 1900.
[5] Rosebery's reaction as described by Lord Kilbracken in his *Reminiscences*, 1931, p. 225.
[6] Cf. J. A. Spender, *The Life of the Right Hon. Sir Henry Campbell-Bannerman*, G.C.B., I [1923], p. 242.
[7] Hirst, *In the Golden Days*, p. 171.

according to recognized and traditional understandings of those terms. We have seen how Morley warned against allowing strong feelings of indignation about social evils to be translated into sweeping and impatient demands for the extension of the activity of the State. In other words, he was frightened about the possible consequences of an involvement of 'conscience' in domestic politics. But with an external issue such as Irish coercion or imperialism there were not the same difficulties. Opposition to imperialism represented a safe harnessing of the force of 'conscience' to political action.

Morley set out to awaken this force, to create out of imperialism a great moral issue. When he saw the 'national conscience' aroused against imperialism, he declared, as he had previously declared in regard to the coercion of the Irish: 'right and wrong are in the nature of things; they are not words and phrases. They are in the nature of things, and if you transgress the laws imposed by the nature of things depend upon it you will pay the penalty.'[1] In his reaction to the South African crisis of 1899 what seemed uppermost was his desire to find a secure relationship between belief and practice, to act in 'a right cause' in obedience to what he termed the 'compulsion of my conscience'.[2] He believed that he had once more discovered a form of 'right conduct' in politics. When he spoke out against imperialism he was doing what he was certain was 'right'.[3] He concluded his great anti-war speech at Manchester on 15 September 1899 with the reiteration of 'the grand potent monosyllable', 'wrong'. No matter what immediate gains might appear to accrue, the war would, he said over and over again, 'be wrong'.[4] He now derived great satisfaction from the feeling of having been able to take a firmly and unequivocally 'right' position on a political issue. In 1902 he said that he was proud to have been in his attitude to the South African war a 'doctrinaire', that is 'a man who believes that there is a relation between cause and effect and that there is some difference between

[1] *The Times*, 7 Nov. 1896, p. 6, cc. 2–4.
[2] To Courtney, 30 Aug. 1899, quoted in G. P. Gooch, *Life of Lord Courtney*, 1920, p. 368.
[3] Cf. Ibid. To Harcourt, 16, 20 Aug. 1899. Hirst, *In the Golden Days*, p. 174.
[4] *The Times*, 16 Sept. 1899, p. 8, c. 3. *Recollections*, II, pp. 86–7.

right and wrong'.¹ Again in 1904 he was to speak of the agitation against the employment of Chinese labour in South Africa as embodying a 'recognition of there being some difference after all—whatever it might amount to—between right and wrong'.² It is significant that other Liberals were observed as having reacted to the issue of imperialism in this way. L. T. Hobhouse later wrote that at the time 'the average Liberal' needed 'the shock of an outspoken violation of right' in order to feel deeply about politics and that Campbell-Bannerman's speech about 'methods of barbarism' marked 'the revival of the idea of justice in the party as an organized force' and 'the reinstatement of the idea of Right in the mind of Liberalism'.³

These aspects of the issue of anti-imperialism make intelligible the existence in his thought and practice of the same ambivalent attitude towards imperialism as an obstruction to progress on domestic reform as had appeared in connection with the Irish question.

In February 1896 he remarked that the Unionists seemed to be looking to foreign affairs for an excuse for not bringing in the domestic legislation which they had promised.⁴ But for Morley anti-imperialism was itself a similar kind of distracting issue. Ireland had gone as an external 'obstruction' on to which he could transfer from the indecision, confusion, and fear of Liberals the blame for lack of progress in the area of social policy. But the indecision, confusion, and fear remained. The emergence of imperialism as a new excuse for inaction and non-commitment in these circumstances can be seen in a speech by Morley to the National Liberal Federation in March 1898. In this he raised the problem of how the Liberals were to refute the allegation that they were 'not a party of social reform'. Although temperance was a great social question, Liberals did not agree on details of temperance reform. They did all want some alteration in the constitutional position of the House of Lords, but, as this scarcely seemed to be an issue that would

---

¹ *The Times*, 22 Nov. 1902, p. 8, c. 4.
² *The Times*, 27 Feb. 1904, p. 14, c. 5.
³ Hobhouse, *Liberalism*, n.d., p. 222.
⁴ *The Times*, 7 Feb. 1896, p. 7, c. 3.

arouse popular enthusiasm, many Liberals would be reluctant to make it 'the question of the next election'. However, perhaps they need not worry too much about the type of reform which they should appear to favour. 'I am not sure that the next election will turn upon legislation at all. When I think of the foreign complications I am not at all sure that the next election will turn upon legislation any more than it did in the great and triumphant year of 1880.'[1] Before this meeting Morley had confessed to finding himself 'not knowing very well what to say to our poor sheep wandering about the wilderness'.[2] But what he had discovered to tell them was a reminder of a great Liberal triumph of the past when anti-imperialism had been the most important issue. The reference to 1880 certainly implies a belief that it would be no bad thing for the party were it to lay aside its problems in the area of domestic policy and concentrate on foreign and imperial affairs. By June 1898 he was declaring that domestic questions were temporarily suspended: 'so far as he could judge, it was very likely that when the next election came it would turn less upon those questions, important as they were, than upon the questions of our national position in the face of Europe and of the world.'[3] That the election did not produce the same kind of triumph for Liberals as had the election of 1880 was attributed by Morley to the weak and divided character of the party. 'If your father had been alive', he told Gladstone's daughter, 'we should have had 1880 over again.'[4] The future of the party depended on its rediscovering its 'soul', formed out of the great principles and traditions of the past, and re-establishing a single, solid, coherent identity.

[1] *The Times*, 24 Mar. 1898, p. 6, cc. 1-2.
[2] To Carnegie, 8 Mar. 1898.
[3] *The Times*, 9 June 1898, p. 11, c. 1.
[4] To Mrs. Drew, 27 Sept. 1900, B.M. Add. MSS. 46240, f. 48.

22

SURVIVING IN A NEW WORLD

MORLEY appeared to be returning to the attitude which he had held towards the Liberal party in the mid 1880s. Once again he showed a strong disposition to welcome the prospect of the disruption of the party as the prelude to its reconstruction around one principle, this time anti-imperialism. At the end of 1898 and beginning of 1899 Harcourt and Morley withdrew from the official councils of the party's leadership in order, as Morley said later, to be 'able to act with a freedom that was impossible so long as we were forced to keep in step with the jingoes in our camp'.[1] This withdrawal marked the culmination of their indignation against the increasingly imperialistic stance of many of their colleagues. A leadership that was part imperialist, part anti-imperialist, seemed to Morley to be no longer tolerable.[2] On 17 January 1899 he explained: 'There are questions which cannot be left open . . . we are now face to face in this most important arena of our national and Imperial affairs with questions on which you must say aye or no. No doubt party unity . . . and comfort would be preserved if questions presented themselves to which you could say both aye and no, but we are not in that position.'[3] He now showed himself convinced that a party without a firm, consistent basis of thought and policy does not deserve to exist. By 1900 he was describing the unifying of the party as it

[1] F. W. Hirst, *In the Golden Days*, 1947, p. 198.

[2] For the development of this rift between Morley and the 'Lib. Imps.', see R. Robinson, J. Gallagher, and A. Denny, *Africa and the Victorians. The Official Mind of Imperialism*, 1961, pp. 353, 358, 377. *The Times*, 10 Dec. 1897, p. 6, c. 2. Haldane to Asquith, 4 Jan. 1898, Haldane MSS. 5904, f. 128. Morley to Sir E. Hamilton, 23 Nov. 1898, B.M. Add. MSS. 48619. Spencer to Asquith, 24 Dec. 1898, Asquith MSS. Dep. 9, f. 147. Morley to Harcourt, 13, 21 Dec. 1898, 24 Nov. 1900; Harcourt to Morley, 21 Dec. 1898. Morley to Carnegie, 27 Jan. 1899. Hirst, *In the Golden Days*, pp. 173–4.

[3] *The Times*, 18 Jan. 1899, p. 6, cc. 1–3.

was then constituted as 'wholly impossible'.[1] To Hirst he expressed the belief that there would probably be new party combinations: ' "The old Liberal party broke up in 1895." It was impossible to say under what form or leadership a new party would arise. He seemed to anticipate the formation of a group like the Peelites. . . .'[2] He scorned the 'rubbish about unity' that was being preached by Sir Henry Campbell-Bannerman, Harcourt's successor as party leader: 'Why should I or anybody else care a straw for a party that has no judgment to pass on the jingo pranks of the last five years?'[3] As the general election approached in 1900, he wrote: 'The Liberal party is where it deserves to be, and I hope the smash will be complete. Then the friends of peace & prudence may try to build another party.' For the existing party was 'a party without principles', and victory for it would therefore be meaningless.[4]

But it became increasingly obvious that Morley himself was not going to take any initiative in forcing on and organizing this work of reconstruction. Withdrawal from contemporary concerns in a mood of high-principled disgust is the predominating feature of his conduct in the period of the South African War. He behaved as one who feels that he is living in a new, alien world, a world in which his own basic assumptions are being upset and undermined by the course of events and discarded by other people as outmoded and irrelevant. For example, the belief in certain progress was giving way to an impression of deterioration, decay, and retrogression. In 1897 Beatrice Webb noted how 'pessimistic' he was and how he 'thinks that all things are going to the bad and that the country has lost its intellect and its character'.[5] In 1901 he wrote that if Britain 'stumbles down hill at the same rate' in the next twenty years as in 'the last 20 years, it won't be a very desirable place to live in'.[6] A few years later A. G. Gardiner

---

[1] To Spencer, 12, 16 May 1900.
[2] Hirst, *In the Golden Days*, pp. 209–10.
[3] To Harcourt, 28 July 1900.
[4] To Harcourt, 10 Sept. 1900. To Bryce, 26 Sept. 1900. To Spencer, 22, 25, 28 Sept. 1900.
[5] B. Webb, *Our Partnership*, 1948, p. 144.
[6] To Frederic Harrison, 25 Dec. 1901.

commented that Morley 'seems to detect in modern life the odour of decay'.¹ The process had begun which was to lead to Morley's saying in 1919: 'As for progress, what signs of it are there now? And all we Victorians believed in it from the Utilitarians onwards.'²

The wave of jingoistic imperialism which swept over the country at the end of the century disgusted and repelled him. England seemed to him by 1899 to be given over to 'all the forces of folly, cant, hypocrisy, and the trickery of politicians'.³ So strongly did he feel alienated from what he described to a friend as 'the new world into which you and I have survived' that he even thought of going abroad: 'The moral and political atmosphere of my own country has become intolerably close and even asphyxiating. . . . The situation is really hellish.'⁴ His belief that democracy was opposed to war and imperialism was now shattered. In 1896 he reflected sadly that the failure of democracy to be 'a guarantee of international peace' was 'widely at variance with confident and reasoned anticipations'.⁵ The South African War 'exhibited English democracy', he had to admit, in a very unexpected light and provoked melancholy thoughts about a connection between democracy and militarism.⁶

He was very concerned about changes in the climate of ideas. In 1896 he wrote of his intention to use his forthcoming Romanes lecture on Machiavelli in order to attack 'the Bismarckian gospel of Force and Fraud, which now masters Europe, and has some foothold in England'.⁷ In *Gladstone*, written around the turn of the century, he deplores the growth of the belief that 'the Real is the only Rational, force is the test of right and wrong, the state has nothing to do with restraints of morals, the ruler is emancipated'. The basic cause of this growth was, he told F. W. Hirst,

---

[1] A. G. Gardiner, *Prophets, Priests and Kings*, 1908, p. 57.
[2] J. H. Morgan, *John, Viscount Morley. An Appreciation and Some Reminiscences*, 1924, p. 37.
[3] *The Times*, 18 Jan. 1899, p. 6, c. 3. To Harrison, 25 Dec. 1898, 27 Dec. 1899.
[4] To Harrison, 23 Dec. 1900. To Harcourt, 6 Nov. 1899.
[5] *Miscellanies Fourth Series*, pp. 214–16.
[6] Ibid., pp. 262–3, 287–9.
[7] To Gladstone, 28 Dec. 1896, B.M. Add. MSS. 44257, f. 228.

that people 'had lost faith without getting a scientific code of morality to substitute for Christian ethics'. 'Speculations in physical science' had been 'distorted for alien purposes', and 'the doctrine of the survival of the fittest had been perverted into "might is right", which includes the right of the strong to kill the weak'.[1]

In these new circumstances Morley appeared increasingly to be himself 'paralysed for the purposes of action'.[2] In 1897 Beatrice Webb discerned a condition of paralysis produced in him by his lack of sympathy with the new 'progressive ideas':

> he dare not pronounce in favour of his own convictions: he feels instinctively the country is against him. To do nothing, and to say nothing, to sit and wait for the tide to ebb from this Government is the long and short of his policy. . . . On politics he is like a theologian who has begun to doubt his theology: in argument he always shrinks away from you, as if he suspected you of laying traps for him out of which he could not struggle. . . . It makes one groan to think of that moral force absolutely useless.[3]

Morley had many years earlier written a description of this particular state of mind. In *On Compromise* he discussed what had happened as 'old hopes have grown pale, the old fears dim; strong sanctions are become weak, and once vivid faiths very numb': 'Those who dwell in the tower of ancient faiths look about them in constant apprehension, misgiving, and wonder, with the hurried uneasy mien of people living amid earthquakes. The air seems to their alarms to be full of missiles, and all is doubt, hesitation, and shivering expectancy. Hence a decisive reluctance to commit one's self. Conscience has lost its strong and on-pressing energy. . . . '[4]

We have seen how his own strong radical impulses of the 1860s and 1870s ebbed away into the 'hesitation' and 'reluctance to commit himself' of 1885 when the time came for translating those impulses into actions. Then the Irish 'obstruction' had served as a justification for divorcing thought from action. By the late

---

[1] *Gladstone*, III, p. 551. Hirst, *In the Golden Days*, p. 209.
[2] Cf. *The Times*, 16 Sept. 1899, p. 8, c. 2.
[3] B. Webb, *Our Partnership*, pp. 143–4.
[4] pp. 36–7. *F.R.*, Apr. 1874, p. 437.

1890s, however, the paralysis of 1885 was once more being exposed to full view. Morley simply did not know how or why he should act in politics. Feeling, that is conviction about 'rightness' and 'wrongness' in regard to certain questions, remained, but not the ability or knowledge for translating it into action relevant to the particular circumstances and climate of opinion of this 'new world' into which he had 'survived'. Hirst noted of him at this time: 'He can touch the hearts of the people. His difficulty or weakness is in taking action'.[1] A wave of strong feeling would sweep over him, only to ebb away before moods of indecision and doubt. For example, according to Labouchere, Morley resolved in a state of great indignation in February 1899 to move a reduction of the vote for the Sudan, but then tried to get someone else to do this for him and finally made a 'not very effective speech' without carrying out a determination expressed just before to read out extracts which he had marked in a speech by Rosebery.[2] Some months later W. S. Blunt found Morley before a speech 'very fierce against Kitchener', but then 'hampered by all sorts of conditions' which made the speech itself seem weak and ineffective.[3] His inability to decide whether or not to act and what form action should take grew more and more paralysing. 'My intentions as to next session', he wrote late in 1899, 'vary from one extreme to another: activity or *bolt*'.[4] Hirst tells how in the spring of 1900 'many of us young Liberals, and some of an older generation too, were distressed by Morley's hesitating mood'. In April 1900 Lloyd George complained that Morley was 'in a very indecisive mood', and Leonard Courtney accused Morley of constantly changing his mind. At a dinner party in January 1901 Hirst noticed Morley wince when Courtney reproached him with 'always shivering on the brink'.[5] Lloyd George himself seemed from now on to feel little but contempt for the perpetually hesitating intellectual in politics. When in 1910 someone remarked to him that

[1] Hirst, *In the Golden Days*, p. 188.
[2] Labouchere to Harcourt, 28 Feb. 1899, Harcourt MSS.
[3] W. S. Blunt, *My Diaries Being a Personal Narrative of Events 1888–1914*, I, 1919, pp. 397–9.
[4] To Dilke, 31 Oct. 1899, B.M. Add. MSS. 43895, f. 218.
[5] Hirst, *In the Golden Days*, pp. 206, 216.

'Morley was wobbly on the question of the Lords', he replied, 'without qualification: "Morley is a funk" '.[1]

In various ways Morley tried to persuade his disillusioned admirers—and himself—that this irresolution did not matter, as any bold action would be futile or even wrong. 'The *entry upon the policy of war* was and remains the initial infamy,' he wrote in 1901. 'I have regarded the sequellae as purely secondary'. People would no longer listen to reason and would have to be left to find out their 'wickedness and folly' for themselves.[2] But, in addition, there was once again an external obstacle which enabled him to associate the expression of strong feeling about the situation with the plea of inability to convert this feeling into action. This was the writing of the *Life of Gladstone*, which, begun as a means of influencing the political debates of the day, developed into a form of escape from them. Thus in August 1899 he wrote that, although he was 'full of this approaching crime in the Transvaal' and 'one ought to raise one's voice', nevertheless 'I must stick to my task'.[3] A year later he wrote that he found himself 'sometimes wondering if I should not be better employed in active politics—where the good cause of peace and sense sadly needs a leader; but never allowing the said wonder to stay my hand'.[4] His literary work obstructed the translation of feeling into political practice. Morley, wrote Hirst in 1901, 'says that but for the pressure of his work, he would write a pamphlet after the manner of Burke to express his *saeva indignatio* against the Boer War'.[5] Frequently he would express his frustration at this imposed impotence.[6] 'It makes me groan' he would tell his friends, 'to think of my hands being tied, when I ought to be up and doing'.[7] One recalls that before he was preoccupied in this way the thought of his 'absolutely useless' and impotent 'moral force' had caused Beatrice Webb to 'groan';

---

[1] L. Masterman, *C. F. G. Masterman A Biography*, 1939, p. 152.

[2] Hirst, *In the Golden Days*, p. 225. To Harrison, 6, 28 July 1901. To Courtney, 8 Mar. 1900, quoted in G. P. Gooch, *Life of Lord Courtney*, 1920, pp. 403–4.

[3] To Carnegie, 17 Aug. 1899.

[4] To Carnegie, 7 July 1900.

[5] Hirst, *In the Golden Days*, p. 225.

[6] e.g. to Harrison, 7 Aug. 1901.

[7] To Spencer, 14 Aug. 1901.

now the preoccupation enabled him to present his impotence as something fastened on him from outside and to describe himself as unable to act, 'tied by my heels with a cannon-ball fastened to my ankle, like a French galley-slave'.[1]

The work on the *Life of Gladstone* provided a protective cocoon for Morley's thought, a means of shielding it from the uncertainties and perils of a 'new world'. Turning away from the contemporary scene, he occupied himself in portraying a man with an extraordinary power of mastering circumstances and producing order out of political confusion. Reverting to a feature of his very early biographical writings, he tried to show how 'character' could be a source of unity and coherence in belief and conduct. His aim was, he said, to present 'a picture of Mr. Gladstone showing that he was a whole man from the beginning to the end of his career, that one set of principles animated him from first to last, and that one set of objects promoted actions'.[2] Accordingly Gladstone is described again and again as one who through the force of his character was able to impose order on the multitudinousness and fragmentariness of political life. Beneath the apparent incongruity of his political and ecclesiastical interests, for example, lay a profound cohering and unifying force: Gladstone's 'genius was one' always. The Gladstone presented in the *Life* is, in fact, very much the kind of man that Morley himself always wanted to be, able to bring diverse and fragmented interests into an organic unity of thought and action. In one passage Morley describes the situation which confronted Gladstone when he first went to the Exchequer: chaos in financial policy, political disagreements, 'party distraction', 'adjournment after adjournment' of decision on 'fundamental maxims'. Such was 'the bewildered scene', in the description of which one can see obvious points of resemblance to the political world in which Morley himself had to work. Gladstone imposed order on this bewilderment, not so much because he was a brilliant financier as because of the power of his personality, his 'practical imagination', his 'habit of unflagging toil', and, above all, his ability to combine analysis with 'the spirit

---

[1] To Carnegie, 21 Sept. 1901.
[2] *The Times*, 19 Jan. 1904, p. 8, c. 1.

of vigorous system'. Thus in Gladstone's personality Morley discerned, as he had also discerned in Mill many years before, a resolution of the problem of combining the destructive, analytical powers of reason with the need for order and a 'spirit of system' in human affairs and ideas. From the scene of confusion and decay which Morley saw about him he turned to contemplate the still, calm, unchanging point of Gladstone's character. Morley's Gladstone is someone unaffected in his innermost being by time and movement and change, in spite of the great length of his public career; someone able nevertheless to respond positively to change, to assimilate new facts and experiences, to extend his range of vision to include 'new social forces', and to retain a vital appreciation of the manifold interests and aspirations of mankind, while never being 'infected' by 'the contagion of the world's slow stain'.[1]

It is not surprising that, as Morley immersed himself in this work of constructing and presenting the great 'system' of thought and practice that was Gladstone's life, his distaste for the squalid, frightening, confused world of politics in which his own life was involved intensified rapidly. He inclined more and more strongly towards retiring permanently from politics into a literary career. The pendulum began to swing again; the familiar oscillation between his two selves, the literary man and the would-be man of action, recommenced. By 1900 he was describing himself as 'drawing more and more within my very humble little shell' and enjoying a 'splendid isolation.'[2] In July he told Harcourt that he felt 'a vehement disposition to withdraw' from Parliament and from 'what is called "politics" '. Harcourt prevailed on him to seek re-election that year; but in August he admitted that it was still very much in his mind to 'cast off the yoke of public life' because of the great difficulty of 'combining a formidable literary task, with the turmoil of affairs'.[3] He felt a revulsion from 'the old game of selfish intrigue'.[4] 'I dread and hate speaking more than I ever did',

[1] *Gladstone*, I, pp. 152, 459–60; III, p. 88.
[2] To Spencer, 26 Jan., 16 May 1900.
[3] To Harcourt, 22 July 1900, 1 Apr. 1904; Harcourt to Morley, 23 July 1900. To Carnegie, 7, 17 Aug. 1900.
[4] To Spencer, 11 Oct. 1900.

he admitted in mid 1901. 'Writing on the other hand, I like *better* than ever.'¹ He resolutely held himself aloof from 'the turmoil of affairs'. '*I will come to no consultations*', he informed the party leader. '*To the best of my knowledge and belief*', he told Lord Spencer in 1902, 'nothing will ever induce me to enter into responsible counsel with the body of those who were once colleagues and friends.' He insisted that he was now 'finished (politically)'.² In 1903 he wrote of his 'invincible loathing' of the political life: 'Why come near such a scene, having once escaped? . . . I want to *write*, which I can & not to speak, which I cannot.'³ He did not intend that the publication of *Gladstone* should mark the termination of his withdrawal into writing. By late 1903 he was saying that he suspected that there was 'one more book left' in him.⁴ In 1904 he asked Campbell-Bannerman to exempt him from parliamentary duties because his writing was 'more fruitful for the universe' than the performing of such duties.⁵ He regarded himself now as merely a 'humble irresponsible man of books'.⁶ In 1905 he began work on a study of Cavour which was intended to complete with *Gladstone* and *Cobden* a trilogy on Liberalism;⁷ and as late as October of that year he was threatening to announce his final 'exit' from politics because 'I have another calling that I do better and like better'.⁸

Nevertheless, within two months after writing this he had sought and been given high office in the new Government of Campbell-Bannerman. The reason why he made this apparent *volte-face* is to be found in part in his abiding desire to prove himself 'practical' as well as 'literary', but also in his attitude towards the condition and future of the Liberal party.

One aspect of Morley's inclination to withdraw personally from

¹ To Spencer, 31 May 1901.
² To Campbell-Bannerman, 15 Jan. 1902, B.M. Add. MSS. 41223, f. 86. To Spencer, 4 Nov. 1902, 6 Feb. 1903.
³ To Campbell-Bannerman, 3 June 1903, B.M. Add. MSS. 41223, ff. 119–22.
⁴ To Carnegie, 5 Dec. 1903.
⁵ 21 May 1904, B.M. Add. MSS. 41223, ff. 130–1.
⁶ To Spencer, 24 Aug. 1904.
⁷ *Recollections*, II, pp. 135–40. W. M. Meredith (ed.), *Letters of George Meredith*, II, 1912, p. 566. To Rosebery, 30 Apr. 1905.
⁸ To Spencer, 11 Oct. 1905.

politics during the South African War had been the fact that in the last resort he had not been prepared to give formal expression to his anti-imperialism by helping to form a new party based on it or to expel imperialists from the existing Liberal party. From the moment when he announced his resignation as an opponent of jingoism from the front bench of the party a conflict had developed in him between the disposition to repeat 1886 and seek the salvation of Liberalism through disruption and reconstruction on a single great issue and, on the other hand, a consciousness of possible dangers and disadvantages in such a course of action. Expressions of contempt for the party in its present condition and for Campbell-Bannerman's efforts to prevent an open split from occurring were strangely interspersed with statements and actions that suggested that he wanted to see the survival of a Liberal party that would include the 'liberal jingoes'. Thus, when in August 1899 he spoke to Hirst about the future of the party, he not only mentioned various domestic issues on which it ought to be developing its ideas but also referred to the desirability of 'avoiding personal acrimony' in case the party should 'come together again' after the Transvaal crisis. A few weeks later Hirst noted that 'Mr. Morley is beginning to fear that the Transvaal question may cause a worse split in the Liberal Party than Home Rule'.[1] The division which at times he seemed ready to welcome at other times he seemed to think of with dread. In January 1901, on finding that Lloyd George and Lehmann were planning to use the *Daily News*, which had just been taken over by the 'pro-Boer' section of the party, 'to declare a new departure and carry fire and sword into the Imp. Country', he advised them 'that the key note at present was unity of the Party: that there must be no abrupt volte face, and no reviling of mistaken friends', 'but gentle argument and persuasion, seasoned with lively attacks on the Government'.[2]

According to Hirst, Morley in July 1901 was 'glad that a split has been avoided, because the longer we hang together the smaller

---

[1] Hirst, *In the Golden Days*, pp. 173, 179.
[2] Campbell-Bannerman to Spencer, 5 Jan. 1901, Spencer MSS. C.-B. to Bryce, 18 Jan. 1901, quoted in J. A. Spender, *The Life of the Right Hon. Sir Henry Campbell-Bannerman, G.C.B.*, I [1923], pp. 317–18.

the split will be; and we cannot afford to lose Asquith'.[1] By the end of that year he was advising Campbell-Bannerman on how to preserve 'the life of the party': 'The party longs for unity, but it longs for an assault on the gov^{mnt}. Will the L. Imps. join in that assault?' When Campbell-Bannerman declared himself 'pretty stiff against inviting' the leading 'L. Imps.', Grey and Asquith, to consultations, Morley urged on him 'my very unhesitating opinion the other way'.[2] Morley clearly now regarded Lloyd George's militant 'pro-Boer' attitude as dangerously disruptive. Early in 1902 Campbell-Bannerman noted with gratification that a speech by Lloyd George attacking the attitude of the party's leadership to the war had caused Morley to 'vote for us'; 'The centre of the party is enlarged and consolidated ... W.V.H[arcourt] and J.M. dined with me on the eve of the Speech among the occupants of the Front Bench, and the Speaker is inviting them to our dinner: both of which events mark a change, for since they rode off into the wilderness they have not dined with us.'[3] Morley explained his attitude frankly in a letter to J. A. Spender in July 1902. He wanted, he wrote, to see a *modus vivendi* established between the sections in the party. With the war over the Liberal imperialists 'and all of us' were 'down in the trough of the sea' together 'and likely to remain there for a period of no short duration'. Since the Liberals could become 'once more a reputable political party with the ordinary prospects and chances', trouble should be taken to keep the party in being. The intra-party quarrels must not be allowed to 'become inveterate'.[4]

Morley had thus reversed his attitude of 1886 and decided to place the preservation of party unity before the advantages of having the party constructed around a single great cause. He realized that the party simply could not afford another split. Morley had shown himself to be aware that 'Socialists' were waiting to replace a Liberal party that became divided or de-

[1] Hirst, *In the Golden Days*, p. 224.
[2] To C.-B., 25 Dec. 1901, B.M. Add. MSS. 41223, f. 80. To Harcourt, 2 Jan. 1902.
[3] C.-B. to Ripon, 24 Jan. 1902, quoted in Spender, *Life of Campbell-Bannerman*, II, p. 25.
[4] 20 July 1902, B.M. Add. MSS. 46391.

moralized or lost its way. A party thus menaced could not afford to lose the talents of Asquith and the other younger Liberals, even if they were imperialists. After all, had not Morley himself seen in them some years earlier the future Liberal élite? Furthermore, home rule had been a much more substantial policy on which to base the reconstruction of the party. Anti-imperialism was altogether too negative and defensive. With the advantage of youth appearing to be on the side of the imperialists, Morley appreciated that the 'pro-Boers' were not strong enough to take a completely independent line and would do better for their own interests if they sought a *modus vivendi* with the imperialists and tried to retain some influence over Liberal policies from within.

The problem of the survival of Liberalism had reached too critical a stage for 'narrow and intolerant definitions' to be any longer safe or wise. Morley came to accept Campbell-Bannerman's attitude—that the party could exist 'whole' 'with all its healthful shades of opinion'. 'We have got to include many shades of opinion in order to make up the Liberal Party', Campbell-Bannerman now argued. 'It always was so and always will be'.[1] There was impatience with Morley's own apparently exclusive standpoint. In July 1901 A. H. D. Acland wrote to Asquith: 'The great bulk of us are not on the one hand reckless like Joe [Chamberlain], or anxious to reiterate the doctrines of Cobden like Morley. There are all sorts of shades of opinion united under a solid Liberalism of a really genuine type.'[2] But it soon became apparent that Morley himself was anxious to help in establishing this unified Liberalism.

Henceforward Morley saw the Liberal party as being essentially a coalition of interests. The holding of these in balance necessitated his own active involvement in Liberal politics, especially when the Liberals returned to power and leading positions had to be given to the imperialists. He himself was generally recognized to represent an important element in the balance. In April 1904 he and Harcourt exchanged letters about their fears of a 'League' ascendancy in the next Liberal Government; and

[1] Spender, *Life of Campbell-Bannerman*, I, pp. 305, 308.
[2] 17 July 1901, Asquith MSS., Dep. 10, f. 27.

Harcourt urged him to stay in politics because of this danger. At this stage they placed much reliance on Lord Spencer, pleading with him, 'in respect to all we wish to prevent' and 'in prospect of future public contingencies', to return to active political life.[1] But in 1905 Spencer was incapacitated by illness. Morley's importance then seemed even greater to the 'pro-Boer' section of the party. In 1907 Lord Loreburn, an anti-imperialist Liberal, was to appeal to him to heed the 'very serious call of duty' and not to resign from the Government: 'The future colour of Liberal official policy largely depends on your presence and influence at a crisis which will get more pronounced before long.'[2] But the leaders of the other section and of the 1905–14 Government itself appeared anxious that Morley should remain one of their colleagues. To them he was a symbol of the 'old' Liberalism who could help to retain the party's traditional support at a time when they themselves were embarking on new departures in Liberal policy. Asquith was to describe Morley in 1914 as 'the greatest source of the moral authority of the Government'.[3] In 1910 Winston Churchill urged Asquith not to allow Morley to leave the Cabinet: 'I am strongly of opinion that Morley's complete detachment from the Government at this stage might prove very disadvantageous to us.'[4]

Morley believed from 1905 on that he must help to maintain what he called 'the strength of the sounder elements in the cabinet'.[5] In 1905 he was active in promoting the claims of Campbell-Bannerman to the premiership, and, having persuaded Asquith to admit the 'necessity for equilibrium between [the] two sections of our party', he agreed to give up his own claims on the Exchequer and to accept the India Office instead so long as the other section abandoned its insistence that Campbell-Bannerman, as Prime Minister, should be in the Lords.[6] But in 1908 Campbell-

[1] To Harcourt, 1, 3 Apr., 14 June, 29 Sept. 1904; Harcourt to Morley, 2 Apr. 1904.
[2] 16 Apr. 1907, I.O.L. MSS. Eur. D. 573/43.
[3] *Memorandum on Resignation*, p. 25.
[4] W. S. Churchill, *Great Contemporaries*, 1938, p. 102.
[5] To Carnegie, 28 Dec. 1906.
[6] On Morley's role in this episode see *Recollections*, II, pp. 132, 142. D. Gwynn, *The Life of John Redmond*, 1932, pp. 112, 117. Haldane to Knollys, 19 Oct. 1905

Bannerman had to resign on account of the illness that was shortly to prove fatal. Morley saw this as producing 'a critical hour for our Party and our Principles'.[1] He was worried about the transference of the leadership to Asquith, because it appeared to 'shift the centre of gravity' in the party. There would therefore, he wrote, 'have to be a little re-adjustment of one or two offices . . . to keep the balance between the two Wings of the Cabinet, the Liberal Leaguers on the one hand, and the Pro-Boers for instance, on the other'. According to Morley's later account, Asquith wanted to give the Exchequer to Haldane, but sent for Lloyd George instead when Morley threatened to resign in protest against what he alleged to be an attempt to create the 'ascendancy of the old Liberal League'.[2]

(draft), Haldane MSS. 5906, f. 222. Grey to Asquith, 25 Nov. 1905, Asquith MSS. Dep. 10, f. 168. Morley to C.-B., 25 Nov. 1905, B.M. Add. MSS. 41223, ff. 164–5. Morley to Carnegie, 3, 24 Nov. 1905. M. V. Brett (ed.), *Journals and Letters of Reginald Viscount Esher*, II, 1934, pp. 121–2.

[1] To R. S. Watson, 22 Mar. 1908, quoted in P. Corder, *The Life of Robert Spence Watson*, 1914, p. 301.

[2] To Minto, 12 Mar. 1908, I.O.L. MSS. Eur. D. 573/3, ff. 66–7. Morgan, *John, Viscount Morley*, p. 48.

23
THE LIBERALS IN OFFICE, 1905-1914

IN the early years of the new century Morley was thinking also of the possible nature and form of the policy with which a reunified party might concern itself. In 1899 he had told F. W. Hirst that, because the party might 'come together again', it ought in his view to be trying to make up its mind on questions 'apart from foreign policy', such as 'Licensing Reform, taxation or rating of ground values, and Old Age Pensions'.[1] But his own preference remained for some single, concentrating issue, and he continued to express opposition to 'programme' politics. In 1900 he criticized Campbell-Bannerman's election address for being 'too diffuse . . . repeating the old error of programme'.[2] Two years later he appealed to the party not to try to construct any positive programme: 'I think a very good working programme for the hour is furnished to us by the Government. Resistance to reaction; that is a very good programme; and that is the programme of to-day . . . I say resistance to the reaction of the Government is in itself a decent sort of programme.' Significantly, however, in the same speech he revived the question of Irish home rule, and, reminding Liberals of 'all the old arguments from 1886 to 1892', warned that the next Liberal Government would be unable to avoid having to deal with the Irish question and that, 'therefore, you had better face it now'.[3] It was almost inevitable that he should revert to these familiar themes as soon as he again considered the problem of unifying Liberal politics. The idea of the Irish policy as imposing priority in Liberal programmes recurred in his thinking. In 1903 he warned Liberals to remember that

[1] F. W. Hirst, *In the Golden Days*, 1947, p. 173.
[2] To Spencer, 22 Sept. 1900.
[3] *The Times*, 9 June 1902, p. 13, c. 2.

'Ireland fixes her own place in our party programmes'.[1] The home-rule policy remained for him both the predominant characteristic of his own Liberal politics and also the most reliable source of 'soundness' in general Liberal practice. In 1905 he told Asquith that 'my polar star was the Irish themselves, as it had been ever since I entered Parliament'; and he advised Campbell-Bannerman that a renewed expression of commitment to securing home rule 'will keep the centre of gravity in the party where it ought to be'.[2]

But Irish policy was now so closely involved with the issue of imperialism that it was for the purposes of Liberal politics as disunifying a factor as was imperialism. In this period Morley was constantly provoked and angered by the Liberal imperialists' opposition to home rule and disposition to ignore Irish policy. In 1903 he condemned them 'for giving Irish policy up at the very moment when the gov$_{mt}$ are forcing it to the front, and in our form too'.[3] But, because they were behaving in this way, Ireland could no longer provide the great unifying policy for a party which Morley knew must continue to include the imperialists.

However, it was in 1903 that Chamberlain launched his campaign for tariff reform, and Morley saw at once the opportunities which this presented for the reunifying of the Liberal party. 'The controversy', he wrote, 'will demand all our guns and all our troops and all our generals.'[4] In October 1903 he wrote of the 'urgency of closing ranks in face of the present real dangers of the country': 'Our best chance now is not to be too hotly *party* in language: but *national* both in language & spirit.'[5] In his speeches he called for the unity of all Liberals in the common interest of the defence of free trade, laid great stress on their opponents' disunity and indecision, and depicted this new issue as one which, like home rule and anti-imperialism before it, solved the Liberals' problems

---

[1] *The Times*, 14 Apr. 1903, p. 8, c. 3.

[2] *Recollections*, II, p. 133. To C.-B., 24 Nov. 1905, B.M. Add. MSS. 41223, f. 162.

[3] To Harcourt, 5 Apr. 1903. See also E. H. Fowler, *The Life of Henry Hartley Fowler, First Viscount Wolverhampton, G.C.S.I.*, 1912, pp. 472–80. To C.-B., 18 Nov. 1902, B.M. Add. MSS. 41223, f. 104. To Carnegie, 3 Nov. 1905.

[4] To Carnegie, 7 June 1903.

[5] To Spencer, 5 Oct. 1903.

THE LIBERALS IN OFFICE, 1905-1914 345

in organizing a coherent domestic policy by enforcing the postponement of commitment and action on all other questions. He declared in characteristic fashion that 'whatever issues might present themselves, until they had secured free trade, all the other questions would lie dormant'. 'It does not seem to me that this is any time for programmes', he advised his colleagues.[1] Nor was he even sure that it was any time for the Irish question. In January 1905 he informed the Irish leaders that he was opposed to the proposal for a parliamentary motion on home rule because of the 'immense disadvantage' that 'it may easily set back the movement from the Unionist camp'; '*the longer it is before the Irish question interrupts the swing* in our direction the better for all of us'.[2]

In fact, the Liberals now found themselves in the fortunate position of not needing to have any positive policies of their own in order to be sure of electoral success, so overwhelming was the reaction of the electorate against the policies and actions of the Unionist Government. Morley was well aware of the negative aspects of the Liberals' electoral triumph of 1906 and knew that the work of constructing coherent, positive domestic policy was still to be done. In 1908 he wrote: 'The Liberal victory two years since was, to the best of my belief, mainly due, in the huge extent of it to furious detestation of Balfour and his tactics. No great issue was really settled, but a good many great issues have been brought into view by the size and the composite nature of the majority.'[3]

Between 1905 and 1910 Morley, as Secretary of State for India, was little more than a spectator of the Liberal Government's efforts to deal with these issues. The Indian post was not the kind of appointment which he had expected or wanted, and, after he had been prevailed upon to take it, he practised the same deliberate aloofness from the activities of his colleagues as he had threatened in 1894 when he retreated into the Irish 'back-kitchen'. In 1906 he wrote of having taken office with the 'very firm intention

---

[1] *The Times*, 20 Oct. 1903, p. 4, c. 1; 26 Mar. 1904, p. 9, c. 6; 21 Jan. 1905, p. 12, c. 3; 4 Feb. 1905, p. 6, c. 1. To Spencer, 8 Oct. 1903.
[2] To Dillon, 26 Jan. 1905, Redmond MSS.
[3] To Minto, 24 Jan. 1908, I.O.L. MSS. Eur. D. 573/3, f. 25.

to become a pure departmental Minister, and to stand aside from other questions', and expressed annoyance at having to attend in the Commons and at Cabinets and at being 'drawn off into all manner of consultations, and all the rest of it'.[1] In 1907 he informed Campbell-Bannerman that he would not speak on, or help with, other subjects, because 'you sent me to the Ganges and Brahmaputra, and I stick to the business of my department'.[2] He later wrote that, while 'the whole range of cabinet work' was part of his responsibility, 'I shirk a good deal of these extraneous affairs'. He admitted that 'my conscience pricks me all the time'; but then he had been 'accustomed for most of my life to concentrate upon one subject at a time'.[3]

He soon became absorbed in his Indian work as if it was his latest single great subject. The 'back-kitchen' attitude quickly gave way to assertions that India was one of the most important political questions requiring the attention of the British Government.[4] In Indian policy he found also a testing-ground for the principles of a true, sound Liberalism.

In Morley's opinion one of the most important and yet most difficult aspects of his conduct of Indian affairs was the preservation of continuity and consistency between his past and present practice as a Liberal. He was desperately concerned to maintain the integrity of his Liberalism. The past loomed large in the judgements and expectations both of himself and of his colleagues and critics. For example, Sir Edward Grey believed that one of the Government's greatest assets for warding off criticism from 'sentimental', anti-imperialist Liberals was the fact that India was governed by a man with an 'unimpeachable record' and known to regard 'the Jingo' as 'the devil incarnate'.[5] In other words, if Morley was in charge, then the Government could not possibly be pursuing a 'Jingo' policy.

[1] To Minto, 22 June 1906, I.O.L. MSS. Eur. D. 573/1, f. 133.
[2] To C.-B., 20 June 1907, B.M. Add. MSS. 41223, f. 252.
[3] To Minto, 7 Apr. 1910, 14 Feb. 1908, I.O.L. MSS. Eur. D. 573/5, f. 55; /3, f. 40.
[4] Cf. Hansard, 4, 161, 570–1; 191, 522. Indian Speeches, p. 40.
[5] To Bryce, 6 Jan. 1908. M. V. Brett (ed.), Journals and Letters of Reginald Viscount Esher, II, 1934, p. 346.

There was a widespread disposition to judge Morley's present conduct in terms of his past. A. G. Gardiner expressed the particular area of interest: how far, under 'the burden of despotic control over a vast subject people, dimly struggling towards freedom', could this 'preacher of political liberty' and 'foe of the "reason of State" ' 'resist the assaults of circumstance and of entrenched officialdom'? For Morley resort to coercion might mean that he 'had begun to dig his own grave'.[1] Soon the disillusionment could be seen emerging. In 1908 H. W. Nevinson remarked to Wilfrid Blunt that 'we were wrong . . . in expecting so much of him'. The Indian nationalist, Gokhale, said that he had once been 'a great believer in Morley and had read all his writings on liberty', but that now his faith was gone. Blunt described Morley's sanctioning of repressive measures in India as surprising in view of the fact that 'his avowed sympathies had always been with liberty', and wrote in 1910 that it had become 'the Irish history over again, with Morley playing the part of Buckshot Forster at the India Office'.[2]

Morley was extremely sensitive to criticism of this kind. In 1907 he complained of how 'I am often wounded in the house of my friends—"shelving the principles of a lifetime", "violently unsaying all that he has been saying for thirty or forty years", and other compliments of that species. This from men to whom I have been attached and with whom I have worked all the time!'[3] In 1909 he published a volume of his own speeches on India 'partly to defend myself against the charge of betraying my Liberal faith'.[4] In one of these speeches he had described his disappointment at finding his 'credit in the bank of public opinion' so low after so many years spent labouring 'for Liberal principles and Liberal causes'.[5] He resorted to such defences as reminding his critics that British rule over India had been approved of by John Stuart Mill,

[1] A. G. Gardiner, *Prophets, Priests and Kings*, 1908, p. 58.
[2] W. S. Blunt, *My Diaries Being a Personal Narrative of Events, 1888–1914*, II, 1920, pp. 203, 212, 227, 229, 299, 328. The Earl of Lytton, *Wilfrid Scawen Blunt A Memoir*, 1961, pp. 178–9.
[3] To Minto, 28 June 1907, I.O.L. MSS. Eur. D. 573/2, ff. 142–3.
[4] To Minto, 18 Nov. 1909, I.O.L. MSS. Eur. D. 573/4, f. 248.
[5] *Indian Speeches*, p. 31.

'a great and benignant lamp of wisdom and humanity' and 'in such ideas as I have about political principles the leader of my generation'. One wonders whether he recalled how in 1881 Chamberlain had tried to make him accept that Mill would not have objected to the coercion then being instituted in Ireland.[1] Certainly he was now very sensitive to allegations that he who had so stoutly opposed the coercion of the Irish was now an 'arch-coercionist' with regard to India. In 1907 he warned the Viceroy, Lord Minto, that, while his 'spotless character as an anti-coercionist in Ireland' was standing him in good stead, 'Tory opponents will scent an inconsistency between deporting Lajpat, and fighting Balfour for locking up William O'Brien'.[2] Two years later he had to tell Minto that on account of his Irish record 'the notion in the present parliamentary circumstances, and with me of all men in the universe as S.S., of our being a party to a new law authorizing "detention without trial", is really too absurd to be thought of'.[3]

Many years previously Morley had told Chamberlain that he was reluctant to give any approval to Irish coercion, because 'I don't want to be dished as a democrat for the rest of my natural life'.[4] Now his political life at least was nearing its end, and he was very worried that the reputation and the organic consistency of principles and action which he had developed during it might be shattered. He pleaded with Minto 'as a sound Whig' to appreciate that they must take care not to 'go down to our graves' 'as imitators of Eldon, Sidmouth, the Six Acts, & all the other men & policies which we were both of us brought up to abhor'.[5] He would remind Minto of the need for 'the utmost care and scruple' in regard to deportations, since it was often some 'momentary slip in vigilance', such as not giving a suspected man the benefit of the doubt in cases of unclear evidence, that 'damaged men's political reputations'.[6]

[1] *Hansard*, 4, 175, 880. Chamberlain to Morley, 22 Oct. 1881.
[2] To Minto, 16, 31 May 1907, I.O.L. MSS. Eur. D. 573/2, f. 107.
[3] To Minto, 26 Aug. 1909, I.O.L. MSS. Eur. D. 573/4, ff. 189–90.
[4] To Chamberlain, 21 Oct. 1881.
[5] 30 July 1908, I.O.L. MSS. Eur. D. 573/3, f. 230.
[6] 13 Jan. 1909, I.O.L. MSS. Eur. D. 573/4, f. 11.

He was concerned about the effect of the compromises with illiberalism which were necessarily entailed in the work of supervising the despotic government of an increasingly turbulent empire. At first he tried resolutely to shut out the voices that would corrupt him into illiberalism: 'Good friends of mine in this Office often say: "Ah, you don't know India", which is true: but then they proceed to impress upon my innocent mind, principles of government that would justify Trepoff at Petersburg, or the Orange Ascendancy, who have made such a detestable mess in Ireland.'[1] But gradually the compromises crept in. Thus in May 1907, after claiming that his parliamentary record showed that 'no one dislikes' detention without trial 'more than I do', he proceeded to justify it for reasons of state.[2] Soon he found himself describing summary jurisdiction as, 'like war, a hateful thing, from which, however, some of the most ardent lovers of peace . . . have not shrunk'.[3] After leaving the India Office in 1910 he said that had he remained there another five years 'even my Liberalism would probably have gone'.[4]

Just as he had not been happy being an 'ordinary' Irish Secretary, so now he was most anxious to develop a distinctive Liberalism in his Indian work. In 1908 he wrote to Minto about the passing of severe sentences on agitators in India:

You will say to me, 'These legal proceedings are at bottom *acts of war* against rebels . . . you must not measure such sentences by the ordinary standards of a law-court . . .' Well, be it so. But if you push me into a position of this sort . . . then I drop reforms . . . ; and I'll tell Asquith that I'm not the man for the work, and that what it needs is a good sound old-fashioned Tory Secretary of State.[5]

Until very recently it has been believed that the chief inspirer of the Minto–Morley reforms was Minto, with Morley following hesitatingly after, prompted by what Blunt called his concern for

[1] To Minto, 3 May 1906, I.O.L. MSS. Eur. D. 573/1, f. 99.
[2] *Hansard*, 4, 174, 613.
[3] *Hansard*, 4, 198, 1977.
[4] Sir A. Fitzroy, *Memoirs*, 3rd edition, II, n.d., p. 458.
[5] 26 Aug. 1908, I.O.L. MSS. Eur. D. 573/3, f. 253.

'saving his own credit as a man of liberal ideas'.[1] In March 1907 Lord Esher noted how 'amazed' Morley was that the proposal for 'a *Native* member of council in India' 'should emanate from Minto'. 'I think J.M. wishes Minto and his proposal to the devil', wrote Esher. 'It places him, as *radical* S. of S., in a most awkward fix.'[2] Recent research, notably by Professor Wolpert, has, however, shown the falseness of this belief about the reforms and has in fact traced its origins to some very skilful manipulating of the situation by Morley to conciliate conservative opinion and thus strengthen his chances of at last accomplishing something by making Minto—who had been appointed Viceroy by the Conservative Government—appear to have been the chief inspirer of the reforms. Dr. R. J. Moore in his book on *Liberalism and Indian Politics 1872–1922*[3] has described how Morley deliberately laid the basis for this 'convenient myth' and how material that would have dispelled it was not published either in Morley's *Recollections* or the Countess of Minto's *India, Minto and Morley*—until recently our main sources of information on the reforms and their genesis.

It often seemed as if there were two Morleys at the India Office. On the one hand, there was the Morley who accepted the assignment in the first place, the would-be practical man of business anxious to free himself of the label of 'doctrinaire'. It is very probable that one reason why, when this anti-imperialist and 'Little Englander' did resume an active political career, he was prepared to do so as the supervisor of the government of a very large portion of the empire, was that he resented the reputation which he had acquired of being a mere theorist and dim-practical doctrinaire as a result of his extreme anti-imperialism. He was as concerned as ever to be accepted as a man of affairs. As early as 1902 he wrote, after having been awarded the Order of Merit, that 'it gives me some satisfaction to think that a good many people less *Sage* than I am, will be inclined to judge more leniently of a Pro-Boer, Little Englander, and all the other abominations, when they hear of him lifting himself up at even-

[1] Lytton, *Wilfrid Scawen Blunt*, p. 181.
[2] Brett, *Journals and Letters of Esher*, II, p. 229.
[3] 1966, pp. 86–7. Cf. S. A. Wolpert, *Morley and India 1906–1910*, California, 1967, Chap. 6.

ing parties with "*Merit*" proclaimed in glittering colours upon his shirt-front'.[1] His longing to be identified with the practical men of the world and not with the impractical intellectuals reasserted itself. In 1904, after quoting some criticisms of tariff reform by the Duke of Devonshire, he reminded his audience that in listening to these 'they were not listening to a lawyer or a theorist, but to a man with great and responsible interests and of enormous social and political experience; and this man was of the same opinion as the people who were called Little Englanders, pro-Boers, and he did not know what'.[2] After 1905 his letters to Lord Minto frequently revealed his extreme annoyance at finding himself placed in the latter category. In one he remarked bitterly that 'I am well known to be a book-man, a theorist, and a mere doctrinaire'. But when he found, after taking office, that his handling of the dispute between Kitchener and Curzon was winning 'universal commendation and applause', he wrote triumphantly: 'So I'm no more to be labelled *doctrinaire*.' In 1907 he was delighted to discover that he had so impressed the editor of the *Daily Mail* with the firmness of his conduct of Indian affairs that in that newspaper 'the humble individual who has usually been pelted as a pure doctrinaire, is hoisted on to a pedestal where he jostles Chatham, Frederick, and men of that lofty breed generally'. Indeed, his letters contain a remarkably large number of references to how 'strong men' such as Chatham and Cromwell and Strafford might have acted had they been in his position.[3]

But, on the other hand, the Morley who was a radical opponent of imperialism was never completely subdued. Indeed, sometimes this Morley would virtually disown the would-be imperialist 'strong man' and support those House of Commons critics who so annoyed and embarrassed the latter. On occasions he found difficulty in concealing his pleasure at having earned or regained the approval of Radicals.[4] He would even admit that their

[1] To Ripon, 1 July 1902, B.M. Add. MSS. 43541, ff. 98-9.
[2] *The Times*, 21 Jan. 1904, p. 10, c. 4.
[3] To Minto, 5 Apr. 1906, 11 July, 23, 28 Aug., 19 Sept. 1907, 3 Jan. 1908, 20 Aug. 1909, I.O.L. MSS. Eur. D. 573/1, f. 76; /2, ff. 153, 206, 223, 238; /3, f. 7; /4, f. 178. To Carnegie, 8 Mar. 1906. *Indian Speeches*, p. 145.
[4] Cf., e.g., to Minto, 14 Nov. 1907, I.O.L. MSS. Eur. D. 573/2, f. 190.

criticisms met with his own approval.[1] 'I was far too long in Opposition', he once explained, 'to think it very criminal to insist at every turn on calling the executive government to account.'[2] In 1909 he threatened that, rather than support the imprisoning of innocent men, he would join the band of Radical critics, 'perhaps with the effect of adding somewhat to their force'.[3] He even sometimes found fault with the Radicals for not showing enough 'force' in their attacks on his own and his officials' conduct of Indian affairs and would reflect on how he would have set about launching these attacks had he been in their position.[4]

For all his determination to instil into himself enthusiasm for the government of an empire which most British official thinking—and Morley's own—still assumed would endure for ever, he was unable to prevent himself from succumbing to moods of pessimism and hopelessness concerning the whole enterprise. His antagonism to imperialism was by now far too deeply entrenched for him to be able easily to replace it by a belief in empire as a good thing. But, in addition, a sense of unreality and strangeness, of being involved with forces that he does not, and can never hope to, understand pervades his observations on India. He found 'the distance and the strangeness' 'terrible' and wrote of himself as 'groping his way in dark places' and 'in twilight'. The Government knew 'so little of the mind of the people', and the people were as ignorant of 'the mind of the Government'. Perhaps 'political machinery' could never bridge this 'tremendous chasm'.[5] The ideals of the British and the Indians were 'divided by a vast gulf', which made the British government of India seem both 'stupendous' and extremely 'artificial'. Morley wondered how something so 'intensely artificial and unnatural' 'can possibly last'.

---

[1] Cf. to Minto, 23 Mar. 1906, 14 Mar. 1907, I.O.L. MSS. Eur. D. 573/1, f. 69; /2, f. 53.

[2] To Minto, 14 Feb. 1908, I.O.L. MSS. Eur. D. 573/3, f. 41.

[3] To Minto, 28 Jan. 1909, I.O.L. MSS. Eur. D. 573/4, ff. 25–6.

[4] e.g. to Minto, 2 Mar. 1906, 12 Apr., 18 July 1907, I.O.L. MSS. Eur. D. 573/1, f. 54; /2, ff. 73, 163.

[5] To Minto, 8 Mar., 15 June, 20 Sept. 1906, 16 May 1907, I.O.L. MSS. Eur. D. 573/1, ff. 58, 128, 196; /2, f. 109. Hansard, 4, 175, 885.

His conclusion shows how deeply imbued with pessimism became his attitude to his Indian work:

> It surely cannot [last], and our only business is to do what we can to make the next transition, whatever it may turn out to be something of an improvement. . . . I cannot say that I feel as if we were doing more than drawing our hands through water. Will your [Minto's] Reform policy, Natives on my Council, Decentralisation, Economising of Taxation, and the rest of our virtuous deeds, really make a pin of difference in their feelings about British rule?[1]

As the construction of the political reforms proceeded, he kept asking himself whether 'any of our work is destined to be fruitful' and whether such reforms could ever interest Indians in 'the durability of the Raj'.[2] 'I did not choose India', he wrote apologetically to a friend at the end of 1908. 'I have no illusions about it. I knew that we are walking in the dark there.' It might even be that the Indians would 'do it better by themselves'. 'But there we are, and it is impossible for us to make a clean bolt.'[3] Enthusiasm never came. Writing to Minto in 1910, Morley gave his final verdict on 'the system that you and I have had to work': 'It is a terribly cumbrous and artificial sort of system, and I am not certain that it will last for ever, or even for many years to come.'[4]

In November 1910 Morley resigned from the India Office and was appointed Lord President of the Council. (He had gone to the House of Lords in 1908 as Viscount Morley of Blackburn.) This new position brought him back into the central councils of the Liberal leadership from which he had preserved a marked aloofness so long as he was at the India Office.

Morley's comments on the domestic policies of the Government since 1905 show clearly that he believed that too much attention was being paid to the interests and demands of labour

---
[1] To Minto, 14 Sept., 9 Nov. 1906, 15 Aug. 1907, I.O.L. MSS. Eur. D. 573/1, ff. 193, 239; /2, f. 198. To Carnegie, 28 Dec. 1906.
[2] To Minto, 2 Apr., 7 May, 24, 30 July 1908, I.O.L. MSS. Eur. D. 573/3, ff. 98, 151, 222, 230.
[3] To Carnegie, 29 Dec. 1908, 15 Jan. 1909.
[4] 19 Oct. 1910, I.O.L. MSS. Eur. D. 573/5, f. 165.

and that the Liberals were running the risk of thereby alienating their essential middle-class support. Thus in September 1906 he wrote in favour of a firm resistance to demands by railway workers for higher wages. Failure to put up such resistance 'will damage us gravely with the middle class, for railways are the middle class investment', and, he added, 'if anybody thinks we can govern this country against the middle class, he is wrong'.[1] He was very concerned that the party should not be identified too closely with 'socialism'. When the independent Socialist Victor Grayson scored his great by-election victory at Colne Valley in 1907, Morley remarked that this would 'frighten people about Socialism, and tho' we are not Socialists, many of our friends live next door, and the frightened people will edge off in the opposite direction'.[2] He feared that at last there might be emerging that domination of politics by social questions that would produce the disruption of Liberalism between the forces of 'socialism' and of embattled property. In 1907 he predicted that 'Socialism', now that it had become 'the key to our politics' and 'the catchword of the hour', would 'split the liberal party, and probably be the means of uniting the other party'.[3]

He became increasingly concerned about the attitude of his colleagues and the party to this situation:

> We are drawing to the edge of that formidable Maelstrom, the Social Question. And opinion is not in the least ripe. Nobody of any political authority has thought out Old Age Pensions, for example; has either thought it out, or worked it out, seriously, in all its ramifications and relations. Yet they are profound, and go to the very roots of our moral, social, and political well-being, or even of our Being at all, whether well or ill. The present House of Commons is not, I much fear, effectively qualified for searching discussion on a deep question of this kind.[4]

Twenty-three years earlier he had rejected Chamberlain's attempt

---

[1] To H. H. Fowler, 30 Sept. 1906, quoted in Fowler, *Life of Viscount Wolverhampton*, p. 505.
[2] To Campbell-Bannerman, 19 July 1907, B.M. Add. MSS. 41223, f. 253.
[3] To Minto, 15 Aug. 1907, I.O.L. MSS. Eur. D. 573/2, f. 199.
[4] To Minto, 24 Jan. 1908, I.O.L. MSS. Eur. D. 573/3, ff. 25–6.

to introduce 'the Social Question' into politics as premature in view of the unpreparedness of Liberal thought. That he was still having to adopt such an attitude in 1908 is a striking commentary on the nature of Liberal politics in the intervening period and on the consequences of the preoccupation with 'obstructions' and excuses for abstention from commitment and decision. Morley wrote now of the dilemma which confronted the still unprepared Liberal party. Old age pensions were, he admitted early in 1908, the issue in which 'the public mind is now most keenly interested and expectant'. But, he continued,

The danger of it to the government & the party is pretty plain. It raises in lively concrete form the burning abstract debates on Socialism, or rather, it does not raise,—it concentrates them. It will be injurious to us with the lower middle-class, who after all are no inconsiderable contingent of our party strength. On the other hand, we shall hardly be able to produce proposals magnificent enough to make the workmen ardently enthusiastic, or even decently satisfied.[1]

When Morley had freed himself from his special responsibility for India the interests of that other country which had been his principal political interest previously were re-emerging into the forefront of debate and action. The great constitutional barrier to the achievement of Irish home rule—the veto of the House of Lords—was removed by the Parliament Act of 1911. But those who were opposed to home rule—the Ulstermen and their allies in the Conservative party—soon revealed a determination to resist if necessary by unconstitutional methods. The Ulster crisis created for the Liberals the embarrassment of their appearing to favour in the case of Ulster that subordination of a minority to a majority section which they so strenuously opposed in the case of Ireland as a whole. The Liberals' desire to conciliate their Irish allies conflicted with their dread of having to coerce Ulster into accepting incorporation in a home-rule Ireland.

In helping to draw up the first Home Rule Bill in 1886 Morley seems to have given almost no thought to the special problem of Ulster. At the 'Round Table' conference in 1887 he seemed

[1] To Bryce, 6 Jan. 1908.

surprised that Ulster was proving to be 'the rock' in the negotiations. He and his colleagues were not even prepared at first with arguments on this aspect of the Irish question. 'I wish you could collect your ideas together about *Ulster*, and the best way of meeting that difficulty', he wrote to Lord Spencer after the conference had begun.[1] And yet he had had experience in 1886 of the violence of feelings against home rule in Ulster. The firm action which he authorized against rioting in Belfast was to be as bitterly remembered against him in Ulster as was Mitchelstown against Balfour in the rest of Ireland.[2] But he refused to take the agitation in Ulster seriously because he regarded it as artificial, deliberately provoked and developed by English Conservatives for their own ends. In 1887 he said that 'a good deal of this zeal for Ulster is artificial' and would be seen to be such once home rule was a *fait accompli*.[3] When the time came for a second Home Rule Bill, Morley again dismissed the agitation as 'heated, aggravated, and encouraged by English statesmen'.[4]

He rejected the suggestion that Protestants would be treated unjustly in a home-rule Ireland. 'I believe', he said, 'if the various forces in Ireland were once allowed to have free play, if laity and clergy met without the disturbing element of a national battle to fight, there would be no more fear of intolerant legislation in the interests of any one particular Church than there is in our own country or in Scotland.' The bitterness of the religious feud stemmed from the association of Protestantism with 'an exclusive and hostile ascendency' which it was the purpose of home rule to bring to an end. Under home rule Roman Catholics would no longer be 'one compact body for persecuting, obscurantist, or any other evil purposes', but would divide into clerical and anti-clerical groups.[5] Before all else he placed the interests of the Irish nation. Ireland needed Ulster. The severance of Ulster 'would

---

[1] To Gladstone, 15 Jan. 1887, B.M. Add. MSS. 44255, f. 178. To Spencer, 15 Jan. 1887.

[2] Cf. *Hansard*, 3, 308, 111–18; (Lords) 14, 1019–20. L. P. Curtis, Jr., *Coercion and Conciliation in Ireland 1880–1892 A Study in Conservative Unionism*, 1963, p. 125.

[3] *The Times*, 7 July 1887, p. 7, c. 4.

[4] *Hansard*, 4, 11, 654.

[5] *The Times*, 22 June 1886, p. 11, c. 3. *Handbook of Home Rule*, p. 256.

destroy the chance of giving full satisfaction to the idea of nationality', 'rob the Dublin body of a valuable element', and 'be a standing affront to the rest of the nation'.[1]

When the details of the third Home Rule Bill were discussed in 1911 Morley appears to have been one of the 'most vehement opponents' of the exclusion of Ulster.[2] But by January 1913 when he spoke in the Lords on the Bill he was having to answer charges that the Liberals were acting illiberally in forcing home rule on the Ulster minority. He argued that, when Liberals had in the past sympathized with peoples 'rightly struggling to be free', this had been in cases of 'actual oppression and hateful misgovernment', which did not exist in Ulster.[3] He thus ignored the fact that the fears of the Ulstermen related to the prospect after the concession of home rule to Ireland. For most of 1913 he remained firm against compromise; but by the end of the year the thought of having to support the use of force against Ulster was weighing on him more and more heavily.[4] In December 1913 he was one of the principal figures in abortive negotiations for a settlement with the Unionists. Austen Chamberlain gained the impression at this time that Morley was extremely 'averse from coercion of Ulster.'[5]

As the Ulster crisis intensified in 1914 Morley was torn between, on the one hand, his fear of violence and coercion and, on the other, his indignation against Ulster and his long-standing enthusiasm for home rule. In January Lord Esher noted that he was 'very undecided and has no clear insight or opinion, at one moment overwhelmed with dismay at the prospect of armed conflict, at another using language of menace towards "rebels" '.[6] He wanted to preserve from the corruption of violence both his own

---

[1] J. L. Garvin, *The Life of Joseph Chamberlain*, II, 1933, p. 287. To Gladstone, 17 Jan. 1887. B.M. Add. MSS. 44255, f. 180. *Hansard*, 4, 11, 656.
[2] D. Gwynn, *The Life of John Redmond*, 1932, p. 236.
[3] *Hansard* (Lords), 13, 810–12.
[4] Cf. to Carnegie, 14, 28 Nov. 1913.
[5] A. Chamberlain, *Politics from Inside. An Epistolary Chronicle 1906–1914*, 1936, pp. 586–94. To Harrison, 10 Dec. 1913. Fitzroy, *Memoirs*, II, p. 531.
[6] Viscount Esher (ed.), *Journals and Letters of Reginald Viscount Esher*, III, 1938, p. 153.

liberal principles and the ideal of home rule with its trust in the reconciling power of reason and the free play of forces. He realized that the success of home rule with Ulster not excluded depended on the development of a liberal spirit in Ireland; the slightest intrusion of violence would, however, render infertile the seed-bed of Liberalism. As for his own Liberal beliefs he came increasingly to feel that their integrity depended on their being kept completely free of compromise or contact with the coercive principle. Thus in March 1914 he was very angry when Winston Churchill declared that 'there are worse things than bloodshed'. This was not Liberalism but 'a Tory platitude'. 'You may talk as you like of bloodshed,' he said to Asquith, 'but I venture to say this, that the first blood shed in Ireland, not in mere civil commotion, but in conflict between the Ulster Volunteers and the forces of the Crown, will mean the end of Home Rule.' Significantly, it was Morley who, alone of the rest of the Cabinet, saw and approved the paragraphs that Seely added to the memorandum on the army crisis in order to assure the officers that they would not be required to participate in the coercion of Ulster.[1]

By July 1914 Morley was aware of a very precarious balance between violence and order in Irish affairs. Since 1886, he told his fellow peers, the Irish issue had involved 'constitutional forms' and 'legitimate methods of agitation and controversy'; but now there was 'another course': 'Resistance by arms is now encouraged against the established Government of the kingdom. This baleful lesson finds encouragement and favour, and the lesson that constitutional methods are no longer to be trusted will be sure to spread. The dark results of appeals to violence and force must spread the dangerous suspicion that constitutional methods are unavailing.'[2] As negotiations commenced, reason appeared to be making its last resistance to the encroaching tide: 'The eight men will all be ready to work their very best for Peace. But there are wild, and perhaps intractable, forces outside the Conference. . . .

[1] Fitzroy, *Memoirs*, II, pp. 541, 545. R. C. K. Ensor, *England 1870–1914*, 1936, p. 478.
[2] *Hansard* (Lords), 16, 532.

The issue of Tyrone &c. is narrow enough, but then, as history so abundantly shows, when men want to fight, a narrow issue will do just as well as a broad one.'[1] But by now this was in effect a microcosm of the entire European situation. A few weeks later wild and intractable forces were unleashed all over Europe when men decided that they wanted to fight over a 'scrap of paper'.

[1] To Carnegie, 20 July 1914.

24

MORLEY AND THE FIRST WORLD WAR: THE LAST YEARS

IN the 1860s Morley had wanted Britain to adopt an interventionist attitude towards the affairs of Europe and be prepared to act as a 'constable' to restrain the 'brawling' nations of that continent. In an article of May 1867 attacking Cobdenite non-interventionism he wrote: 'The confusion and alarm which reign throughout the continent of Europe at this moment are the deplorably expressive commentary upon England's deliberate and sustained withdrawal from her place in the European State-System.' He alleged that Europe was in a condition of anarchy mainly on account of 'the premeditated absence from the scene of the only nation which could possibly quell or restrain the violence of these detestable animosities'. England should 'stand forth in Europe as the high-minded, benignant, and virile guardian of the European Peace', prepared to employ force against any disturber of that peace.[1]

But all this was changed abruptly by the victory of Prussia over France in 1870–1. For a 'constable' must be neutral in his attitude to the personal characteristics of the combatants, whereas Morley found his own sympathies now actively engaged on the side of Purssia, even though Prussian victory threatened the establishment of the hegemony of that country in Europe and an end to a balance of power. He applauded Prussia's conduct towards France after Sedan as 'the just and stern retribution wh. a wholesome and robust morality never forbids us to exact, when its exaction may teach a lesson'. Prussia's war aims were described by him as essentially 'moral'.[2] In other words, it was now Prussia, not England, that was acting as the 'high-minded, benignant, and

[1] F.R., May 1867, pp. 621–8.
[2] To Harrison, 26 Apr. 1871.

virile guardian of the European Peace', the enforcer of a stern international morality upon a power whose 'cause and aims were immoral'. Morley seemed quite prepared to see the role which he had envisaged for his own country in 1867 transferred now to Prussia. By 1877 he was arguing in favour of a British policy of 'non-intervention, tempered by a close friendly understanding with Germany'.[1] As his own opposition to militarism and conscription grew, he argued that, since, 'if we are going to operate in Europe at all, we shall have to militarize', it was Britain's 'true interest and duty' to leave the Prussians alone to impose order and stability in Europe.[2] The cause of Germany was the cause of 'the order, discipline, loyalty, steady development of Europe'.[3]

This development he continued to see as menaced principally by France. He dismissed fears of danger from aggressive German militarism, arguing that it was French aggressiveness and provocativeness that was responsible for the German military stance and that the Germans were naturally pacific and averse from meddling in the affairs of other people. Bismarck's policy was one of peace and non-interference, and German public opinion would always guard against Germany's entering upon foreign adventures. According to Morley, Prussian '*militarismus*' was 'only the natural condition of her stage of development, and the indispensable guarantee (from geographical reasons) against the jealousy of reactionary courts and princelets & kinglings'. The growth of the Liberal movement in Germany, checked by a decade of war, would now be resumed, and militarism would gradually disappear. 'The Hohenzollern method, civilized and modernized as there seems reason to hope it may be in the hands of the Crown Prince, appears to me likely', Morley wrote in 1871, 'to prove much more veritably republican, than any system that can be worked among a people so intolerant of difference of opinion as the French are.' He rejoiced that it would now be Germany and not France which would be the cultural centre of Europe and the model of social development. German military hegemony was

[1] *F.R.*, Jan. 1877, p. 140.
[2] *F.R.*, Oct. 1870, pp. 480 ff. To Harrison, 22 Feb. 1871.
[3] To Harrison, 26 Apr. 1871.

acceptable in part because it would give scope for German social and cultural dominance in Europe. Compared to 'the issue whether the French or the German is the more hopeful type of political & social condition', 'the minor controversies as to the origin of the [Franco-Prussian] war, its continuance since Sédan, and so on, seem to me to be secondary', he wrote. 'My own sympathies are strongly with German ideas of society, and even of government', he once confessed, adding: 'of course I mean liberal German, not German Junker ideas'. The French were far too unstable and too inclined to veer between the extremes of revolution and reaction, whereas the Prussians were sober, disciplined, and orderly. 'French republicanism is hollow, heady, intolerant,' he wrote, 'and I at least have no faith in its stability, nor in its virtue, if it be stable.' When the Paris Commune was set up, he referred contemptuously to these 'phrase-mongering curs, whom an Uhlan or two will suffice to send howling back into their dens'. He predicted that the Commune would fail because of the 'weakness of faith inside'. It was not the way of social progress: 'The new society will have to be perfected . . . not by Celts, but by Teutons, who can take deeper draughts.'[1]

His support of the Prussian cause led to a series of sharp disagreements between himself and the positivists, who were passionately pro-French.[2] One reason for his turning away from positivism was his fear of being handicapped in his contact with English opinion by appearing to have the 'taint' of association with French revolutionary political thought.[3]

The connection between Morley's support of German military hegemony and his belief in the desirability of a predominance of German social and cultural values is seen further in his attitude towards Russia and his arguments on the social implications of

[1] *F.R.*, Sept. 1870, pp. 369–76; June 1875, pp. 899–907. To Harrison, 22 Feb., 20, 29 Mar., 14, 26 Apr., 25 June, 23 July 1871, 5, 10 Jan. 1872. To Lady Amberley, 20 Dec. 1870, and to Lord Amberley, 9 Jan. 1871, B. and P. Russell (edd.), *The Amberley Papers. The Letters and Diaries of Lord and Lady Amberley*, II, 1937, pp. 387, 443–4. *P.M.G.*, 12, 28 Aug. 1882, 5 Jan. 1883. E. V. Lucas, *The Colvins and Their Friends*, 1928, pp. 48–9.

[2] See to Harrison, 22 Feb., 14, 25, 26 Apr. 1871, 10 Jan. 1872, 6 Sept. 1873. To Congreve, 4 Feb. 1874, B.M. Add. MSS. 45241, ff. 61–2.

[3] Cf. to Harrison, 26 July, 9 Dec. 1871.

Russian influence in Europe. In 1870 he wrote that a weak Germany 'means preponderating Russia'. The 'interests of the highest civilisation' called for 'the interposition in the heart of the European state-system' of a strong German nation which would not only serve as a barrier 'between the western nations and the half-barbarous Russian Swarms' but would also 'spread eastwards' civilizing ideas.[1] In January 1871 he published an article in the *Fortnightly Review* by a German professor, Von Sybel, alleging that had France defeated Prussia the 'Russian democracy' 'would have been ready and eager to fraternise with the Parisian Socialist'.[2] This appears to have reflected Morley's own attitude very closely, for a month later he wrote to Harrison on the dangers of a Franco-Russian alliance, which he thought might emerge within the next twenty years:

The Slav peoples are the most instinctively and phrenetically communistic in their aspirations. Add to these Slav aspirations French form, grace, practical enthusiasm, always eager to move in the communistic direction. Do you—who are not a communist—think there is not far more peril to the foundations of Europe in this politico-social alliance of peoples with such ideas, than in the Prussian Junkers?[3]

In June 1871 he published another article, anonymous and intensely pro-German, which claimed that a Franco-Russian alliance 'would instantaneously associate the modern communism of France, which has hitherto been revolutionary, with the ancient communism of all the Slav races, which is generic and historical'.[4] From a letter which he wrote to Harrison at this time we can see how Morley himself associated the revolutionary outbreak of Parisian Communism with the fear of an invasion of Europe by a swarm of barbarous Russians. He suggested that the Commune was 'a type of those Gothic, Visigothic, Ostrogothic, barbarous, invasions of the decaying empire—wh. had no polity nor plan, but that of destroying and taking possession'. Perhaps, he wrote, just as 'a new christian organisation arose out of the chaos & con-

[1] *F.R.*, Sept. 1870, p. 371.
[2] *F.R.*, Jan. 1871, p. 3.
[3] 22 Feb. 1871.
[4] *F.R.*, June 1871, pp. 677 ff.

fusion' of the disintegrated Roman empire, so, in the disruption of 'the social empire of to-day', 'some new and as yet unforeseen system will rise out of the many wild and purposeless outbreaks of wh. the Commune is a type'.[1] Russia seemed to him very likely to be the source of such a new system. In 1877 he wrote that it was certain that Russia would follow 'a path of her own' in social development, 'whether to higher social forms than our own or not, none of us will live to know'; and he remarked in particular on 'the circumstance of the Commune in Russia having survived in full vigour as the social unit, down to a time when the English economist comes upon no more than broken traces of it in other lands'. In the same essay he observed concerning the condition of western Europe that 'the miseries and iniquities of a state of much inequality of wealth are not less glaring in 1877 then they were in 1848' when 'Mr. Mill talked about a general reconsideration of all the first principles of society being felt to be inevitable'.[2] It is not surprising that in this situation he should have wanted the example and contagion of Russian Communism to be kept well away from western Europe; hence the importance of a strong Germany spreading a civilizing influence eastwards from a dominant position in the European state system. In another article in 1877 he referred to what he had written in 1870 about Germany as a bulwark against Russia, and, remarking that 'everybody to-day sees how just that was', claimed again that 'Germany is the power in whose strength, prosperity, and vigorous government, Europe has the most vital interest, because she is the Power best able from her position to deal with' Russia.[3]

From this time on Morley became extremely isolationist in his attitude to the affairs of Europe. They are almost completely ignored in his writing and speeches. But when after 1905 there was increasing discussion of the need to prepare for war with Germany, his former feelings about that country underwent a remarkable revival. He dismissed his colleagues' apprehensions about the 'German danger'. In 1907 he wrote after the Kaiser's

[1] 16 July 1871.
[2] *F.R.*, Feb. 1877, pp. 264, 266.
[3] *F.R.*, Jan. 1877, p. 139.

visit that the Kaiser had left people in London with the 'golden impression' that 'he does really desire and intend *Peace*'. As for the German naval programme, he remarked that, 'for my own part, the American Fleet in the Pacific makes me a good deal more uncomfortable than German battleships on paper'.[1] The tendency of the Foreign Office to see everywhere 'the finger of the German' began to anger him: 'The anti-German bias, prejudice, and suspicion will soon become as great a nuisance as any of the other biases, &c., with which John Bull has befooled himself.'[2] He complained to Sir Edward Grey himself that 'the anti-German aspect' of British foreign policy was becoming far too pronounced.[3] Even his old trust in the ultimate liberalization of Germany had survived. Writing to Andrew Carnegie about the 'fight for Peace' in which Carnegie was involved, he said: 'Some day a great ruler will arise at Berlin, and he will fire the train for your ideas.'[4] The frame of mind which he had revealed in his quarrels with the positivists also reappeared. Austin Harrison, son of Frederic Harrison, visited Morley in 1909 and wrote afterwards of having been 'astonished to find how "unrealistic" (as I thought) his views were about Germany's attitude' and 'how far more he leaned towards Goethe than towards Comte'.[5]

As once he had blamed French aggressiveness for the persistence of German militarism, which he was sure would otherwise have been gradually diminishing in the natural evolution of Germany towards a higher stage of social development, so now he blamed British provocations and imperialistic behaviour. From 1909 on he made repeated protests against what he considered 'provocative' language and conduct towards Germany.[6] He was later to allege that in the Agadir crisis the Kaiser had wanted peace but had been forced by the Junkers into belligerence because of the attitude of

[1] To Minto, 20 Dec. 1907, I.O.L. MSS. Eur. D. 573/2, ff. 323-4.
[2] To Minto, 6 Feb., 4 Mar. 1908, I.O.L. MSS. Eur. D. 573/3, ff. 36, 65.
[3] To Grey, 22 June 1909, Grey MSS, Vol. 59. Cf. to Minto, 21 May 1909, I.O.L. MSS. Eur. D. 573/4, f. 112.
[4] 7 July 1909.
[5] A. Harrison, *Frederic Harrison. Thoughts and Memories*, 1926, p. 177.
[6] To Minto, 21 May 1909, I.O.L. MSS. Eur. D. 573/4, f. 112. To Grey, 22 June 1909, Grey MSS., vol. 59. To Carnegie, 7 Jan. 1910. To Asquith, 27 July 1911, Asquith MSS, Dep. 13, f. 39.

Britain and that Morocco, Agadir, and finally Belgium were regarded by the British Government as pretexts for a war which it wanted all the time.[1] He himself from within that Government opposed preparation for war. In 1911 he insisted that no further military conversations be held with France. Later he accused his colleagues, especially Grey, Asquith, and Haldane, of having deceived him as to the nature of the conversations that were held and the extent of the military commitments entered into. Although Haldane denied this charge, it does appear that on a number of occasions the 'imperialist' wing of the Cabinet did try to exclude Morley and others from knowledge of the military planning that was being undertaken at the time.[2]

Morley laid great stress on the conciliation of Germany. In November 1911 Lord Esher noted the participation of Morley, who 'believes in capturing German sentiment', in a 'Cabinet cabal against the Entente with France' and against preparations for war with Germany.[3] Speaking in the Lords on relations with Germany, Morley urged that any apparent conflict of interests between the two countries be not resolved either by war or 'by diplomacy starting from fixed antipathies and prepossessions'. The foundation of a Europe 'inhabited by good Europeans' must, he said, be an Anglo-German understanding. He declared that Germany's 'national ideals' deserved 'a supreme place among the greatest ideals that now animate and guide the world', and praised 'Germany's high and strict standard of competency, the purity and vigour of her administration of affairs', the great achievements of German art, science, and letters, and 'the fixed strength of character and duty in the German people'.[4]

[1] J. H. Morgan, *John, Viscount Morley, An Appreciation and Some Reminiscences*, 1924, p. 98. *Memorandum on Resignation*, p. 14.

[2] Cf. J. P. Mackintosh, *The British Cabinet*, 1962, pp. 316-22. Sir A. Fitzroy, *Memoirs*, 3rd edition, II, n.d., pp. 461, 466, 485-6, 581. Memo. by John Burns on a conversation with Morley, 14 June 1916, B. M. Add. MSS. 46283, ff. 73-4. Viscount Esher (ed.), *Journals and Letters of Reginald Viscount Esher*, III, 1938, p. 74. Morgan, *John, Viscount Morley*, pp. 43-7. [Lord Haldane], *Richard Burdon Haldane. An Autobiography*, 1929, pp. 228-9. *Memorandum on Resignation*, p. 18. To Haldane, 16 Aug. 1920, Haldane MSS. 5914, f. 244.

[3] Esher, *Journals and Letters of Viscount Esher*, III, p. 74.

[4] *Hansard* (Lords), 10, 383-5.

As the crisis of July and early August 1914 developed, Morley insisted on the wrongness of war between Britain and Germany. In 1871 he had described the two countries as fitted to be allies 'by geographical position, by slow Teutonic ponderosity, by common sense, and true scientific training'.[1] Now he argued that they were 'better fitted to understand one another than any other pair in Europe'.[2] He also still believed that the need for a bulwark against Russian expansion into Europe made the avoidance of any action that might weaken Germany one of Britain's most vital interests. When late in July the cabinet decided to initiate the precautionary stage of preparation for war, Morley told Sir Almeric Fitzroy that he did not approve because 'he cannot brook this country becoming a party to what he regards as a Slavonic movement against Teuton influence'. Fitzroy discovered that 'Russia and all she stands for is still for him identified with barbarism, and he looks upon any tendency hostile to Germany that has its roots in Slav aspirations as prejudicial to the interests of civilization'.[3] When he argued with his colleagues against war, he found that 'they were rather surprised at the stress I laid upon the Russian side of things'. ' "Have you ever thought", I put to them, "what will happen if Russia wins? If Germany is beaten and Russia is beaten, it is not England and France who will emerge pre-eminent in Europe. It will be Russia. Will that be good for Western civilisation? I at least don't think so. . . . " '[4] In his letter of resignation of 4 August he drew attention to one 'cardinal difference' between himself and his colleagues: 'To bind ourselves to France is at the same time to bind ourselves to Russia, and to whatever demands may be made by Russia on France.'[5] 'We are only playing Russia's game', he told Asquith.[6] After the outbreak of war he continued to insist that Russia was 'the real aggressor' and the country which 'stands most to gain out of this war'. The

[1] To Harrison, 22 Feb. 1871.
[2] *Memorandum on Resignation*, p. 19.
[3] Fitzroy, *Memoirs*, II, p. 557.
[4] *Memorandum on Resignation*, p. 6.
[5] The Earl of Oxford and Asquith, *Memories and Reflections, 1852–1927*, II, 1928, pp. 10–14.
[6] Morgan, *John, Viscount Morley*, p. 50.

preponderance of Russia 'must follow', he argued, 'from a successful war', and would that not be 'a greater menace to Europe than any Germany could offer'?[1]

To the end, he opposed entry into war with Germany, even maintaining that no *casus belli* need be found in German aggression against Belgium. He warned his colleagues of the effect that war would have on the British economy: ' "In the present temper of labour", said I, "this tremendous dislocation of industrial life must be fraught with public danger. The atmosphere of war cannot be friendly to order, in a democratic system that is verging on the humour of '48" .' When a declaration of war became certain, he determined to resign. On the occasion of John Bright's resignation in 1882 in protest against the bombardment of Alexandria the editor of the *Pall Mall Gazette* had acknowledged that even 'a practical statesman owes a debt to the moral unity of his life'. So now Morley found himself under pressure from friends and from 'conscience' to be consistent with what Fitzroy called 'all the antecedent tendencies of his faith'. John Burns told him that the 'Peace Party' 'look to you to stand firm'; and Morley after reflecting that he was, after all, 'a notorious peace-man and little-Englander, etc.', and after spending 'two hours' rumination' remembering what Gladstone used to say about leaving a Cabinet 'on public grounds', decided that he was 'bound to go'.[2]

'What use should I be', Morley wrote to Margot Asquith on 9 August, 'in the Council of War, into which unhappy circumstances have transformed the Cabinet? I've run my course and kept the faith. That's enough.'[3] He was later to claim that in early August perfectly good terms of settlement with Germany were 'already within reach of reason and persistent patience'.[4] But a Liberal Government had decided that force, not reason, must be

[1] Ibid., p. 42. Fitzroy, *Memoirs*, II, p. 571.
[2] *Memorandum on Resignation*, pp. 3–25. Fitzroy, *Memoirs*, II, pp. 557–62. Esher, *Journals and Letters of Viscount Esher*, III, pp. 205–6. To Bryce, 24 Nov. 1914. P.M.G., 15 July 1882. Morgan, *John, Viscount Morley*, pp. 119–20.
[3] M. Asquith, *Autobiography*, II, 1922, pp. 184–5.
[4] *Memorandum on Resignation*, p. 19.

the arbiter; and Morley felt that he had nothing in common with Liberalism of this kind.

After his resignation Morley felt that he was watching the final collapse and extinction of nineteenth-century Liberalism. He had thought that resignation might be a last means of saving the 'soul' of Liberalism, that 'the break-up of the Ministry' would be 'less of an evil both for Liberal principles, and the prospects and power of the Liberal party, than their wholesale identification with a Cabinet committed to intervention in arms by sea and land in Central Europe and all the meshes of the Continental system'.[1] But only John Burns went out with Morley. Lloyd George remained in the Cabinet; and Morley's resignation appeared as no more than a personal gesture. Morley now believed, however, that the 'prospects' of the Liberal party were ended. 'The old Liberalism had done its work', he wrote later, 'and the time had come for openly changing imperial landmarks, and extinguishing beacons that needed new luminants.'[2] The decisive act, in his opinion, was the formation of the Coalition Government in 1915. The 'new Liberals', the 'apostles of Efficiency', had to 'seek deliverance' from their inability to apply force effectively in the support of 'the opposing party that counted Liberalism, old or new, for dangerous and deluding moonshine'.[3] 'Liberalism, as we have known it, is dead beyond resurrection', Morley now told his friends.[4]

It appeared, however, that he might be looking now towards Labour as a possible source of 'new luminants' for the beacons of political faith. He had long been opposed to any development of independent Labour politics and had told working men that they would be 'better off if they had the Liberal strength on their side'.[5] But what if the Liberals had no strength, either in ideas or in practice? Gradually since 1905 the essential conservatism of the British working man had been impressing itself on him. After the

[1] Ibid., p. 17.
[2] Ibid., p. 28.
[3] *Recollections*, II, p. 81.
[4] Morgan, *John, Viscount Morley*, p. 99.
[5] *The Times*, 20 Apr. 1903, p. 7, c. 2.

1906 elections he wrote that, although 'the Labour Party has now at last assumed definite shape' and there would certainly be 'some wild-cat talk', he was sure 'that the British workmen are essentially *bourgeois*, without a bit of the French Red about them'.[1] He told Winston Churchill that 'the English working man', unlike 'the French "Red" ', did not think of new systems but only of fairer treatment in the existing system.[2] In 1908 he wrote to Lord Minto: 'Don't believe that Socialism, in any deep or definable sense, will go far with our working men. I have had many chances of knowing them well. They are most emphatically Individualist in practice and aim, and only Socialist in the sense—and a grand sense—of being readily stirred by sympathy and pity for their comrades. In all this, I should venture to put them well above their "betters". '[3] In 1909 and 1910 he asked the Lords not to be afraid of 'Socialism' in England, for 'the English working man ... is not in the least a Phrygian with a red cap'.[4]

The disintegration of Liberalism during and after the war found Morley prepared to look sympathetically on Labour as a new political force. Ramsay MacDonald, whom Morley considered to be a parliamentarian 'of very superior quality' with 'a front-bench mind', became very friendly with Morley in his retirement and paid 'periodic visits' to his home. According to Harold Laski, 'few would have rejoiced' as Morley to see MacDonald Prime Minister, for the 'old man had talked of it so eagerly and so often'. Prompted by Haldane and MacDonald and by Morley's own willingness to come to terms with the world of Labour, other Labour leaders found their way to Morley's home at Wimbledon. Philip Snowden struck up 'an intimate acquaintance' with Morley and often visited him. On one occasion Morley asked MacDonald to bring out the miners' leader, Robert Smillie, for a talk. Smillie later told how at this meeting Morley expressed regret for having opposed eight hours legislation many years before.[5]

[1] To Minto, 16 Jan. 1906, I.O.L. MSS. Eur. D. 573/1, f. 21.
[2] W. S. Churchill, *Great Contemporaries*, 1938, p. 100.
[3] 24 Jan. 1908, I.O.L. MSS. Eur. D. 573/3, ff. 26–7.
[4] *Hansard* (Lords), 4, 1144; 6, 992.
[5] To Minto, 20 Aug. 1909, I.O.L. MSS. Eur. D. 573/4, f. 184. R. Smillie, *My Life For Labour*, 1924, pp. 261–2. Morgan, *John, Viscount Morley*, pp. 79–80. M. D.

So anxious was he now to establish contact with this new force in politics that he even tried to overcome his long-standing dislike of Socialist intellectuals. Early in 1919 he expressed a wish to see the Webbs, and Haldane brought them out to Wimbledon. Beatrice Webb was surprised. 'We have never been on terms of friendship with John Morley', she wrote. 'We have neither liked nor disliked him; and we have always assumed a similar attitude on his part.' On speaking to him, they found that he was 'pathetically anxious to make his peace with the new world of social democracy', and that he appeared to be now 'more open-minded to the new thought than he was when he had the vigour to grasp its meaning'. Beatrice Webb thought that it was the war which had 'compelled his pacifist soul to seek comradeship in the international socialist movement'. 'As Sidney said goodbye', she wrote, Morley 'said wistfully "There is no malice between us?"—as if our visit had been one of reconciliation after personal estrangement. We have been quite unconscious of any relationship—good or bad—between us and him.'[1] In 1920 Haldane introduced Harold Laski to him. He was at once very impressed by Laski,[2] and a very close friendship developed between them.

But for Morley the spirit of Labour politics could never—except, of course, for the devotion to international peace—be other than completely opposed to the spirit of Liberalism. In the *Recollections*, written at this period, he defines Liberalism as the 'pursuit of social good against class interest or dynastic interest'.[3] In the crisis over the powers of the House of Lords he had stated, his abhorrence of 'class prejudice' in politics.[4] But Labour politics were class politics and could only have the effect of making 'class prejudice' the determinant of political divisions. National unity would be endangered by such a development. In 1903 Morley had declared that he 'hated and detested the notion of setting

---

Howe (ed.), *Holmes-Laski Letters* . . . *1916–1935*, I, 1953, pp. 570, 593. Viscount Snowden, *An Autobiography*, I, 1934, pp. 143, 444–5, 505.

[1] M. I. Cole (ed.), *Beatrice Webb's Diaries 1912–1924*, 1952, p. 158.
[2] To Haldane, 28 Aug. 1920, Haldane MSS. 5914, f. 247.
[3] I, p. 21.
[4] *Hansard* (Lords), 6, 992.

Labour apart as a sort of scowling and sullen class'. Liberalism was a national creed, which 'comprehended labour and a great many things besides', both 'the best interests of the whole community, and the specified interests of labour'.[1] In 1914 he wrote that 'the resolve of the Labour men to quarrel with Liberalism, makes a bad look-out for the nation as a whole'.[2] After the war Morley was on better terms with middle-class Labour leaders than he was with working men themselves, whom he clearly still regarded as too much imbued with class feelings. In 1919, after Smillie's visit, Morley told a friend that such men reminded him of Louis Blanc, whom he had known and who 'thought of nothing but the ends of his own trade and class and never of the effect on the country'. Smillie, he complained, 'talked to me just as Louis Blanc talked to me—as if we were all coal-miners'.[3]

It seemed to Morley as if the only place where he could still find the spirit of Liberalism was within himself. After the beginning of the war he watched with horror the collapse of the world in which he had thought and worked. It was the experience of the South African War over again, but a hundred times more terrible. 'You cannot', he wrote to friends in America, 'imagine any change more extraordinary than the change in thought, feeling, interests, that has come over us here.' '*Our* world has fallen to pieces, we—elders like me at any rate—cannot reasonably hope for even a glimpse of its restoration.' He would refer to 'the frantic demoralisations' of the world around him and even confess to feeling 'half sorry that I have lived long enough to see such shipwreck'. The dark forces that menaced the light of reason with extinction now seemed overwhelming. Of Britain he wrote: 'No such storm of unreason has swept over it in my long life.' 'Life here is rather a heavy burden', he wrote in 1915. 'Political perplexities, military horrors, ruinous waste of Treasure, the desperate outlook for the European world and its civilisation, with all the ideas and material

---

[1] *The Times*, 16 Apr. 1903, p. 4, c. 2; 20 Apr. 1903, p. 7, c. 2.
[2] To Carnegie, 26 Feb. 1914.
[3] Morgan, *John, Viscount Morley*, p. 100.

means of civilisation,—make miserable companionship for day or night, and the pressure on one's fortitude is sharp.' Depressed, he withdrew inwards to endeavour to cultivate within himself some area of calmness and order. 'I practise self-command', he wrote; 'the horror of it all afflicts me at least as sorely as anybody in the world, but it is a mistake to add to all the other break-down of one's hope, the break-down of one's own vigorous self-command.'[1]

Sometimes he tried publicly to uphold Liberal values and principles. In November 1915 he spoke in the House of Lords in protest against censorship. Good government, he argued, 'demands in the foreground and in the background the support of public opinion'. Government 'must lean on public opinion, good or bad'; but 'how in the world', he asked, 'are you to get and lean upon a free, full, and correct public opinion unless the public has free, full, and correct information as to the facts on which that public opinion is founded?'[2] Thus he tried to ignore the special conditions of the war emergency and to detach from this corrupting context and maintain uncontaminated the values of a normal, Liberal England, the values of a free and open society. Seldom, however, was his desire to make this detachment apparent in public utterance. For the most part he preferred to preserve his vision of a Liberal England through withdrawal into himself away from the forces that were demolishing the reality of that England. Just as during the South African war he turned to preoccupying himself with the *Life of Gladstone,* so now he again took up literary work and, looking inwards and to the past, tried to recapture and give expression to the spirit of Victorian Liberalism. So intent was he now on detaching himself from the contemporary world that he even feared the effect of publishing his memoirs. 'I only want to end my days in quiet', he told a friend, 'and to call attention to my existence is not the way to quiet.'[3]

---

[1] To Carnegie, 13, 30 Nov. 1914, 3, 31 Dec. 1915, 2 Nov. 1916. To Mrs. Carnegie, 28 May, 29 June, 9 Nov. 1915.

[2] *Hansard* (Lords), 20, 132–3.

[3] To Bryce, 19 Aug. 1917. See also to Carnegie, 13 Nov. 1914, 3 Dec. 1915, 2 Nov. 1916; to Mrs. Carnegie, 29 June 1915.

However, he believed that he would not merely be calling attention to his own existence. He defined one of the purposes of the *Recollections* as to keep bright for 'younger readers with their lives before them' 'the lamp of loyalty to Reason'.[1]

Once more he renounced completely involvement in responsibility for a society given over to 'war fever' and the 'the exasperation of hate'. He reverted to an *'iron silence,* and resolved to 'watch the hideous struggle, as I should watch a devastating Plague or Famine—with a Stoic's fortitude'. 'Fate must run its course', he wrote; the public must be left to find out for itself 'the criminal folly' of the war.[2] His resignation in August 1914 became his justification for detachment and the rock on which he built his estimation of the continuing integrity of his Liberalism. 'I took a decisive step three years ago', he wrote in 1917, 'and if anybody cares to know what I thought of it all, that act is left to testify.' 'I cannot but rejoice', he would say, 'that I had no part or lot in the catastrophe.' His deliberate disengagement from a society given over to force and violence seemed to him to be the crowning expression of his Liberal faith. He wrote to Andrew Carnegie:

There is a story of the death of Pericles. When he lay on his couch, nearing his end, his friends gathered round, and talked to one another of the great good things that had filled his life. They did not know that he overheard. Suddenly he raised himself and said—'You miss the greatest of all. No Athenian by my means was ever made to put on the apparel of mourning'. You guess that I recall this in thinking how I exult that I never sat for an hour in a war cabinet . . .[3]

He carried to considerable lengths his effort to dissociate his political practice and free his political 'conscience' from any suggestion of involvement in the use of force. Even comparatively minor incidents when he had been thus involved in the past now returned to torment him. For example, in the letter just quoted he admitted to having once been 'responsible for a frontier war' in India but added that 'it only lasted a fortnight, and only cost £35,000'. In 1916, speaking in the House of Lords about the

[1] *Recollections*, I, p. X.
[2] To Carnegie, 28 Aug., 10 Oct., 6, 13 Nov. 1914, 12 Jan. 1915.
[3] To Mrs. Carnegie, 10 Aug. 1917, 30 July 1915. To Carnegie, 6 Mar. 1916.

unrest in Ireland, he asked if the best course might not be to 'let things come to a still graver head' rather than employ 'severe, drastic, repressive measures'. He referred to an occasion when he himself had sanctioned the use of force, and he tried by recanting to expunge it from his conscience:

I look back upon one action in my experience . . . I refer to riotous proceedings which went on day after day in the city of Belfast in the year 1886. . . . I wondered then, and I wonder now, looking back upon it after all these years, whether it would not have been wiser to tolerate a great deal of violence and lawlessness in Belfast in 1886 than to have taken the severe proceedings that we felt ourselves obliged to take.[1]

In 1921 he reappeared in the Lords to speak of the 'ugly failure' of the renewed coercion in Ireland and to declare that only through ending this resort to force could Britain again have 'a good conscience'.[2]

Those who visited Morley in his last years carried away the impression of a man struggling in his seclusion to cherish and preserve the values and principles of a lifetime, to create within himself, within his own personal corner of existence, a microcosm of the order that could not be found outside. In the *Recollections* appear some thoughts set down in the 'falling daylight' of his life on the philosophy of Marcus Aurelius, 'the saint of Agnosticism': 'With patient and penetrating gaze he watches the recurrent motions of the universe, not sure whether it is all entanglement, confusion, dispersion; or is it unity, order, providence? Is it a well-arranged cosmos, or chaos? . . . His moral stands good in either case. If all is random, be not random thou. . . .'[3] After 1914, when all outside was 'random' and chaotic, Morley seemed to be applying this 'moral' to his own existence and respecting the 'commanding principle' which he had once praised Rousseau for never forgetting, 'that a man's life ought to be steadily composed to oneness with itself in all its parts'.[4] In January 1915 Lord Esher

[1] *Hansard* (Lords), 21, 831.
[2] Ibid., 48, 6–8.
[3] II, pp. 363–4.
[4] *Rousseau*, I, pp. 207–8. *F.R.*, Nov. 1872, p. 580.

visited him at Wimbledon and found him 'an impressive figure; uncompromising in his adherence to lifelong principles of political conduct; firm in the faith of that Cobden school of political thought of which he is at once the historian and the sole relic'.[1] On his first visit to Morley, in 1920, Laski too noted that 'the pure milk of the Cobdenite word remains pure even in the midst of changes'. The devotion to reason remained equally pure. 'Would it not have been better for the world', he would say to friends, 'if Rousseau had never been born?' Voltaire, on the other hand, was 'the type of man this generation most needed'. No epitaph on his career would therefore have pleased him more than Laski's observation after his death that 'the lamp of reason burned the more brightly for his presence'.[2]

[1] Esher, *Journals and Letters of Viscount Esher*, III, p. 204.
[2] Howe, *Holmes-Laski Letters*, I, pp. 278, 349, 438, 542. H. J. Massingham (ed.), *H.W.M. A Selection From the Writings of H. W. Massingham*, 1925, p. 24.

CONCLUSION

IN spite of the prominent position which Morley attained during his lengthy political career, his record is not one of substantial practical achievement. In part, the reasons for this can be found in the particular political circumstances of the time. His opportunities for positive political work were admittedly limited, since his party was out of office for all but seven of his first twenty-three years as an M.P. and what should have been his most mature and productive years as a politician were therefore spent largely on the Opposition benches. His first two terms in office were devoted almost exclusively to Irish affairs and the home-rule policy, but the dissentient Liberals and the House of Lords between them ensured that very little of what he then tried to achieve passed on to the statute book. The Indian reforms seemed to be his most substantial accomplishment, but the intention that they would be only a first, very cautious step on a long, gradual process towards some very limited form of self-government was soon swept away by the pressure of events.[1] It is in regard to domestic affairs that the barrenness of his record is most obvious, however; and here the reasons are also clearly in part subjective. In the first place, we have seen how a diversion from domestic policies was frequently welcomed and fostered. Secondly, it must be recognized that, if the Liberals spent so much of this period out of office, that was where many of them, including Morley, often wanted to be. We have noted the recurring desire to seek purge and reconstruction of the party through defeat or schism and the constant fear of the consequences of the pursuit of electoral success.

In 1919 Balfour summed up Morley's career by saying: 'His fault in politics is that he's too negative.'[2] Indeed, much of his

---

[1] Cf. Morley's criticism of the Montagu-Chelmsford reforms in 1921: 'My reforms were quite enough for a generation at least.' J. H. Morgan, *John, Viscount Morley An Appreciation and Some Reminiscences*, 1924, p. 21.

[2] Ibid., p. 102.

activity can be most aptly described in terms of negativism or opposition—anti-coercion, anti-intervention, anti-imperialism, opposition to social legislation and to tariff reform. His were the politics of Liberalism fighting a rearguard action, the politics of resistance to positive policies as they were initiated or demanded by other people. His career became increasingly characterized by defensiveness. He himself in his writings on politics had shown an awareness of the difficulties of a practical politician who has to react to events and demands and 'emergencies' as they arise without the guidance of any general, comprehensive system of principles. Having failed to find such a system relevant to the conditions of the late nineteenth century, he tried at least to make something systematic out of the 'emergencies'. Each would be fitted into a pattern as an 'obstruction' to what he alleged would otherwise be orderly progress. The Irish question is the outstanding example of how in his politics confusion and negativism in the area of domestic policy could be obscured by the theory of the obstruction to progress.

To what extent are Morley's weaknesses as a practical politician attributable to his being an 'intellectual in politics'? Undoubtedly one significant point is that he was an intellectual first, and then a politician. In other words, the division between these two aspects of his career is virtually a chronological division. He came into politics in early middle age after his basic ideas had been formed. His intellectual development was not determined to any important degree by involvement in political practice. There was no really effective interplay between ideas and practice, perhaps because he had embarked so late on a political career. Obsessed by the need to be consistent and to adhere to principles which he had already worked out and established, he lacked flexibility in his response to the circumstances which he encountered as a politician. What the chronological division meant was that he was a mid-Victorian Liberal intellectual in late Victorian politics, and much about his political career is explicable if we think of him as working in one period with ideas derived from another. In the 1860s he made much of the necessity of having a mind open to 'new ideas', but his own thinking appears to have been little

CONCLUSION 379

affected by the new ideas that were coming up in the 1880s and 1890s, especially those which concerned the responsibilities of the State with regard to social welfare. H. J. Laski once described thus what he considered had gone wrong in Morley's career: 'he was content to stop at J. S. Mill and not reexamine his foundations once he had reached middle age. But all the great events of his life happened after he had reached that post.'[1]

Morley adhered to what might be called a classic Liberalism. It was very strongly individualistic, and it put most emphasis on the extension of a freedom defined in the classic sense: free trade, 'free land', free education, freedom from privilege and artificial restrictions. These were the principles that guided him in an age of greater emphasis on society, greater concern with social problems, and new understandings of social limitations on individual freedom. It is not surprising, therefore, that as a politician Morley often seemed bewildered and unsure of himself.

One paralysing factor was his inheritance from the previous age of a very limited conception of what a politician can and ought to do. He professed himself 'cool and sceptical about *political* change',[2] preferring to rely on change by 'natural' processes, which would be organic, not imposed, and in which he believed there to be inherent the principle of progress. He believed that the 'very nature of things' imposes strict limits on the extent to which legislation can achieve what its authors intend it to achieve, since the artificial must always struggle in vain against such overwhelming natural forces as habit and tradition and organic social growths and the limits of pliancy in the condition of human nature.[3] His pessimism about his Indian reforms and about the future of the 'intensely artificial and unnatural' British government of India is an excellent example of this attitude. His view of legislation was often either that it went in advance of opinion and would therefore prove 'impotent' or that it was 'superfluous' and unnecessary because it reflected an already existent opinion which could be left to work its own change organically within the natural

---

[1] M. D. Howe (ed.), *Holmes–Laski Letters 1916–1935*, I, 1953, p. 751.
[2] To Lord Minto, 26 Mar. 1908, I.O.L. MSS. Eur. D. 573/3, ff. 83–4.
[3] Cf. *Studies in Literature*, p. 76; *Rousseau*, II, pp. 125–6.

processes of community life.¹ One of his most profound beliefs was that legislative action is an interference with nature and is therefore to be avoided if at all possible. He himself was handicapped as a politician by his perpetual indecision and fear of commitment to a course of action, and he became obsessed with devices that had the effect of impeding and delaying action—the 'polity of discussion', and the obstructions to progress which he so often represented himself as working to overcome.

Morley's greatest distrust and antagonism were always reserved for those who wished to impose change rather than to encourage an organic evolution. He especially disliked impatience. Early in his career he opposed system-mongers, such as the positivists, who refused to 'abide in patient contentment' with 'an uncompleted interpretation of existence', 'leaving reconstruction, its form, its modes, its epoch, for the fulness of time and maturity of effort to disclose', and insisted on 'a hasty supplement of unconcluded analysis' by artificially constructed systems.² Later he became the antagonist of politicians, such as Chamberlain and the Socialists, who wished to use the power of the State to accelerate and direct social and economic changes of a particular, preconceived kind. There was 'no short cut in life', he once remarked. 'It was useless', he said, 'to attempt "sudden reformation" or "reformatory rebellion". There was no such thing as progress "by force, or book, or candle".'³

Morley's understanding of the means and instruments necessary for a determined course of constructive political action was quite inadequate. His political thinking remained basically concerned with the individual, and social and institutional considerations never attained much prominence in it. He himself, as we have seen, was very much aware of the advantage for a politician of possessing systematic principles for guidance in political conduct and he often complained of the absence of 'system' in contemporary politics. Under Mill's influence, he came to realize that the only kind of system which he would find satisfactory would be

[1] Cf. *F.R.*, May 1879, p. 663.
[2] *Voltaire*, p. 38.
[3] A. Harrison, *Frederic Harrison. Thoughts and Memories*, 1926, p. 177.

CONCLUSION 381

one which had developed organically out of a state of intellectual 'liberty', out of the free play of opinion and reason. But such a system did not emerge, and Morley was left, like Byron, without 'practical strength', because he was 'conscious of gaps and cataclysms in the structure of his belief'.[1] In order to have firmness and coherence in his political action he had recourse to those provisional substitutes for system, the single great questions, with which this study has been so much concerned.

At the very heart of Morley's thinking lay the principle of allowing free scope for 'natural' and 'organic' development. For all that he was so strong an individualist and so determined an advocate of the supremacy of reason, he was never able to follow out these beliefs into a creed based on the idea of the aloneness of man and his reason. He could not shake off the effects of the mid-Victorian intellectual crisis within which his early intellectual development took place, in particular the assumption that what was occurring was a transition from one religion to another. His belief in progress, natural evolution, and the emergence of order out of a 'free play of forces' was, as he later admitted, virtually a religious belief. And it had inhibiting consequences for his own political activity. Towards the end of his career he came to recognize that, as a 'superstition' or 'kind of fatalism', 'faith in Progress' had had a harmful effect both on 'the effective sense of individual responsibility' and on 'the successful working of principles and institutions of which that responsibility is the vital step'.[2] The essence of Morley's Liberalism had been 'individual responsibility', but what weakened it and made it less and less relevant to the conditions of his own day was his inability because of his faith in natural improvement to extend it into the acceptance by the individual of responsibility as a voter in a democratic political system for the welfare of his fellow men. For to have advocated legislative action and State intervention in social and economic affairs to a more positive degree than the 'setting free' on which classic Liberalism was based would have been to admit far more than Morley was ever prepared to admit, namely that progress and

[1] *F.R.*, Dec. 1870, p. 665.
[2] *Miscellanies Fourth Series*, p. 293. Cf. above, p. 47.

improvement in human affairs depend on man and on man alone.

Morley wanted to believe that in history and in change there was some pattern such as a religion traces, and therefore he clung to his belief in natural development. We have seen, for example, how he tried to preserve a sense of order and progress in change by reacting to particular political phenomena or situations as if they involved 'obstructions'. Thus the solving of the Irish question was presented as the key that would unlock the door to certain progress.

He did not, of course, believe in any abstract or primitive 'Nature', such as that from which the French revolutionaries—and Joseph Chamberlain—claimed to be able to derive certain human 'rights'. Nor was his 'natural' development Social Darwinism, for he very much disliked the application to human affairs of speculations in physical science.[1] It was rather a Comtist process, governed by 'stages' and expressed in laws, customs, and institutions, which evolved to fit the changes in man's ideas about the world. 'Only "stages" mattered,' he once said; 'it was idle to be in advance of one's time.'[2] The desire to discover what was 'organic' change in his own day was obviously a major source of the emphasis which he placed on continuity with the past. Wanting to believe that lines of development and improvement did run through human affairs, but lacking a system that would explain to him where those lines were leading in present and future, he tended to look to the only phase of human activity about which he could feel that he possessed some certain knowledge and to judge the present in terms of the past. In default of any other understanding, the lines of the past were made to do service as the lines of the present and future as well. We have seen what effect this had on his political thinking. The past increasingly overlaid the reality of the present, which he found himself unable to understand in its own terms and about which he grew bewildered and frightened.

For Morley the great problem was that change had occurred so rapidly in recent times that discontinuity between present and past was everywhere apparent and new ways of looking at human

[1] Cf. above, p. 10.
[2] Harrison, *Frederic Harrison*, p. 177.

affairs were constantly being demanded. As Morley recognized, the formulation of ideas and principles for guidance in political practice was falling farther and farther behind social, economic, and political changes. We can see his awareness of this in his association of nostalgia for the Benthamites' systematization of thought and practice with the admission that their system was not relevant to the problems of his own day. He showed himself also very sensitive to alterations in concepts of morality, stemming, in particular, from the impact of Darwinism and Socialist thought. He saw that 'the Darwinism hypothesis and the mass of evidence for it' had 'given a tremendous shake' to established ideas about 'right and wrong'.[1] In 1896 he observed that, whereas to writers such as W. E. H. Lecky 'the sense of right and wrong' was 'the basis of respect for property and for the obligation of contract', Socialists were now appealing to a very different 'sense of right and wrong' which, 'so far from being the root of respect for property, is hostile to it, and is at this moment shaking it to its foundation all over the modern world'.[2] Another example of his awareness of discontinuity and of changes in fundamentals in his disillusionment with the results of great Liberal reforms. In 1891 he described a change of mood which he had noticed in his generation:

They have ceased either to trust or to distrust liberty, and have come to the mind that it matters little either way. Men are disenchanted. They have got what they wanted in the days of their youth, yet what of it, they ask? France has thrown off the Empire, but the statesmen of the republic are not a great breed. Italy has gained her unity, yet unity has not been followed by thrift, wisdom, or large increase of public virtue or happiness. America has purged herself of slavery, yet life in America is material, prosaic. . . .[3]

But even quite early in his career he sensed the existence of such a disenchantment. In *On Compromise*[4] he remarked that over the previous forty years the enthusiasm of Englishmen for such

[1] *F.R.*, Aug. 1877, p. 271.
[2] *Miscellanies Fourth Series*, pp. 212–13.
[3] *Gladstone*, III, p. 475.
[4] p. 14.

principles as nationalism, anti-slavery, and parliamentary reform had declined because the results of the putting into practice of these principles had been 'so disappointing as to make us wonder whether it is really worth while to pray, when to have our prayers granted carries the world so very slight a way forward'. 'The old aspirations have vanished, and no new ones have arisen in their place', he wrote. In other words, new theories, new principles, new systems of analysis and interpretation, were needed to enable men to understand and act in the very strange and different world that had developed after the advent of 'liberty'; but men who had expected continuity of mood and spirit were bewildered and disillusioned.

Morley was not an original political thinker, but his thinking is well worth studying in so far as it does involve the interaction of several major schools of thought and does also provide the basis for a substantial practical career. Burke was obviously one of the principal sources of Morley's respect for 'organic growth' in society. His concern with the past contained more than an element of Burkean conservatism. When a friend once taxed him with having departed from the ways of his 'vigorous revolutionary youth', he declared, in order to give proof of consistency: 'The man whose first literary task and first success was a glorification of Burke can never have been at heart a revolutionary champion.'[1] But his interest in social development owed much also to Comte. His loss of faith in the Comtist system greatly weakened, however, that one aspect of his thought which did offer a theory about society as a guide for action in present and future. Burke offered no system and no guidance for the practice of a would-be progressive politician (except, perhaps, in respect of anti-imperialism). Morley did not even attempt to develop the tendencies in Mill's thinking discernible in the 'Essays on Socialism'. His individualism, which had, of course, begun by being predominantly Millite, as in 'New Ideas' and *On Compromise*, moved away from Mill's influence after the early 1870s and became Cobdenite when involved in economic and social questions.

[1] To Carnegie, 9 Oct. 1909.

Morley never succeeded in fusing into a comprehensive synthesis of his own the diverse intellectual influences to which he was subjected. But it was never, in fact, his aim to achieve this. For him order in thought could come only through relating ideas to practical conditions and testing them in action, not through relating them to one another and constructing a harmonious arrangement of them in isolation.

In practical politics Morley's greatest positive contribution lay in the examples which he gave of ways of approaching and thinking about political problems. Here the influences were both Burkean and rationalist—Burkean in that his respect for 'organic' social development made him especially sensitive to the effects of alien domination of Ireland and India and the empire; and rationalist in that his cool, unemotional manner of writing and arguing about Ireland and India probably in the end had a more substantial effect, in helping to change the climate of opinion, than the actual policy proposals which he made. At the end of his career he himself saw his achievement in this way. He spoke of the 'disappearance of that horrible prejudice and superstition' that had been so prevalent before 1886, 'namely, that the Irish had nothing human about them but the form', and declared: 'I often think for my own part that, though all the effort that has been expended over Home Rule in all these years were to come to naught, even supposing Home Rule does break down, the toil and labour of the noble spirit by which it was started in 1886 would have been well worth undertaking for the sake of this reward.'[1]

[1] Hansard (Lords), 16, 531–2 (1 July 1914).

APPENDIX

Entries in Morley's Commonplace Book

Morley's entire library was bequeathed by him to the University of Manchester and is now housed at Ashburne Hall, Fallowfield. Included in the library is a commonplace book in which Morley entered under various headings quotations from books and notes and references which he felt might be useful to him in his own literary work. I append below a selection of Morley's notes on themes which are relevant to various discussions in this book. These are referred to in square brackets.

1. *'Decentralisation'* (from pages 89–90)
    'It is not wonderful nor discreditable that persons who are dissatisfied with the conditions of political life at present, cry for a return to the solid and organic life of old society, based on the spirit of religion, the spirit of the family, of the trade guild, of the municipality. They are quite right in thinking the suffrage too weak a bond between public and private interests. But it is impossible to return to the past, because industrial conditions are wholly changed, and with them the conditions of the family have changed also: the religious conditions are transformed &c. Burke believed rashly that the old order cd. be preserved, tho' its bases were gone: Comte believed rashly that the old order cd. be restored with the old bases transformed: Mill thought that a new and better order wd. gradually arise, in course of experiment, on condition of leaving individuals free.' [cf. above p. 29]
    'The towns have grown large, and unmanageable; their size, e.g. London, indisposes people to take a part in a business where the individual is so small a fraction of the effective power'. [p. 249]
    'Minority representat[n]. an excuse for fastidious indolence: a

dilettante way for getting an ineffectual *hearing* for opinions, wh. it ought to be your object to persuade the majority not only to hear but to *realise*—and you ought to be content with nothing less.'

'Relations of Disestablishm^t. to decentralisat^n. of the state—as well as its secularisat^n.'

2. *Decision-making* (from page 155—no heading in the book)
'While cultivating a balanced habit of mind—a disposition to hearken to both sets of arguments—don't forget that you have to decide—and that the decision is at last the most important part of the matter.'
'Danger of Mill's temper in this respect.' [cf. above. p. 30]

3. '*England*' (from page 100)
'England. Two peculiar difficulties.
   1. An industrial society, yet with a purely military empire in the east.
   2. Obliged to watch foreign affairs, and yet compelled to non-intervention, (a.) by the excitable and various temper of her people, wh. cannot be trusted, and (b.) by the publicity of the parliamentary system, and the peculiar conditions of parliamentary control.'

4. '*History*' (from page 54)
'No political history ought to be written, and no good one has bn. written, by a man who has not been either himself a participator in practical politics, whether the politics of government or of agitation, or else the habitual intimate of men who were engaged in this active participation (as Hallam, for instance.)' [cf. above p. 126]

5. '*J. S. Mill*' (from page 60)
'It is worthy of remark that in the only institution with whose working he was practically connected, J. S. Mill was distinctly and emphatically conservative—the East India Company.' [cf. above, p. 49]

6. *'Literature'* (from page 47)
    '. . . The balance has to be struck between the service of literature in disciplining and fertilising the intellect, and its disservice in blunting and enervating the readiness of the practical energies.'

7. *'Parliamentary Reform'* (from page 76)
    'Evils in sight:—Mere local popularity, limiting the area of possible candidates. [cf. above, p. 125]
    Power of the publicans over the newly admitted voters.'
    And opposite this:—'Explain the fact that tho' power is ultimately and theoretically in the hands of the popular party, yet it constantly finds its way in practice to the Conservative party.'

8. *'Political Progress'* (from page 82)
    'The state represents physical force together with moral authority. That state is most civilised where moral authority is most potent, and physical force least required.'

9. *'Political Religionists'* (from page 88)
    'If ever you meet a man who insists with special vehemence on the necessity of religion for keeping society together, you may be sure in nine cases out of ten that he is one of those who does his best to pull society to pieces by his rapacity for anti-social acquisitions (speculation &c.) and the extent of his anti-social expenditure.'

10. *'Positivism'* (from page 111)
    'The present condition of English society offers all the signs that precede a strong moral and spiritual reaction against luxury, materialism, and secularity. The spiritual and devout element in humanity will inevitably raise its voice, as it did in Florence by Savonarola.
    'Will this inevitable uprising be kindled by Positivism or the Religion of Humanity, even supposing that doctrine one day to produce a man of apostolical genius?

'No; it will spring from the old source, this time and perhaps the next and the next. Positivism has no *book*, rich, noble, and eloquent with the spiritual outpourings of eastern fervour and imagination. It has no history of martyrs and high examples. Above all, it is not ascetic. We want a new manner of life, as well as a new teaching and preaching. Comtism is not ascetic, but indulgent, casuistic, and politic. It does not strike the imaginat^n. enough to catch any of the vast mass of indifferents who can only be seized by the external.'

11. '*Progress*' (from page 144)
'It is all important that a young man sh^d. start life with a general faith in the principle of social improvement; he may decline in the energy of his faith, as the years wear out the edge of his mind. But if a man starts with a predisposition to regard improvement as moonshine, there is no limit to the hold wh. stupidity and obstruct^n. may get upon him'.

12. '*Shortness of Life*' (from page 42)
'The worst of all the evils connected with the short duration of human life is the impatience and hurry wh. it breeds in some of the noblest and most ardent minds. The mischief of this is visible when we reflect that for the consummation of all great improvements the lapse of many scores of years is often necessary, after the propriety of the improvement has once occurred to the more enlightened spirits.'
This is ticked in a different ink, and Morley has written at the foot:
'Yes, indeed—
Circumspice.—1887.' [An obvious reference to Chamberlain's behaviour—cf. above. p. 157]

SELECT BIBLIOGRAPHY

The material is arranged as follows:

- A. Manuscript collections.
- B. Official papers.
- C. Newspapers and periodicals.
- D. Works by Morley.
- E. Books and articles on Morley.
- F. Memoirs, diaries, biographies, collections of letters, and other sources in which primary material is to be found.
- G. Secondary works on the intellectual, literary, and political background.

A. *Manuscript collections.* (Figures in brackets indicate the location of correspondence with Morley)

Letters written by and to Morley can be found in numerous collections. Those listed here are the more important such collections as far as the study of Morley's career is concerned.

Asquith Papers in the Bodleian Library, Oxford. (Deposits 9 to 13)
Balfour Papers in the British Museum. (B.M. Add. MSS. 49778)
Bryce Papers in the Bodleian Library, Oxford.
Burns (John) Papers in the British Museum. (B.M. Add. MSS. 46283)
Campbell-Bannerman Papers in the British Museum. (B.M. Add. MSS. 41223)
Carnegie (Andrew) Papers in the Library of Congress, Washington. Micro-films of letters from Morley to Carnegie in the Bodleian Library, Oxford.
Chamberlain (Joseph) Papers in the Birmingham University Library.
Congreve (Richard) Papers—the Positivist Archive—in the British Museum. (B.M. Add. MSS. 45241)
Dilke Papers in the British Museum. (B.M. Add. MSS. 43895)
Fisher (H. A. L.) Papers in the Bodleian Library, Oxford. (Boxes 2 and 3)
Gladstone (Mary) Papers in the British Museum. (B.M. Add. MSS. 46226 and 46240)

SELECT BIBLIOGRAPHY 391

Gladstone (Viscount) Papers in the British Museum. (B.M. Add. MSS. 46019)
Gladstone (W. E.) Papers in the British Museum. (B.M. Add. MSS. 44255-7)
Haldane Papers in the National Library of Scotland, Edinburgh. (MSS. 5903-17)
Hamilton (Sir E. W.) Papers in the British Museum. (B.M. Add. MSS. 48619)
Harcourt Papers at Stanton Harcourt, Oxfordshire. In the private possession of Viscount Harcourt.
Harrison (Frederic) Papers in the British Library of Political and Economic Science, L.S.E., London.
Huxley (T. H.) Papers in the Library of the Imperial College of Science and Technology, London. (General Correspondence, Vol. 23)
Mill (John Stuart) Papers in the British Library of Political and Economic Science, L.S.E., London. (Vols. 2 and 5)
Morley Papers in the India Office Library. (MSS. Eur. D. 573/1-43)
Ripon Papers in the British Museum. (B.M. MSS. 43541)
Rosebery Papers in the National Library of Scotland, Edinburgh.
Spencer Papers at Althorp, Northamptonshire. In the private possession of Earl Spencer.
Spender (J. A.) Papers in the British Museum. (B.M. Add. MSS. 46391)

B. *Official papers*
Hansard's Parliamentary Debates, *Third and Fourth Series, and House of Lords*.

C. *Newspapers and periodicals*
a. Newspapers
Newcastle Daily Chronicle
Pall Mall Gazette
The Times

b. Periodicals
The Fortnightly Review. The more important articles written by Morley for the *Fortnightly* between 1866 and 1882 are as follows:

'England and the Annexation of Mysore', Old Series, No. 33, 15 Sept. 1866.
'France in the Seventeenth Century' (a review of *France Under Richelieu and Colbert* by J. H. Bridges), New Series, No 1, Jan. 1867.

'Edmund Burke', Part I, 2,* Feb. 1867.
'Edmund Burke', Part II, 3, Mar. 1867.
'Edmund Burke', Part III, 4, Apr. 1867.
'Young England and the Political Future' (a review of *Essays on Reform*), 4, Apr. 1867.
'England and the European Crisis', 5, May 1867.
'Edmund Burke', Part IV, 7, July 1867.
Review of *Dissertations and Discussions* by J. S. Mill, vol. III, 7, July 1867.
'Mr. Froude on the Science of History', 8, Aug. 1867.
'Anonymous Journalism', 9, Sept. 1867.
'The Liberal Programme', 9, Sept. 1867.
Review of *Three English Statesmen* by Goldwin Smith, 9, Sept. 1867.
'A Fragment on the Genesis of Morals', 15, Mar. 1868.
'Joseph de Maistre', I, 17, May 1868.
'Joseph de Maistre', II, 18, June 1868.
'The Political Prelude', 19, July 1868.
'Old Parties and New Policy', 21, Sept. 1868.
'Joseph de Maistre', III, 22, Oct. 1868.
'The Chamber of Mediocrity', 24, Dec. 1868.
'Mr. Lecky's First Chapter', 29, May 1869.
'Condorcet', Part I, 37, Jan. 1870.
'Condorcet', Part II, 38, Feb. 1870.
'A Short Letter to Some Ladies', 39, Mar. 1870.
'Vauvenargues', 40, Apr. 1870.
'Carlyle', 43, July 1870.
'The Fortnightly Review and Positivism: A Note', 43, July 1870.
'The Life of Turgot', 44, Aug. 1870.
'France and Germany', 45, Sept. 1870.
'England and the War', 46, Oct. 1870.
'A Note to Colonel Chesney's Letter', 47, Nov. 1870.
'Byron', 48, Dec. 1870.
'Turgot's Two Discourses at the Sorbonne', 57, Sept. 1871.
'Voltaire at Berlin. A Chapter from a Forthcoming Monograph', 58, Oct. 1871.
'Irish Policy in the Eighteenth Century', 62, Feb. 1872.
'Rousseau's Influence on European Thought', 65, May 1872.
'Rousseau at Les Charmettes. A Chapter from a Forthcoming Monograph', 69, Sept. 1872.

SELECT BIBLIOGRAPHY

'Rousseau and Theresa de Vasseur', 70, Oct. 1872.
'Rousseau in Paris (1744–56)', 71, Nov. 1872.
'The New Heloïsa', 72, Dec. 1872.
'The Five Gas-Stokers', 73, Jan. 1873.
'Mr. Pater's Essays' (a review of *Studies in the History of the Renaissance* by W. H. Pater), 76, Apr. 1873.
'The Death of Mr. Mill', 78, June 1873.
'The Struggle for National Education', I, 80, Aug. 1873.
'Mr. Mill's Doctrine of Liberty', 80, Aug. 1873.
'The Struggle for National Education', II, 81, Sept. 1873.
'The Struggle for National Education', III, 82, Oct. 1873.
'Mr. Mill's Autobiography', 85, Jan. 1874.
'M. Victor Hugo's New Romance', 87, Mar. 1874.
'On Compromise', I, 88, Apr. 1874.
'On Compromise', II, 90, June 1874.
'On Compromise', III, 91, July 1874.
'On Compromise', Conclusion, 92, Aug. 1874.
'Mr. Flint's Philosophy of History', 93, Sept. 1874.
'A Recent Work on Supernatural Religion' (a review of *Supernatural Religion: an Inquiry into the Reality of Divine Revelation*), 94, Oct. 1874.
'Mr. Mill's Three Essays on Religion', 95, Nov. 1874.
'Mr. Mill's Three Essays on Religion', 97, Jan. 1875.
'Diderot', I, 98, Feb. 1875.
'The Liberal Eclipse', 98, Feb. 1875.
'Diderot', II, 100, Apr. 1875.
'Diderot', III, 101, May 1875.
'A Day at Sedan', 102, June 1875.
'Diderot', IV, 105, Sept. 1875.
'Diderot', V, 107, Nov. 1875.
'M. Taine's New Work', 111, Mar. 1876.
'Macaulay', 112, Apr. 1876.
'Some Recent Travels', 113, May 1876.
'Robespierre', I, 116, Aug. 1876.
'Robespierre', II, 117, Sept. 1876.
'On Popular Culture: An Address', 119, Nov. 1876.
'A New Work on Russia' (a review of *Russia* by D. Mackenzie Wallace), 122, Feb. 1877.
'An Address to Some Miners', 123, Mar. 1877.
'Turgot in Limousin', 125, May 1877.

'Three Books of the Eighteenth Century. I. Holbach's System of Nature', 128, Aug. 1877.
'Three Books of the Eighteenth Century. II. Raynal's History of the Indies', 131, Nov. 1877.
'Memorials of a Man of Letters', 136, Apr. 1878.
'Diderot at St. Petersburg', 137, May 1878.
'Lancashire', 139, July 1878.
'A Political Epilogue', 141, Sept. 1878.
'An Economic Address: With Some Notes', 142, Oct. 1878.
'The Impoverishment of India Not Proven', 144, Dec. 1878.
'The Plain Story of the Zulu War', 147, Mar. 1879.
'Further Remarks on Zulu Affairs', 148, Apr. 1879.
'The French Republic and the Catholic Church', 149, May 1879.
'The House of Commons', 152, Aug. 1879.
'A Word with some Critics', 154, Oct. 1879.
'A Note on the Preceding Article' ('The England of To-day' by H. D. Traill), 157, Jan. 1880.
'England and Ireland', 172, Apr. 1881.
'Cobden's First Pamphlets', 173, May 1881.
'On the Policy of Commercial Treaties', 174, June 1881.
'Conciliation with Ireland', 175, July 1881.
'The Journals of Caroline Fox', 181, Jan. 1882.
'The Life of James Mill', 184, Apr. 1882.
'Egyptian Policy: A Retrospect', 187, July 1882.
'Valedictory', 190, Oct. 1882.

* All numbers given henceforth are in the New Series.

The Liberator.

Macmillan's Magazine. Articles by Morley which appeared in this journal include:
'W. R. Greg: A Sketch', Vol. XLVIII, June 1883.
'The Expansion of England', Vol. XLIX, Feb. 1884.
'The Life of George Eliot', Vol. LI, Feb. 1885.
'On Pattison's Memoirs', Vol. LI, Apr. 1885.

The Nineteenth Century. Articles by Morley include:
'Irish Revolution and English Liberalism', Nov. 1882.
'A New Calendar of Great Men', Feb. 1892.
'Matthew Arnold', Dec. 1895.
'Lecky on Democracy' (a review of *Democracy and Liberty* by W. E. H. Lecky), May 1896.

SELECT BIBLIOGRAPHY 395

'Arbitration with America', Aug. 1896.
'Guicciardini', Nov. 1897.
'Mr. Harrison's Historical Romance', Oct. 1904.
'British Democracy and Indian Government', Feb. 1911.

D. *Works by Morley*

All were published in London. The edition referred to is the one quoted from in this book.

Burke, 1879 (in the 'English Men of Letters' series).
Critical Miscellanies, 3 vols., 1886 (Vols. I and II first published in 1877).
Vol. I includes 'Robespierre', 'Carlyle', 'Byron', and 'Macaulay', all reprinted from the *Fortnightly Review*, and also an essay on 'Emerson'.
Vol. II includes 'Vauvenargues', 'Turgot', 'Condorcet', and 'Joseph de Maistre', also all from the *Fortnightly Review*.
Vol. III includes 'On Popular Culture', 'The Death of Mr. Mill', 'Mr. Mill's Autobiography', and 'France in the Eighteenth Century' from the *Fortnightly Review*, 'The Life of George Eliot', 'On Pattison's Memoirs', 'W. R. Greg: A Sketch', and 'The Expansion of England' from *Macmillan's Magazine*, 'Auguste Comte' from an article written by Morley for the *Encyclopaedia Britannica*, and 'Harriet Martineau'.
Diderot and the Encyclopaedists, 2 vols., 1878.
Edmund Burke: A Historical Study. 1867.
Indian Speeches (1907–1909), 1909.
The Life of Richard Cobden, 2 vols., 1881.
The Life of William Ewart Gladstone, 3 vols., 1903.
Memorandum on Resignation. August 1914, 1928.
Miscellanies Fourth Series, 1908.
This includes 'Machiavelli', 'Guicciardini', 'A New Calendar of Great Men', 'John Stuart Mill: An Anniversary', 'Lecky on Democracy', 'A Historical Romance', and 'Democracy and Reaction'.
Modern Characteristics. A Serious of Short Essays from the Saturday Review, published anonymously, 1865.
Notes on Politics and History: A University Address, 1913.
Oliver Cromwell, 2nd ed., 1904 (1st ed. was published in 1900).
On Compromise, 1874.
Politics and History, 1921 (in the de luxe edition of Morley's works).

Recollections, 2 vols., 1917.
Rousseau, 1st ed., 2 vols., 1873., 2nd ed., 2 vols., 1886.
The Struggle for National Education, 1873.
Studies in Conduct. Short essays from the 'Saturday Review', published anonymously, 1867 (attributed to Morley in the British Museum printed catalogue).
Studies in Literature, 1891.
   This includes 'Wordsworth', 'Aphorisms', 'Maine on Popular Government', 'A Few Words on French Models', 'On the Study of Literature', 'Victor Hugo's *Ninety-Three*', 'On *The Ring and The Book*', 'Memorials of a Man of Letters', and 'Valedictory'.
Voltaire, 1872.
Walpole, 1889.

E. *Books and articles on Morley* (Place of publication London unless otherwise indicated)

Ausubel, H., and others	*Some Modern Historians of Britain*, New York, 1951 (includes an essay on Morley).
Braybrooke, P.	*Lord Morley. Writer and Thinker* [1924].
Gardiner, A. G.	*Prophets, Priests and Kings*, 1908 (includes an essay on Morley).
Harper, G. M.	*John Morley and Other Essays*, Princeton, New Jersey, and London, 1920.
Hirst, F. W.	Article on Morley in the *Dictionary of National Biography, 1922–1930*.
	Early Life and Letters of John Morley, 2 vols., 1927.
Knickerbocker, F. W.	*Free Minds John Morley and his Friends*, Cambridge, Mass., 1943.
Koss, S. E.	'Morley in the Middle', *English Historical Review*, Vol. 82, No. 324, July 1967.
Massingham, H. J. (ed.)	*H. W. M. A Selection from the Writing of H. W. Massingham*, 1925 (includes an essay on 'Morley the Humanist').
Minto, Mary, Countess of	*India Minto and Morley 1905–1910 Compiled from the Correspondence Between the Viceroy and the Secretary of State with Extracts from her Indian Journal*, 1934.
Morgan, J. H.	*John, Viscount Morley. An Appreciation and Some Reminiscences*, 1924.

Morison, J. L.	*John Morley: A Study in Victorianism*, Kingston, Ontario, 1920.
Scott, J. W. Robertson	*The Life and Death of a Newspaper. An Account of the Temperaments, Perturbations and Achievements of John Morley, W. T. Stead, E. T. Cook, Harry Cust, J. L. Garvin and three other Editors of the Pall Mall Gazette* . . . , 1952.
Sirdar, Ali Khan Sayed	*Life of Lord Morley*, 1923.
Staebler, W.	*The Liberal Mind of John Morley*, Princeton, 1943.
Willey, B.	*More Nineteenth-Century Studies: A Group of Honest Doubters*, 1956 (includes an essay on Morley).
Wolpert, S. A.	*Morley and India 1906–1910*, Berkeley and Los Angeles, 1967.

Numerous articles on Morley were written by his contemporaries, mostly at the time of his death. There is a useful list of these in Wolpert's bibliography.

F. *Memoirs, biographies, diaries, collections of letters, and other printed sources in which is to be found material of a primary nature relating to Morley, e.g. letters written by or to him, recollections of him, references to him in diaries or memoranda (Place of publication London unless otherwise stated)*

[Aberdare, Lord]	*Letters of the Rt. Hon. Henry Austin Bruce G.C.B. Lord Aberdare of Duffryn*, printed for private circulation, Oxford, 1902.
Askwith, Lord	*Lord James of Hereford*, 1930.
Asquith, M.	*Autobiography*, 2 vols., 1922.
Birrell, A.	*Things Past Redress*, 1937.
Blunt, W. S.	*My Diaries. Being a Personal Narrative of Events, 1888–1914*, 2 vols., 1919, 1920.
Brett, M. V. [Oliver, Viscount Esher]	*Journals and Letters of Reginald Viscount Esher*, Vol. I, 1934; Vol. II, 1934; Vol. III, 1938.
Chamberlain, A.	*Down the Years*, 1935.
	Politics from Inside. An Epistolary Chronicle 1906–1914, 1936.
Churchill, R. S.	*Winston S. Churchill*, Vol. II, 1967.
Churchill, W. S.	*Great Contemporaries*, 1938.

SELECT BIBLIOGRAPHY

Cole, M. I.	*Beatrice Webb's Diaries 1912–1924*, 1952.
Corder, P.	*The Life of Robert Spence Watson*, 1914.
Crewe, Marquess of	*Lord Rosebery*, 2 vols., 1931.
Elliot, H. S. R. (ed.)	*The Letters of John Stuart Mill*, 2 vols., 1910.
Fisher, H. A. L.	*James Bryce (Viscount Bryce of Dechmont, O. M.)*, 1927.
	An Unfinished Autobiography, 1948.
Fitzroy, A.	*Memoirs*, 2 vols., 3rd ed. [1925].
Fowler, E. H.	*The Life of Henry Hartley Fowler, First Viscount Wolverhampton, G.C.S.I.*, 1912.
Fraser, P.	*Joseph Chamberlain Radicalism and Empire, 1868–1914*, 1966.
Gardiner, A. G.	*The Life of Sir William Harcourt*, 2 vols., 1923.
Garvin, J. L., and Amery, J.	*The Life of Joseph Chamberlain*, Vol. I, 1932; Vol. II, 1933; Vol. IV, 1951.
Gladstone, Viscount	*After Thirty Years*, 1929.
Gooch, G. P.	*Life of Lord Courtney*, 1920.
Gwynn, D.	*The Life of John Redmond*, 1932.
Gwynn, S., and Tuckwell, G. M.	*The Life of the Rt. Hon. Sir Charles W. Dilke, Bart., M.P.*, 2 vols., 1917.
Haight, G. S. (ed.)	*The George Eliot Letters*, 7 vols., 1956.
Haldane, E. S.	*From One Century to Another. Reminiscences*, 1937.
[Haldane, Lord]	*Richard Burdon Haldane. An Autobiography*, 1929.
Hamer, F. E. (ed.)	*The Personal Papers of Lord Rendel*, 1931.
Hamilton, M. A.	*Remembering My Good Friends*, 1944.
Hammond, J. L.	*C. P. Scott of the Manchester Guardian*, 1934.
Hardy, F. E.	*The Early Life of Thomas Hardy. 1840–1891 . . .*, 1928.
	The Later Years of Thomas Hardy. 1892–1928, 1930.
Harris, S. H.	*Auberon Herbert: Crusader for Liberty*, 1943.
Harris, W.	*J. A. Spender*, 1946.
Harrison, A.	*Frederic Harrison. Thoughts and Memories*, 1926.
Haultain, A. (ed.)	*A Selection from Goldwin Smith's Correspondence Comprising Letters Chiefly To and From His English Friends, Written between the Years 1846 and 1910* [1913].

SELECT BIBLIOGRAPHY

Healy, T. M.	*Letters and Leaders of My Day*, 2 vols. [1928].
Helps, E. A. (ed.)	*Correspondence of Sir Arthur Helps, K.C.B., D.C.L.*, 1917.
Hendrick, B. J.	*The Life of Andrew Carnegie*, 2 vols., New York, 1932.
Hirst, F. W.	*In the Golden Days*, 1947.
Howard, C. H. D. (ed.)	*A Political Memoir 1880–92 by Joseph Chamberlain*, 1953.
Howe, M. D. (ed.)	*Holmes-Laski Letters. The Correspondence of Mr. Justice Holmes and Harold J. Laski 1916–1935*, 2 vols., 1953.
Hughes, E.	*Keir Hardie*, 1956.
Hutchinson, H. G. (ed.)	*Private Diaries of the Rt. Hon. Sir Algernon West, G.C.B.*, 1922.
James, R. R.	*Lord Randolph Churchill*, 1959.
	Rosebery. A Biography of Archibald Philip, Fifth Earl of Rosebery, 1963.
Jenkins, R.	*Asquith*, 1964.
	Sir Charles Dilke. A Victorian Tragedy, 1958.
Kilbracken, Lord	*Reminiscences*, 1931.
Lang, C. Y. (ed.)	*The Swinburne Letters*, 6 vols., New Haven, 1959–62.
Lee, S.	*King Edward VII. A Biography*, Vol. II, 1927.
Lucas, E. V.	*The Colvins and Their Friends*, 1928.
Lucy, Sir Henry	*The Balfourian Parliament 1900–1905*, 1906.
	A Diary of the Home Rule Parliament, 1892–1895, 1896.
	A Diary of the Salisbury Parliament, 1886–1892, 1892.
	A Diary of Two Parliaments, Vol. II, 1886.
	A Diary of the Unionist Parliament, 1895–1900, Bristol, 1901.
Lytton, Earl of	*Wilfred Scawen Blunt. A Memoir*, 1961.
Maitland, F. W.	*The Life and Letters of Leslie Stephen*, 1906.
Mallet, C.	*Herbert Gladstone. A Memoir*, 1932.
Masterman, L.	*C. F. G. Masterman. A Biography*, 1939.
Meredith, W. M. (ed.)	*Letters of George Meredith*, 2 vols., 1912.
Mill, J. S.	*Autobiography*, 6th ed., 1879.
Mills, J. Saxon	*Sir Edward Cook, K.B.E. A Biography*, 1921.

Nowell-Smith, S. (ed.)	*Letters to Macmillan*, 1967.
O'Connor, T. P.	*Memoirs of an Old Parliamentarian*, 2 vols., 1929.
Oxford and Asquith, Earl of	*Memories and Reflections, 1852–1927*, 2 vols., 1928.
Pease, A. E.	*Elections and Recollections*, 1932.
Pope-Hennessey, J.	*Lord Crewe, 1858–1945: The Likeness of a Liberal*, 1955.
Rait, R. S. (ed.)	*Memorials of Albert Venn Dicey. Being Chiefly Letters and Diaries*, 1925.
Ramm, A. (ed.)	*The Political Correspondence of Mr. Gladstone and Lord Granville 1876–1886*, 2 vols., Oxford, 1962.
Rogers, J. Guiness	*An Autobiography*, 1903.
Russell, B. and P. (edd.)	*The Amberley Papers. The Letters and Diaries of Lord and Lady Amberley*, 2 vols., 1937.
Russell, G. W. E. (ed.)	*Letters of Matthew Arnold 1848–1888*, 2 vols., 1901.
	Malcolm MacColl Memoirs and Correspondence, 1914.
Samuel, Viscount	*Memoirs*, 1945.
Smillie, R.	*My Life For Labour*, 1924.
Snowden, Viscount	*An Autobiography*, Vol. I, 1934.
Sommer, D.	*Haldane of Cloan. His Life and Times 1856–1928*, 1960.
Spender, J. A.	*Life, Journalism and Politics*, Vol. I, 1927.
	The Life of the Rt. Hon. Sir Henry Campbell-Bannerman, G.C.B., 2 vols. [1923].
Spender, J. A., and Asquith, C.	*Life of Herbert Henry Asquith, Lord Oxford and Asquith*, Vol. I, 1932.
Sydenham, Lord	*My Working Life*, 1927.
Thorold, A. L.	*The Life of Henry Labouchere*, 1913.
Trevelyan, G. M.	*Grey of Fallodon Being the Life of Sir Edward Grey Afterwards Viscount Grey of Fallodon*, 1937.
Webb, B.	*My Apprenticeship*, 1929.
	Our Partnership, 1948.
Wolf, L.	*Life of the First Marquess of Ripon, K.G., P.C., G.C.S.I., D.C.L., Etc.*, Vol. II, 1921.

SELECT BIBLIOGRAPHY   401

G. *Secondary works* on the intellectual, literary, and political background in each of which some aspect of Morley's career is discussed within the wider treatment of some general theme (Place of publication London unless otherwise indicated)

Arnstein, W. L.	*The Bradlaugh Case A Study in Late Victorian Opinion and Politics*, Oxford, 1965.
Bevington, M. M.	*The Saturday Review 1855–1868. Representative Educated Opinion in Victorian England*, New York, 1941.
Brown, A. W.	*The Metaphysical Society. Victorian Minds in Crisis, 1869–1880*, New York, 1947.
Bullock, A., and Shock, M. (edd.)	*The Liberal Tradition From Fox to Keynes*, 1956.
Curtis, L. P., Jr.	*Coercion and Conciliation in Ireland 1880–1892: A Study in Conservative Unionism*, Princeton and London, 1963.
Das, M. N.	*India under Morley and Minto: Politics behind Revolution, Repression and Reforms*, 1964.
Everett, E. M.	*The Party of Humanity. The Fortnightly Review and its Contributors 1865–1874*, Chapel Hill, North Carolina, 1939.
Hammond, J. L.	*Gladstone and the Irish Nation*, 1938.
Harrison, R.	*Before the Socialists: Studies in Labour and Politics 1861–1881*, 1965.
Houghton, W. E.	*The Victorian Frame of Mind 1830–1870*, New Haven and London, 1957.
Hurst, M.	*Joseph Chamberlain and Liberal Reunion The Round Table Conference of 1887*, 1967.
Lyons, F. S. L.	*The Fall of Parnell 1890–91*, 1960.
McBriar, A. M.	*Fabian Socialism and English Politics 1884–1918*, Cambridge, 1962.
Magnus, P.	*Gladstone. A Biography*, 1954. *King Edward the Seventh*, 1964. *Kitchener: Portrait of an Imperialist*, 1958.
Moody, T. W.	'Michael Davitt and the British Labour Movement 1882–1906', *Transactions of the Royal Historical Society*, 5th Series, Vol. 3, 1953.
Morgan, C. L.	*The House of Macmillan, 1843–1943*, 1943.

Ostrogorski, M.	*Democracy and the Organization of Political Parties,* Vol. I, 1902.
Pelling, H.	*Social Geography of British Elections 1885–1910,* 1967.
Shannon, R. T.	*Gladstone and the Bulgarian Agitation 1876,* 1963.
Stansky, P.	*Ambitions and Strategies The struggle for the leadership of the Liberal Party in the 1890s,* Oxford, 1964.
Wasti, S. R.	*Lord Minto and the Indian Nationalist Movement, 1905 to 1910,* Oxford, 1964.

INDEX

N.B. Morley is referred to throughout as M.

Acland, A. H. D., 247, 340
Acton, Lord, 210, 281
Agadir, crisis over, 365-6
Annan, Noel, 43, 87
Anti-Corn Law League, M. on, 76, 253
Argyll, 8th Duke of, 178
Arnold, Matthew, cited, 7, 38 n., 55, 77, 86; *Culture and Anarchy*, 42, 72; and M., 72
Asquith, H. H., on M., 57, 341; M.'s relations with, 245-8; and home rule in 1892, 281; and M. in the Liberal succession crisis, 287-8; M.'s anxiety that party should not lose, 339-40; M. influences to maintain balance in party, 342; becomes Prime Minister, 342; and Ulster crisis, 1914, 358; mentioned, 291, 340, 344, 349, 366-7
Asquith, Margot, 368

Bagehot, Walter, cited, 3, 6, 42, 81; on the 'polity of discussion', 200, 240-2
Balfour, A. J., cited, 7; on M. as a home-rule advocate, 210; M. and the Irish policy of, 217, 348; on M. 377; mentioned, 300, 345, 356
Barnes, George, 325
Barry, Maltman, 276
Beesly, E. S., 20, 102
Belfast, M. and 1886 riots in, 356, 375
Benthamites, M. on, 48, 68, 383
Birrell, A., 3 n.
Bismarck, and the Roman Catholic Church, 28; M.'s attitude to, 54-6, 331
Blanc, Louis, 372
Blatchford, Robert, 276
Blunt, W. S., on M., 333; on M.'s Indian policy, 347, 349

Boswell, James, 44
Bradlaugh, Charles, 277
Brett, Reginald, *see* Esher, Lord
Bridges, J. H., 11, 20, 38 n.
Briggs, Professor Asa, 250
Bright, John, M. on relationship of with Cobden, 115; warns M. to be consistent on Irish coercion, 145; dislike of programmes, 196; mentioned, 71, 95, 368
Buffon, 44
Burke, Edmund, M. on early career of, 2, 126; his 'passion', 15; M.'s admiration for, 37, 40-2; M. on, 45, 60, 66, 115, 386; on prejudice, 65, 292; influence of ideas of on M., 65-6, 68, 384-5; M. on relations of with Lord Rockingham, 85, 115; and party, 126; opposes coercion of the Americans, 133; break with Whig party, 138, 207; M. thinks of imitating during South African War, 334
Burns, John, M. envies, 60; opposes M. at Newcastle, 276; and the crisis of Aug. 1914, 368-9
Buxton, Sydney, 266
Byron, Lord, M. on, 34, 65, 381

Caine, W. S., 265
Campbell-Bannerman, Sir Henry, on M., 14, 57; efforts to keep party united after 1898, 330, 338, 340; 'methods of barbarism' speech, 337; M. advises on party unity, 339; becomes Prime Minister, 341; M. criticizes 1900 election address of, 343; M. advises on Irish policy, 1905, 344; M. and, 1905-8, 346

Carlyle, Thomas, M. on 'heroes' of, 45–6, 93; influence on M., 62, 88–90; M. condemns, 68; on 'anarchy', 86; mentioned, 38 n., 96

Carnegie, Andrew, 181, 365, 374

Cavour, M. plans study of, 337

Chamberlain, Austen, 114, 118, 357

Chamberlain, Joseph, M.'s complementary relationship with, 77, 99, 113–19, 122, 174–5, 289–90; and the *Fortnightly Review*, 83, 99, 119–20; on Liberal disunity in the 1870s, 92, 104, 136, 203; M. advises in the 1870s and early 1880s, 94–5, 104, 117–19; M. first meets, 99; M. on as a Radical leader, 99, 113; and Radicalism in the 1870s, 103–11, 125; urges M. to enter Parliament, 123–5; helps M. financially, 122–3; on M.'s 'non-belief' as a political handicap, 124; development of rift between M. and, 127–8, 141–6, 150–63, 181; in office, 1880–85, 134; Radical programme and campaign of, 1885, 150–62, 188–9, 244, 382; and Irish policy, 1885, 166; and the rift with M., 1885–6, 168–78, 190, 195, 197, 207, 221–3, 289, 293, 354, 380, 389; and the Catholic University question, 1898, 187; M. attacks Irish policy of after 1886, 191; attacks the Liberals' Irish preoccupation, 200, 202; position of in politics after 1886 schism, 218; and Liberal reunion, 219–27; 288, and 'anarchic' Radicalism in London, 251; tariff reform campaign of, 344; mentioned, 100, 126, 212, 229, 264, 267, 300, 340, 348

Chatham, Lord, 118, 351

Christianity, M.'s views on, 1, 4–6, 17–18, 38; Rousseau and, 36; mentioned, 43

Churchill, Lord Randolph, 173, 193, 210, 218

Churchill, Winston, on *On Compromise*, 246; against Morley's leaving Government in 1910, 341; 'worse things than bloodshed' speech, 358; mentioned, 370

Church in England, M. on, 96–9, 106

Cobden, Richard, as a 'one question at a time' reformer, 93, 95, 161; M. on relationship of with Bright, 115; M. on ideas and principles of, 121–2, 142; influence of ideas of on M., 141–2, 309–10, 340, 376, 384; mentioned, 208

Coercion, M. opposes in Ireland, 91, 127, 129–34, 144–6, 164–6, 210–12, 232–8, 326, 347–8, 375, 378; M. and in India, 347–9

Collings, Jesse, 122, 124, 213

Communards of Paris, 1870–71, M. and the positivists' sympathy for, 28; M. condemns behaviour of, 67, 362; mentioned, 97, 363

Comte, Auguste, M.'s interest in ideas of, 16–21, 382, 384; M. dissociates himself from, 27–32, 36, 386; attitude of to Voltaire, 29; and construction of a system, 34; on the Encyclopaedia, 73, 119; influence of on M.'s élitism, 78; on role of the editor, 119; M. prefers Goethe to, 365; mentioned, 96, 159

Condorcet, 34, 39, 115

Congreve, Richard, 20, 27–8, 96, 103

Conservative party, M. on natural coherence of, 135; M. on impact of 'Tory Democracy' on, 160; in 1885 elections, 188; M. contrasts with Liberal party in Irish policy, 193–4; and the Irish preoccupation after 1885, 218; predominance of in London, 251; frequency of attaining power, 388

Courtney, Leonard, 143, 267, 280, 323–4

Cowen, Joseph, 122–3, 128, 135

Craig, M.P. for Newcastle, 276–7, 305

Cromer, Lord, 321

Cromwell, Oliver, M. on, 46, 55–6, 61

Curran, P., 277

Curzon, Lord, 351

Daily Mail, 351

INDEX 405

Daily News, 171–2, 180, 231, 338
Dale, R. W., 110
Danton, 223
Darwinian ideas, M. on impact of, 10, 382–3
Davitt, Michael, 279
De Maistre, Joseph, M.'s reasons for writing on, 16, 42
Descartes, 35
Devonshire, Duke of, *see* Hartington, Marquis of
Diamond, Charles, 279
Diderot, M. on, 1, 35, 39, 119
Dilke, Ashton, 128
Dilke, Sir Charles, and the Radical campaign of 1885, 151–2, 166, 169–70; appeals to M. in 1886 to continue working for Radical principles, 174; mentioned, 77, 120, 134, 146, 291
Disestablishment, M.'s support for, 91, 106, 387; of Church in Ireland, 98; the movement for, 106–11, 119, 139; and Radicalism in the 1880s, 159, 161, 189; subordinated after 1885, 205

Edinburgh Review, 120
Education, M.'s views on, 105–6
Education Act of 1870, M. and the agitation against, 96–9, 104–7, 116, 138
Egypt, M. opposes intervention in and annexation of in 1880s, 131, 133, 138, 141; M. and Chamberlain differ on, 141–4; M. wants evacuation of in 1890s, 321
Eight Hours Bills, M.'s opposition to, 197, 230, 243, 254–62, 275–6, 291, 309
Eliot, George, 16
Encyclopaedia, The, as model for the *Fortnightly Review*, 72–3, 119; mentioned, 1, 119
Esher, Lord, 14, 169, 173, 176, 288–9, 293, 350, 357, 366, 375

Fabianism, 248, 277 n.
Ferguson, R. Munro, 270 n.
Fitzroy, Sir Almeric, 367–8
Forster, W. E., warns M. about disestablishment campaign, 111; M. opposes Irish policy of, 1881–2, 127, 144, 146, 211; mentioned, 180, 347
Fortnightly Review, G. H. Lewes first editor of, 16; M.'s editorship of, 26, 66, 70–4, 98, 112, 119–21, 127, 205; as a forum for 'the instructed', 79–85; 'safety' of the radicalism of, 80; Radicalism in the 1870s and, 99, 103, 108, 110; M.'s commentaries in, 115; and 'free thinkers', 124; mentioned, 42, 81, 83–4, 102, 112, 123–4, 161, 200, 289, 363
Fowler, H. H., congratulates M., 1886, 212; and the 'Round Table' conference, 220, 228; and the younger Liberals, 247; predicts disruption of Liberal party, 1898, 306; and Irish policy, 1896–7, 319
Fox, Charles James, M. on, 138, 207
France, in 18th century, 24; M.'s attitude to role of in European state-system, 360–4
Franco-Prussian War, 28, 360, 362
Frederick the Great, quarrel of with Voltaire, 44; M.'s attitude to, 55–6, 351
Free trade, M. defends, 312–13, 344–5
French politics, M. on contemporary, 135, 383
French revolution, M.'s interest in, 39; M. on excesses of, 68, 76; M.'s projected history of, 122, 126; mentioned, 66, 80, 155, 166
French thinking, M.'s dislike of, 27–9, 154, 362–3
Frere, Sir Bartle, M. demands recall of, 127, 321
Fromm, Erich, 12
Froude, J. A., 43

Gardiner, A. G., on M., 330, 347
Garvin, J. L., 175
George V, King, on M., 293
George, Henry, 140
Germany, M. favours hegemony of in Europe, 361–4; M.'s attitude to, 1905–14, 364–6; M. opposes entry into war with, 1914, 367–9

Gladstone, Herbert, and the 'Hawarden Kite', 169–70; welcomes defeat, 1895, 304

Gladstone, W. E., M. attracted to in 1876, 40; M.'s 'reverence' for, 43; idealized by M., 45, 182; thinks M. should leave politics, 1895, 58; on party's disunity in 1870s, 92, 203; M. asks to write for the *Fortnightly*, 120; M. supports in opposition to Irish coercion in early 1890s, 127, 179–80; agrees with M. on Egyptian policy, 1884, 142; M. urges to create peers, 1884, 149; and the political crisis of 1885, 152, 160, 178; M. supports over Irish home rule, 167, 170–4, 189–90, 210; intrigues concerning in Dec. 1885, 169–70; M. rallies to in 1886 as a conservative force, 176–8, 292; his 'one idea at a time faculty', 178–9; relationship with M. after 1885, 178–82, 281–2; M. and before 1885, 179–80; on Ireland as the great obstruction, 204–5; M. on the prospect after the retirement of, 213, 264, 281–2, 293–4; Irish policy of after 1886, 214, 229; M. advises on handling of dissentient Liberals, 218, 225; concentrates on opposing coercion, 1887, 233; and the development of Liberal policy after 1886, 245; bored by S. Webb, 248; and the Parnell divorce crisis, 263–5, 267; as Liberal leader in the 1890s, 268–9; and the 1892 election result, 280; fourth ministry of, 1892–4, 280–3; retirement of, 1894, 285–8, 296, 305; favours M. for the Foreign Office in 1894, 287; advocates anti-Lords campaign, 1893–4, 302; M. on taxation policy of, 312; and M. after 1894, 317; rebukes M. for wanting to resign on Uganda in 1892, 321; M. upholds principles of, 325, 328; mentioned, 67, 70, 133, 150, 162 n., 176, 219–20, 222, 275, 280–1, 304, 368. *See also* Morley, J.: *Gladstone, Life of William Ewart*

Glasier, J. B., 324

Goethe, M. prefers to Comte, 365

Gokhale, disillusioned with M., 347

Goschen, G. J., 172, 294

Graham, R. B. Cunninghame, opposes M. in Newcastle, 230–1, 261–2, 276–8

Granville, Lord, 179

Grayson, Victor, 354

Grey, Sir Edward, M.'s relations with and influence on, 245–7; against taking office dependent on the Irish, 318; as Liberal imperialist, 339; on M. as Indian Secretary, 346; M. and the foreign policy of, 365–6

Haldane, Elizabeth, 248

Haldane, R. B., on M., 55, 58, 213; M.'s relations with, 245–8; and the eight hours question, 258; on construction of a new party, 1895, 304; M. persuades Asquith not to give Exchequer to, 1908, 342; M. accuses of concealing commitments to France, 366; introduces Labour leaders and Socialists to M., 370–1

Hamond, C. F., 276–7

Harcourt, Lewis, 286–7

Harcourt, Sir William, blames M. for Forster's resignation, 146; dispute with M. over Irish policy after Parnell divorce crisis, 183, 223, 266–9; after 1885 exploits M.'s anti-coercion record, 210–12; on M.'s position in the party in 1887, 212; and the 'Round Table' conference, 220–1,; opposes the Liberal preoccupation with Ireland, 228–30, 234; opposes Irish coercion, 233; fears about effects of 'plan of campaign', 234–5; disagrees with M. on eight hour day, 257; and Liberal policy, 1892–5, 280–1; and the succession crisis, 1894, 287–8; M. prefers Rosebery to in 1894, 288–95; M.'s relationship with and attitude to, 288–91; M.'s political relationship with after 1894, 297, 319; indifference of to fate of Government, 1894–5, 303–4; and Irish policy after

1894, 318; resignation of, 1898, 329–30; persuades M. not to retire in 1900, 336; and the reunifying of the party 339–41; mentioned, 152, 222, 248, 321

Hardie, J. Keir, 276–8, 324

Hardy, Thomas, on M., 58

Harrison, Austin, 68, 365

Harrison, Frederic, early career of, 4; friendship of with M., 4, 16; cited, 6–7; urges M. to take up positivism, 11, 26–32, 67; as a positivist, 20; quarrels with M. over German Church laws, 28, 66; and the life of action, 61; M. on, 68; and Radicalism in the 1870s, 99, 113; and the Sudan crisis of 1885, 143; mentioned, 40, 66, 70, 73, 103, 165, 363

Hartington, Marquis of, in the 1885 crisis, 152, 172, 189; M. praises, 157, 351; as 'bulwark' against socialism, 157, 176, 293–4; mentioned, 221, 293

Healy, T. M., 57, 299

Henderson, Arthur, 305

Herschell, Farrer, 220

Hirst, F. W., on M., 22, 43–4, 64, 311, 313, 333; mentioned, 117, 320, 325, 330–1, 334, 338, 343

Hobhouse, L. T., 327

Holbach, 9, 39, 62

Houghton, W. E., 3, 11

House of Lords, M. and agitation against, 1883–5, 147, 149–50, 159; M. and the question of reforming in the 1890s, 265–6; rejection of Home Rule Bill by, 1893, 283–4; M. not in favour of campaign against in the 1890s, 302, 327; M. and the crisis over powers of, 1909–11, 334, 371

Huxley, T. H., cited, 8, 87; influence of on M., 21; and positivism, 21, 27

Illingworth, Alfred, 224

Imperialism, M. opposes in Southern Africa, 67; M.'s reasons for opposing, 91, 131–4; opposition to in 1885, 162–3; opposition to in the late 1890s and early 20th century, 310–34, 350–1

India, M. and, 341, 345–53, 374, 377, 379, 385

Ireland, M. on need for 'peculiar ways of dealing with', 66, 165, 256; M. on English rule over, 164–6, 184–8

Irish home rule, M. and before 1885, 163–6; M. and in 1885, 163–8; M. as advocate of, 1885–6, 171–4; opposition of Chamberlain to, 171–3; M.'s reasons for advocating, 183–93, 205–8, 215; as the Liberals' great preoccupation, Chapters 13, 14, and 15, 318; disagreements over details of, 213–18; the Liberal party and after 1885, 242–4; as affected by the Parnell divorce crisis, 264–9; M. defends as the great Liberal policy and commitment in the 1890s, 274–5, 283, 303; the Liberal leaders and, 1892–5, 281–3; position of after rejection of 1893 Bill, 283–4, 297–9; M. tries to keep alive between 1895 and 1905, 318–19, 343–5; crisis concerning, 1910–14, 355–9

Irish home rule party, alliance of with Liberal party after 1885, 107, 225, 228, 231–2, 267–8; and the 1885 elections, 168–9; M. tries to maintain alliance with in 1890s, 274, 299–301, 318–19; mentioned, 92

Irish Land League, M. on, 130–1, 164

Irish question, as a 'microcosm', 90; and 'Ultramontanism', 97; M. and before 1886, Chapter 9; as the great obstruction in British politics, 201–5, 242

James, Sir Henry, 264, 293

Jameson raid, M.'s reaction to, 233

Johnson, Dr., 115

Kimberley, Lord, 287

Kitchener, Lord, 333, 351

Labouchere, Henry, and the Radical split, 1886, 172; on lack of an 'urban cow' in 1885, 189; attitude of to the home-rule policy, 236; younger Liberals' dislike of in the late 1880s,

INDEX

245, 290; M.'s dislike of radicalism of, 290–1; on M., 333
Labour, M. and anti-imperialism of, 324–5; M.'s attitude to in politics after 1905, 369–72
Laffitte, Pierre, 16
Laidler, J., 261
Lajpat, M. and the deportation of, 348
Land reform, M. and, 139–40, 155–6
Laski, Harold, on M., 44, 45 n., 49, 57, 370, 376, 379, M.'s friendship with; 294 n., 371
Lawson, Sir Wilfrid, 143
Lecky, W. E. H., 383
Leeds Mercury. 169–70
Lehmann, R. C., 338
Lewes, G. H., 16, 70
Liberal imperialists, emergence of, 245–6; M. opposes, 322–3, 325; M. on place of in party, 338–42; and Irish policy in early 20th century, 344
Liberalism, M. on principles of, 47; 'anarchy' in, 92; debased by party, 101; and anti-denominationalism, 105; and State intervention, 158–9
Liberal party, disunity of in the 1870s, 92–3, 104; M. on in the 1870s, 103, 108–9; disorganization of before 1886, 135–7; M. on possible disruption of before 1886, 137–8; opposition to House of Lords and, 1884–5, 149–50; the Radicals and in 1885, 151–2, 160, 167; M.'s anxieties concerning future of after 1885, 176, 293–4; and the preoccupation with Irish policy after 1885, 188, Chapter 9, 269–70, 298–9; sectionalism in, 197, 264–5; growth of discontent in with Irish preoccupation, 227–30; search for new policy for after 1886, Chapter 16; the middle class and, 251–2; and the Parnell divorce crisis, 263–8; policy of in the early 1890s, 271–3; threat of split in if Irish policy shelved, 274–5, 288, 296; and the 1892 elections, 280; impatience in with home rule, 1892–3, 280–1; and home rule after rejection of 1893 Bill, 283–4; sectionalism and disunity in after Gladstone's retirement, 301–2; prospects for after defeat in 1895, 305–6; imperialism and, 322–8, 338–40; M.'s views on future of in early 20th century, 338–41, 343; and the balance of sections, 1901–14, 340–2; reunified over tariff reform, 344–5; election triumph of in 1906, 345; M. on, 1905–14, 353–5; the First World War and, 369
Liberal Unionists, M. and, 218–27
Liberation Society, M. and, 107–10; mentioned, 92
Lloyd George, David, on M.'s indecisiveness, 333; warned by M. not to worsen party split, 1901, 338; M. regards as too extremist, 339; becomes Chancellor, 342; remains in Cabinet, August 1914, 369
Local government reform, M. and, 265, 308–9
London, M. and, 248–54, 265–6, 386
Loreburn, Lord, 341
Low, Sir Sidney, on M., 294 n.

Macaulay, 60, 138
MacDonald, J. Ramsay, M. and, 370
Machiavelli, M.'s Romanes lecture on, 54, 331
Macmillan and Co., M. as reader for, 123
Macmillan Magazine, M.'s editorship of, 124
Magnus, Sir Philip, 182
Maine, Sir Henry, 195
Manchester School, 122, 257
Marcus Aurelius, 375
Massingham, H. W., on M., 256
Metaphysical Society, M. as member of, 39–40
Mill, John Stuart, cited, 6–8; influence of on M., 8, 20–31, 51–2, 62, 76, 379–80, 384, 386; and positivism, 16, 27, 67; *On Liberty*, 20, 42, 51–2; *Auguste Comte and Positivism*, 21; M. on strength of character of, 40, 336; M.'s 'reverence' for, 43; M. defends principles of, 49, 86; *Representative Government*, 51, 183; on effort and

energy, 55; on the intellectual élite, 78; not a specialist, 89; rebukes M. for referring to 'the Revolution', 93; on the Radicals of the 1830s, 112–13; view of on party, 125; and land reform, 140; and Irish coercion, 145; M. refers to views of on India, 347–8; 'Essays on Socialism', 384; mentioned, 70–1, 114, 364, 387
Minto, Countess of, 350
Minto, Lord, 293, 348–53, 370
Montagu-Chelmsford reforms, M. on, 377 n.
Montrose Burghs, M. M.P. for, 320
Moore, Dr. R. J., 350
Morgan, J. H., on M., 55, 57
Morison, James Cotter, 16
Morley, Arnold, 125, 220, 224, 275
Morley, John (for M.'s connection with particular themes, episodes, organizations, and people not referred to here see under appropriate headings), consequences for of loss of religious faith, Chapters 1 and 2; on the need for system in thought, 9–11; proneness of to melancholy and emotional instability, 12–15; difficulties found by in accepting systems of thought, 33–7; against interfering with 'natural' processes and order, 33–6, 131–2, 380–1; world-view of diminishes, 37–9; as biographer, 39–45, 48–9; on character, 40–2; fails to find general context for studies of individuals, 45–8; puts emphasis on the individual, 49–50, 52; élitism of, 50–2; attitude of to energy and power, 53–5; admires 'men of iron', 55–7; femininity of character of, 57; craves a life of action—his two selves, 57–9; tendency of to disparage the literary life, 59–60; fears self-consciousness of man of letters, 60–1; seeks relief in life of action, 61–3; as an intellectual in politics, 63, 378; on absence of systematic principles in politics, 64, 378; indecisiveness of, 64; opposes abstract phrases, 65–7; on feeling in politics, 67–8; and the principles of 'utility' and 'expediency', 68–9; hesitates between a literary and a political career, 70–2, 122–3, 126; on political situation after 1867 Reform Act, 74–6; on the work of preparing opinion, 76–85; on relations between intellectuals and politicians, 84–5, 112–19; and the single great question, 86–93; on 'one question at a time' as the best kind of reform politics, 93–5, 104; and Nonconformity, 96; attitude of to party organization and conflict, 99–103, 125–6, 138; and Radicalism in the 1870s, 103–4, 112; financial position of, 123–4; effects of views of on religion on political career, 124; fails to secure nomination at Nottingham, 1880, 124–5; how anti-coercion and anti-imperialism became the preoccupations of, 133–4, 137–9; and the disorganization of Radicalism in the early 1880s, 134–7; political thinking of relates more and more to the past, 148–9; reaction of to Chamberlain's references to 'natural rights', 153–6; views of on State intervention and 'the Social Question', 158–9, 255–7; how preoccupation of with Irish question emerges in 1885, 160–8; and the political crisis of Dec. 1885–Jan. 1886, 168–76; becomes Irish Secretary, 180; and the preoccupation of country and Liberal party with Ireland after 1885, 187–8, 191–4, 197–200, 205–8; and the 1885 elections, 188–92; on lack of system and order in politics, 1886, 195; prefers a single question to a programme, 1886, 195–6; on the 'Irish obstruction' and its implications for Liberal politics, 200–5, 208–9, 240, 242; position of in Liberal party, 1886, 210–13, 219; becomes excessively preoccupied with Irish question, 213; and details of Irish policy, 213–18, 232; and the 'polity of discussion', 240–3, 258–9; looks

for new policies and principles after 1886, 243–5, 247–9, 271–3; relations of with young Liberals, 1886–95, 245–8; 'provincial' Liberalism of, 249–52; and the widening of the Liberal programme, 1891–2, 264–9, 272–3, 280; and the 1892 elections, 276–80; and the Liberal succession crisis, 1894, 285–95; and Irish policy, 1892–5, 299–301; indifferent to prospect of defeat, 1894–5, 302–4; on party and class divisions in the 1890s, 305–7; on social-reform policies in late 1890s, 306–10; on increased State expenditure and taxation, 311–14; on imperialism and social reform, 315–16; effect of South African War and new climate of opinion on, 330–2, 336–7; indecision and irresolution of during South African War, 332–5; favours and works for maintenance of unity of Liberal party in early 20th century, 337–41; position and influence of in 1905–14 Government, 341–2, 345–6; on problems of Liberal policy and politics 1905–14, 345, 353–5; why opposed to entry into war in 1914, 367–9; during the First World War, 372–5; negativism of career of, 377–8; disillusioned by results of great reforms, 382–4

Writings of: *Burke*, 125–6, 151, 175; *Cobden, Life of Richard*, 76, 93, 95, 123, 253, 309, 337; *Cromwell, Oliver*, 13, 46; *Diderot*, 119; *Gladstone, Life of William Ewart*, 40, 45, 60, 190, 222, 320, 325, 331, 334–7, 373; *Modern Characteristics*, 13; *On Compromise*, 2–6, 8, 12, 24–6, 36, 38–9, 42, 50–1, 74, 127, 196, 203, 223, 246, 289, 291, 332, 383–4; *Recollections*, 13, 17, 47, 49, 59, 72, 210, 219, 350, 371, 373–5; *Rousseau*, 14, 30, 35, 50, 55, 60, 93; *Voltaire*, 13, 29–30, 39, 43–4, 46, 59–61, 88

Morley, Samuel, 125

National Education League, 92, 99, 107

National Liberal Federation, Chamberlain, and, 136; M. on role of in and after 1885–6 crisis, 196; Newcastle programme of, 1891, 272–3; mentioned, 197 n., 206, 221 n., 235, 245, 247, 250, 254, 263, 273, 327–8

Nevinson, H. W., 347

Newcastle, M. suggested as candidate for, 1877, 122–3; M. becomes M.P. for, 128, 135; labour agitation and opposition to M. in, 201, 204, 228, 230–1, 240, 243, 254, 260–2, 275–6; elections of 1892 in, 276–80; M. loses seat at, 1895, 280, 304–5; mentioned, 143

Nineteenth Century, The, 165

Nonconformity, M. and, 96, 124

Nottingham Liberals, M. refused nomination by, 124–5

O'Brien, W., 348
O'Connor, T. P., on M., 14, 59, 64
Ostrogorski, M., 128

Pall Mall Gazette, Arnold advises M. to become editor of, 72; M.'s editorship of, 123, 127, 144, 179–80; cited, 132, 138, 141, 145–6, 154, 156, 165, 177, 234, 290, 368

Palmerston, Lord, M. on foreign policy of, 54

Parnell, Charles Stewart, M. on, 57; and Gladstone, 1885–6, 169; crisis over divorce of, 1890–1, 213, 254, 263–7, 274, 321; uneasy about Liberal reunion, 225; M. and, 234–5; mentioned, 219

Pericles, 374
Perks, R. W., 316 n.
Peter the Great, 56
Pitt, William, the Younger, M. on relations of with Adam Smith, 85, 115
'Plan of Campaign', M.'s attitude to, 206, 234
Positivism, M. and, Chapter 2, 43, 50, 362, 388–9; mentioned, 6, 11

Positivists, M. and, 16, 26–31, 66–7, 380; and the cult of great men, 43; M. clashes with over attitude to France, 362, 365; mentioned, 8, 61, 149, 214
Potter, Beatrice, see Webb, Beatrice
Progress, M.'s belief in, 17–19, 47–8, 62, 148, 201–2, 230–1, 381–2, 389
Protestantism, M. on, 28, 96
Prussia, M.'s admiration for, 28, 360–3
Pym, John, 113

Quarterly Review, 99

Radical Club, 112
Radical Programme, The, 161
Reay, Lord, 143
Reid, T. Wemyss, 169–70
Rendel, Lord, on M., 57, 288; mentioned, 180, 317
Ripon, Lord, opposes Liberal reunion in 1887, 224; opposes Irish coercion, 233; M. and, 293; mentioned, 60, 221
Robespierre, M. on, 37, 39, 67, 223
Rockingham, Lord, M. on relations of with Burke, 85, 115
Roman Catholicism, 28, 97
Rosebery, Lord, on M., 14, 57; and the young Liberals, 245, 247; M. prefers as leader in 1894, 247, Chapter 19; and London, 252; M. appeals to for 'a practicable socialism', 271; lacks enthusiasm for home rule, 281; and Irish policy, 1894–5, 297, 303; and the Lords question in the 1890s, 302; M. conflicts with over imperialism, 315, 333; mentioned, 13
Rousseau, 11, 35–7, 39, 42, 53–4, 62, 68, 375–6
Russia, M.'s attitude to role of in European state-system, 362–8

Salisbury, Lord, 99, 210, 293
Saturday Review, 3, 13, 21
Schnadhorst, F., 213
Seely, J., 358
Shakespeare, M.'s opinion of *Measure for Measure* by, 181–2

Shaw-Lefevre, G., and the Radical campaign of, 1885, 151–2, 169
Sheffield Liberals, will not have M. as candidate, 124
Sidgwick, Henry, 8
Smillie, Robert, 370
Smith, Adam, M. on relations of with Pitt the younger, 85, 115
Smith, Goldwin, 55, 77, 107, 200
Snowden, Philip, 370
South African War, M. on the consequences of, 311; M.'s opposition to, 326–7; M.'s behaviour during, 330–7
Spencer, Herbert, influence of on M., 21; and positivism, 27
Spencer, Lord, and Forster's resignation, 1882, 146; attacked by *Pall Mall Gazette*, 1883, 146; and M.'s pre-1886 anti-coercion record, 210–12; and the 1886 land purchase plan, 217; and the 'Round Table' conference, 1887, 220, 356; commitment of to home rule, 269, 272, 282; M.'s admiration of, 293; and the party in the early 20th century, 341; mentioned, 166, 297, 387
Spender, J. A., 57, 287, 339
Stephen, James Fitzjames, *Liberty, Equality, Fraternity*, 7, 86; M. defends Mill against, 49, 51, 86
Stephen, Leslie, 3
Strafford, Lord, M. on, 55–6, 351
Sudan, 132, 143

Tariff reform, 312–13, 344, 378
Taylor, Helen, 26
Temperance reform, M. and, 244–5, 265–6, 271–2, 307, 327
Times, The, 141, 235
Trade unionism, M. on, 79, 98, 258; the campaign against Irish coercion and, 236–8
Trevelyan, G. M., 246
Trevelyan, Sir George O., M. on 'House of Commons tone' of, 134; M. on Irish policy of, 1883, 146, 166; and the Radical campaign of 1885, 151; mentioned, 224, 227

Turgot, M. on, 23-4, 39, 60, 62, 115
Tyndall, J., 21

Uganda, the Liberal Government of 1892-5 and, 282, 321
Ulster, M.'s attitude to, 218, 355-7; crisis over, 1910-14, 355-9

Vauvenargues, 39
Voltaire, M. on, 29, 35, 39, 44, 60, 376
Von Sybel, Professor, 363

Wadham College, 20
Wallace, A. R., 140
Watson, Robert Spence, 128, 143, 169-70
Webb, Beatrice, on M., 85, 243, 260, 324, 330, 332, 334; visit of to M. in 1919, 371; mentioned, 62
Webb, Sidney, M. and, 248, 371
West, Sir Algernon, 57, 59, 281-2, 286, 321
Westminster Gazette, 310
Wolpert, S. A., 349

www.ingramcontent.com/pod-product-compliance
Lightning Source LLC
Chambersburg PA
CBHW070007010526
44117CB00011B/1451